PRISON MEMOIRS
OF AN ANARCHIST

Alexander Berkman

ALEXANDER BERKMAN

PRISON MEMOIRS

OF AN

ANARCHIST

Introductory by Hutchins Hapgood
With a new Introduction by Paul Goodman

SCHOCKEN BOOKS · NEW YORK

Studies in the Libertarian and Utopian Tradition

Originally published in 1912 by the
Mother Earth Publishing Association

First SCHOCKEN edition 1970
Introduction Copyright © 1970 by Dissent Publishing Corporation
Library of Congress Catalog Card No. 77-130206

Manufactured in the United States of America

The Introduction by Paul Goodman was
originally published as "Memoirs from Prison,"
in *Dissent,* July-August 1970, pp. 368-371.

Second Printing, 1972

To all those who in and out of prison
fight against their bondage

"But this I know, that every Law
   That men have made for Man,
Since first Man took his brother's life,
   And the sad world began,
But straws the wheat and saves the chaff
   With a most evil fan."

OSCAR WILDE

CONTENTS

CONTENTS

ILLUSTRATIONS

AS INTRODUCTORY

I wish that everybody in the world would read this book. And my reasons are not due to any desire on my part that people should join any group of social philosophers or revolutionists. I desire that the book be widely read because the general and careful reading of it would definitely add to true civilization.

It is a contribution to the writings which promote civilization; for the following reasons:

It is a human document. It is a difficult thing to be sincere. More than that, it is a valuable thing. To be so, means unusual qualities of the heart and of the head; unusual qualities of character. The books that possess this quality are unusual books. There are not many deliberately autobiographical writings that are markedly sincere; there are not many direct human documents. This is one of these few books.

Not only has this book the interest of the human document, but it is also a striking proof of the power of the human soul. Alexander Berkman spent fourteen years in prison; under perhaps more than commonly harsh and severe conditions. Prison life tends to destroy the body, weaken the mind and pervert the character. Berkman consciously struggled with these adverse, destructive conditions. He took care of his body. He took care of his mind. He did so strenuously. It was a moral effort. He felt insane ideas trying to take possession of him. Insanity is a natural result of prison life. It always tends to come. This man felt it, consciously struggled against it, and overcame it. That the prison affected him is true. It always does. But he saved himself, essentially. Society tried to destroy him, but failed.

If people will read this book carefully it will tend to do away with prisons. The public, once vividly conscious of what prison life is and must be, would not be willing to maintain prisons. This is the only book that I know which goes deeply into the corrupting, demoralizing psychology of prison life. It shows, in picture after picture, sketch after sketch, not only the obvious brutality, stupidity, ugliness permeating the institution, but, very touching, it shows the good qualities and instincts of the human heart perverted, demoralized, helplessly struggling for life; beautiful tendencies basely expressing themselves. And the personality of Berkman goes through it all; idealistic, courageous, uncompromising, sincere, truthful; not untouched, as I have said, by his surroundings, but remaining his essential self.

What lessons there are in this book! Like all truthful documents it makes us love and hate our fellow men, doubt ourselves, doubt our society, tends to make us take a strenuous, serious attitude towards life, and not be too quick to judge, without going into a situation painfully, carefully. .It tends to complicate the present simplicity of our moral attitudes. It tends to make us more mature.

The above are the main reasons why I should like to have everybody read this book.

But there are other aspects of the book which are interesting and valuable in a more special, more limited way; aspects in which only comparatively few persons will be interested, and which will arouse the opposition and hostility of many. The Russian Nihilistic origin of Berkman, his Anarchistic experience in America, his attempt on the life of Frick—an attempt made at a violent

industrial crisis, an attempt made as a result of a sincere
if fanatical belief that he was called on by his destiny
to strike a psychological blow for the oppressed of the
community—this part of the book will arouse extreme
disagreement and disapproval of his ideas and his act.
But I see no reason why this, with the rest, should not
rather be regarded as an integral part of a human document, as part of the record of a life, with its social and
psychological suggestions and explanations. Why not
try to understand an honest man even if he feels called
on to kill? There, too, it may be deeply instructive.
There, too, it has its lessons. Read it not in a combative
spirit. Read to understand. Do not read to agree, of
course, but read to see.

HUTCHINS HAPGOOD.

INTRODUCTION
TO THE 1970 EDITION
by Paul Goodman

i

THE extraordinary, appalling beginning of this extraordinary book—I can't conceive of any other way to make credible the *Attentat* on Frick by the compassionate, sensitive, and intellectual young man, and the author succeeds in making it totally credible. No novelist of the period could have accomplished it, but Berkman was able to remember a style from the high Romantic period of Robert Schumann and E. T. A. Hoffmann, onrushing impetuosity luridly lit by flashes of childhood and early adolescent traumas from the unconscious, leading to an explosive act. And writing it down was an overflow of strong feelings recollected in tranquility, as Wordsworth defined poetry. (Did he find the tranquility, from time to time, in jail?) It is a vivid poem of adolescent infatuation, seeking to repair the self and be a Man, as he says. It puts the act beyond moral approval or condemnation; it is so.

My guess is that such writing is, for its author, a catharsis of pity and fear, and he is afterwards in the world differently.

Prison literature is an old genre among human beings. And our century, and maybe especially the coming generation, is producing more and more examples. They write well, these pacifists, blacks, anarchists, free speakers, fighters for justice, whether in corporate liberal, fascist, or socialist countries. The regimes of the world evidently cannot put up with some beautiful human spirits.

In one important respect, I think there is a notable difference between our contemporaries and the prison writers of a few generations back. Men like Kropotkin,

INTRODUCTION TO THE 1970 EDITION

Berkman, and Debs were quite certain, both by their philosophy and the evidence of their senses, that the concept of punishment is worthless and the jails must simply be abolished. The Bastille is the essence of what is rotten and must be stormed first. Except in a few cases, jails do not reform. They always hinder rehabilitation. Far from protecting society, they create more and more serious crimes. They cause immense, unnecessary suffering, and the effect on the warders is also humanly disastrous. Big, isolated jails do not even provide public revenge, and putting trouble out of sight heightens social anxiety rather than allays it. If every citizen would make occasional visits to the prisons and mass insane asylums, I think that, corrupt as we are, these institutions would not endure. What to do with hard cases is a real question, but it is better to do nothing at all than to continue what does more harm than good. Debs said, "So long as one person is in prison, I am not free." In our times, however, even thoughtful pacifists and libertarian socialists hardly mention the abolition of jails. For instance, unlike fifty years ago when it was common, there is almost never a plank in a radical platform on the subject of prisons. (A single exception was the platform of Dave McReynolds, of the War Resisters League, running for Congress in 1968.) How is this?

One possible explanation is that our militants are so stupid that they take prison for an acceptable institution for their enemies. I have seen a sign at a demonstration, "Free Such and Such! Put District Attorney X in jail!" Black militants demand the right for black juries to put black people in black jails. To my surprise, Coretta King did not ask for amnesty for Ray. And apparently it is all right for Cuba to keep enemies of the Revolution in cages. Certainly Berkman or Debs would not have accepted such a notion of revolution.

But I doubt that our present radicals really are this stupid. I suspect that the truth is more terrible.

INTRODUCTION TO THE 1970 EDITION

Rather, the jails, like the high schools, like the swollen cities, like the polluted rivers, like the congested traffic, like the TV, like slow or quick violence, are taken for granted as the nature of things. People are so swamped by the conditions of modern life, that they do not really believe these evils are human artifacts and could be otherwise. And when in daily life people are harried, circumscribed, bored, and threatened anyway, the difference between being out of jail and in jail tends to diminish. I wonder whether, to a frank glance, the routine of most of us in New York does not seem very like jail, some with privileges, some in solitary. Hobbes had a salutary doctrine that a prisoner has a moral duty to escape, by force or fraud, and return to the "state of nature"; but this does not apply if there is no state of nature.

ii

"Often I think that we revolutionists are like the capitalist system. We drain men and women of the best that is in them, and then stand quietly by and and see them end their last days in destitution and loneliness."

It was Emma Goldman, the "Girl" in Berkman's book, who made this remark in 1933, a couple of years before Berkman killed himself. (I quote it from Paul Avrich's *The Russian Anarchists.*) It was the sad time when the surviving Russian anarchists, those who had not been slaughtered or imprisoned, were scattered in exile—by the Workers' State that they had done much to bring into power.

"Gray are the passing days," wrote Berkman in his diary, after Lenin and Trotsky's slaughter of the libertarian sailors at Kronstadt in 1921—after he and Emma Goldman had vainly tried to mediate. "One by one the embers of hope have died out. Terror and despotism have crushed the life born in October. The slogans of the Revolution are forsworn, its ideals stifled in the blood of the people. The breath of yesterday is dooming millions to death; the shadow of today hangs like a pall over the country. Dictatorship is trampling the masses under foot. The Revolution is dead; its spirit cries in the wilderness. . . . I have decided to leave Russia" (Avrich, *op. cit.*, p. 233).

The high pitch of this rhetoric—it was written for himself, not for publication—is not exaggerated, considering the magnitude of the events and the truth of his statements.

A few years before, he had again been arrested in New York for violating the draft law. He was deported from the United States in 1919.

Yet the same disappointment is already fully explicit in the early days of the *Prison Memoirs*. In Chapter VI he describes his dismay at the cowardice, venality, and ignorance of their own interests, of his fellow prisoners—the Negro, the Thief, and (alas!) the noble Homestead Workman. As a writer, he obviously does not know whether to laugh or to cry at his own naïveté; and neither does the reader, for it is told with such frankness and irony. But the young man, sentenced to 22 years, is

pacing the floor in agitation over the conversation with his fellow-prisoners. Why can't they understand the motives that prompted his act? Their manner of pitying condescension is aggravating. . . .

He passes a sleepless night. The events of the day have stirred him to the very depths. Bitterness and anger against the Homestead striker fill his heart. His hero of yesterday, the hero of the glorious struggle of the People—how contemptible he has proved himself, how cravenly small! No consciousness of the great mission of his class, no proud realization of the part he himself had acted in the noble struggle. A cowardly, overgrown boy, terrified at to-morrow's punishment for the prank he has played!

INTRODUCTION TO THE 1970 EDITION

Politically, to be sure, there is also another side to the story. In the web of history, Berkman's sacrifice is a bright one in the millions of strands. The considerable gains of labor in the United States stemmed from such acts and lives, although their outcome toward a worthier society has been far short of, in some ways counter to, what he wanted. I think we have to say four different and contradictory things: If people had followed Berkman's way, there would be a better world. The fact that they did not, and presumably could not, follow it means that he was wrongheaded, he suffered from ideas. Because of him, there is more value in the world than there would be otherwise; the noble cause has been kept alive for another generation. And human beings do not *know* any better process than this blundering and tormented process of history.

iii

But the most impressive news of Berkman's as of other prison books is not blundering and tormented at all. It is how human beings are made of rubber and bounce. Given any resources of physical health, moral conviction, or intellectual alertness, they make do in a shaking bad environment without being personally destroyed. Naturally those who survive to write memoirs have already proved they have survivability.

The bouncy resiliency is most exhibited in this genre when there is a project of escape, however far-fetched. In Berkman's book, when the escape plot begins, the abrupt reversal of the prose is almost comic, as if years of repression and dejection had had no effect at all. But it is so whenever there is sudden hope, however far-fetched. In the winter of '67 and the spring of '68 we saw it among the youth of Czechoslovakia. Most of them had been born since 1947, when the Russians took over, and on any sociological theory whatever, they should have been brainwashed and internally cowed, rather than just bowing to the inevitable and biding their time. But they were not.

In my opinion, the flood of excitement occurs just because there is a possibility of doing something that makes a modicum of sense, instead of the utter waste and endless senselessness in which one has been doing time, whether in jail or under a tyranny. The need to make sense *is* the craving for freedom.

Berkman's story, where the far-fetched plot to escape falls through, is especially instructive. For there is no collapse of spirit, but just a somber return to his more profound humane concerns that have also begun to make sense. In the best cases, like his, what seems to occur over the weeks and months and years is just the opposite of the dreary sentiment that I referred to above, i.e., that the outside world is nearly as much of a prison as the prison. It is rather the philosophical discovery that wherever one is is a sample of all the reality that there is.

It is a useless question whether or not it is a good or adequate sample. In prison, fork, shoelace, radiator pipe, and clove of nutmeg become important objects of study and use. "Ten steps from one corner to another is already something," says Kropotkin. "If I repeat them one hundred fifty times I shall have walked a verst." Jim Peck, who does not tend to poetry and rapture, seems in his prison to be enraptured by windows: "I used to go and gaze eagerly at the valley below and the hills beyond" or "After the sun dropped behind the prison building, we waited for the orange and pink clouds to fade into gray. The tension of the day would ease as we stood by our windows." Activists who like to devise obstructive tactics also find in prison the means for fun and games—in recent literature, this activity seems to take the place of the older intricate schemes of escape, which would tend to confirm my hunch that they judge inside and outside as fairly equivalent aspects of the same System. Political prisoners engage in political actions relevant to the local circumstances—sabotage, petitions, boycotts, hunger strikes about segregation, maltreatment, lousy food. We have been seeing political action in military jails.

Predictably, as an anarchist and a poet, Berkman devotes most of his pages to the characters and stories of men, his fellows: their loyalty and fortitude, their pettiness and duplicity, the brutality of the powerful, the suffering of the powerless. Remarkably for his time, he seems to make no distinction at all in his mind between "political prisoners" and "common criminals," though in their paranoid treatment of him, the authorities continually keep making the distinction—to his disadvantage (their panic about his ideology is very American). In contemporary social psychology, needless to say, we understand that they are *all* political prisoners, which Berkman, as an anarchist, knew. In the older theology, we are all common criminals.

His telling of the sexual scenes is especially notable. Most of the prison writers treat homosexuality with varying degrees of tolerance or matter-of-factness; it is rare that they are outraged or censorious like the do-good investigators. But Berkman alone unsophisticatedly goes to the essence, the longing, being in love, and love, that would inevitably occur. His embarrassed conversations are quite wonderful; I do not know any novels of sixty years ago to equal them. He does not mention any scenes of sexual brutality, however, though this also would be the nature of the case where men are not free. Being in prison is one of the conditions that most need fellow-feeling, but it is one of the worst conditions for it.

And the last episode of prison books is getting out, when it turns out that after all one has not come back to freedom. Not because the outside world is a prison, but because one is oneself not all there. And the Girl is no longer all there. . . . This is why the writers write. Men returned from the front lines do the same.

PART 1

THE AWAKENING AND ITS TOLL

ALEXANDER BERKMAN
At the time of the Homestead Strike

CHAPTER I

THE CALL OF HOMESTEAD

I

CLEARLY every detail of that day is engraved on my mind. It is the sixth of July, 1892. We are quietly sitting in the back of our little flat—Fedya and I—when suddenly the Girl enters. Her naturally quick, energetic step sounds more than usually resolute. As I turn to her, I am struck by the peculiar gleam in her eyes and the heightened color.

"Have you read it?" she cries, waving the half-open newspaper.

"What is it?"

"Homestead. Strikers shot. Pinkertons have killed women and children."

She speaks in a quick, jerky manner. Her words ring like the cry of a wounded animal, the melodious voice tinged with the harshness of bitterness—the bitterness of helpless agony.

I take the paper from her hands. In growing excitement I read the vivid account of the tremendous struggle, the Homestead strike, or, more correctly, the lockout. The report details the conspiracy on the part of the Carnegie Company to crush the Amalgamated Association of Iron and Steel Workers; the selection, for the purpose, of Henry Clay Frick, whose attitude toward labor is implacably hostile; his secret military preparations while designedly prolonging the peace negotiations with the Amalgamated; the fortification of the Homestead steel-works; the erection of a high board fence, capped by barbed wire and provided with loopholes for sharpshooters; the hiring of an army of Pinkerton thugs; the attempt to smuggle them, in the dead of night, into Homestead; and, finally, the terrible carnage.

I pass the paper to Fedya. The Girl glances at me. We sit in silence, each busy with his own thoughts. Only now and then we exchange a word, a searching, significant look.

II

It is hot and stuffy in the train. The air is oppressive with tobacco smoke; the boisterous talk of the men playing cards near by annoys me. I turn to the window. The gust of perfumed air, laden with the rich aroma of fresh-mown hay, is soothingly invigorating. Green woods and yellow fields circle in the distance, whirl nearer, close, then rush by, giving place to other circling fields and woods. The country looks young and alluring in the early morning sunshine. But my thoughts are busy with Homestead.

The great battle has been fought. Never before, in all its history, has American labor won such a signal victory. By force of arms the workers of Homestead have compelled three hundred Pinkerton invaders to surrender, to surrender most humbly, ignominiously. What humiliating defeat for the powers that be! Does not the Pinkerton janizary represent organized authority, forever crushing the toiler in the interest of the exploiters? Well may the enemies of the People be terrified at the unexpected awakening. But the People, the workers of America, have joyously acclaimed the rebellious manhood of Homestead. The steel-workers were not the aggressors. Resignedly they had toiled and suffered. Out of their flesh and bone grew the great steel industry; on their blood fattened the powerful Carnegie Company. Yet patiently they had waited for the promised greater share of the wealth they were creating. Like a bolt from a clear sky came the blow: wages were to be reduced! Peremptorily the steel magnates refused to continue the sliding scale previously agreed upon as a guarantee of peace. The Carnegie firm challenged the Amalgamated Association by the submission of conditions which it knew the workers could not accept. Foreseeing refusal, it flaunted warlike preparations to crush the union under the iron heel. Perfidious Carnegie shrank from the task, having recently proclaimed the gospel of good will and harmony. "I would lay it down as a maxim," he had declared, "that there is no excuse for a strike or a lockout until arbitration of differences has been offered by one party and refused by the other. The right of the workingmen to combine and to form trades-unions is no less sacred than the right of the manufacturer to enter into association and conference with his fellows, and it must sooner or later be conceded. Manufacturers should meet their men *more than half-way.*"

With smooth words the great philanthropist had persuaded the workers to indorse the high tariff. Every product of his mills protected, Andrew Carnegie secured a reduction in the duty on steel billets, in return for his generous contribution to the Republican campaign fund. In complete control of the billet market, the Carnegie firm engineered a depression of prices, as a seeming consequence of a lower duty. But *the market price of billets was the sole standard of wages in the Homestead mills.* The wages of the workers must be reduced! The offer of the Amalgamated Association to arbitrate the new scale met with contemptuous refusal: there was nothing to arbitrate; the men must submit unconditionally; the union was to be exterminated. And Carnegie selected Henry C. Frick, the bloody Frick of the coke regions, to carry the program into execution.

Must the oppressed forever submit? The manhood of Homestead rebelled: the millmen scorned the despotic ultimatum. Then Frick's hand fell. The war was on! Indignation swept the country. Throughout the land the tyrannical attitude of the Carnegie Company was bitterly denounced, the ruthless brutality of Frick universally execrated.

I could no longer remain indifferent. The moment was urgent. The toilers of Homestead had defied the oppressor. They were awakening. But as yet the steel-workers were only blindly rebellious. The vision of Anarchism alone could imbue discontent with conscious revolutionary purpose; it alone could lend wings to the aspirations of labor. The dissemination of our ideas among the proletariat of Homestead would illumine the great struggle, help to clarify the issues, and point the way to complete ultimate emancipation.

My days were feverish with anxiety. The stirring call, "Labor, Awaken!" would fire the hearts of the disinherited, and inspire them to noble deeds. It would carry to the oppressed the message of the New Day, and prepare them for the approaching Social Revolution. Homestead might prove the first blush of the glorious Dawn. How I chafed at the obstacles my project encountered! Unexpected difficulties impeded every step. The efforts to get the leaflet translated into popular English proved unavailing. It would endanger me to distribute such a fiery appeal, my friend remonstrated. Impatiently I waived aside his objections. As if personal considerations could for an instant be weighed in the scale of the great Cause! But in vain I argued and pleaded. And all the while precious moments were being wasted, and new obstacles barred the way. I rushed frantically from printer to compositor, begging, imploring. None dared print the appeal. And time was fleeting. Suddenly flashed the news of the Pinkerton carnage. The world stood aghast.

The time for speech was past. Throughout the land the toilers echoed the defiance of the men of Homestead. The steel-workers had rallied bravely to the defence; the murderous Pinkertons were driven from the city. But loudly called the blood of Mammon's victims on the banks of the Monongahela. Loudly it calls. It is the People calling. Ah, the People! The grand, mysterious, yet so near and real, People. . . .

In my mind I see myself back in the little Russian college town, amid the circle of Petersburg students, home for their vacation, surrounded by the halo of that vague and wonderful something we called "Nihilist." The rushing train, Homestead, the five years passed in America, all turn into a mist, hazy with the distance of unreality, of centuries; and again I sit among superior beings, reverently listening to the impassioned discussion of dimly understood high themes, with the oft-recurring refrain of "Bazarov, Hegel, Liberty, Chernishevsky, *v naród.*" To the People! To the beautiful, simple People, so noble in spite of centuries of brutalizing suffering! Like a clarion call the note rings in my ears, amidst the din of contending views and obscure phraseology. The People! My Greek mythology moods have often pictured HIM to me as the mighty Atlas, supporting on his shoulders the weight of the world, his back bent, his face the mirror of unutterable misery, in his eye the look of hopeless anguish, the dumb, pitiful appeal for help. Ah, to help this helplessly suffering giant, to lighten his burden! The way is obscure, the means uncertain, but in the heated student debate the note rings clear: To the People, become one of them, share their joys and sorrows, and thus you will teach them. Yes, that is the solution! But what is that red-headed Misha from Odessa saying? "It is all good and well about going to the People, but the energetic men of the deed, the Rakhmetovs, blaze the path of popular revolution by individual acts of revolt against—"

"Ticket, please!" A heavy hand is on my shoulder. With an effort I realize the situation. The card-players are exchanging angry words. With a deft movement the conductor unhooks the board, and calmly walks away with it under his arm. A roar of laughter greets the players. Twitted by the other passengers, they soon subside, and presently the car grows quiet.

I have difficulty in keeping myself from falling back into reverie. I must form a definite plan of action. My purpose is quite clear to me. A tremendous struggle is taking place at Homestead: the People are manifesting the right spirit in resisting tyranny and invasion. My heart exults. This is, at last, what I have always hoped for from the American workingman: once aroused, he will brook no interference; he will fight all obstacles, and conquer even more than his original demands. It is the spirit of the heroic past reincarnated in the steel-workers of Homestead, Pennsylvania. What supreme joy to aid in this work! That is my natural mission. I feel the strength of a great undertaking. No shadow of doubt crosses my mind. The People—the toilers of the world, the producers—comprise, to me, the universe. They alone count. The rest are parasites, who have no right to exist. But to the People belongs the earth—by right, if not in fact. To make it so in fact, all means are justifiable; nay, advisable, even to the point of taking life. The question of moral right in such matters often agitated the revolutionary circles I used to frequent. I had always taken the extreme view. The more radical the treatment, I held, the quicker the cure. Society is a patient; sick constitutionally and functionally. Surgical treatment is often imperative. The removal of a tyrant is not merely justifiable; it is the highest duty of every true revolutionist. Human life is, indeed, sacred and inviolate. But the killing of a tyrant, of an enemy of the People, is in no way to be considered as the taking of a life. A revolutionist would rather perish a thousand times than be guilty of what is ordinarily called murder. In truth, murder and *Attentat** are to me opposite terms. To remove a tyrant is an act of liberation, the giving of life and opportunity to an oppressed people. True, the Cause often calls upon the revolutionist to commit an unpleasant act; but it is the test of a true revolutionist— nay, more, his pride—to sacrifice all merely human feeling at the call of the People's Cause. If the latter demand his life, so much the better.

Could anything be nobler than to die for a grand, a sublime Cause? Why, the very life of a true revolutionist has no other purpose, no significance whatever, save to sacrifice it on the altar of the beloved People. And what could be higher in life than to be a true revolutionist? It is to be a *man*,

---

* An act of political assassination.

a complete MAN. A being who has neither personal interests nor desires above the necessities of the Cause; one who has emancipated himself from being merely human, and has risen above that, even to the height of conviction which excludes all doubt, all regret; in short, one who in the very inmost of his soul feels himself revolutionist first, human afterwards.

Such a revolutionist I feel myself to be. Indeed, far more so than even the extreme radicals of my own circle. My mind reverts to a characteristic incident in connection with the poet Edelstadt. It was in New York, about the year 1890. Edelstadt, one of the tenderest of souls, was beloved by every one in our circle, the *Pioneers of Liberty,* the first Jewish Anarchist organization on American soil. One evening the closer personal friends of Edelstadt met to consider plans for aiding the sick poet. It was decided to send our comrade to Denver, some one suggesting that money be drawn for the purpose from the revolutionary treasury. I objected. Though a dear, personal friend of Edelstadt, and his former roommate, I could not allow—I argued— that funds belonging to the movement be devoted to private purposes, however good and even necessary those might be. The strong disapproval of my sentiments I met with this challenge: "Do you mean to help Edelstadt, the poet and man, or Edelstadt the revolutionist? Do you consider him a true, active revolutionist? His poetry is beautiful, indeed, and may indirectly even prove of some propagandistic value. Aid our friend with your private funds, if you will; but no money from the movement can be given, except for direct revolutionary activity."

"Do you mean that the poet is less to you than the revolutionist?" I was asked by Tikhon, a young medical student, whom we playfully dubbed "Lingg," because of his rather successful affectation of the celebrated revolutionist's physical appearance.

"I am revolutionist first, man afterwards," I replied, with conviction.

"You are either a knave or a hero," he retorted.

"Lingg" was quite right. He could not know me. To his *bourgeois* mind, for all his imitation of the Chicago martyr, my words must have sounded knavish. Well, some day he may know which I am, knave or revolutionist. I do not think in the term "hero," for though the type of revolutionist I feel myself to be might popularly be so called, the word has no significance for me. It merely means a revolutionist who does his duty. There is no heroism in that: it is neither more nor less than a revolutionist should do. Rakhmetov did more, too much. In spite of my great admiration for Chernishevsky, who had so strongly influenced the Russian youth of my time, I can not suppress the touch of resentment I feel because the author of "What's To Be Done?" represented his arch-revolutionist Rakhmetov as going through a system of unspeakable, self-inflicted torture to prepare himself for future exigencies. It was a sign of weakness. Does a real revolutionist need to prepare himself, to steel his nerves and harden his body? I feel it almost a personal insult, this suggestion of the revolutionist's mere human clay.

No, the thorough revolutionist needs no such self-doubting preparations. For I know *I* do not need them. The feeling is quite impersonal, strange as it may seem. My own individuality is entirely in the background; aye, I am not conscious of any personality in matters pertaining to the Cause. I am simply a revolutionist, a terrorist by conviction, an instrument for furthering the cause of humanity; in short, a Rakhmetov.   Indeed, I shall assume that name upon my arrival in Pittsburgh.

.   .   .   .

The piercing shrieks of the locomotive awake me with a start. My first thought is of my wallet, containing important addresses of Allegheny comrades, which I was trying to memorize when I must have fallen asleep. The wallet is gone! For a moment I am overwhelmed with terror. What if it is lost? Suddenly my foot touches something soft. I pick it up, feeling tremendously relieved to find all the contents safe: the precious addresses, a small newspaper lithograph of Frick, and a dollar bill. My joy at recovering the wallet is not a whit dampened by the meagerness of my funds. The dollar will do to get a room in a hotel for the first night, and in the morning I'll look up Nold or Bauer. They will find a place for me to stay a day or two. "I won't remain there long," I think, with an inward smile.

We are nearing Washington, D. C. The train is to make a six-hour stop there. I curse the stupidity of the delay: something may be happening in Pittsburgh or Homestead. Besides, no time is to be lost in striking a telling blow, while public sentiment is aroused at the atrocities of the Carnegie Company, the brutality of Frick.

Yet my irritation is strangely dispelled by the beautiful picture that greets my eye as I step from the train. The sun has risen, a large ball of deep red, pouring a flood of gold upon the Capitol. The cupola rears its proud head majestically above the pile of stone and marble. Like a living thing the light palpitates, trembling with passion to kiss the uppermost peak, striking it with blinding brilliancy, and then spreading in a broadening embrace down the shoulders of the towering giant. The amber waves entwine its flanks with soft caresses, and then rush on, to right and left, wider and lower, flashing upon the stately trees, dallying amid leaves and branches, finally unfolding themselves over the broad avenue, and ever growing more golden and generous as they scatter. And cupola-headed giant, stately trees, and broad avenue quiver with new-born ecstasy, all nature heaves the contented sigh of bliss, and nestles closer to the golden giver of life.

At this moment I realize, as perhaps never before, the great joy, the surpassing gladness, of being. But in a trice the picture changes. Before my eyes rises the Monongahela river, carrying barges filled with armed men. And I hear a shot. A boy falls to the gangplank. The blood gushes from the centre of his forehead. The hole ploughed by the bullet yawns black on the crimson face. Cries and wailing ring in my ears. I see men running toward the river, and women kneeling by the side of the dead.

The horrible vision revives in my mind a similar incident, lived through in imagination before. It was the sight of an executed Nihilist. The Nihilists! How much of their precious blood has been shed, how many thousands of them line the road of Russia's suffering! Inexpressibly near and soul-kin I feel to those men and women, the adored, mysterious ones of my youth, who had left wealthy homes and high station to "go to the People," to become one with them, though despised by all whom they held dear, persecuted and ridiculed even by the benighted objects of their great sacrifice.

Clearly there flashes out upon my memory my first impression of Nihilist Russia. I had just passed my second year's gymnasium examinations. Overflowing with blissful excitement, I rushed into the house to tell mother the joyful news. How happy it will make her! Next week will be my twelfth birthday, but mother need give me no present. I have one for her, instead. "Mamma, mamma!" I called, when suddenly I caught her voice, raised in anger. Something has happened, I thought; mother never speaks so loudly. Something very peculiar, I felt, noticing the door leading from the broad hallway to the dining-room closed, contrary to custom. In perturbation I hesitated at the door. "Shame on you, Nathan," I heard my mother's voice, "to condemn your own brother because he is a Nihilist. You are no better than"—her voice fell to a whisper, but my straining ear distinctly caught the dread word, uttered with hatred and fear—"a *palátch.*"*

I was struck with terror. Mother's tone, my rich uncle Nathan's unwonted presence at our house, the fearful word *palátch*—something awful must have happened. I tiptoed out of the hallway, and ran to my room. Trembling with fear, I threw myself on the bed. What has the *palátch* done? I moaned. *"Your* brother," she had said to uncle. Her own youngest brother, my favorite uncle Maxim. Oh, what has happened to him? My excited imagination conjured up horrible visions. There stood the powerful figure of the giant *palátch*, all in black, his right arm bare to the shoulder, in his hand the uplifted ax. I could see the glimmer of the sharp steel as it began to descend, slowly, so torturingly slowly, while my heart ceased beating and

---

* Hangman.

my feverish eyes followed, bewitched, the glowing black coals in the *palátch's* head. Suddenly the two fiery eyes fused into a large ball of flaming red; the figure of the fearful one-eyed cyclop grew taller and stretched higher and higher, and everywhere was the giant—on all sides of me was he—then a sudden flash of steel, and in his monster hand I saw raised a head, cut close to the neck, its eyes incessantly blinking, the dark-red blood gushing from mouth and ears and throat. Something looked ghastly familiar about that head with the broad white forehead and expressive mouth, so sweet and sad. "Oh, Maxim, Maxim!" I cried, terror-stricken: the next moment a flood of passionate hatred of the *palátch* seized me, and I rushed, head bent, toward the one-eyed monster. Nearer and nearer I came,—another quick rush, and then the violent impact of my body struck him in the very centre, and he fell, forward and heavy, right upon me, and I felt his fearful weight crushing my arms, my chest, my head. . . .

"Sasha! Sashenka! What is the matter, *golub-chik?*" I recognize the sweet, tender voice of my mother, sounding far away and strange, then coming closer and growing more soothing. I open my eyes. Mother is kneeling by the bed, her beautiful black eyes bathed in tears. Passionately she showers kisses upon my face and hands, entreating: "*Golubchik,* what is it?"

"Mamma, what happened to Uncle Maxim?" I ask, breathlessly watching her face.

Her sudden change of expression chills my heart with fear. She turns ghostly white, large drops of perspiration stand on her forehead, and her eyes grow large and round with terror. "Mamma!" I cry, throwing my arms around her. Her lips move, and I feel her warm breath on my cheek; but, without uttering a word, she bursts into vehement weeping.

"Who—told—you? You—know?" she whispers between sobs.

.   .   ..

The pall of death seems to have descended upon our home. The house is oppressively silent. Everybody walks about in slippers, and the piano is kept locked. Only monosyllables, in undertone, are exchanged at the dinner-table. Mother's seat remains vacant. She is very ill, the nurse informs us; no one is to see her.

The situation bewilders me. I keep wondering what has happened to Maxim. Was my vision of the *palátch* a presentiment, or the echo of an accomplished tragedy? Vaguely I feel guilty of mother's illness. The shock of my question may be responsible for her condition. Yet there must be more to it, I try to persuade my troubled spirit. One afternoon, finding my eldest brother Maxim, named after mother's favorite brother, in a very cheerful mood, I call him aside and ask, in a boldly assumed confidential manner: "Maximushka, tell me, what is a Nihilist?"

"Go to the devil, *molokossoss** you!" he cries, angrily. With a show of violence, quite inexplicable to me, Maxim throws his paper on the floor, jumps from his seat, upsetting the chair, and leaves the room.

.   .   .   .

The fate of Uncle Maxim remains a mystery, the question of Nihilism unsolved. I am absorbed in my studies. Yet a deep interest, curiosity about the mysterious and forbidden, slumbers in my consciousness, when quite unexpectedly it is roused into keen activity by a school incident. I am fifteen now, in the fourth. grade of the classic gymnasium at Kovno. By direction

---

* Literally, milk-sucker. A contemptuous term applied to inexperienced youth.

of the Ministry of Education, compulsory religious instruction is being introduced in the State schools. Special classes have been opened at the gymnasium for the religious instruction of Jewish pupils. The parents of the latter resent the innovation; almost every Jewish child receives religious training at home or in *cheidar*.* But the school authorities have ordered the gymnasiasts of Jewish faith to attend classes in religion.

The roll-call at the first session finds me missing. Summoned before the Director for an explanation, I state that I failed to attend because I have a private Jewish tutor at home, and,—anyway, I do not believe in religion. The prim Director looks inexpressibly shocked.

"Young man," he addresses me in the artificial guttural voice he affects on solemn occasions. "Young man, when, permit me to ask, did you reach so profound a conclusion?"

His manner disconcerts me; but the sarcasm of his words and the offensive tone rouse my resentment. Impulsively, defiantly, I discover my cherished secret. "Since I wrote the essay, 'There Is No God,'" I reply, with secret exultation. But the next instant I realize the recklessness of my confession. I have a fleeting sense of coming trouble, at school and at home. Yet somehow I feel I have acted like a *man*. Uncle Maxim, the Nihilist, would act so in my position. I know his reputation for uncompromising candor, and love him for his bold, frank ways.

"Oh, that is interesting," I hear, as in a dream, the unpleasant guttural voice of the Director. "When did you write it?"

"Three years ago."

"How old were you then?"

———

* Schools for instruction in Jewish religion and laws.

"Twelve."

"Have you the essay?"

"Yes."

"Where?"

"At home."

"Bring it to me to-morrow. Without fail, remember."

His voice grows stern. The words fall upon my ears with the harsh metallic sound of my sister's piano that memorable evening of our musicale when, in a spirit of mischief, I hid a piece of gas pipe in the instrument tuned for the occasion.

"To-morrow, then. You are dismissed."

The Educational Board, in conclave assembled, reads the essay. My disquisition is unanimously condemned. Exemplary punishment is to be visited upon me for "precocious godlessness, dangerous tendencies, and insubordination." I am publicly reprimanded, and reduced to the third class. The peculiar sentence robs me of a year, and forces me to associate with the "children" my senior class looks down upon with undisguised contempt. I feel disgraced, humiliated.

.   .   .   .

Thus vision chases vision, memory succeeds memory, while the interminable hours creep towards the afternoon, and the station clock drones like an endless old woman.

III

Over at last. "All aboard!"

On and on rushes the engine, every moment bringing me nearer to my destination. The conductor drawling out the stations, the noisy going and coming produce almost no conscious impression on my senses. Seeing and hearing every detail of my surroundings, I am nevertheless oblivious to them. Faster than the train rushes my fancy, as if reviewing a panorama of vivid scenes, apparently without organic connection with each other, yet somehow intimately associated in my thoughts of the past. But how different is the present! I am speeding toward Pittsburgh, the very heart of the industrial struggle of America. America! I dwell wonderingly on the unuttered sound. Why in America? And again unfold pictures of old scenes.

I am walking in the garden of our well-appointed country place, in a fashionable suburb of St. Petersburg, where the family generally spends the summer months. As I pass the veranda, Dr. Semeonov, the celebrated physician of the resort, steps out of the house and beckons to me.

"Alexander Ossipovitch," he addresses me in his courtly manner, "your mother is very ill. Are you alone with her?"

"We have servants, and two nurses are in attendance," I reply.

"To be sure, to be sure," the shadow of a smile hovers about the corners of his delicately chiseled lips. "I mean of the family."

"Oh, yes! I am alone here with my mother."

"Your mother is rather restless to-day, Alexander Ossipovitch. Could you sit up with her to-night?"

"Certainly, certainly," I quickly assent, wondering at the peculiar request. Mother has been improving, the nurses have assured me. My presence at her bedside may prove irksome to her. Our relations have been strained since the day when, in a fit of anger, she slapped Rose, our new chambermaid, whereupon I resented mother's right to inflict physical punishment on the servants. I can see her now, erect and haughty, facing me across the dinner-table, her eyes ablaze with indignation.

"You forget you are speaking to your mother, Al-ex-an-der"; she pronounces the name in four distinct syllables, as is her habit when angry with me.

"You have no right to strike the girl," I retort, defiantly.

"You forget yourself. My treatment of the menial is no concern of yours."

I cannot suppress the sharp reply that springs to my lips: "The low servant girl is as good as you."

I see mother's long, slender fingers grasp the heavy ladle, and the next instant a sharp pain pierces my left hand. Our eyes meet. Her arm remains motionless, her gaze directed to the spreading blood stain on the white table-cloth. The ladle falls from her hand. She closes her eyes, and her body sinks limply to the chair.

Anger and humiliation extinguish my momentary impulse to rush to her assistance. Without uttering a word, I pick up the heavy saltcellar, and fling it violently against the French mirror. At the crash of the glass my mother opens her eyes in amazement. I rise and leave the house.

My heart beats fast as I enter mother's sick-room. I fear she may resent my intrusion: the shadow of the past stands between us. But she is lying quietly on the bed, and has apparently not noticed my entrance. I sit down at the bedside. A long time passes in silence. Mother seems to be asleep. It is growing dark in the room, and I settle down to pass the night in the chair. Suddenly I hear "Sasha!" called in a weak, faint voice. I bend over her. "Drink of water." As I hold the glass to her lips, she slightly turns away her head, saying very low, "Ice water, please." I start to leave the room. "Sasha!" I hear behind me, and, quickly tiptoeing to the bed, I bring my face closely, very closely to hers, to catch the faint words: "Help me turn to the wall." Tenderly I wrap my arms around the weak, emaciated body, and an overpowering longing seizes me to touch her hand with my lips and on my knees beg her forgiveness. I feel so near to her, my heart is overflowing with compassion and love. But I dare not kiss her—we have become estranged. Affectionately I hold her in my arms for just the shadow of a second, dreading lest she suspect the storm of emotion raging within me. Caressingly I turn her to the wall, and, as I slowly withdraw, I feel as if some mysterious, yet definite, something has at the very instant left her body.

In a few minutes I return with a glass of ice water. I hold it to her lips, but she seems oblivious of my presence. "She cannot have gone to sleep so quickly," I wonder. "Mother!" I call, softly. No reply. "Little mother! Mamotchka!" She does not appear to hear me. "Dearest, *golubchick!*" I cry, in a paroxysm of sudden fear, pressing my hot lips upon her face. Then I become conscious of an arm upon my shoulder, and hear the measured voice of the doctor: "My boy, you must bear up. She is at rest."

IV

"Wake up, young feller! Whatcher sighin' for?" Bewildered I turn around to meet the coarse, yet not unkindly, face of a swarthy laborer in the seat back of me.

"Oh, nothing; just dreaming," I reply. Not wishing to encourage conversation, I pretend to become absorbed in my book.

How strange is the sudden sound of English!

Almost as suddenly had I been transplanted to American soil. Six months passed after my mother's death. Threatened by the educational authorities with a "wolf's passport" on account of my "dangerous tendencies"— which would close every professional avenue to me, in spite of my otherwise very satisfactory standing—the situation aggravated by a violent quarrel with my guardian, Uncle Nathan, I decided to go to America. There, beyond the ocean, was the land of noble achievement, a glorious free country, where men walked erect in the full stature of manhood,—the very realization of my youthful dreams.

And now I am in America, the blessed land. The disillusionment, the disappointments, the vain struggles! . . . The kaleidoscope of my brain unfolds them all before my view. Now I see myself on a bench in Union Square Park, huddled close to Fedya and Mikhail, my roommates. The night wind sweeps across the cheerless park, chilling us to the bone. I feel hungry and tired, fagged out by the day's fruitless search for work. My heart sinks within me as I glance at my friends. "Nothing," each had morosely reported at our nightly meeting, after the day's weary tramp. Fedya groans in uneasy sleep, his hand groping about his knees. I pick up the newspaper that had fallen under the seat, spread it over his legs, and tuck the ends underneath. But a sudden blast tears the paper away, and whirls it off into the darkness. As I press Fedya's hat down on his head, I am struck by his ghastly look. How these few weeks have changed the plump, rosy-cheeked youth! Poor fellow, no one wants his labor. How his mother would suffer if she knew that her carefully reared boy passes the nights in the . . . What is that pain I feel? Some one is bending over me, looming unnaturally large in the darkness. Half-dazed I see an arm swing to and fro, with short, semicircular backward strokes, and with every movement I feel a sharp sting, as of a lash. Oh, it's in my soles! Bewildered I spring to my feet. A rough hand grabs me by the throat, and I face a policeman.

"Are you thieves?" he bellows.

Mikhail replies, sleepily: "We Russians. Want work."

"Git out o' here! Off with you!"

Quickly, silently, we walk away, Fedya and I in front, Mikhail limping behind us. The dimly lighted streets are deserted, save for a hurrying figure here and there, closely wrapped, flitting mysteriously around the corner. Columns of dust rise from the gray pavements, are caught up by the wind, rushed to some distance, then carried in a spiral upwards, to be followed by another wave of choking dust. From somewhere a tantalizing odor reaches my nostrils. "The bakery on Second Street," Fedya remarks. Unconsciously our steps quicken. Shoulders raised, heads bent, and shivering, we keep on to the lower Bowery. Mikhail is steadily falling behind. "Dammit, I feel bad," he says, catching up with us, as we step into an open hallway. A thorough inspection of our pockets reveals the possession of twelve cents, all around. Mikhail is to go to bed, we decide, handing him a dime. The cigarettes purchased for the remaining two cents are divided equally, each taking a few puffs of the "fourth" in the box. Fedya and I sleep on the steps of the city hall.

.   .   .   .

"Pitt-s-burgh! Pitt-s-burgh!"

The harsh cry of the conductor startles me with the violence of a shock. Impatient as I am of the long journey, the realization that I have reached my destination comes unexpectedly, overwhelming me with the dread of unpreparedness. In a flurry I gather up my things, but, noticing that the other passengers keep their places, I precipitately resume my seat, fearful lest my agitation be noticed. To hide my confusion, I turn to the open window. Thick clouds of smoke overcast the sky, shrouding the morning with sombre gray. The air is heavy with soot and cinders; the smell is nauseating. In the distance, giant furnaces vomit pillars of fire, the lurid flashes accentuating a line of frame structures, dilapidated and miserable. They are the homes of the workers who have created the industrial glory of Pittsburgh, reared its millionaires, its Carnegies and Fricks.

The sight fills me with hatred of the perverse social justice that turns the needs of mankind into an Inferno of brutalizing toil. It robs man of his soul, drives the sunshine from his life, degrades him lower than the beasts, and between the millstones of divine bliss and hellish torture grinds flesh and blood into iron and steel, transmutes human lives into gold, gold, countless gold.

The great, noble People! But is it really great and noble to be slaves and remain content? No, no! They are awakening, awakening!

CHAPTER II

THE SEAT OF WAR

CONTENTEDLY peaceful the Monongahela stretches before me, its waters lazily rippling in the sunlight, and softly crooning to the murmur of the woods on the hazy shore. But the opposite bank presents a picture of sharp contrast. Near the edge of the river rises a high board fence, topped with barbed wire, the menacing aspect heightened by warlike watch-towers and ramparts. The sinister wall looks down on me with a thousand hollow eyes, whose evident murderous purpose fully justifies the name of "Fort Frick." Groups of excited people crowd the open spaces between the river and the fort, filling the air with the confusion of many voices. Men carrying Winchesters are hurrying by, their faces grimy, eyes bold yet anxious. From the mill-yard gape the black mouths of cannon, dismantled breastworks bar the passages, and the ground is strewn with burning cinders, empty shells, oil barrels, broken furnace stacks, and piles of steel and iron. The place looks the aftermath of a sanguinary conflict,—the symbol of our industrial life, of the ruthless struggle in which the *stronger,* the sturdy man of labor, is always the victim, because he acts *weakly.* But the charred hulks of the Pinkerton barges at the landing-place, and the blood-bespattered gangplank, bear mute witness that for once the battle went to the *really strong, to the victim who dared.*

A group of workingmen approaches me. Big, stal-

23

wart men, the power of conscious strength in their step
and bearing. Each of them carries a weapon: some Winchesters, others shotguns. In the hand of one I notice
the gleaming barrel of a navy revolver.

"Who are you?" the man with the revolver sternly
asks me.

"A friend, a visitor."

"Can you show credentials or a union card?"

Presently, satisfied as to my trustworthiness, they
allow me to proceed.

In one of the mill-yards I come upon a dense crowd
of men and women of various types: the short, broad-
faced Slav, elbowing his tall American fellow-striker;
the swarthy Italian, heavy-mustached, gesticulating and
talking rapidly to a cluster of excited countrymen. The
people are surging about a raised platform, on which
stands a large, heavy man.

I press forward. "Listen, gentlemen, listen!" I hear
the speaker's voice. "Just a few words, gentlemen!
You all know who I am, don't you?"

"Yes, yes, Sheriff!" several men cry. "Go on!"

"Yes," continues the speaker, "you all know who I
am. Your Sheriff, the Sheriff of Allegheny County, of
the great Commonwealth of Pennsylvania."

"Go ahead!" some one yells, impatiently.

"If you don't interrupt me, gentlemen, I'll go ahead."

"S-s-sh! Order!"

The speaker advances to the edge of the platform.
"Men of Homestead! It is my sworn duty, as Sheriff,
to preserve the peace. Your city is in a state of lawless-
ness. I have asked the Governor to send the militia and
I hope—"

"No! No!" many voices protest. "To hell with you!"
The tumult drowns the words of the Sheriff. Shaking
his clenched fist, his foot stamping the platform, he

shouts at the crowd, but his voice is lost amid the general uproar.

"O'Donnell! O'Donnell!" comes from several sides, the cry swelling into a tremendous chorus, "O'Donnell!"

I see the popular leader of the strike nimbly ascend the platform. The assembly becomes hushed.

"Brothers," O'Donnell begins in a flowing, ingratiating manner, "we have won a great, noble victory over the Company. We have driven the Pinkerton invaders out of our city—"

"Damn the murderers!"

"Silence! Order!"

"You have won a big victory," O'Donnell continues, "a great, significant victory, such as was never before known in the history of labor's struggle for better conditions."

Vociferous cheering interrupts the speaker. "But," he continues, "you must show the world that you desire to maintain peace and order along with your rights. The Pinkertons were invaders. We defended our homes and drove them out; rightly so. But you are law-abiding citizens. You respect the law and the authority of the State. Public opinion will uphold you in your struggle if you act right. Now is the time, friends!" He raises his voice in waxing enthusiasm, "Now is the time! Welcome the soldiers. They are not sent by that man Frick. They are the people's militia. They are our friends. Let us welcome them as friends!"

Applause, mixed with cries of impatient disapproval, greets the exhortation. Arms are raised in angry argument, and the crowd sways back and forth, breaking into several excited groups. Presently a tall, dark man appears on the platform. His stentorian voice gradually draws the assembly closer to the front. Slowly the tumult subsides.

"Don't you believe it, men!" The speaker shakes his finger at the audience, as if to emphasize his warning. "Don't you believe that the soldiers are coming as friends. Soft words these, Mr. O'Donnell. They'll cost us dear. Remember what I say, brothers. The soldiers are no friends of ours. I know what I am talking about. They are coming here because that damned murderer Frick wants them."

"Hear! Hear!"

"Yes!" the tall man continues, his voice quivering with emotion, "I can tell you just how it is. The scoundrel of a Sheriff there asked the Governor for troops, and that damned Frick paid the Sheriff to do it, I say!"

"No! Yes! No!" the clamor is renewed, but I can hear the speaker's voice rising above the din: "Yes, bribed him. You all know this cowardly Sheriff. Don't you let the soldiers come, I tell you. First *they'll* come; then the blacklegs. You want 'em?"

"No! No!" roars the crowd.

"Well, if you don't want the damned scabs, keep out the soldiers, you understand? If you don't, they'll drive you out from the homes you have paid for with your blood. You and your wives and children they'll drive out, and out you will go from these"—the speaker points in the direction of the mills—"that's what they'll do, if you don't look out. We have sweated and bled in these mills, our brothers have been killed and maimed there, we have made the damned Company rich, and now they send the soldiers here to shoot us down like the Pinkerton thugs have tried to. And you want to welcome the murderers, do you? Keep them out, I tell you!"

Amid shouts and yells the speaker leaves the platform.

"McLuckie! 'Honest' McLuckie!" a voice is heard on the fringe of the crowd, and as one man the assembly takes up the cry, " 'Honest' McLuckie!"

I am eager to see the popular Burgess of Homestead, himself a poorly paid employee of the Carnegie Company. A large-boned, good-natured-looking working-man elbows his way to the front, the men readily making way for him with nods and pleasant smiles.

"I haven't prepared any speech," the Burgess begins haltingly, "but I want to say, I don't see how you are going to fight the soldiers. There is a good deal of truth in what the brother before me said; but if you stop to think on it, he forgot to tell you just one little thing. The *how?* How is he going to do it, to keep the soldiers out? That's what I'd like to know. I'm afraid it's bad to let them in. The blacklegs *might* be hiding in the rear. But then again, it's bad *not* to let the soldiers in. You can't stand up against 'em: they are not Pinkertons. And we can't fight the Government of Pennsylvania. Perhaps the Governor won't send the militia. But if he does, I reckon the best way for us will be to make friends with them. Guess it's the only thing we can do. That's all I have to say."

The assembly breaks up, dejected, dispirited.

CHAPTER III

THE SPIRIT OF PITTSBURGH

I

LIKE a gigantic hive the twin cities jut out on the banks of the Ohio, heavily breathing the spirit of feverish activity, and permeating the atmosphere with the rage of life. Ceaselessly flow the streams of human ants, meeting and diverging, their paths crossing and recrossing, leaving in their trail a thousand winding passages, mounds of structure, peaked and domed. Their huge shadows overcast the yellow thread of gleaming river that curves and twists its painful way, now hugging the shore, now hiding in affright, and again timidly stretching its arms toward the wrathful monsters that belch fire and smoke into the midst of the giant hive. And over the whole is spread the gloom of thick fog, oppressive and dispiriting—the symbol of our existence, with all its darkness and cold.

This is Pittsburgh, the heart of American industrialism, whose spirit moulds the life of the great Nation. The spirit of Pittsburgh, the Iron City! Cold as steel, hard as iron, its products. These are the keynote of the great Republic, dominating all other chords, sacrificing harmony to noise, beauty to bulk. Its torch of liberty is a furnace fire, consuming, destroying, devastating: a country-wide furnace, in which the bones and marrow of the producers, their limbs and bodies, their health and blood, are cast into Bessemer steel, rolled into armor plate, and converted into engines of murder to be consecrated to Mammon by his high priests, the Carnegies, the Fricks.

The spirit of the Iron City characterizes the negotiations carried on between the Carnegie Company and the Homestead men. Henry Clay Frick, in absolute control of the firm, incarnates the spirit of the furnace, is the living emblem of his trade. The olive branch held out by the workers after their victory over the Pinkertons has been refused. The ultimatum issued by Frick is the last word of Caesar: the union of the steelworkers is to be crushed, completely and absolutely, even at the cost of shedding the blood of the last man in Homestead; the Company will deal only with individual workers, who must accept the terms offered, without question or discussion; he, Frick, will operate the mills with non-union labor, even if it should require the combined military power of the State and the Union to carry the plan into execution. Millmen disobeying the order to return to work under the new schedule of reduced wages are to be discharged forthwith, and evicted from the Company houses.

II

In an obscure alley, in the town of Homestead, there stands a one-story frame house, looking old and forlorn. It is occupied by the widow Johnson and her four small children. Six months ago, the breaking of a crane buried her husband under two hundred tons of metal. When the body was carried into the house, the distracted woman refused to recognize in the mangled remains her big, strong "Jack." For weeks the neighborhood resounded with her frenzied cry, "My husband! Where's my husband?" But the loving care of kind-hearted neighbors has now somewhat restored the poor woman's reason. Accompanied by her four little orphans, she recently gained admittance to Mr. Frick. On her knees she implored him not to drive her out of her home. Her poor husband was dead, she pleaded; she could not pay off the mortgage; the children were too young to work; she herself was hardly able to walk. Frick was very kind, she thought; he had promised to see what could be done. She would not listen to the neighbors urging her to sue the Company for damages. "The crane was rotten," her husband's friends informed her; "the government inspector had condemned it." But Mr. Frick was kind, and surely he knew best about the crane. Did he not say it was her poor husband's own carelessness?

She feels very thankful to good Mr. Frick for extending the mortgage. She had lived in such mortal dread lest her own little home, where dear John had been such a kind husband to her, be taken away, and her children driven into the street. She must never forget to ask the Lord's blessing upon the good Mr. Frick. Every day she repeats to her neighbors the story of her visit to the great man; how kindly he received her, how simply he talked with her. "Just like us folks," the widow says.

She is now telling the wonderful story to neighbor Mary, the hunchback, who, with undiminished interest, hears the recital for the twentieth time. It reflects such importance to know some one that had come in intimate contact with the Iron King; why, into his very presence! and even talked to the great magnate!

" 'Dear Mr. Frick,' says I," the widow is narrating,

" 'dear Mr. Frick,' I says, 'look at my poor little angels—' "

A knock on the door interrupts her. "Must be one-eyed Kate," the widow observes. "Come in! Come in!" she calls out, cheerfully. "Poor Kate!" she remarks with a sigh. "Her man's got the consumption. Won't last long, I fear."

A tall, rough-looking man stands in the doorway. Behind him appear two others. Frightened, the widow rises from the chair. One of the children begins to cry, and runs to hide behind his mother.

"Beg pard'n, ma'am," the tall man says. "Have no fear. We are Deputy Sheriffs. Read this." He produces an official-looking paper. "Ordered to dispossess you. Very sorry, ma'am, but get ready. Quick, got a dozen more of—"

There is a piercing scream. The Deputy Sheriff catches the limp body of the widow in his arms.

III

East End, the fashionable residence quarter of Pittsburgh, lies basking in the afternoon sun. The broad avenue looks cool and inviting: the stately trees touch their shadows across the carriage road, gently nodding their heads in mutual approval. A steady procession of equipages fills the avenue, the richly caparisoned horses and uniformed flunkies lending color and life to the scene. A cavalcade is passing me. The laughter of the ladies sounds joyous and care-free. Their happiness irritates me. I am thinking of Homestead. In mind I see the sombre fence, the fortifications and cannon; the piteous figure of the widow rises before me, the little children weeping, and again I hear the anguished cry of a broken heart, a shattered brain. . . .

And here all is joy and laughter. The gentlemen seem pleased; the ladies are happy. Why should they concern themselves with misery and want? The common folk are fit only to be their slaves, to feed and clothe them, build these beautiful palaces, and be content with the charitable crust. "Take what I give you," Frick commands. Why, here is his house! A luxurious place, with large garden, barns, and stable. That stable there,—it is more cheerful and habitable than the widow's home. Ah, life could be made livable, beautiful! Why should it not be? Why so much misery and strife? Sunshine, flowers, beautiful things are all around me. That is life! Joy and peace. . . . No! There can be no peace with such as Frick and these parasites in carriages riding on our backs, and sucking the blood of the workers. Fricks, vampires, all of them—I almost shout aloud —they are all one class. All in a cabal against *my* class, the toilers, the producers. An impersonal conspiracy, perhaps; but a conspiracy nevertheless. And the fine ladies on horseback smile and laugh. What is the misery of the People to *them?* Probably they are laughing at me. Laugh! Laugh! You despise me. I am of the People, but you belong to the Fricks. Well, it may soon be our turn to laugh. . . .

Returning to Pittsburgh in the evening, I learn that the conferences between the Carnegie Company and the Advisory Committee of the strikers have terminated in the final refusal of Frick to consider the demands of the millmen. The last hope is gone! The master is determined to crush his rebellious slaves.

CHAPTER IV

THE ATTENTAT

The door of Frick's private office, to the left of the reception-room, swings open as the colored attendant emerges, and I catch a flitting glimpse of a black-bearded, well-knit figure at a table in the back of the room.

"Mistah Frick is engaged. He can't see you now, sah," the negro says, handing back my card.

I take the pasteboard, return it to my case, and walk slowly out of the reception-room. But quickly retracing my steps, I pass through the gate separating the clerks from the visitors, and, brushing the astounded attendant aside, I step into the office on the left, and find myself facing Frick.

For an instant the sunlight, streaming through the windows, dazzles me. I discern two men at the further end of the long table.

"Fr—," I begin. The look of terror on his face strikes me speechless. It is the dread of the conscious presence of death. "He understands," it flashes through my mind. With a quick motion I draw the revolver. As I raise the weapon, I see Frick clutch with both hands the arm of the chair, and attempt to rise. I aim at his head. "Perhaps he wears armor," I reflect. With a look of horror he quickly averts his face, as I pull the trigger. There is a flash, and the high-ceilinged

33

room reverberates as with the booming of cannon. I hear a sharp, piercing cry, and see Frick on his knees, his head against the arm of the chair. I feel calm and possessed, intent upon every movement of the man. He is lying head and shoulders under the large armchair, without sound or motion. "Dead?" I wonder. I must make sure. About twenty-five feet separate us. I take a few steps toward him, when suddenly the other man, whose presence I had quite forgotten, leaps upon me. I struggle to loosen his hold. He looks slender and small. I would not hurt him: I have no business with him. Suddenly I hear the cry, "Murder! Help!" My heart stands still as I realize that it is Frick shouting. "Alive?" I wonder. I hurl the stranger aside and fire at the crawling figure of Frick. The man struck my hand,—I have missed! He grapples with me, and we wrestle across the room. I try to throw him, but spying an opening between his arm and body, I thrust the revolver against his side and aim at Frick, cowering behind the chair. I pull the trigger. There is a click— but no explosion! By the throat I catch the stranger, still clinging to me, when suddenly something heavy strikes me on the back of the head. Sharp pains shoot through my eyes. I sink to the floor, vaguely conscious of the weapon slipping from my hands.

"Where is the hammer? Hit him, carpenter!" Confused voices ring in my ears. Painfully I strive to rise. The weight of many bodies is pressing on me. Now—it's Frick's voice! Not dead? . . . I crawl in the direction of the sound, dragging the struggling men with me. I must get the dagger from my pocket—I have it! Repeatedly I strike with it at the legs of the man near the window. I hear Frick cry out in pain— there is much shouting and stamping—my arms are pulled and twisted, and I am lifted bodily from the floor.

Police, clerks, workmen in overalls, surround me. An officer pulls my head back by the hair, and my eyes meet Frick's. He stands in front of me, supported by several men. His face is ashen gray; the black beard is streaked with red, and blood is oozing from his neck. For an instant a strange feeling, as of shame, comes over me; but the next moment I am filled with anger at the sentiment, so unworthy of a revolutionist. With defiant hatred I look him full in the face.

"Mr. Frick, do you identify this man as your assailant?"

Frick nods weakly.

The street is lined with a dense, excited crowd. A young man in civilian dress, who is accompanying the police, inquires, not unkindly:

"Are you hurt? You're bleeding."

I pass my hand over my face. I feel no pain, but there is a peculiar sensation about my eyes.

"I've lost my glasses," I remark, involuntarily.

"You'll be damn lucky if you don't lose your head," an officer retorts.

CHAPTER V

THE THIRD DEGREE

I

The clanking of the keys grows fainter and fainter; the sound of footsteps dies away. The officers are gone. It is a relief to be alone. Their insolent looks and stupid questions, insinuations and threats,—how disgusting and tiresome it all is! A sense of complete indifference possesses me. I stretch myself out on the wooden bench, running along the wall of the cell, and at once fall asleep.

I awake feeling tired and chilly. All is quiet and dark around me. Is it night? My hand gropes blindly, hesitantly. Something wet and clammy touches my cheek. In sudden affright I draw back. The cell is damp and musty; the foul air nauseates me. Slowly my foot feels the floor, drawing my body forward, all my senses on the alert. I clutch the bars. The feel of iron is reassuring. Pressed close to the door, my mouth in the narrow opening, I draw quick, short breaths. I am hot, perspiring. My throat is dry to cracking; I cannot swallow. "Water! I want water!" The voice frightens me. Was it I that spoke? The sound rolls up; it rises from gallery to gallery, and strikes the opposite corner under the roof; now it crawls underneath, knocks in the distant hollows, and abruptly ceases.

"Holloa, there! Whatcher in for?"

The voice seems to issue at once from all sides of the corridor. But the sound relieves me. Now the air feels better; it is not so difficult to breathe. I begin to distinguish the outline of a row of cells opposite mine. There are dark forms at the doors. The men within look like beasts restlessly pacing their cages.

"Whatcher in for?" It comes from somewhere alongside. "Can't talk, eh? 'Sorderly, guess."

What am I in for? Oh, yes! It's Frick. Well, I shall not stay *here* long, anyhow. They will soon take me out—they will lean me against a wall—a slimy wall like this, perhaps. They will bandage my eyes, and the soldiers there. . . . No: they are going to hang me. Well, I shall be glad when they take me out of here. I am so dry. I'm suffocating. . . .

. . . The upright irons of the barred door grow faint, and melt into a single line; it adjusts itself crosswise between the upper and side sills. It resembles a scaffold, and there is a man sinking the beam into the ground. He leans it carefully against the wall, and picks up a spade. Now he stands with one foot in the hole. It is the carpenter! He hit me on the head. From behind, too, the coward. If he only knew what he had done. He is one of the People: we must go to them, enlighten them. I wish he'd look up. He doesn't know his real friends. He looks like a Russian peasant, with his broad back. What hairy arms he has! If he would only look up. . . . Now he sinks the beam into the ground; he is stamping down the earth. I will catch his eye as he turns around. Ah, he didn't look! He has his eyes always on the ground. Just like the *muzhik*. Now he is taking a few steps backward, critically examining his work. He seems pleased. How peculiar the cross-piece looks. The horizontal beam seems too long; out of proportion. I hope it won't break. I remember the feeling I had when my brother once showed me the picture of a man dangling from the branch of a tree. Underneath was inscribed, *The Execution of Stenka Razin.* "Didn't the branch break?" I asked. "No, Sasha," mother replied, "Stenka—well, he weighed nothing"; and I wondered at the peculiar look she exchanged with Maxim. But mother smiled sadly at me, and wouldn't explain. Then she turned to my brother: "Maxim, you must not bring Sashenka such pictures. He is too young." "Not too young, mamotchka, to learn that Stenka was a great man." "What! You young fool," father bristled with anger, "he was a murderer, a common rioter." But mother and Maxim bravely defended Stenka, and I was deeply incensed at father, who despotically terminated the discussion. "Not another word, now! I won't hear any more of that peasant criminal." The peculiar divergence of opinion perplexed me. Anybody could tell the difference between a murderer and a worthy man. Why couldn't they agree? He must have been a good man, I finally decided. Mother wouldn't cry over a hanged murderer: I saw her stealthily wipe her eyes as she looked at that picture. Yes, Stenka Razin was surely a noble man. I cried myself to sleep over the unspeakable injustice, wondering how I could ever forgive "them" the killing of the good Stenka, and why the weak-looking branch did not break with his weight. Why didn't it break? . . . The scaffold they will prepare for me might break with my weight. They'll hang me like Stenka, and perhaps a little boy will some day see the picture—and they will call me murderer—and only a few will know the truth—and the picture will show me hanging from . . . No, they shall not hang me!

My hand steals to the lapel of my coat, and a deep sense of gratification comes over me, as I feel the nitro-glycerine cartridge secure in the lining. I smile at the imaginary carpenter. Useless preparations! I have, myself, prepared for the event. No, they won't hang me. My hand caresses the long, narrow tube. Go ahead! Make your gallows. Why, the man is putting on his coat. Is he done already? Now he is turning around. He is looking straight at me. Why, it's Frick! Alive? . . .

My brain is on fire. I press my head against the bars, and groan heavily. Alive? Have I failed? Failed? . . .

II

Heavy footsteps approach nearer; the clanking of the keys grows more distinct. I must compose myself. Those mocking, unfriendly eyes shall not witness my agony. They could allay this terrible uncertainty, but I must seem indifferent.

Would I "take lunch with the Chief"? I decline, requesting a glass of water. Certainly; but the Chief wishes to see me first. Flanked on each side by a policeman, I pass through winding corridors, and finally ascend to the private office of the Chief. My mind is busy with thoughts of escape, as I carefully note the surroundings. I am in a large, well-furnished room, the heavily curtained windows built unusually high above the floor. A brass railing separates me from the roll-top desk, at which a middle-aged man, of distinct Irish type, is engaged with some papers.

"Good morning," he greets me, pleasantly. "Have a seat," pointing to a chair inside the railing. "I understand you asked for some water?"

"Yes."

"Just a few questions first. Nothing important. Your pedigree, you know. Mere matter of form. Answer frankly, and you shall have everything you want."

His manner is courteous, almost ingratiating.

"Now tell me, Mr. Berkman, what is your name? Your real name, I mean."

"That's my real name."

"You don't mean you gave your real name on the card you sent in to Mr. Frick?"

"I gave my real name."

"And you are an agent of a New York employment firm?"

"No."

"That was on your card."

"I wrote it to gain access to Frick."

"And you gave the name 'Alexander Berkman' to gain access?"

"No. I gave my real name. Whatever might happen, I did not want anyone else to be blamed."

"Are you a Homestead striker?"

"No."

"Why did you attack Mr. Frick?"

"He is an enemy of the People."

"You got a personal grievance against him?"

"No. I consider him an enemy of the People."

"Where do you come from?"

"From the station cell."

"Come, now, you may speak frankly, Mr. Berkman. I am your friend. I am going to give you a nice, comfortable cell. The other—"

"Worse than a Russian prison," I interrupt, angrily.

"How long did you serve there?"

"Where?"

"In the prison in Russia."

"I was never before inside a cell."

"Come, now, Mr. Berkman, tell the truth."

He motions to the officer behind my chair. The window curtains are drawn aside, exposing me to the full glare of the sunlight. My gaze wanders to the clock on the wall. The hour-hand points to V. The calendar on the desk reads, July—23—Saturday. Only three hours since my arrest? It seemed so long in the cell. . . .

"You can be quite frank with me," the inquisitor is saying. "I know a good deal more about you than you think. We've got your friend Rak-metov."

With difficulty I suppress a smile at the stupidity of the intended trap. In the register of the hotel where I passed the first night in Pittsburgh, I signed "Rakhmetov," the name of the hero in Chernishevsky's famous novel.

"Yes, we've got your friend, and we know all about you."

"Then why do you ask me?"

"Don't you try to be smart now. Answer my questions, d'ye hear?"

His manner has suddenly changed. His tone is threatening.

"Now answer me. Where do you live?"

"Give me some water. I am too dry to talk."

"Certainly, certainly," he replies, coaxingly. "You shall have a drink. Do you prefer whiskey or beer?"

"I never drink whiskey, and beer very seldom. I want water."

"Well, you'll get it as soon as we get through. Don't let us waste time, then. Who are your friends?"

"Give me a drink."

"The quicker we get through, the sooner you'll get a drink. I am having a nice cell fixed up for you, too. I want to be your friend, Mr. Berkman. Treat me right, and I'll take care of you. Now, tell me, where did you stop in Pittsburgh?"

"I have nothing to tell you."

"Answer me, or I'll—"

His face is purple with rage. With clenched fist he leaps from his seat; but, suddenly controlling himself, he says, with a reassuring smile:

"Now be sensible, Mr. Berkman. You seem to be an intelligent man. Why don't you talk sensibly?"

"What do you want to know?"

"Who went with you to Mr. Frick's office?"

Impatient of the comedy, I rise with the words:

"I came to Pittsburgh alone. I stopped at the Merchants' Hotel, opposite the B. and O. depot. I signed the name Rakhmetov in the register there. It's a fictitious name. My real name is Alexander Berkman. I went to Frick's office alone. I had no helpers. That's all I have to tell you."

"Very good, very good. Take your seat, Mr. Berkman. We're not in any hurry. Take your seat. You may as well stay here as in the cell; it's pleasanter. But I am going to have another cell fixed up for you. Just tell me, where do you stay in New York?"

"I have told you all there is to tell."

"Now. don't be stubborn. Who are your friends?"

"I won't say another word."

"Damn you, you'll think better of it. Officers, take him back. Same cell."

Every morning and evening, during three days, the scene is repeated by new inquisitors. They coax and threaten, they smile and rage in turn. I remain indifferent. But water is refused me, my thirst aggravated by the salty food they have given me. It consumes me, it tortures and burns my vitals through the sleepless nights passed on the hard wooden bench. The foul air of the cell is stifling. The silence of the grave torments me; my soul is in an agony of uncertainty.

CHAPTER VI

THE JAIL

I

THE days ring with noisy clamor. There is constant going and coming. The clatter of levers, the slamming of iron doors, continually reverberates through the corridors. The dull thud of a footfall in the cell above hammers on my head with maddening regularity. In my ears is the yelling and shouting of coarse voices.

"Cell num-ber ee-e-lev-ven! To court! Right a-way!"

A prisoner hurriedly passes my door. His step is nervous, in his look expectant **fear**.

"Hurry, there! To court!"

"Good luck, Jimmie."

The man flushes and averts his face, as he passes **a** group of visitors clustered about an overseer.

"Who is that, Officer?" One of the ladies advances, lorgnette in hand, and stares boldly at the prisoner. Suddenly she shrinks back. A man is being led past by the guards. His face is bleeding from a deep gash, his head swathed in bandages. The officers thrust him violently into a cell. He falls heavily against the bed. "Oh, don't! For Jesus' sake, don't!" The shutting of the heavy door drowns his cries.

The visitors crowd about the cell.

"What did he do? He can't come out now, Officer?"

44

"No, ma'am. He's safe."

The lady's laugh rings clear and silvery. She steps closer to the bars, eagerly peering into the darkness. A smile of exciting security plays about her mouth.

"What has he done, Officer?"

"Stole some clothes, ma'am."

Disdainful disappointment is on the lady's face. "Where is that man who—er—we read in the papers yesterday? You know—the newspaper artist who killed—er—that girl in such a brutal manner."

"Oh, Jack Tarlin. Murderers' Row, this way, ladies."

II

The sun is slowly nearing the blue patch of sky, visible from my cell in the western wing of the jail. I stand close to the bars to catch the cheering rays. They glide across my face with tender, soft caress, and I feel something melt within me. Closer I press to the door. I long for the precious embrace to surround me, to envelop me, to pour its soft balm into my aching soul. The last rays are fading away, and something out of my heart is departing with them. . . . But the lengthening shadows on the gray flagstones spread quiet. Gradually the clamor ceases, the sounds die out. I hear the creaking of rusty hinges, there is the click of a lock, and all is hushed and dark.

.   .   .   .

The silence grows gloomy, oppressive. It fills me with mysterious awe. It lives. It pulsates with slow, measured breathing, as of some monster. It rises and falls; approaches, recedes. It is Misery asleep. Now it presses heavily against my door. I hear its quickened breathing. Oh, it is the guard! Is it the death watch? His outline is lost in the semi-darkness, but I see the whites of his eyes. They stare at me, they watch and follow me. I feel their gaze upon me, as I nervously pace the floor. Unconsciously my step quickens, but I cannot escape that glint of steel. It grimaces and mocks me. It dances before me: it is here and there, all around me. Now it flits up and down; it doubles, trebles. The fearful eyes stare at me from a hundred depressions in the wall. On every side they surround me, and bar my way.

I bury my head in the pillow. My sleep is restless and broken. Ever the terrible gaze is upon me, watching, watching, the white eyeballs turning with my every movement.

III

The line of prisoners files by my cell. They walk in twos, conversing in subdued tones. It is a motley crowd from the ends of the world. The native of the western part of the State, the "Pennsylvania Dutchman," of stolid mien, passes slowly, in silence. The son of southern Italy, stocky and black-eyed, alert suspicion on his face, walks with quick, nervous step. The tall, slender Spaniard, swarthy and of classic feature, looks about him with suppressed disdain. Each, in passing, casts a furtive glance into my cell. The last in the line is a young negro, walking alone. He nods and smiles broadly at me, exposing teeth of dazzling whiteness. The guard brings up the rear. He pauses at my door, his sharp eye measuring me severely, critically.

"You may fall in."

The cell is unlocked, and I join the line. The

negro is at my side. He loses no time in engaging
me in conversation. He is very glad, he assures me,
that they have at last permitted me to "fall in." It
was a shame to deprive me of exercise for four days.
Now they will "call de night-dog off. Must been afeared
o' soocide," he explains.

His flow of speech is incessant; he seems not a
whit disconcerted by my evident disinclination to talk.
Would I have a cigarette? May smoke in the cell.
One can buy "de weed" here, if he has "de dough";
buy anything 'cept booze. He is full of the prison
gossip. That tall man there is Jack Tinford, of
Homestead—sure to swing—threw dynamite at the
Pinkertons. That little "dago" will keep Jack company—
cut his wife's throat. The "Dutchy" there is "bugs"—
choked his son in sleep. Presently my talkative companion volunteers the information that he also is
waiting for trial. Nothing worse than second degree
murder, though. Can't hang him, he laughs gleefully.
"His" man didn't "croak" till after the ninth day.
He lightly waves aside my remark concerning the
ninth-day superstition. He is convinced they won't
hang him. "Can't do't," he reiterates, with a happy
grin. Suddenly he changes the subject. "Wat am
yo doin' heah? Only murdah cases on dis ah gal'ry.
Yuh man didn' croak!" Evidently he expects no
answer, immediately assuring me that I am "all right."
"Guess dey b'lieve it am mo' safe foah yo. But can't
hang yo, can't hang yo." He grows excited over the
recital of his case. Minutely he describes the details.
"Dat big niggah, guess 'e t'ot I's afeared of 'm. He
know bettah now," he chuckles. "Dis ah chile am
afeared of none ov'm. Ah ain't. 'Gwan 'way, niggah,'
Ah says to 'm; 'yo bettah leab mah gahl be.' An' dat
big black niggah grab de cleaveh,—we's in d'otel

kitchen, yo see. 'Niggah, drop dat,' Ah hollos, an' he come at me. Den dis ah coon pull his trusty li'lle brodeh," he taps his pocket significantly, "an' Ah lets de ornery niggah hab it. Plum' in de belly, yassah, Ah does, an' he drop his cleaveh an' Ah pulls mah knife out, two inches, 'bout, an' den Ah gives it half twist like, an' shoves it in 'gen." He illustrates the ghastly motion. "Dat bad niggah neveh botheh *me* 'gen, noh nobody else, Ah guess. But dey can't hang me, no sah, dey can't, 'cause mah man croak two weeks later. Ah's lucky, yassah, Ah is." His face is wreathed in a broad grin, his teeth shimmer white. Suddenly he grows serious. "Yo am strikeh? No-o-o? Not a steel-woikeh?" with utter amazement. "What yo wan' teh shoot Frick foah?" He does not attempt to disguise his impatient incredulity, as I essay an explanation. "Afeared t' tell. Yo am deep all right, Ahlick—dat am yuh name? But yo am right, yassah, yo am right. Doan' tell nobody. Dey's mos'ly crooks, dat dey am, an' dey need watchin' sho'. Yo jes' membuh dat."

There is a peculiar movement in the marching line. I notice a prisoner leave his place. He casts an anxious glance around, and disappears in the niche of the cell door. The line continues on its march, and, as I near the man's hiding place, I hear him whisper, "Fall back, Aleck." Surprised at being addressed in such familiar manner, I slow down my pace. The man is at my side.

"Say, Berk, you don't want to be seen walking with that 'dinge.' "

The sound of my shortened name grates harshly on my ear. I feel the impulse to resent the mutilation. The man's manner suggests a lack of respect, offensive to my dignity as a revolutionist.

"Why?" I ask, turning to look at him.

He is short and stocky. The thin lips and pointed chin of the elongated face suggest the fox. He meets my gaze with a sharp look from above his smoked-glass spectacles. His voice is husky, his tone unpleasantly confidential. It is bad for a white man to be seen with a "nigger," he informs me. It will make feeling against me. He himself is a Pittsburgh man for the last twenty years, but he was "born and raised" in the South, in Atlanta. They have no use for "niggers" down there, he assures me. They must be taught to keep their place, and they are no good, anyway. I had better take his advice, for he is friendly disposed toward me. I must be very careful of appearances before the trial. My inexperience is quite evident, but he "knows the ropes." I must not give "them" an opportunity to say anything against me. My behavior in jail will weigh with the judge in determining my sentence. He himself expects to "get off easy." He knows some of the judges. Mostly good men. He ought to know: helped to elect one of them; voted three times for him at the last election. He closes the left eye, and playfully pokes me with his elbow. He hopes he'll "get before that judge." He will, if he is lucky, he assures me. He had always had pretty good luck. Last time he got off with three years, though he nearly killed "his" man. But it was in self-defence. Have I got a chew of tobacco about me? Don't use the weed? Well, it'll be easier in the "pen." What's the pen? Why, don't I know? The penitentiary, of course. I should have no fear. Frick ain't going to die. But what did I want to kill the man for? I ain't no Pittsburgh man, that he could see plain. What did I want to "nose in" for? Help the strikers? I must be crazy to talk that way.

Why, it was none of my "cheese." Didn't I come from
New York? Yes? Well, then, how could the strike
concern me? I must have some personal grudge
against Frick. Ever had dealings with him? No?
Sure? Then it's plain "bughouse," no use talking.
But it's different with his case. It was his partner
in business. He knew the skunk meant to cheat him
out of money, and they quarreled. Did I notice the
dark glasses he wears? Well, his eyes are bad. He
only meant to scare the man. But, damn him, he
croaked. Curse such luck. His third offence, too.
Do I think the judge will have pity on him? Why,
he is almost blind. How did he manage to "get
his man"? Why, just an accidental shot. He didn't
mean to—

The gong intones its deep, full bass.

"All in!"

The line breaks. There is a simultaneous clatter
of many doors, and I am in the cell again.

IV

Within, on the narrow stool, I find a tin pan filled
with a dark-brown mixture. It is the noon meal, but
the "dinner" does not look inviting: the pan is old
and rusty; the smell of the soup excites suspicion.
The greasy surface, dotted here and there with specks
of vegetable, resembles a pool of stagnant water covered
with green slime. The first taste nauseates me, and I
decide to "dine" on the remnants of my breakfast—a
piece of bread.

I pace the floor in agitation over the conversation
with my fellow-prisoners. Why can't they understand

the motives that prompted my act? Their manner of pitying condescension is aggravating. My attempted explanation they evidently considered a waste of effort. Not a striker myself, I could and should have had no interest in the struggle,—the opinion seemed final with both the negro and the white man. In the purpose of the act they refused to see any significance,—nothing beyond the mere physical effect. It would have been a good thing if Frick had died, because "he was bad." But it is "lucky" for me that he didn't die, they thought, for now "they" can't hang me. My remark that the probable consequences to myself are not to be weighed in the scale against the welfare of the People, they had met with a smile of derision, suggestive of doubt as to my sanity. It is, of course, consoling to reflect that neither of those men can properly be said to represent the People. The negro is a very inferior type of laborer; and the other—he is a *bourgeois,* "in business." He is not worth while. Besides, he confessed that it is his third offence. He is a common criminal, not an honest producer. But that tall man— the Homestead steel-worker whom the negro pointed out to me—oh, *he* will understand: he is of the real People. My heart wells up in admiration of the man, as I think of his participation in the memorable struggle of Homestead. He fought the Pinkertons, the myrmidons of Capital. Perhaps he helped to dynamite the barges and drive those Hessians out of town. He is tall and broad-shouldered, his face strong and determined, his body manly and powerful. He is of the true spirit; the embodiment of the great, noble People: the giant of labor grown to his full stature, conscious of his strength. Fearless, strong, and proud, he will conquer all obstacles; he will break his chains and liberate mankind.

V

Next morning, during exercise hour, I watch with beating heart for an opportunity to converse with the Homestead steel-worker. I shall explain to him the motives and purpose of my attempt on Frick. He will understand me; he will himself enlighten his fellow-strikers. It is very important *they* should comprehend my act quite clearly, and he is the very man to do this great service to humanity. He is the rebel-worker; his heroism during the struggle bears witness. I hope the People will not allow the enemy to hang him. He defended the rights of the Homestead workers, the cause of the whole working class. No, the People will never allow such a sacrifice. How well he carries himself! Erect, head high, the look of conscious dignity and strength—

"Cell num-b-ber fi-i-ve!"

The prisoner with the smoked glasses leaves the line, and advances in response to the guard's call. Quickly I pass along the gallery, and fall into the vacant place, alongside of the steel-worker.

"A happy chance," I address him. "I should like to speak to you about something important. You are one of the Homestead strikers, are you not?"

"Jack Tinford," he introduces himself. "What's your name?"

He is visibly startled by my answer. "The man who shot Frick?" he asks.

An expression of deep anxiety crosses his face. His eye wanders to the gate. Through the wire network I observe visitors approaching from the Warden's office.

"They'd better not see us together," he says, impatiently. "Fall in back of me. Then we'll talk."

Pained at his manner, yet not fully realizing its significance, I slowly fall back. His tall, broad figure completely hides me from view. He speaks to me in monosyllables, unwillingly. At the mention of Homestead he grows more communicative, talking in an undertone, as if conversing with his neighbor, the Sicilian, who does not understand a syllable of English. I strain my ear to catch his words. The steel-workers merely defended themselves against armed invaders, I hear him say. They are not on strike: they've been locked out by Frick, because he wants to non-unionize the works. That's why he broke the contract with the Amalgamated, and hired the damned Pinkertons two months before, when all was peace. They shot many workers from the barges before the millmen "got after them." They deserved roasting alive for their unprovoked murders. Well, the men "fixed them all right." Some were killed, others committed suicide on the burning barges, and the rest were forced to surrender like whipped curs. A grand victory all right, if that coward of a sheriff hadn't got the Governor to send the militia to Homestead. But it was a victory, you bet, for the boys to get the best of three hundred armed Pinkertons. He himself, though, had nothing to do with the fight. He was sick at the time. They're trying to get the Pinkertons to swear his life away. One of the hounds has already made an affidavit that he saw him, Jack Tinford, throw dynamite at the barges, before the Pinkertons landed. But never mind, he is not afraid. No Pittsburgh jury will believe those lying murderers. He was in his sweetheart's house, sick abed. The girl and her mother will prove an alibi for him. And the Advisory Committee of the Amalgamated, too. They know he wasn't on the shore. They'll swear to it in court, anyhow—

Abruptly he ceases, a look of fear on his face. For a moment he is lost in thought. Then he gives me a searching look, and smiles at me. As we turn the corner of the walk, he whispers: "Too bad you didn't kill him. Some business misunderstanding, eh?" he adds, aloud.

Could he be serious, I wonder. Does he only pretend? He faces straight ahead, and I am unable to see his expression. I begin the careful explanation I had prepared:

"Jack, it was for you, for your people that I—"

Impatiently, angrily he interrupts me. I'd better be careful not to talk that way in court, he warns me. If Frick should die, I'd hang myself with such "gab." And it would only harm the steel-workers. They don't believe in killing; they respect the law. Of course, they had a right to defend their homes and families against unlawful invaders. But they welcomed the militia to Homestead. They showed their respect for authority. To be sure, Frick deserves to die. He is a murderer. But the mill-workers will have nothing to do with Anarchists. What did I want to kill him for, anyhow? I did not belong to the Homestead men. It was none of my business. I had better not say anything about it in court, or—

The gong tolls.

"All in!"

VI

I pass a sleepless night. The events of the day have stirred me to the very depths. Bitterness and anger against the Homestead striker fill my heart. My hero of yesterday, the hero of the glorious struggle of the People,—how contemptible he has proved himself, how cravenly small! No consciousness of the great mission of his class, no proud realization of the part he himself had acted in the noble struggle. A cowardly, overgrown boy, terrified at to-morrow's punishment for the prank he has played! Meanly concerned only with his own safety, and willing to resort to lying, in order to escape responsibility.

The very thought is appalling. It is a sacrilege, an insult to the holy Cause, to the People. To myself, too. Not that lying is to be condemned, provided it is in the interest of the Cause. All means are justified in the war of humanity against its enemies. Indeed, the more repugnant the means, the stronger the test of one's nobility and devotion. All great revolutionists have proved that. There is no more striking example in the annals of the Russian movement than that peerless Nihilist—what was his name? Why, how peculiar that it should escape me just now! I knew it so well. He undermined the Winter Palace, beneath the very dining-room of the Tsar. What debasement, what terrible indignities he had to endure in the rôle of the servile, simple-minded peasant carpenter. How his proud spirit must have suffered, for weeks and months,—all for the sake of his great purpose. Wonderful man! To be worthy of your comradeship. . . . But this Homestead worker, what a pigmy by comparison. He is absorbed in the single thought of saving himself, the traitor. A veritable Judas, preparing to forswear his people and their cause, willing to lie and deny his participation. How proud I should be in his place: to have fought on the barricades, as he did! And then to die for it,—ah, could there be a more glorious fate for a man, a real man? To serve even as the least stone in the foundation of a free society, or as a plank in the bridge across which the triumphant People shall finally pass into the land of promise?

A plank in the bridge. . . . In the *most*.* What a significant name! How it impressed me the first time I heard it! No, I saw it in print, I remember quite clearly. Mother had just died. I was dreaming of the New World, the Land of Freedom. Eagerly I read every line of "American news." One day, in the little Kovno library—how distinctly it all comes back to me—I can see myself sitting there, perusing the papers. Must get acquainted with the country. What is this? "Anarchists hanged in Chicago." There are many names—one is "Most." "What is an Anarchist?" I whisper to the student near by. He is from Peter,** he will know. "S—sh! Same as Nihilists." "In free America?" I wondered.

How little I knew of America then! A free country, indeed, that hangs its noblest men. And the misery, the exploitation,—it's terrible. I must mention all this in court, in my defence. No, not defence—some fitter word. Explanation! Yes, my explanation. I need no defence: I don't consider myself guilty. What did the Warden mean? Fool for a client, he said, when I told him that I would refuse legal aid. He thinks I am a fool. Well, he's a *bourgeois,* he can't understand. I'll tell him to leave me alone. He belongs to the enemy. The lawyers, too. They are all in the capitalist camp. I need no lawyers. They couldn't explain my case. I shall not talk to the reporters, either. They are a lying pack, those journalistic hounds of capitalism. They always misrepresent us. And they know better, too. They wrote columns of interviews with Most when he went to prison. All lies. I saw him off myself; he didn't say a word to them. They are our worst enemies. The Warden said that they'll

* Russian for "bridge."
** Popular abbreviation of St. Petersburg.

come to see me to-morrow. I'll have nothing to say
to them. They're sure to twist my words, and thus
impair the effect of my act. It is not complete without
my explanation. I shall prepare it very carefully. Of
course, the jury won't understand. They, too, belong
to the capitalist class. But I must use the trial to
talk to the People. To be sure, an *Attentat* on a Frick
is in itself splendid propaganda. It combines the
value of example with terroristic effect. But very
much depends upon my explanation. It offers me a
rare opportunity for a broader agitation of our ideas.
The comrades outside will also use my act for
propaganda. The People misunderstand us: they have
been prejudiced by the capitalist press. They must
be enlightened; that is our glorious task. Very difficult
and slow work, it is true; but they will learn. Their
patience will break, and then—the good People, they
have always been too kind to their enemies. And brave,
even in their suffering. Yes, very brave. Not like that
fellow, the steel-worker. He is a disgrace to Homestead,
the traitor. . . .

I pace the cell in agitation. The Judas-striker is
not fit to live. Perhaps it would be best they should
hang him. His death would help to open the eyes of the
People to the real character of legal justice. Legal
justice—what a travesty! They are mutually exclusive
terms. Yes, indeed, it would be best he should be
hanged. The Pinkerton will testify against him. He
saw Jack throw dynamite. Very good. Perhaps others
will also swear to it. The judge will believe the Pinkertons. Yes, they will hang him.

The thought somewhat soothes my perturbation.
At least the cause of the People will benefit to some
extent. The man himself is not to be considered.

He has ceased to exist: his interests are exclusively
personal; he can be of no further benefit to the People.
Only his death can aid the Cause. It is best for him
to end his career in the service of humanity. I hope
he will act like a man on the scaffold. The enemy
should not gloat over his fear, his craven terror.
They'll see in him the spirit of the People. Of course,
he is not worthy of it. But he must die like a rebel-
worker, bravely, defiantly. I must speak to him about it.

The deep bass of the gong dispels my reverie.

VII

There is a distinct sense of freedom in the solitude
of the night. The day's atmosphere is surcharged with
noisome anxiety, the hours laden with impending
terrors. But the night is soothing. For the first time I
feel alone, unobserved. The "night-dog has been called
off." How refinedly brutal is this constant care lest the
hangman be robbed of his prey! A simple precaution
against suicide, the Warden told me. I felt the naïve
stupidity of the suggestion like the thrust of a dagger.
What a tremendous chasm in our mental attitudes!
His mind cannot grasp the impossibility of suicide
before I have explained to the People the motive and
purpose of my act. Suicide? As if the mere death
of Frick was my object! The very thought is impossible, insulting. It outrages me that even a *bourgeois*
should so meanly misjudge the aspirations of an active
revolutionist. The insignificant reptile, Frick,—as if
the mere man were worth a terroristic effort! I aimed
at the many-headed hydra whose visible representative
was Frick. The Homestead developments had given
him temporary prominence, thrown this particular hydra-
head into bold relief, so to speak. That alone made him

worthy of the revolutionist's attention. Primarily, as
an object lesson; it would strike terror into the soul
of his class. They are craven-hearted, their conscience
weighted with guilt,—and life is dear to them. Their
strangling hold on labor might be loosened. Only for
a while, no doubt. But that much would be gained,
due to the act of the *Attentäter*. The People could not
fail to realize the depth of a love that will give its
own life for their cause. To give a young life, full of
health and vitality, to give all, without a thought of self;
to give all, voluntarily, cheerfully; nay, enthusiastically—
could any one fail to understand such a love?

But this is the first terrorist act in America. The
People may fail to comprehend it thoroughly. Yet they
will know that an Anarchist committed the deed. I will
talk to them from the courtroom. And my comrades
at liberty will use the opportunity to the utmost to shed
light on the questions involved. Such a deed must draw
the attention of the world. This first act of voluntary
Anarchist sacrifice will make the workingmen think
deeply. Perhaps even more so than the Chicago martyrdom. The latter was preëminently a lesson in capitalist
justice. The culmination of a plutocratic conspiracy,
the tragedy of 1887 lacked the element of voluntary
Anarchist self-sacrifice in the interests of the People.
In that distinctive quality my act is initial. Perhaps
it will prove the entering wedge. The leaven of
growing oppression is at work. It is for us, the
Anarchists, to educate labor to its great mission. Let the
world learn of the misery of Homestead. The sudden
thunderclap gives warning that beyond the calm horizon
the storm is gathering. The lightning of social protest—

"Quick, Ahlick! Plant it." Something white flutters
between the bars. Hastily I read the newspaper clipping.

Glorious! Who would have expected it? A soldier in one of the regiments stationed at Homestead called upon the line to give "three cheers for the man who shot Frick." My soul overflows with beautiful hopes. Such a wonderful spirit among the militia; perhaps the soldiers will fraternize with the strikers. It is by no means an impossibility: such things have happened before. After all, they are of the People, mostly workingmen. Their interests are identical with those of the strikers, and surely they hate Frick, who is universally condemned for his brutality, his arrogance. This soldier—what is his name? Iams, W. L. Iams—he typifies the best feeling of the regiment. The others probably lack his courage. They feared to respond to his cheers, especially because of the Colonel's presence. But undoubtedly most of them feel as Iams does. It would be dangerous for the enemy to rely upon the Tenth Pennsylvania. And in the other Homestead regiments, there must also be such noble Iamses. They will not permit their comrade to be court-martialed, as the Colonel threatens. Iams is not merely a militia man. He is a citizen, a native. He has the right to express his opinion regarding my deed. If he had condemned it, he would not be punished. May he not, then, voice a favorable sentiment? No, they can't punish him. And he is surely very popular among the soldiers. How manfully he behaved as the Colonel raged before the regiment, and demanded to know who cheered for "the assassin of Mr. Frick," as the imbecile put it. Iams stepped out of the ranks, and boldly avowed his act. He could have remained silent, or denied it. But he is evidently not like that cowardly steel-worker. He even refused the Colonel's offer to apologize.

Brave boy! He is the right material for a revolutionist. Such a man has no business to belong to the militia. He should know for what purpose it is intended: a tool of capitalism in the enslavement of labor. After all, it will benefit him to be court-martialed. It will enlighten him. I must follow the case. Perhaps the negro will give me more clippings. It was very generous of him to risk this act of friendship. The Warden has expressly interdicted the passing of newspapers to me, though the other prisoners are permitted to buy them. He discriminates against me in every possible way. A rank ignoramus: he cannot even pronounce "Anarchist." Yesterday he said to me: "The Anachrists are no good. What do they want, anyhow?" I replied, angrily: "First you say they are no good, then you ask what they want." He flushed. "Got no use for them, anyway." Such an imbecile! Not the least sense of justice—he condemns without knowing. I believe he is aiding the detectives. Why does he insist I should plead guilty? I have repeatedly told him that, though I do not deny the act, I am innocent. The stupid laughed outright. "Better plead guilty, you'll get off easier. You did it, so better plead guilty." In vain I strove to explain to him: "I don't believe in your laws, I don't acknowledge the authority of your courts. I am innocent, morally." The aggravating smile of condescending wisdom kept playing about his lips. "Plead guilty. Take my advice, plead guilty."

Instinctively I sense some presence at the door. The small, cunning eyes of the Warden peer intently through the bars. I feel him an enemy. Well, he may have the clipping now if he wishes. But no torture shall draw from me an admission incriminating the negro. The name Rakhmetov flits through my mind. I shall be true to that memory.

"A gentleman in my office wishes to see you," the Warden informs me.

"Who is he?"

"A friend of yours, from Pittsburgh."

"I know no one in Pittsburgh. I don't care to see the man."

The Warden's suave insistence arouses my suspicions. Why should he be so much interested in my seeing a stranger? Visits are privileges, I have been told. I decline the privilege. But the Warden insists. I refuse. Finally he orders me out of the cell. Two guards lead me into the hallway. They halt me at the head of a line of a dozen men. Six are counted off, and I am assigned to the seventh place. I notice that I am the only one in the line wearing glasses. The Warden enters from an inner office, accompanied by three visitors. They pass down the row, scrutinizing each face. They return, their gaze fixed on the men. One of the strangers makes a motion as if to put his hand on the shoulder of the man on my left. The Warden hastily calls the visitors aside. They converse in whispers, then walk up the line, and pass slowly back, till they are alongside of me. The tall stranger puts his hand familiarly on my shoulder, exclaiming:

"Don't you recognize me, Mr. Berkman? I met you on Fifth Avenue, right in front of the Telegraph building."*

"I never saw you before in my life."

"Oh, yes! You remember I spoke to you—"

"No, you did not," I interrupt, impatiently.

"Take him back," the Warden commands.

---

* The building in which the offices of the Carnegie Company were located.

I protest against the perfidious proceeding. "A positive identification," the Warden asserts. The detective had seen me "in the company of two friends, inspecting the office of Mr. Frick." Indignantly I deny the false statement, charging him with abetting the conspiracy to involve my comrades. He grows livid with rage, and orders me deprived of exercise that afternoon.

The Warden's rôle in the police plot is now apparent to me. I realize him in his true colors. Ignorant though he is, familiarity with police methods has developed in him a certain shrewdness: the low cunning of the fox seeking its prey. The good-natured smile masks a depth of malice, his crude vanity glorying in the successful abuse of his wardenship over unfortunate human beings.

This new appreciation of his character clarifies various incidents heretofore puzzling to me. My mail is being detained at the office, I am sure. It is impossible that my New York comrades should have neglected me so long: it is now over a week since my arrest. As a matter of due precaution, they would not communicate with me at once. But two or three days would be sufficient to perfect a *Deckadresse*.* Yet not a line has reached me from them. It is evident that my mail is being detained.

My reflections rouse bitter hatred of the Warden. His infamy fills me with rage. The negro's warning against the occupant of the next cell assumes a new aspect. Undoubtedly the man is a spy; placed there by the Warden, evidently. Little incidents, insignificant in themselves, add strong proof to justify the suspicion. It grows to conviction as I review various circumstances

---

* A "disguise" address, to mask the identity of the correspondent.

concerning my neighbor. The questions I deemed foolish, prompted by mere curiosity, I now see in the light of the Warden's rôle as volunteer detective. The young negro was sent to the dungeon for warning me against the spy in the next cell. But the latter is never reported, notwithstanding his continual knocking and talking. Specially privileged, evidently. And the Warden, too, is hand-in-glove with the police. I am convinced he himself caused the writing of those letters he gave me yesterday. They were postmarked Homestead, from a pretended striker. They want to blow up the mills, the letter said; good bombs are needed. I should send them the addresses of my friends who know how to make effective explosives. What a stupid trap! One of the epistles sought to involve some of the strike leaders in my act. In another, John Most was mentioned. Well, I am not to be caught with such chaff. But I must be on my guard. It is best I should decline to accept mail. They withhold the letters of my friends, anyhow. Yes, I'll refuse all mail.

I feel myself surrounded by enemies, open and secret. Not a single being here I may call friend; except the negro, who, I know, wishes me well. I hope he will give me more clippings,—perhaps there will be news of my comrades. I'll try to "fall in" with him at exercise to-morrow. . . . Oh! they are handing out tracts. To-morrow is Sunday,—no exercise!

VIII

The Lord's day is honored by depriving the prisoners of dinner. A scanty allowance of bread, with a tincupful of black, unsweetened coffee, constitutes breakfast. Supper is a repetition of the morning meal, except that the coffee looks thinner, the tincup more rusty. I force myself to swallow a mouthful by shutting my eyes. It tastes like greasy dishwater, with a bitter suggestion of burnt bread.

Exercise is also abolished on the sacred day. The atmosphere is pervaded with the gloom of unbroken silence. In the afternoon, I hear the creaking of the inner gate. There is much swishing of dresses: the good ladies of the tracts are being seated. The doors on Murderers' Row are opened partly, at a fifteen-degree angle. The prisoners remain in their cells, with the guards stationed at the gallery entrances.

All is silent. I can hear the beating of my heart in the oppressive quiet. A faint shadow crosses the darksome floor; now it oscillates on the bars. I hear the muffled fall of felt-soled steps. Silently the turnkey passes the cell, like a flitting mystery casting its shadow, athwart a troubled soul. I catch the glint of a revolver protruding from his pocket.

Suddenly the sweet strains of a violin resound in the corridor. Female voices swell the melody, "Nearer my God to Thee, nearer to Thee." Slowly the volume expands; it rises, grows more resonant in contact with the gallery floor, and echoes in my cell, "Nearer to Thee, to Thee."

The sounds die away. A deep male voice utters, "Let us pray." Its metallic hardness rings like a command. The guards stand with lowered heads. Their lips mumble after the invisible speaker, "Our Father who art in Heaven, give us this day our daily bread. . . . Forgive us our trespasses as we forgive those that trespass against us——"

"Like hell you do!" some one shouts from the upper gallery. There is suppressed giggling in the cells. Pellmell the officers rush up the stairs. The uproar

increases. "Order!" Yells and catcalls drown the
Warden's voice. Doors are violently opened and shut.
The thunder of rattling iron is deafening. Suddenly all
is quiet: the guards have reached the galleries. Only
hasty tiptoeing is heard.

The offender cannot be found. The gong rings the
supper hour. The prisoners stand at the doors, cup in
hand, ready to receive the coffee.

"Give the s—— of b—— no supper! No supper!"
roars the Warden.

Sabbath benediction!

The levers are pulled, and we are locked in for
the night.

IX

In agitation I pace the cell. Frick didn't die! He
has almost recovered. I have positive information: the
"blind" prisoner gave me the clipping during exercise.
"You're a poor shot," he teased me.

The poignancy of the disappointment pierces my
heart. I feel it with the intensity of a catastrophe. My
imprisonment, the vexations of jail life, the future—
all is submerged in the flood of misery at the realization
of my failure. Bitter thoughts crowd my mind; self-
accusation overwhelms me. I failed! Failed! . . . It
might have been different, had I gone to Frick's residence. It was my original intention, too. But the house
in the East End was guarded. Besides, I had no time to
wait: that very morning the papers had announced
Frick's intended visit to New York. I was determined
he should not escape me. I resolved to act at once. It
was mainly his cowardice that saved him—he hid under
the chair! Played dead! And now he lives, the vampire. . . . And Homestead? How will it affect condi-

tions there? If Frick had died, Carnegie would have hastened to settle with the strikers. The shrewd Scot only made use of Frick to destroy the hated union. He himself was absent, he could not be held accountable. The author of "Triumphant Democracy" is sensitive to adverse criticism. With the elimination of Frick, responsibility for Homestead conditions would rest with Carnegie. To support his rôle as the friend of labor, he must needs terminate the sanguinary struggle. Such a development of affairs would have greatly advanced the Anarchist propaganda. However some may condemn my act, the workers could not be blind to the actual situation, and the practical effects of Frick's death. But his recovery . . . .

Yet, who can tell? It may perhaps have the same results. If not, the strike was virtually lost when the steel-workers permitted the militia to take possession of Homestead. It afforded the Company an opportunity to fill the mills with scabs. But even if the strike be lost,—our propaganda is the chief consideration. The Homestead workers are but a very small part of the American working class. Important as this great struggle is, the cause of the whole People is supreme. And their true cause is Anarchism. All other issues are merged in it; it alone will solve the labor problem. No other consideration deserves attention. The suffering of individuals, of large masses, indeed, is unavoidable under capitalist conditions. Poverty and wretchedness must constantly increase; it is inevitable. A revolutionist cannot be influenced by mere sentimentality. We bleed for the People, we suffer for them, but we know the real source of their misery. Our whole civilization, false to the core as it is, must be destroyed, to be born anew. Only with the abolition of exploitation will labor gain justice. Anarchism alone can save the world.

These reflections somewhat soothe me. My failure
to accomplish the desired result is grievously exasperat-
ing, and I feel deeply humiliated. But I shall be the
sole sufferer. Properly viewed, the merely physical
result of my act cannot affect its propagandistic value;
and that is, always, the supreme consideration. The
chief purpose of my *Attentat* was to call attention to our
social iniquities; to arouse a vital interest in the sufferings
of the People by an act of self-sacrifice; to stimulate
discussion regarding the cause and purpose of the act,
and thus bring the teachings of Anarchism before the
world. The Homestead situation offered the psychologic
social moment. What matter the personal consequences
to Frick? the merely physical results of my *Attentat?*
The conditions necessary for propaganda are there: the
act is accomplished.

As to myself—my disappointment is bitter, indeed.
I wanted to die for the Cause. But now they will send
me to prison—they will bury me alive. . . .

Involuntarily my hand reaches for the lapel of my
coat, when suddenly I remember my great loss. In
agony, I live through again the scene in the police station, on the third day after my arrest. . . . Rough hands
seize my arms, and I am forced into a chair. My head
is thrust violently backward, and I face the Chief. He
clutches me by the throat.

"Open your mouth! Damn you, open your mouth!"

Everything is whirling before me, the desk is circling
the room, the bloodshot eyes of the Chief gaze at me
from the floor, his feet flung high in the air, and
everything is whirling, whirling. . . .

"Now, Doc, quick!"

There is a sharp sting in my tongue, my jaws are
gripped as by a vise, and my mouth is torn open.

"What d'ye think of *that,* eh?"

The Chief stands before me, in his hand the dynamite cartridge.

"What's this?" he demands, with an oath.

"Candy," I reply, defiantly.

X

How full of anxiety these two weeks have been! Still no news of my comrades. The Warden is not offering me any more mail; he evidently regards my last refusal as final. But I am now permitted to purchase papers; they may contain something about my friends. If I could only learn what propaganda is being made out of my act, and what the Girl and Fedya are doing! I long to know what is happening with them. But my interest is merely that of the revolutionist. They are so far away,—I do not count among the living. On the outside, everything seems to continue as usual, as if nothing had happened. Frick is quite well now; at his desk again, the press reports. Nothing else of importance. The police seem to have given up their hunt. How ridiculous the Chief has made himself by kidnaping my friend Mollock, the New York baker! The impudence of the authorities, to decoy an unsuspecting workingman across the State line, and then arrest him as my accomplice! I suppose he is the only Anarchist the stupid Chief could find. My negro friend informed me of the kidnaping last week. But I felt no anxiety: I knew the "silent baker" would prove deaf and dumb. Not a word could they draw from him. Mollock's discharge by the magistrate put the Chief in a very ludicrous position. Now he is thirsting for revenge, and probably seeking a victim nearer home, in Allegheny. But if the comrades preserve silence, all will be well, for I was careful to leave no clew. I had told them that my destination was Chicago, where I expected to secure a position. I can depend on Bauer and Nold. But that man E., whom I found living in the same house with Nold, impressed me as rather unreliable. I thought there was something of the hang-dog look about him. I should certainly not trust him, and I'm afraid he might compromise the others. Why are they friendly, I wonder. He is probably not even a comrade. The Allegheny Anarchists should have nothing in common with him. It is not well for us to associate with the *bourgeois*-minded.

My meditation is interrupted by a guard, who informs me that I am "wanted at the office." There is a letter for me, but some postage is due on it. Would I pay?

"A trap," it flits through my mind, as I accompany the overseer. I shall persist in my refusal to accept decoy mail.

"More letters from Homestead?" I turn to the Warden.

He quickly suppresses a smile. "No, it is post-marked, Brooklyn, N. Y."

I glance at the envelope. The writing is apparently a woman's, but the chirography is smaller than the Girl's. I yearn for news of her. The letter is from Brooklyn —perhaps a *Deckadresse!*

"I'll take the letter, Warden."

"All right. You will open it here."

"Then I don't want it."

I start from the office, when the Warden detains me:

"Take the letter along, but within ten minutes you must return it to me. You may go now."

I hasten to the cell. If there is anything important in the letter, I shall destroy it: I owe the enemy no

obligations. As with trembling hand I tear open the
envelope, a paper dollar flutters to the floor. I glance
at the signature, but the name is unfamiliar. Anxiously
I scan the lines. An unknown sympathizer sends greetings, in the name of humanity. "I am not an Anarchist,"
I read, "but I wish you well. My sympathy, however,
is with the man, not with the act. I cannot justify your
attempt. Life, human life, especially, is sacred. None
has the right to take what he cannot give."

I pass a troubled night. My mind struggles with
the problem presented so unexpectedly. Can any one
understanding my motives, doubt the justification of the
Attentat? The legal aspect aside, can the morality of
the act be questioned? It is impossible to confound
law with right; they are opposites. The law is immoral:
it is the conspiracy of rulers and priests against the
workers, to continue their subjection. To be law-
abiding means to acquiesce, if not directly participate,
in that conspiracy. A revolutionist is the truly moral
man: to him the interests of humanity are supreme;
to advance them, his sole aim in life. Government, with
its laws, is the common enemy. All weapons are justifiable in the noble struggle of the People against this
terrible curse. The Law! It is the arch-crime of the
centuries. The path of Man is soaked with the blood it
has shed. Can this great criminal determine Right? Is
a revolutionist to respect such a travesty? It would
mean the perpetuation of human slavery.

No, the revolutionist owes no duty to capitalist
morality. He is the soldier of humanity. He has consecrated his life to the People in their great struggle.
It is a bitter war. The revolutionist cannot shrink from
the service it imposes upon him. Aye, even the duty
of death. Cheerfully and joyfully he would die a

thousand times to hasten the triumph of liberty. His life belongs to the People. He has no right to live or enjoy while others suffer.

How often we had discussed this, Fedya and I. He was somewhat inclined to sybaritism; not quite emancipated from the tendencies of his *bourgeois* youth. Once in New York—I shall never forget—at the time when our circle had just begun the publication of the first Jewish Anarchist paper in America, we came to blows. We, the most intimate friends; yes, actually came to blows. Nobody would have believed it. They used to call us the Twins. If I happened to appear anywhere alone, they would inquire, anxiously, "What is the matter? Is your chum sick?" It was so unusual; we were each other's shadow. But one day I struck him. He had outraged my most sacred feelings: to spend twenty cents for a meal! It was not mere extravagance; it was positively a crime, incredible in a revolutionist. I could not forgive him for months. Even now,—two years have passed,—yet a certain feeling of resentment still remains with me. What right had a revolutionist to such self-indulgence? The movement needed aid; every cent was valuable. To spend twenty cents for a single meal! He was a traitor to the Cause. True, it was his first meal in two days, and we were economizing on rent by sleeping in the parks. He had worked hard, too, to earn the money. But he should have known that he had no right to his earnings while the movement stood in such need of funds. His defence was unspeakably aggravating: he had earned ten dollars that week—he had given seven into the paper's treasury—he needed three dollars for his week's expenses—his shoes were torn, too. I had no patience with such arguments. They merely proved his *bourgeois* predilections. Personal comforts could not be of any consideration to a true revolutionist. It was a question of the movement; *its* needs, the first issue. Every penny spent for ourselves was so much taken from the Cause. True, the revolutionist must live. But luxury is a crime; worse, a weakness. One could exist on five cents a day. Twenty cents for a single meal! Incredible. It was robbery.

Poor Twin! He was deeply grieved, but he knew that I was merely just. The revolutionist has no personal right to anything. Everything he has or earns belongs to the Cause. Everything, even his affections. Indeed, these especially. He must not become too much attached to anything. He should guard against strong love or passion. The People should be his only great love, his supreme passion. Mere human sentiment is unworthy of the real revolutionist: he lives for humanity, and he must ever be ready to respond to its call. The soldier of Revolution must not be lured from the field of battle by the siren song of love. Great danger lurks in such weakness. The Russian tyrant has frequently attempted to bait his prey with a beautiful woman. Our comrades there are careful not to associate with any woman, except of proved revolutionary character. Aye, her mere passive interest in the Cause is not sufficient. Love may transform her into a Delilah to shear one's strength. Only with a woman consecrated to active participation may the revolutionist associate. Their perfect comradeship would prove a mutual inspiration, a source of increased strength. Equals, thoroughly solidaric, they would the more successfully serve the Cause of the People. Countless Russian women bear witness—Sophia Perovskaya, Vera Figner, Zassulitch, and many other heroic martyrs, tortured in the casemates of Schlüsselburg, buried alive in the Petropavlovka. What devotion, what fortitude! Perfect comrades they were, often stronger than the men. Brave, noble women that fill the prisons and *étapes*, tramp the toilsome road. . . .

The Siberian steppe rises before me. Its broad expanse shimmers in the sun's rays, and blinds the eye with white brilliancy. The endless monotony agonizes the sight, and stupefies the brain. It breathes the chill of death into the heart, and grips the soul with the terror of madness. In vain the eye seeks relief from the white Monster that slowly tightens his embrace, and threatens to swallow you in his frozen depth. . . . There, in the distance, where the blue meets the white, a heavy line of crimson dyes the surface. It winds along the virgin bosom, grows redder and deeper, and ascends the mountain in a dark ribbon, twining and wreathing its course in lengthening pain, now disappearing in the hollow, and again rising on the height. Behold a man and a woman, hand in hand, their heads bent, on their shoulders a heavy cross, slowly toiling the upward way, and behind them others, men and women, young and old, all weary with the heavy task, trudging along the dismal desert, amid death and silence, save for the mournful clank, clank of the chains. . . .

"Get out now. Exercise!"

As in a dream I walk along the gallery. The voice of my exercise mate sounds dully in my ears. I do not understand what he is saying. Does he know about the Nihilists, I wonder?

"Billy, have you ever read anything about Nihilists?"

"Sure, Berk. When I done my last bit in the dump below, a guy lent me a book. A corker, too, it was. Let's see, what you call 'em again?"

"Nihilists."

"Yes, sure. About some Nihirists. The book's called Aivan Strodjoff."

"What was the name?"

"Somethin' like that. Aivan Strodjoff or Strogoff."

"Oh, you mean Ivan Strogov, don't you?"

"That's it. Funny names them foreigners have. A fellow needs a cast-iron jaw to say it every day. But the story was a corker all right. About a Rooshan patriot or something. He was hot stuff, I tell you. Overheard a plot to kill th' king by them fellows—er— what's you call 'em?"

"Nihilists?"

"Yep. Nihilist plot, you know. Well, they wants to kill his Nibs and all the dookes, to make one of their own crowd king. See? Foxy fellows, you bet. But Aivan was too much for 'em. He plays detective. Gets in all kinds of scrapes, and some one burns his eyes out. But he's game. I don't remember how it all ends, but—"

"I know the story. It's trash. It doesn't tell the truth about—"

"Oh, t'hell with it! Say, Berk, d'ye think they'll hang me? Won't the judge sympathize with a blind man? Look at me eyes. Pretty near blind, swear to God, I am. Won't hang a blind man, will they?"

The pitiful appeal goes to my heart, and I assure him they will not hang a blind man. His eyes brighten, his face grows radiant with hope.

Why does he love life so, I wonder. Of what value is it without a high purpose, uninspired by revolutionary ideals? He is small and cowardly: he lies to save his neck. There is nothing at all wrong with his eyes. But why should *I* lie for his sake?

My conscience smites me for the moment of weak-

ness. I should not allow inane sentimentality to influence me: it is beneath the revolutionist.

"Billy," I say with some asperity, "many innocent
people have been hanged. The Nihilists, for instance—"

"Oh, damn 'em! What do *I* care about 'em! Will
they hang *me,* that's what I want to know."

"May be they will," I reply, irritated at the profana-
tion of my ideal. A look of terror spreads over his
face. His eyes are fastened upon me, his lips parted.
"Yes," I continue, "perhaps they will hang you. Many
innocent men have suffered such a fate. I don't think
you are innocent, either; nor blind. You don't need
those glasses; there is nothing the matter with your
eyes. Now understand, Billy, I don't want them to
hang you. I don't believe in hanging. But I must tell
you the truth, and you'd better be ready for the worst."

Gradually the look of fear fades from his face. Rage
suffuses his cheeks with spots of dark red.

"You're crazy! What's the use talkin' to you, anyhow? You are a damn Anarchist. I'm a good Catholic,
I want you to know that! I haven't always did right,
but the good father confessed me last week. I'm no
damn murderer like you, see? It was an accident. I'm
pretty near blind, and this is a Christian country, thank
God! They won't hang a blind man. Don't you ever
talk to *me* again!"

XI

The days and weeks pass in wearying monotony,
broken only by my anxiety about the approaching trial.
It is part of the designed cruelty to keep me ignorant
of the precise date. "Hold yourself ready. You may
be called any time," the Warden had said. But the

shadows are lengthening, the days come and go, and still my name has not appeared on the court calendar. Why this torture? Let me have over with it. My mission is almost accomplished,—the explanation in court, and then my life is done. I shall never again have an opportunity to work for the Cause. I may therefore leave the world. I should die content, but for the partial failure of my plans. The bitterness of disappointment is gnawing at my heart. Yet why? The physical results of my act cannot affect its propagandistic value. Why, then, these regrets? I should rise above them. But the gibes of officers and prisoners wound me. "Bad shot, ain't you?" They do not dream how keen their thoughtless thrusts. I smile and try to appear indifferent, while my heart bleeds. Why should I, the revolutionist, be moved by such remarks? It is weakness. They are so far beneath me; they live in the swamp of their narrow personal interests; they cannot understand. And yet the croaking of the frogs may reach the eagle's aerie, and disturb the peace of the heights.

The "trusty" passes along the gallery. He walks slowly, dusting the iron railing, then turns to give my door a few light strokes with the cat-o'-many-tails. Leaning against the outer wall, he stoops low, pretending to wipe the doorsill,—there is a quick movement of his hand, and a little roll of white is shot between the lower bars, falling at my feet. "A stiff," he whispers.

Indifferently I pick up the note. I know no one in the jail; it is probably some poor fellow asking for cigarettes. Placing the roll between the pages of a newspaper, I am surprised to find it in German. From whom can it be? I turn to the signature. Carl Nold? It's impossible; it's a trap! No, but that

handwriting,—I could not mistake it: the small, clear
chirography is undoubtedly Nold's. But how did he
smuggle in this note? I feel the blood rush to my head
as my eye flits over the penciled lines: Bauer and he are
arrested; they are in the jail now, charged with conspiracy to kill Frick; detectives swore they met them in
my company, in front of the Frick office building. They
have engaged a lawyer, the note runs on. Would I
accept his services? I probably have no money, and I
shouldn't expect any from New York, because Most—
what's this?—because Most has repudiated the act—

The gong tolls the exercise hour. With difficulty
I walk to the gallery. I feel feverish: my feet drag
heavily, and I stumble against the railing.

"Is yo sick, Ahlick?" It must be the negro's voice.
My throat is dry; my lips refuse to move. Hazily I see
the guard approach. He walks me to the cell, and lowers
the berth. "You may lie down." The lock clicks, and
I'm alone.

The line marches past, up and down, up and down.
The regular footfall beats against my brain like hammer
strokes. When will they stop? My head aches dread-
fully—I am glad I don't have to walk—it was good of
the negro to call the guard—I felt so sick. What was it?
Oh, the note! Where is it?

The possibility of loss dismays me. Hastily I pick
the newspaper up from the floor. With trembling hands
I turn the leaves. Ah, it's here! If I had not found it,
I vaguely wonder, were the thing mere fancy?

The sight of the crumpled paper fills me with dread.
Nold and Bauer here! Perhaps—if they act discreetly—
all will be well. They are innocent; they can prove
it. But Most! How can it be possible? Of course,
he was displeased when I began to associate with the

autonomists. But how can that make any difference?
At such a time! What matter personal likes and dis-
likes to a revolutionist, to a Most—the hero of my first
years in America, the name that stirred my soul in that
little library in Kovno—Most, the Bridge of Liberty!
My teacher—the author of the *Kriegswissenschaft*—
the ideal revolutionist—he to denounce me, to repudiate
propaganda by deed?

It's incredible! I cannot believe it. The Girl will not
fail to write to me about it. I'll wait till I hear from
her. But, then, Nold is himself a great admirer of
Most; he would not say anything derogatory, unless
fully convinced that it is true. Yet—it is barely con-
ceivable. How explain such a change in Most? To
forswear his whole past, his glorious past! He was
always so proud of it, and of his extreme revolu-
tionism. Some tremendous motive must be back of such
apostasy. It has no parallel in Anarchist annals. But
what can it be? How boldly he acted during the Haymarket tragedy—publicly advised the use of violence to
avenge the capitalist conspiracy. He must have realized
the danger of the speech for which he was later doomed
to Blackwell's Island. I remember his defiant manner
on the way to prison. How I admired his strong spirit,
as I accompanied him on the last ride! That was only
a little over a year ago, and he is just out a few months.
Perhaps—is it possible? A coward? Has that prison
experience influenced his present attitude? Why, it is
terrible to think of. Most—a coward? He who has
devoted his entire life to the Cause, sacrificed his seat in
the Reichstag because of uncompromising honesty, stood
in the forefront all his life, faced peril and danger,—
he a coward? Yet, it is impossible that he should have
suddenly altered the views of a lifetime. What could
have prompted his denunciation of my act? Personal

dislike? No, that was a matter of petty jealousy. His confidence in me, as a revolutionist, was unbounded. Did he not issue a secret circular letter to aid my plans concerning Russia? That was proof of absolute faith. One could not change his opinion so suddenly. Moreover, it can have no bearing on his repudiation of a terrorist act. I can find no explanation, unless—can it be?—fear of personal consequences. Afraid *he* might be held responsible, perhaps. Such a possibility is not excluded, surely. The enemy hates him bitterly, and would welcome an opportunity, would even conspire, to hang him. But that is the price one pays for his love of humanity. Every revolutionist is exposed to this danger. Most especially; his whole career has been a duel with tyranny. But he was never before influenced by such considerations. Is he not prepared to take the responsibility for his terrorist propaganda, the work of his whole life? Why has he suddenly been stricken with fear? Can it be? Can it be? . . .

My soul is in the throes of agonizing doubt. Despair grips my heart, as I hesitatingly admit to myself the probable truth. But it cannot be; Nold has made a mistake. May be the letter is a trap; it was not written by Carl. But I know his hand so well. It is his, his! Perhaps I'll have a letter in the morning. The Girl—she is the only one I can trust—she'll tell me—

My head feels heavy. Wearily I lie on the bed. Perhaps to-morrow . . . a letter . . .

XII

"Your pards are here. Do you want to see them?" the Warden asks.

"What 'pards'?"

"Your partners, Bauer and Nold."

"My comrades, you mean. I have no partners."

"Same thing. Want to see them? Their lawyers are here."

"Yes, I'll see them."

Of course, I myself need no defence. I will conduct my own case, and explain my act. But I shall be glad to meet my comrades. I wonder how they feel about their arrest,—perhaps they are inclined to blame me. And what is their attitude toward my deed? If they side with Most—

My senses are on the alert as the guard accompanies me into the hall. Near the wall, seated at a small table, I behold Nold and Bauer. Two other men are with them; their attorneys, I suppose. All eyes scrutinize me curiously, searchingly. Nold advances toward me. His manner is somewhat nervous, a look of intense seriousness in his heavy-browed eyes. He grasps my hand. The pressure is warm, intimate, as if he yearns to pour boundless confidence into my heart. For a moment a wave of thankfulness overwhelms me: I long to embrace him. But curious eyes bore into me. I glance at Bauer. There is a cheerful smile on the good-natured, ruddy face. The guard pushes a chair toward the table, and leans against the railing. His presence constrains me: he will report to the Warden everything said.

I am introduced to the lawyers. The contrast in their appearance suggests a lifetime of legal wrangling. The younger man, evidently a recent graduate, is quick, alert, and talkative. There is an air of anxious expectancy about him, with a look of Semitic shrewdness in the long, narrow face. He enlarges upon the kind consent of his distinguished colleague to take charge of my case. His demeanor toward the elder lawyer is deeply respectful, almost reverential. The latter looks bored, and is silent.

"Do you wish to say something, Colonel?" the young lawyer suggests.

"Nothing."

He ejects the monosyllable sharply, brusquely. His colleague looks abashed, like a schoolboy caught in a naughty act.

"You, Mr. Berkman?" he asks.

I thank them for their interest in my case. But I need no defence, I explain, since I do not consider myself guilty. I am exclusively concerned in making a public statement in the courtroom. If I am represented by an attorney, I should be deprived of the opportunity. Yet it is most vital to clarify to the People the purpose of my act, the circumstances—

The heavy breathing opposite distracts me. I glance at the Colonel. His eyes are closed, and from the parted lips there issues the regular respiration of sound sleep. A look of mild dismay crosses the young lawyer's face. He rises with an apologetic smile.

"You are tired, Colonel. It's awfully close here."

"Let us go," the Colonel replies.

Depressed I return to the cell. The old lawyer,— how little my explanation interested him! He fell asleep! Why, it is a matter of life and death, an issue that involves the welfare of the world! I was so happy at the opportunity to elucidate my motives to intelligent Americans,—and he was sleeping! The young lawyer, too, is disgusting, with his air of condescending pity toward one who "will have a fool for a client," as he characterized my decision to conduct my own case. He may think such a course suicidal. Perhaps it is, in regard to consequences. But the length of the sentence is a matter of indifference to me: I'll die soon, anyway. The only thing of importance now is my explanation. And that man fell asleep! Perhaps he considers me a criminal. But what can I expect of a lawyer, when even the steel-worker could not understand my act? Most himself—

With the name, I recollect the letters the guard had given me during the interview. There are three of them; one from the Girl! At last! Why did she not write before? They must have kept the letter in the office. Yes, the postmark is a week old. She'll tell me about Most,—but what is the use? I'm sure of it now; I read it plainly in Nold's eyes. It's all true. But I must see what she writes.

How every line breathes her devotion to the Cause! She is the real Russian woman revolutionist. Her letter is full of bitterness against the attitude of Most and his lieutenants in the German and Jewish Anarchist circles, but she writes words of cheer and encouragement in my imprisonment. She refers to the financial difficulties of the little commune consisting of Fedya, herself, and one or two other comrades, and closes with the remark that, fortunately, I need no money for legal defence or attorneys.

The staunch Girl! She and Fedya are, after all, the only true revolutionists I know in our ranks. The others all possess some weakness. I could not rely on them. The German comrades,—they are heavy, phlegmatic; they lack the enthusiasm of Russia. I wonder how they ever produced a Reinsdorf. Well, he is the exception. There is nothing to be expected from the German movement, excepting perhaps the autonomists. But they are a mere handful, quite insignificant, kept alive mainly by the Most and Peukert feud. Peukert, too, the life of

their circle, is chiefly concerned with his personal rehabilitation. Quite natural, of course. A terrible injustice has been done him.* It is remarkable that the false
accusations have not driven him into obscurity. There
is great perseverance, aye, moral courage of no mean
order, in his survival in the movement. It was that
which first awakened my interest in him. Most's explanation, full of bitter invective, suggested hostile personal feeling. What a tremendous sensation I created
at the first Jewish Anarchist Conference by demanding
that the charges against Peukert be investigated! The
result entirely failed to substantiate the accusations. But
the Mostianer were not convinced, blinded by the vitu-
perative eloquence of Most. And now . . . now, again,
they will follow, as blindly. To be sure, they will not
dare take open stand against my act; not the Jewish
comrades, at least. After all, the fire of Russia still
smolders in their hearts. But Most's attitude toward
me will influence them: it will dampen their enthusiasm,
and thus react on the propaganda. The burden of
making agitation through my act will fall on the Girl's
shoulders. She will stand a lone soldier in the field.
She will exert her utmost efforts, I am convinced. But
she will stand alone. Fedya will also remain loyal. But
what can he do? He is not a speaker. Nor the rest
of the commune circle. And Most? We had all been
so intimate. . . . It's his cursed jealousy, and cowardice,
too. Yes, mostly cowardice—he can't be jealous of me

---

* Joseph Peukert, at one time a leading Anarchist of Austria,
was charged with betraying the German Anarchist Neve into the
hands of the police. Neve was sentenced to ten years' prison.
Peukert always insisted that the accusation against him originated
with some of his political enemies among the Socialists. It is
certain that the arrest of Neve was not due to calculated
treachery on the part of Peukert, but rather to indiscretion.

now! He recently left prison,—it must have terrorized him. The weakling! He will minimize the effect of my act, perhaps paralyze its propagandistic influence altogether. . . . Now I stand alone—except for the Girl —quite alone. It is always so. Was not "he" alone, my beloved, "unknown" Grinevitzky, isolated, scorned by his comrades? But his bomb . . . how it thundered. . . .

I was just a boy then. Let me see,—it was in 1881. I was about eleven years old. The class was assembling after the noon recess. I had barely settled in my seat, when the teacher called me forward. His long pointer was dancing a fanciful figure on the gigantic map of Russia.

"What province is that?" he demanded.

"Astrakhan."

"Mention its chief products."

Products? The name Chernishevsky flitted through my mind. He was in Astrakhan,—I heard Maxim tell mother so at dinner.

"Nihilists," I burst out.

The boys tittered; some laughed aloud. The teacher grew purple. He struck the pointer violently on the floor, shivering the tapering end. Suddenly there broke a roll of thunder. One—two— With a terrific crash, the window panes fell upon the desks; the floor shook beneath our feet. The room was hushed. Deathly pale, the teacher took a step toward the window, but hastily turned, and dashed from the room. The pupils rushed after him. I wondered at the air of fear and suspicion on the streets. At home every one spoke in subdued tones. Father looked at mother severely, reproachfully, and Maxim was unusually silent, but his face seemed radiant, an unwonted brilliancy in his eye. At night, alone with me in the dormitory, he rushed to my bed,

knelt at my side, and threw his arms around me and
kissed me, and cried, and kissed me. His wildness
frightened me. "What is it, Maximotchka?" I breathed
softly. He ran up and down the room, kissing me and
murmuring, "Glorious, glorious! Victory!"

Between sobs, solemnly pledging me to secrecy, he
whispered mysterious, awe-inspiring words: Will of the
People—tyrant removed—Free Russia. . . .

XIII

The nights overwhelm me with the sense of solitude.
Life is so remote, so appallingly far away—it has abandoned me in this desert of silence. The distant puffing
of fire engines, the shrieking of river sirens, accentuate
my loneliness. Yet it feels so near, this monster Life,
huge, palpitating with vitality, intent upon its wonted
course. How unmindful of myself, flung into the darkness,—like a furnace spark belched forth amid fire and
smoke into the blackness of night.

The monster! Its eyes are implacable; they watch
every gate of life. Every approach they guard, lest
I enter back—I and the others here. Poor unfortunates,
how irritated and nervous they are growing as their
trial day draws near! There is a hunted look in their
eyes; their faces are haggard and anxious. They walk
weakly, haltingly, worn with the long days of waiting.
Only "Blackie," the young negro, remains cheerful. But
I often miss the broad smile on the kindly face. I am
sure his eyes were moist when the three Italians returned
from court this morning. They had been sentenced to
death. Joe, a boy of eighteen, walked to the cell with
a firm step. His brother Pasquale passed us with both
hands over his face, weeping silently. But the old man,

their father—as he was crossing the hallway, we saw him suddenly stop. For a moment he swayed, then lurched forward, his head striking the iron railing, his body falling limp to the floor. By the arms the guards dragged him up the stairway, his legs hitting the stone with a dull thud, the fresh crimson spreading over his white hair, a glassy torpor in his eyes. Suddenly he stood upright. His head thrown back, his arms upraised, he cried hoarsely, anguished, "O Santa Maria! Sio innocente, inno—"

The guard swung his club. The old man reeled and fell.

"Ready! Death-watch!" shouted the Warden.

"In-no-cente! Death-watch!" mocked the echo under the roof.

The old man haunts my days. I hear the agonized cry; its black despair chills my marrow. Exercise hour has become insupportable. The prisoners irritate me: each is absorbed in his own case. The deadening monotony of the jail routine grows unbearable. The constant cruelty and brutality is harrowing. I wish it were all over. The uncertainty of my trial day is a ceaseless torture. I have been waiting now almost two months. My court speech is prepared. I could die now, but they would suppress my explanation, and the People thus remain ignorant of my aim and purpose. I owe it to the Cause—and to the true comrades—to stay on the scene till after the trial. There is nothing more to bind me to life. With the speech, my opportunities for propaganda will be exhausted. Death, suicide, is the only logical, the sole possible, conclusion. Yes, that is self-evident. If I only knew the date of my trial,—that day will be my last. The poor old Italian,—he and his sons, they at least know when they are to die. They count each day; every hour brings them closer to the end. They will be hanged here, in the jail yard. Perhaps they killed under great provocation, in the heat of passion. But the sheriff will murder them in cold blood. The law of peace and order!

I shall not be hanged—yet I feel as if I were dead. My life is done; only the last rite remains to be performed. After that—well, I'll find a way. When the trial is over, they'll return me to my cell. The spoon is of tin: I shall put a sharp edge on it—on the stone floor —very quietly, at night—

"Number six, to court! Num-ber six!"

Did the turnkey call "six"? Who is in cell six? Why, it's *my* cell! I feel the cold perspiration running down my back. My heart beats violently, my hands tremble, as I hastily pick up the newspaper. Nervously I turn the pages. There must be some mistake: my name didn't appear yet in the court calendar column. The list is published every Monday—why, this is Saturday's paper—yesterday we had service—it must be Monday to-day. Oh, shame! They didn't give me the paper to-day, and it's Monday—yes, it's Monday—

The shadow falls across my door. The lock clicks.

"Hurry, To court!"

CHAPTER VII

THE TRIAL

THE courtroom breathes the chill of the graveyard. The stained windows cast sickly rays into the silent chamber. In the sombre light the faces look funereal, spectral.

Anxiously I scan the room. Perhaps my friends, the Girl, have come to greet me. . . . Everywhere cold eyes meet my gaze. Police and court attendants on every side. Several newspaper men draw near. It is humiliating that through them I must speak to the People.

"Prisoner at the bar, stand up!"

The Commonwealth of Pennsylvania—the clerk vociferates—charges me with felonious assault on H. C. Frick, with intent to kill; felonious assault on John G. A. Leishman; feloniously entering the offices of the Carnegie Company on three occasions, each constituting a separate indictment; and with unlawfully carrying concealed weapons.

"Do you plead guilty or not guilty?"

I protest against the multiplication of the charges. I do not deny the attempt on Frick, but the accusation of having assaulted Leishman is not true. I have visited the Carnegie offices only—

"Do you plead guilty or not guilty?" the judge interrupts.

"Not guilty. I want to explain—"

"Your attorneys will do that."

"I have no attorney."

"The Court will appoint one to defend you."

"I need no defence. I want to make a statement."

"You will be given an opportunity at the proper time."

Impatiently I watch the proceedings. Of what use are all these preliminaries? My conviction is a foregone conclusion. The men in the jury box there, they are to decide my fate. As if they could understand! They measure me with cold, unsympathetic looks. Why were the talesmen not examined in my presence? They were already seated when I entered.

"When was the jury picked?" I demand.

"You have four challenges," the prosecutor retorts.

The names of the talesmen sound strange. But what matter who are the men to judge me? They, too, belong to the enemy. They will do the master's bidding. Yet I may, even for a moment, clog the wheels of the Juggernaut. At random, I select four names from the printed list, and the new jurors file into the box.

The trial proceeds. A police officer and two negro employees of Frick in turn take the witness stand. They had seen me three times in the Frick office, they testify. They speak falsely, but I feel indifferent to the hired witnesses. A tall man takes the stand. I recognize the detective who so brazenly claimed to identify me in the jail. He is followed by a physician who states that each wound of Frick might have proved fatal. John G. A. Leishman is called. I attempted to kill him, he testifies. "It's a lie!" I cry out, angrily, but the guards force me into the seat. Now Frick comes forward. He seeks to avoid my eye, as I confront him.

The prosecutor turns to me. I decline to examine the witnesses for the State. They have spoken falsely; there is no truth in them, and I shall not participate in the mockery.

"Call the witnesses for the defence," the judge commands.

I have no need of witnesses. I wish to proceed with my statement. The prosecutor demands that I speak English. But I insist on reading my prepared paper, in German. The judge rules to permit me the services of the court interpreter.

"I address myself to the People," I begin. "Some may wonder why I have declined a legal defence. My reasons are twofold. In the first place, I am an Anarchist: I do not believe in man-made law, designed to enslave and oppress humanity. Secondly, an extraordinary phenomenon like an *Attentat* cannot be measured by the narrow standards of legality. It requires a view of the social background to be adequately understood. A lawyer would try to defend, or palliate, my act from the standpoint of the law. Yet the real question at issue is not a defence of myself, but rather the *explanation* of the deed. It is mistaken to believe *me* on trial. The actual defendant is Society—the system of injustice, of the organized exploitation of the People."

The voice of the interpreter sounds cracked and shrill. Word for word he translates my utterance, the sentences broken, disconnected, in his inadequate English. The vociferous tones pierce my ears, and my heart bleeds at his meaningless declamation.

"Translate sentences, not single words," I remonstrate.

With an impatient gesture he leaves me.

"Oh, please, go on!" I cry in dismay.

He returns hesitatingly.

"Look at my paper," I adjure him, "and translate each sentence as I read it."

The glazy eyes are turned to me, in a blank, unseeing stare. The man is blind!

"Let—us—continue," he stammers.

"We have heard enough," the judge interrupts.

"I have not read a third of my paper," I cry in consternation.

"It will do."

"I have declined the services of attorneys to get time to—"

"We allow you five more minutes."

"But I can't explain in such a short time. I have the right to be heard."

"We'll teach you differently."

I am ordered from the witness chair. Several jurymen leave their seats, but the district attorney hurries forward, and whispers to them. They remain in the jury box. The room is hushed as the judge rises.

"Have you anything to say why sentence should not be passed upon you?"

"You would not let me speak," I reply. "Your justice is a farce."

"Silence!"

In a daze, I hear the droning voice on the bench. Hurriedly the guards lead me from the courtroom.

"The judge was easy on you," the Warden jeers. "Twenty-two years! Pretty stiff, eh?"

PART II

THE PENITENTIARY

WESTERN PENITENTIARY OF PENNSYLVANIA—MAIN BUILDING

CHAPTER I

DESPERATE THOUGHTS

I

"Make yourself at home, now. You'll stay here a while, huh, huh!"

As in a dream I hear the harsh tones. Is the man speaking to me, I wonder. Why is he laughing? I feel so weary, I long to be alone.

Now the voice has ceased; the steps are receding. All is silent, and I am alone. A nameless weight oppresses me. I feel exhausted, my mind a void. Heavily I fall on the bed. Head buried in the straw pillow, my heart breaking, I sink into deep sleep.

.   .   .   .

My eyes burn as with hot irons. The heat sears my sight, and consumes my eyelids. Now it pierces my head; my brain is aflame, it is swept by a raging fire. Oh!

I wake in horror. A stream of dazzling light is pouring into my face. Terrified, I press my hands to my eyes, but the mysterious flow pierces my lids, and blinds me with maddening torture.

"Get up and undress. What's the matter with you, anyhow?"

The voice frightens me. The cell is filled with a continuous glare. Beyond, all is dark, the guard invisible.

95

"Now lay down and go to sleep."

Silently I obey, when suddenly all grows black before my eyes. A terrible fear grips my heart. Have I gone blind? I grope for the bed, the wall . . . I can't see! With a desperate cry I spring to the door. A faint click reaches my tense ear, the streaming lightning burns into my face. Oh, I can see! I can see!

"What t' hell's the matter with you, eh? Go to sleep. You hear?"

Quiet and immovable I lie on the bed. Strange horrors haunt me. . . . What a terrible place this must be! This agony— I cannot support it. Twenty-two years! Oh, it is hopeless, hopeless. I must die. I'll die to-night. . . . With bated breath I creep from the bed. The iron bedstead creaks. In affright I draw back, feigning sleep. All remains silent. The guard did not hear me. I should feel the terrible bull's-eye even with closed lids. Slowly I open my eyes. It is dark all around. I grope about the cell. The wall is damp, musty. The odors are nauseating. . . . I cannot live here. I must die. This very night . . . . Something white glimmers in the corner. Cautiously I bend over. It is a spoon. For a moment I hold it indifferently; then a great joy overwhelms me. Now I can die! I creep back into bed, nervously clutching the tin. My hand feels for my heart. It is beating violently. I will put the narrow end of the spoon over here—like this— I will force it in—a little lower—a steady pressure—just between the ribs. . . . The metal feels cold. How hot my body is! Caressingly I pat the spoon against my side. My fingers seek the edge. It is dull. I must press it hard. Yes, it is very dull. If I only had my revolver. But the cartridge might fail to explode. That's why Frick is now well, and I must die. How he looked at me in court! There was hate in his eyes, and fear, too. He turned his head away, he could not face me. I saw that he felt guilty. Yet he lives. I didn't crush him. Oh, I failed, I failed. . . .

"Keep quiet there, or I'll put you in the hole."

The gruff voice startles me. I must have been moaning. I'll draw the blanket over my head, so. What was I thinking about? Oh, I remember. He is well, and I am here. I failed to crush him. He lives. Of course, it does not really matter. The opportunity for propaganda is there, as the result of my act. That was the main purpose. But I meant to kill him, and he lives. My speech, too, failed. They tricked me. They kept the date secret. They were afraid my friends would be present. It was maddening the way the prosecuting attorney and the judge kept interrupting me. I did not read even a third of my statement. And the whole effect was lost. How that man interpreted! The poor old man! He was deeply offended when I corrected his translation. I did not know he was blind. I called him back, and suffered renewed torture at his screeching. I was almost glad when the judge forced me to discontinue. That judge! He acted as indifferently as if the matter did not concern him. He must have known that the sentence meant death. Twenty-two years! As if it is possible to survive such a sentence in this terrible place! Yes, he knew it; he spoke of making an example of me. The old villain! He has been doing it all his life: making an example of social victims, the victims of his own class, of capitalism. The brutal mockery of it—had I anything to say why sentence should not be passed? Yet he wouldn't permit me to continue my statement. "The court has been very patient!" I am glad I told him that I didn't expect justice, and did not get it. Perhaps I should have thrown in his face the epithet that sprang to my lips. No, it was best that I controlled my anger. Else they would have rejoiced to proclaim the Anarchists vulgar criminals. Such things help to prejudice the People against us. We, criminals? We, who are ever ready to give our lives for liberty, criminals? And they, our accusers? They break their own laws: they knew it was not legal to multiply the charges against me. They made six indictments out of one act, as if the minor "offences" were not included in the major, made necessary by the deed itself. They thirsted for blood. Legally, they could not give me more than seven years. But I am an Anarchist. I had attempted the life of a great magnate; in him capitalism felt itself attacked. Of course, I knew they would take advantage of my refusal to be legally represented. Twenty-two years! The judge imposed the maximum penalty on each charge. Well, I expected no less, and it makes no difference now. I am going to die, anyway.

I clutch the spoon in my feverish hand. Its narrow end against my heart, I test the resistance of the flesh. A violent blow will drive it between the ribs. . . .

One, two, three—the deep metallic bass floats upon the silence, resonant, compelling. Instantly all is motion: overhead, on the sides, everything is vibrant with life. Men yawn and cough, chairs and beds are noisily moved about, heavy feet pace stone floors. In the distance sounds a low rolling, as of thunder. It grows nearer and louder. I hear the officers' sharp command, the familiar click of locks, doors opening and shutting. Now the rumbling grows clearer, more distinct. With a moan the heavy bread-wagon stops at my cell. A guard unlocks the door. His eyes rest on me curiously, suspiciously, while the trusty hands me a small loaf of bread. I have barely time to withdraw my arm before the door is closed and locked.

"Want coffee? Hold your cup."

Between the narrow bars, the beverage is poured into
my bent, rusty tin can. In the semi-darkness of the cell
the steaming liquid overflows, scalding my bare feet.
With a cry of pain I drop the can. In the dimly-lit hall
the floor looks stained with blood.

"What do you mean by that?" the guard shouts
at me.

"I couldn't help it."

"Want to be smart, don't you? Well, we'll take it
out of you. Hey, there, Sam," the officer motions to the
trusty, "no dinner for A 7, you hear!"

"Yes, sir. Yes, sir!"

"No more coffee, either."

"Yes, sir."

The guard measures me with a look of scornful
hatred. Malice mirrors in his face. Involuntarily I step
back into the cell. His gaze falls on my naked feet.

"Ain't you got no shoes?"

"Yes."

"Ye-e-s! Can't you say 'sir'? Got shoes?"

"Yes."

"Put 'em on, damn you."

His tongue sweeps the large quid of tobacco from one
cheek to the other. With a hiss, a thick stream of brown
splashes on my feet. "Damn you, put 'em on."

The clatter and noises have ceased; the steps have
died away. All is still in the dark hall. Only occasional
shadows flit by, silent, ghostlike.

II

"Forward, march!"

The long line of prisoners, in stripes and lockstep,
resembles an undulating snake, wriggling from side to

side, its black-and-gray body moving forward, yet apparently remaining in the same spot. A thousand feet strike the stone floor in regular tempo, with alternate rising and falling accent, as each division, flanked by officers, approaches and passes my cell. Brutal faces, repulsive in their stolid indifference or malicious leer. Here and there a well-shaped head, intelligent eye, or sympathetic expression, but accentuates the features of the striped line: coarse and sinister, with the guilty-treacherous look of the ruthlessly hunted. Head bent, right arm extended, with hand touching the shoulder of the man in front, all uniformly clad in horizontal black and gray, the men seem will-less cogs in a machine, oscillating to the shouted command of the tall guards on the flanks, stern and alert.

The measured beat grows fainter and dies with the hollow thud of the last footfall, behind the closed double door leading into the prison yard. The pall of silence descends upon the cell-house. I feel utterly alone, deserted and forsaken amid the towering pile of stone and iron. The stillness overwhelms me with almost tangible weight. I am buried within the narrow walls; the massive rock is pressing down upon my head, my sides. I cannot breathe. The foul air is stifling. Oh, I can't, I can't live here! I can't suffer this agony. Twenty-two years! It is a lifetime. No, it's impossible. I must die. I will! Now!

Clutching the spoon, I throw myself on the bed. My eyes wander over the cell, faintly lit by the light in the hall: the whitewashed walls, yellow with damp—the splashes of dark-red blood at the head of the bed— the clumps of vermin around the holes in the wall—the small table and the rickety chair—the filthy floor, black and gray in spots. . . . Why, it's stone! I can sharpen

the spoon. Cautiously I crouch in the corner. The tin
glides over the greasy surface, noiselessly, smoothly,
till the thick layer of filth is worn off. Then it scratches
and scrapes. With the pillow I deaden the rasping
sound. The metal is growing hot in my hand. I pass
the sharp edge across my finger. Drops of blood trickle
down to the floor. The wound is ragged, but the blade
is keen. Stealthily I crawl back into bed. My hand
gropes for my heart. I touch the spot with the blade.
Between the ribs—here—I'll be dead when they find
me. . . . If Frick had only died. So much propaganda
could be made—that damned Most, if he hadn't turned
against me! He will ruin the whole effect of the act.
It's nothing but cowardice. But what is he afraid of?
They can't implicate him. We've been estranged for
over a year. He could easily prove it. The traitor!
Preached propaganda by deed all his life—now he
repudiates the first *Attentat* in this country. What
tremendous agitation he could have made of it! Now
he denies me, he doesn't know me. The wretch! He
knew me well enough and trusted me, too, when together
we set up the secret circular in the *Freiheit* office.
It was in William Street. We waited for the other
compositors to leave; then we worked all night. It was
to recommend me: I planned to go to Russia then.
Yes, to Russia. Perhaps I might have done something
important there. Why didn't I go? What was it?
Well, I can't think of it now. It's peculiar, though. But
America was more important. Plenty of revolutionists in
Russia. And now. . . . Oh, I'll never do anything more.
I'll be dead soon. They'll find me cold—a pool of blood
under me—the mattress will be red—no, it will be
dark-red, and the blood will soak through the straw . . .
I wonder how much blood I have. It will gush from
my heart—I must strike right here—strong and quick

—it will not pain much. But the edge is ragged—it may catch—or tear the flesh. They say the skin is tough. I must strike hard. Perhaps better to fall against the blade? No, the tin may bend. I'll grasp it close—like this—then a quick drive—right into the heart—it's the surest way. I must not wound myself—I would bleed slowly—they might discover me still alive. No, no! I must die at once. They'll find me dead—my heart—they'll feel it—not beating—the blade still in it—they'll call the doctor—"He's dead." And the Girl and Fedya and the others will hear of it—she'll be sad—but she will understand. Yes, she will be glad—they couldn't torture me here—she'll know I cheated them—yes, she. . . . Where is she now? What does she think of it all? Does she, too, think I've failed? And Fedya, also? If I'd only hear from her—just once. It would be easier to die. But she'll understand, she—

"Git off that bed! Don't you know the rules, eh? Get out o' there!"

Horrified, speechless, I spring to my feet. The spoon falls from my relaxed grip. It strikes the floor, clinking on the stone loudly, damningly. My heart stands still as I face the guard. There is something repulsively familiar about the tall man, his mouth drawn into a derisive smile. Oh, it's the officer of the morning!

"Foxy, ain't you? Gimme that spoon."

The coffee incident flashes through my mind. Loathing and hatred of the tall guard fill my being. For a second I hesitate. I must hide the spoon. I cannot afford to lose it—not to this brute—

"Cap'n, here!"

I am dragged from the cell. The tall keeper carefully examines the spoon, a malicious grin stealing over his face.

"Look, Cap'n. Sharp as a razor. Pretty des-
p'rate, eh?"

"Take him to the Deputy, Mr. Fellings."

III

In the rotunda, connecting the north and south
cell-houses, the Deputy stands at a high desk. Angular
and bony, with slightly stooped shoulders, his face is
a mass of minute wrinkles seamed on yellow parchment.
The curved nose overhangs thin, compressed lips. The
steely eyes measure me coldly, unfriendly.

"Who is this?"

The low, almost feminine, voice sharply accentuates
the cadaver-like face and figure. The contrast is
startling.

"A 7."

"What is the charge, Officer?"

"Two charges, Mr. McPane. Layin' in bed and
tryin' soocide."

A smile of satanic satisfaction slowly spreads over
the Deputy's wizened face. The long, heavy fingers of
his right hand work convulsively, as if drumming stiffly
on an imaginary board.

"Yes, hm, hm, yes. A 7, two charges. Hm, hm.
How did he try to, hm, hm, to commit suicide?"

"With this spoon, Mr. McPane. Sharp as a razor."

"Yes, hm, yes. Wants to die. We have no such
charge as, hm, hm, as trying suicide in this institution.
Sharpened spoon, hm, hm; a grave offence. I'll see
about that later. For breaking the rules, hm, hm, by
lying in bed out of hours, hm, hm, three days. Take him
down, Officer. He will, hm, hm, cool off."

I am faint and weary. A sense of utter indifference possesses me. Vaguely I am conscious of the guards leading me through dark corridors, dragging me down steep flights, half undressing me, and finally thrusting me into a black void. I am dizzy; my head is awhirl. I stagger and fall on the flagstones of the dungeon.

.   .   .   .

The cell is filled with light. It hurts my eyes. Some one is bending over me.

"A bit feverish. Better take him to the cell."

"Hm, hm, Doctor, he is in punishment."

"Not safe, Mr. McPane."

"We'll postpone it, then. Hm, hm, take him to the cell, Officers."

"Git up."

My legs seem paralyzed. They refuse to move. I am lifted and carried up the stairs, through corridors and halls, and then thrown heavily on a bed.

I feel so weak. Perhaps I shall die now. It would be best. But I have no weapon! They have taken away the spoon. There is nothing in the cell that I could use. These iron bars—I could beat my head against them. But oh! it is such a horrible death. My skull would break, and the brains ooze out. . . . But the bars are smooth. Would my skull break with one blow? I'm afraid it might only crack, and I should be too weak to strike again. If I only had a revolver; that is the easiest and quickest. I've always thought I'd prefer such a death—to be shot. The barrel close to the temple —one couldn't miss. Some people have done it in front of a mirror. But I have no mirror. I have no revolver, either. . . . Through the mouth it is also

fatal. . . . That Moscow student—Russov was his
name; yes, Ivan Russov—he shot himself through
the mouth. Of course, he was foolish to kill himself
for a woman; but I admired his courage. How coolly he
had made all preparations; he even left a note directing
that his gold watch be given to the landlady, because—
he wrote—after passing through his brain, the bullet
might damage the wall. Wonderful! It actually
happened that way. I saw the bullet imbedded in the
wall near the sofa, and Ivan lay so still and peaceful,
I thought he was asleep. I had often seen him like that
in my brother's study, after our lessons. What a
splendid tutor he was! I liked him from the first, when
mother introduced him: "Sasha, Ivan Nikolaievitch will
be your instructor in Latin during vacation time." My
hand hurt all day; he had gripped it so powerfully, like
a vise. But I was glad I didn't cry out. I admired
him for it; I felt he must be very strong and manly to
have such a handshake. Mother smiled when I told
her about it. Her hand pained her too, she said. Sister
blushed a little. "Rather energetic," she observed. And
Maxim felt so happy over the favorable impression
made by his college chum. "What did I tell you?" he
cried, in glee; "Ivan Nikolaievitch *molodetz!** Think
of it, he's only twenty. Graduates next year. The
youngest alumnus since the foundation of the university.
Molodetz!" But how red were Maxim's eyes when he
brought the bullet home. He would keep it, he said,
as long as he lived: he had dug it out, with his own
hands, from the wall of Ivan Nikolaievitch's room. At
dinner he opened the little box, unwrapped the cotton,
and showed me the bullet. Sister went into hysterics,
and mamma called Max a brute. "For a woman, an

---

* Clever, brave lad.

unworthy woman!" sister moaned. I thought he was
foolish to take his life on account of a woman. I felt
a little disappointed: Ivan Nikolaievitch should have been
more manly. They all said she was very beautiful, the
acknowledged belle of Kovno. She was tall and stately,
but I thought she walked too stiffly; she seemed self-
conscious and artificial. Mother said I was too young
to talk of such things. How shocked she would have
been had she known that I was in love with Nadya, my
sister's chum. And I had kissed our chambermaid, too.
Dear little Rosa,—I remember she threatened to tell
mother. I was so frightened, I wouldn't come to dinner.
Mamma sent the maid to call me, but I refused to go
till Rosa promised not to tell. . . . The sweet girl, with
those red-apple cheeks. How kind she was! But the
little imp couldn't keep the secret. She told Tatanya,
the cook of our neighbor, the Latin instructor at the
gymnasium. Next day he teased me about the servant
girl. Before the whole class, too. I wished the floor
would open and swallow me. I was so mortified.

. . . How far off it all seems. Centuries away.
I wonder what has become of her. Where is Rosa now?
Why, she must be here, in America. I had almost forgotten,—I met her in New York. It was such a surprise.
I was standing on the stoop of the tenement house where
I boarded. I had then been only a few months in the
country. A young lady passed by. She looked up at me,
then turned and ascended the steps. "Don't you know
me, Mr. Berkman? Don't you really recognize me?"
Some mistake, I thought. I had never before seen this
beautiful, stylish young woman. She invited me into
the hallway. "Don't tell these people here. I am Rosa.
Don't you remember? Why, you know, I was your
mother's—your mother's maid." She blushed violently.

Those red cheeks—why, certainly, it's Rosa! I thought of the stolen kiss. "Would I dare it now?" I wondered, suddenly conscious of my shabby clothes. She seemed so prosperous. How our positions were changed! She looked the very *barishnya,** like my sister. "Is your mother here?" she asked. "Mother? She died, just before I left." I glanced apprehensively at her. Did she remember that terrible scene when mother struck her? "I didn't know about your mother." Her voice was husky; a tear glistened in her eye. The dear girl, always generous-hearted. I ought to make amends to her for mother's insult. We looked at each other in embarrassment. Then she held out a gloved hand. Very large, I thought; red, too, probably. "Good-bye, *Gospodin*† Berkman," she said. "I'll see you again soon. Please don't tell these people who I am." I experienced a feeling of guilt and shame. *Gospodin* Berkman— somehow it echoed the servile *barinya*‡ with which the domestics used to address my mother. For all her finery, Rosa had not gotten over it. Too much bred in, poor girl. She has not become emancipated. I never saw her at our meetings; she is conservative, no doubt. She was so ignorant, she could not even read. Perhaps she has learned in this country. Now she will read about me, and she'll know how I died. . . . Oh, I haven't the spoon! What shall I do, what shall I do? I can't live. I couldn't stand this torture. Perhaps if I had seven years, I would try to serve the sentence. But I couldn't, anyhow. I might live here a year, or two. But twenty-two, twenty-two years! What is the use? No man could survive it. It's terrible, twenty-two years! Their cursed justice—they always talk of law. Yet legally I shouldn't have gotten more than seven years. Legally!

---

*Young lady. † Mister. ‡ Lady.

As if *they* care about "legality." They wanted to make an example of me. Of course, I knew it beforehand; but if I had seven years—perhaps I might live through it; I would try. But twenty-two—it's a lifetime, a whole lifetime. Seventeen is no better. That man Jamestown got seventeen years. He celled next to me in the jail. He didn't look like a highway robber, he was so small and puny. He must be here now. A fool, to think he could live here seventeen years. In this hell—what an imbecile he is! He should have committed suicide long ago. They sent him away before my trial; it's about three weeks ago. Enough time; why hasn't he done something? He will soon die here, anyway; it would be better to suicide. A strong man might live five years; I doubt it, though; perhaps a very strong man might. *I* couldn't; no, I know I couldn't; perhaps two or three years, at most. We had often spoken about this, the Girl, Fedya, and I. I had then such a peculiar idea of prison: I thought I would be sitting on the floor in a gruesome, black hole, with my hands and feet chained to the wall; and the worms would crawl over me, and slowly devour my face and my eyes, and I so helpless, chained to the wall. The Girl and Fedya had a similar idea. She said she might bear prison life a few weeks. I could for a year, I thought; but was doubtful. I pictured myself fighting the worms off with my feet; it would take the vermin that long to eat all my flesh, till they got to my heart; that would be fatal. . . . And the vermin here, those big, brown bedbugs, they must be like those worms, so vicious and hungry. Perhaps there are worms here, too. There must be in the dungeon: there is a wound on my foot. I don't know how it happened. I was unconscious in that dark hole—it was just like my old idea of prison. I couldn't live even a week there: it's awful. Here it is a little better; but it's never light in this cell,—always

in semidarkness. And so small and narrow; no
windows; it's damp, and smells so foully all the time.
The walls are wet and clammy; smeared with blood, too.
Bedbugs—augh! it's nauseating. Not much better than
that black hole, with my hands and arms chained to the
wall. Just a trifle better,—my hands are not chained.
Perhaps I could live here a few years: no more than
three, or may be five. But these brutal officers! No, no,
I couldn't stand it. I want to die! I'd die here soon,
anyway; they will kill me. But I won't give the enemy
the satisfaction; they shall not be able to say that they
are torturing me in prison, or that they killed me. No!
I'd rather kill myself. Yes, kill myself. I shall have
to do it—with my head against the bars—no, not now!
At night, when it's all dark,—they couldn't save me then.
It will be a terrible death, but it must be done. . . .
If I only knew about "them" in New York—the Girl
and Fedya—it would be easier to die then. . . . What are
they doing in the case? Are they making propaganda
out of it? They must be waiting to hear of my suicide.
They know I can't live here long. Perhaps they wonder
why I didn't suicide right after the trial. But I could
not. I thought I should be taken from the court to my
cell in jail; sentenced prisoners usually are. I had
prepared to hang myself that night, but they must have
suspected something. They brought me directly here
from the courtroom. Perhaps I should have been
dead now—

"Supper! Want coffee? Hold your tin!" the trusty
shouts into the door. Suddenly he whispers, "Grab it,
quick!" A long, dark object is shot between the bars
into the cell, dropping at the foot of the bed. The man
is gone. I pick up the parcel, tightly wrapped in brown
paper. What can it be? The outside cover protects
two layers of old newspaper; then a white object comes

to view. A towel! There is something round and
hard inside—it's a cake of soap. A sense of thankfulness
steals into my heart, as I wonder who the donor may
be. It is good to know that there is at least one being
here with a friendly spirit. Perhaps it's some one I
knew in the jail. But how did he procure these things?
Are they permitted? The towel feels nice and soft; it
is a relief from the hard straw bed. Everything is so
hard and coarse here—the language, the guards. . . .
I pass the towel over my face; it soothes me somewhat.
I ought to wash up—my head feels so heavy—I haven't
washed since I got here. When did I come? Let me
see; what is to-day? I don't know, I can't think. But
my trial—it was on Monday, the nineteenth of September. They brought me here in the afternoon; no, in
the evening. And that guard—he frightened me so with
the bull's-eye lantern. Was it last night? No, it must
have been longer than that. Have I been here only
since yesterday? Why, it seems such a long time! Can
this be Tuesday, only Tuesday? I'll ask the trusty the
next time he passes. I'll find out who sent this towel,
too. Perhaps I could get some cold water from him;
or may be there is some here—

My eyes are growing accustomed to the semi-
darkness of the cell. I discern objects quite clearly.
There is a small wooden table and an old chair; in
the furthest corner, almost hidden by the bed, is the
privy; near it, in the center of the wall opposite the
door, is a water spigot over a narrow, circular basin.
The water is lukewarm and muddy, but it feels refreshing. The rub-down with the towel is invigorating.
The stimulated blood courses through my veins with a
pleasing tingle. Suddenly a sharp sting, as of a needle,
pricks my face. There's a pin in the towel. As I draw
it out, something white flutters to the floor. A note!

With ear alert for a passing step, I hastily read the penciled writing:

Be shure to tare this up as soon as you reade it, it's from a friend. We is going to make a break and you can come along, we know you are on the level. Lay low and keep your lamps lit at night, watch the screws and the stools they is worse than bulls. Dump is full of them and don't have nothing to say. So long, will see you tomorrow. A true friend.

I read the note carefully, repeatedly. The peculiar language baffles me. Vaguely I surmise its meaning: evidently an escape is being planned. My heart beats violently, as I contemplate the possibilities. If I could escape. . . . Oh, I should not have to die! Why haven't I thought of it before? What a glorious thing it would be! Of course, they would ransack the country for me. I should have to hide. But what does it matter? I'd be at liberty. And what tremendous effect! It would make great propaganda: people would become much interested, and I—why, I should have new opportunities—

The shadow of suspicion falls over my joyous thought, overwhelming me with despair. Perhaps a trap! I don't know who wrote the note. A fine conspirator I'd prove, to be duped so easily. But why should they want to trap me? And who? Some guard? What purpose could it serve? But they are so mean, so brutal. That tall officer—the Deputy called him Fellings—he seems to have taken a bitter dislike to me. This may be his work, to get me in trouble. Would he really stoop to such an outrage? These things happen—they have been done in Russia. And he looks like a *provocateur,* the scoundrel. No, he won't get me that way. I must read the note again. It contains so many expressions I don't understand. I should "keep my lamps lit." What lamps? There are none in the cell; where am I to get them? And what "screws" must I watch? And the "stools,"—I have only a chair here. Why should I watch it? Perhaps it's to be used as a weapon. No, it must mean something else. The note says he will call to-morrow. I'll be able to tell by his looks whether he can be trusted. Yes, yes, that will be best. I'll wait till to-morrow. Oh, I wish it were here!

CHAPTER II

THE WILL TO LIVE

I

THE days drag interminably in the semidarkness of the cell. The gong regulates my existence with depressing monotony. But the tenor of my thoughts has been changed by the note of the mysterious correspondent. In vain I have been waiting for his appearance,—yet the suggestion of escape has germinated hope. The will to live is beginning to assert itself, growing more imperative as the days go by. I wonder that my mind dwells upon suicide more and more rarely, ever more cursorily. The thought of self-destruction fills me with dismay. Every possibility of escape must first be exhausted, I reassure my troubled conscience. Surely I have no fear of death—when the proper time arrives. But haste would be highly imprudent; worse, quite unnecessary. Indeed, it is my duty as a revolutionist to seize every opportunity for propaganda: escape would afford me many occasions to serve the Cause. It was thoughtless on my part to condemn that man Jamestown. I even resented his seemingly unforgivable delay in committing suicide, considering the impossible sentence of seventeen years. Indeed, I was unjust: Jamestown is, no doubt, forming his plans. It takes time to mature such an undertaking: one must first familiarize himself with the new surroundings, get one's bearings in the prison. So far I have had but little chance to do so. Evidently, it is the policy of the authorities to keep me in solitary confinement, and in consequent ignorance of the intricate system of hallways, double gates, and winding passages. At liberty to leave this place, it would prove difficult for me to find, unaided, my way out. Oh, if I possessed the magic ring I dreamed of last night! It was a wonderful talisman, secreted—I fancied in the dream—by the goddess of the Social Revolution. I saw her quite distinctly: tall and commanding, the radiance of all-conquering love in her eyes. She stood at my bedside, a smile of surpassing gentleness suffusing the queenly countenance, her arm extended above me, half in blessing, half pointing toward the dark wall. Eagerly I looked in the direction of the arched hand—there, in a crevice, something luminous glowed with the brilliancy of fresh dew in the morning sun. It was a heart-shaped ring cleft in the centre. Its scintillating rays glorified the dark corner with the aureole of a great hope. Impulsively I reached out, and pressed the parts of the ring into a close-fitting whole, when, lo! the rays burst into a fire that spread and instantly melted the iron and steel, and dissolved the prison walls, disclosing to my enraptured gaze green fields and woods, and men and women playfully at work in the sunshine of freedom. And then . . . something dispelled the vision.

Oh, if I had that magic heart now! To escape, to be free! May be my unknown friend will yet keep his word. He is probably perfecting plans, or perhaps it is not safe for him to visit me. If my comrades could aid me, escape would be feasible. But the Girl and Fedya will never consider the possibility. No doubt they refrain from writing because they momentarily expect to hear of my suicide. How distraught the poor

Girl must be! Yet she should have written: it is now four days since my removal to the penitentiary. Every day I anxiously await the coming of the Chaplain, who distributes the mail.—There he is! The quick, nervous step has become familiar to my ear. Expectantly I follow his movements; I recognize the vigorous slam of the door and the click of the spring lock. The short steps patter on the bridge connecting the upper rotunda with the cell-house, and pass along the gallery. The solitary footfall amid the silence reminds me of the timid haste of one crossing a graveyard at night. Now the Chaplain pauses: he is comparing the number of the wooden block hanging outside the cell with that on the letter. Some one has remembered a friend in prison. The steps continue and grow faint, as the postman rounds the distant corner. He passes the cell-row on the opposite side, ascends the topmost tier, and finally reaches the ground floor containing my cell. My heart beats faster as the sound approaches: there must surely be a letter for me. He is nearing the cell—he pauses. I can't see him yet, but I know he is comparing numbers. Perhaps the letter is for me. I hope the Chaplain will make no mistake: Range K, Cell 6, Number A 7. Something light flaps on the floor of the next cell, and the quick, short step has passed me by. No mail for me! Another twenty-four hours must elapse before I may receive a letter, and then, too, perhaps the faint shadow will not pause at my door.

II

The thought of my twenty-two-year sentence is driving me desperate. I would make use of any means, however terrible, to escape from this hell, to regain liberty. Liberty! What would it not offer me after this experience? I should have the greatest opportunity for revolutionary activity. I would choose Russia. The Mostianer have forsaken me. I will keep aloof, but they shall learn what a true revolutionist is capable of accomplishing. If there is a spark of manhood in them, they will blush for their despicable attitude toward my act, their shameful treatment of me. How eager they will then be to prove their confidence by exaggerated devotion, to salve their guilty conscience! I should not have to complain of a lack of financial aid, were I to inform our intimate circles of my plans regarding future activity in Russia. It would be glorious, glorious! S—sh—

It's the Chaplain. Perhaps he has mail for me to-day. . . . May be he is suppressing letters from my friends; or probably it is the Warden's fault: the mailbag is first examined in his office.—Now the Chaplain is descending to the ground floor. He pauses. It must be Cell 2 getting a letter. Now he is coming. The shadow is opposite my door,—gone!

"Chaplain, one moment, please."

"Who's calling?"

"Here, Chaplain. Cell 6 K."

"What is it, my boy?"

"Chaplain, I should like something to read."

"Read? Why, we have a splendid library, m' boy; very fine library. I will send you a catalogue, and you can draw one book every week."

"I missed library day on this range. I'll have to wait another week. But I'd like to have something in the meantime, Chaplain."

"You are not working, m' boy?"

"No."

"You have not refused to work, have you?"

"No, I have not been offered any work yet."

"Oh, well, you will be assigned soon. Be patient, m' boy."

"But can't I have something to read now?"

"Isn't there a Bible in your cell?"

"A Bible? I don't believe in it, Chaplain."

"My boy, it will do you no harm to read it. It may do you good. Read it, m' boy."

For a moment I hesitate. A desperate idea crosses my mind.

"All right, Chaplain, I'll read the Bible, but I don't care for the modern English version. Perhaps you have one with Greek or Latin annotations?"

"Why, why, m' boy, do you understand Latin or Greek?"

"Yes, I have studied the classics."

The Chaplain seems impressed. He steps close to the door, leaning against it in the attitude of a man prepared for a long conversation. We talk about the classics, the sources of my knowledge, Russian schools, social conditions. An interesting and intelligent man, this prison Chaplain, an extensive traveler whose visit to Russia had impressed him with the great possibilities of that country. Finally he motions to a guard:

"Let A 7 come with me."

With a suspicious glance at me, the officer unlocks the door. "Shall I come along, Chaplain?" he asks.

"No, no. It is all right. Come, m' boy."

Past the tier of vacant cells, we ascend the stairway to the upper rotunda, on the left side of which is the Chaplain's office. Excited and alert, I absorb every detail of the surroundings. I strive to appear indifferent, while furtively following every movement of the Chaplain, as he selects the rotunda key from the large bunch in his hand, and opens the door. Passionate longing for liberty is consuming me. A plan of escape is maturing in my mind. The Chaplain carries all the keys—he lives in the Warden's house, connected with the prison—he is so fragile—I could easily overpower him—there is no one in the rotunda—I'd stifle his cries— take the keys—

"Have a seat, my boy. Sit down. Here are some books. Look them over. I have a duplicate of my personal Bible, with annotations. It is somewhere here."

With feverish eyes I watch him lay the keys on the desk. A quick motion, and they would be mine. That large and heavy one, it must belong to the gate. It is so big,—one blow would kill him. Ah, there is a safe! The Chaplain is taking some books from it. His back is turned to me. A thrust—and I'd lock him in. . . . Stealthily, imperceptibly, I draw nearer to the desk, my eyes fastened on the keys. Now I bend over them, pretending to be absorbed in a book, the while my hand glides forward, slowly, cautiously. Quickly I lean over; the open book in my hands entirely hides the keys. My hand touches them. Desperately I clutch the large, heavy bunch, my arm slowly rises—

"My boy, I cannot find that Bible just now, but I'll give you some other book. Sit down, my boy. I am so sorry about you. I am an officer of the State, but I think you were dealt with unjustly. Your sentence is quite excessive. I can well understand the state of mind that actuated you, a young enthusiast, in these exciting times. It was in connection with Homestead, is it not so, m' boy?"

I fall back into the chair, shaken, unmanned. That deep note of sympathy, the sincerity of the trembling voice—no, no, I cannot touch him. . . .

III

At last, mail from New York! Letters from the
Girl and Fedya. With a feeling of mixed anxiety
and resentment, I gaze at the familiar handwriting.
Why didn't they write before? The edge of expectancy
has been dulled by the long suspense. The Girl and
the Twin, my closest, most intimate friends of yesterday,
—but the yesterday seems so distant in the past, its very
reality submerged in the tide of soul-racking events.

There is a note of disappointment, almost of bitterness, in the Girl's letter. The failure of my act will
lessen the moral effect, and diminish its propagandistic
value. The situation is aggravated by Most. Owing
to his disparaging attitude, the Germans remain indifferent. To a considerable extent, even the Jewish
revolutionary element has been influenced by him. The
Twin, in veiled and abstruse Russian, hints at the attempted completion of my work, planned, yet impossible
of realization.

I smile scornfully at the "completion" that failed
even of an attempt. The damningly false viewpoint of
the Girl exasperates me, and I angrily resent the dis-
approving surprise I sense in both letters at my continued
existence.

I read the lines repeatedly. Every word drips
bitterness into my soul. Have I grown morbid, or do
they actually presume to reproach me with my failure
to suicide? By what right? Impatiently I smother the
accusing whisper of my conscience, "By the right of
revolutionary ethics." The will to live leaps into being
peremptorily, more compelling and imperative at the
implied challenge.

No, I will struggle and fight! Friend or enemy,
they shall learn that I am not so easily done for. I will
live, to escape, to conquer!

CHAPTER III

SPECTRAL SILENCE

THE silence grows more oppressive, the solitude unbearable. My natural buoyancy is weighted down by a nameless dread. With dismay I realize the failing elasticity of my step, the gradual loss of mental vivacity. I feel worn in body and soul.

The regular tolling of the gong, calling to toil or meals, accentuates the enervating routine. It sounds ominously amid the stillness, like the portent of some calamity, horrible and sudden. Unshaped fears, the more terrifying because vague, fill my heart. In vain I seek to drown my riotous thoughts by reading and exercise. The walls stand, immovable sentinels, hemming me in on every side, till movement grows into torture. In the constant dusk of the windowless cell the letters dance before my eyes, now forming fantastic figures, now dissolving into corpses and images of death. The morbid pictures fascinate my mind. The hissing gas jet in the corridor irresistibly attracts me. With eyes half shut, I follow the flickering light. Its diffusing rays form a kaleidoscope of variegated pattern, now crystallizing into scenes of my youth, now converging upon the image of my New York life, with grotesque illumination of the tragic moments. Now the flame is swept by a gust of wind. It darts hither and thither, angrily contending with the surrounding darkness. It whizzes and strikes into its adversary, who falters, then advances with giant shadow, menacing the light with frenzied threats on the whitewashed wall. Look! The shadow grows and grows, till it mounts the iron gates that fall heavily behind me, as the officers lead me through the passage. "You're home now," the guard mocks me. I look back. The gray pile looms above me, cold and forbidding, and on its crest stands the black figure leering at me in triumph. The walls frown upon me. They seem human in their cruel immobility. Their huge arms tower into the night, as if to crush me on the instant. I feel so small, unutterably weak and defenceless amid all the loneliness,—the breath of the grave is on my face, it draws closer, it surrounds me, and shuts the last rays from my sight. In horror I pause. . . . The chain grows taut, the sharp edges cut into my wrist. I lurch forward, and wake on the floor of the cell.

Restless dream and nightmare haunt the long nights. I listen eagerly for the tolling of the gong, bidding darkness depart. But the breaking day brings neither hope nor gladness. Gloomy as yesterday, devoid of interest as the to-morrows at its heels, endlessly dull and leaden: the rumbling carts, with their loads of half-baked bread; the tasteless brown liquid; the passing lines of striped misery; the coarse commands; the heavy tread; and then—the silence of the tomb.

Why continue the unprofitable torture? No advantage could accrue to the Cause from prolonging this agony. All avenues of escape are closed; the institution is impregnable. The good people have generously fortified this modern bastille; the world at large may sleep in peace, undisturbed by the anguish of Calvary. No cry of tormented soul shall pierce these walls of stone, much less the heart of man. Why, then, prolong the agony? None heeds, none cares, unless perhaps my comrades,—and they are far away and helpless.

Helpless, quite helpless. Ah, if our movement were strong, the enemy would not dare commit such outrages, knowing that quick and merciless vengeance would retaliate for injustice. But the enemy realizes our weakness. To our everlasting shame, the crime of Chicago has not yet been avenged. *Vae victis!* They shall forever be the victims. Only might is respected; it alone can influence tyrants. Had we strength,—but if the judicial murders of 1887 failed to arouse more than passive indignation, can I expect radical developments in consequence of my brutally excessive sentence? It is unreasonable. Five years, indeed, have passed since the Haymarket tragedy. Perhaps the People have since been taught in the bitter school of oppression and defeat. Oh, if labor would realize the significance of my deed, if the worker would understand my aims and motives, he could be roused to strong protest, perhaps to active demand. Ah, yes! But when, when will the dullard realize things? When will he open his eyes? Blind to his own slavery and degradation, can I expect him to perceive the wrong suffered by others? And who is to enlighten him? No one conceives the truth as deeply and clearly as we Anarchists. Even the Socialists dare not advocate the whole, unvarnished truth. They have clothed the Goddess of Liberty with a fig-leaf; religion, the very fountain-head of bigotry and injustice, has officially been declared *Privatsache*. Henceforth these timid world-liberators must be careful not to tread upon the toes of prejudice and superstition. Soon they will grow to *bourgeois* respectability, a party of "practical" politics and "sound" morality. What a miserable descent from the peaks of Nihilism that proclaimed defiance of all established institutions, *because* they were established, hence wrong. Indeed, there is not a single institution in our pseudo-civilization that deserves to exist. But only the Anarchists dare wage war upon all and every form of wrong, and they are few in number, lacking in power. The internal divisions, too, aggravate our weakness; and now, even Most has turned apostate. The Jewish comrades will be influenced by his attitude. Only the Girl remains. But she is young in the movement, and almost unknown. Undoubtedly she has talent as a speaker, but she is a woman, in rather poor health. In all the movement, I know of no one capable of propaganda by deed, or of an avenging act, except the Twin. At least I can expect no other comrade to undertake the dangerous task of a rescue. The Twin is a true revolutionist; somewhat impulsive and irresponsible, perhaps, with slight aristocratic leanings, yet quite reliable in matters of revolutionary import. But he would not harbor the thought. We held such queer notions of prison: the sight of a police uniform, an arrest, suggested visions of a bottomless pit, irrevocable disappearance, as in Russia. How can I broach the subject to the Twin? All mail passes through the hands of the censor; my correspondence, especially —a long-timer and an Anarchist—will be minutely scrutinized. There seems no possibility. I am buried alive in this stone grave. Escape is hopeless. And this agony of living death—I cannot support it. . . .

CHAPTER IV

A RAY OF LIGHT

I yearn for companionship. Even the mere sight
of a human form is a relief. Every morning, after
breakfast, I eagerly listen for the familiar swish-swash
on the flagstones of the hallway: it is the old rangeman*
"sweeping up." The sensitive mouth puckered up in
an inaudible whistle, the one-armed prisoner swings the
broom with his left, the top of the handle pressed under
the armpit.

"Hello, Aleck! How're you feeling to-day?"

He stands opposite my cell, at the further end of
the wall, the broom suspended in mid-stroke. I catch
an occasional glance of the kind blue eyes, while his
head is in constant motion, turning to right and left,
alert for the approach of a guard.

"How're you, Aleck?"

"Oh, nothing extra."

"I know how it is, Aleck, I've been through the
mill. Keep up your nerve, you'll be all right, old boy.
You're young yet."

"Old enough to die," I say, bitterly.

"S—sh! Don't speak so loud. The screw's got
long ears."

---

*Prisoner taking care of a range or tier of cells.

"The screw?"

A wild hope trembles in my heart. The "screw"! The puzzling expression in the mysterious note,—perhaps this man wrote it. In anxious expectancy, I watch the rangeman. His back turned toward me, head bent, he hurriedly plies the broom with the quick, short stroke of the one-armed sweeper. "S—sh!" he cautions, without turning, as he crosses the line of my cell.

I listen intently. Not a sound, save the regular swish-swash of the broom. But the more practiced ear of the old prisoner did not err. A long shadow falls across the hall. The tall guard of the malicious eyes stands at my door.

"What you pryin' out for?" he demands.

"I am not prying."

"Don't you contradict me. Stand back in your hole there. Don't you be leanin' on th' door, d'ye hear?"

Down the hall the guard shouts: "Hey you, cripple! Talkin' there, wasn't you?"

"No, sir."

"Don't you dare lie to me. You was."

"Swear to God I wasn't."

"W-a-all, if I ever catch you talkin' to that s—— of a b——, I'll fix you."

The scratching of the broom has ceased. The rangeman is dusting the doors. The even strokes of the cat-o'-nine-tails sound nearer. Again the man stops at my door, his head turning right and left, the while he diligently plies the duster.

"Aleck," he whispers, "be careful of that screw. He's a ——. See him jump on me?"

"What would he do to you if he saw you talking to me?"

"Throw me in the hole, the dungeon, you know. I'd lose my job, too."

"Then better don't talk to me."

"Oh, I ain't scared of him. He can't catch *me*, not he. He didn't see me talkin'; just bluffed. Can't bluff *me*, though."

"But be careful."

"It's all right. He's gone out in the yard now. He has no biz in the block,* anyhow, 'cept at feedin' time. He's jest lookin' for trouble. Mean skunk he is, that Cornbread Tom."

"Who?"

"That screw Fellings. We call him Cornbread Tom, b'cause he swipes our corn dodger."

"What's corn dodger?"

"Ha, ha! Toosdays and Satoordays we gets a chunk of cornbread for breakfast. It ain't much, but better'n stale punk. Know what punk is? Not long on lingo, are you? Punk's bread, and then some kids is punk."

He chuckles, merrily, as at some successful *bon mot*. Suddenly he pricks up his ears, and with a quick gesture of warning, tiptoes away from the cell. In a few minutes he returns, whispering:

"All O. K. Road's clear. Tom's been called to the shop. Won't be back till dinner, thank th' Lord. Only the Cap is in the block, old man Mitchell, in charge of this wing. North Block it's called."

"The women are in the South Block?"

"Nope. Th' girls got a speshal building. South Block's th' new cell-house, just finished. Crowded already, an' fresh fish comin' every day. Court's busy in Pittsburgh all right. Know any one here?"

"No."

---

* Cell-house.

"Well, get acquainted, Aleck. It'll give you an interest. Guess that's what you need. I know how you feel, boy. Thought I'd die when I landed here. Awful dump. A guy advised me to take an interest an' make friends. I thought he was kiddin' me, but he was on the level, all right. Get acquainted, Aleck; you'll go bugs if you don't. Must vamoose now. See you later. My name's Wingie."

"Wingie?"

"That's what they call me here. I'm an old soldier; was at Bull Run. Run so damn fast I lost my right wing, hah, hah, hah! S'long."

Eagerly I look forward to the stolen talks with Wingie. They are the sole break in the monotony of my life. But days pass without the exchange of a word. Silently the one-armed prisoner walks by, apparently oblivious of my existence, while with beating heart I peer between the bars for a cheering sign of recognition. Only the quick wink of his eye reassures me of his interest, and gives warning of the spying guard.

By degrees the ingenuity of Wingie affords us more frequent snatches of conversation, and I gather valuable information about the prison. The inmates sympathize with me, Wingie says. They know I'm "on th' level." I'm sure to find friends, but I must be careful of the "stool pigeons," who report everything to the officers. Wingie is familiar with the history of every keeper. Most of them are "rotten," he assures me. Especially the Captain of the night watch is "fierce an' an ex-fly."* Only three "screws" are on night duty in each block, but there are a hundred overseers to "run th' dump" during the day. Wingie promises to be my friend, and to furnish "more pointers bymby."

---

* Fly or fly-cop, a detective.

CHAPTER V

THE SHOP

I

I STAND in line with a dozen prisoners, in the ante-room of the Deputy's office. Humiliation overcomes me as my eye falls, for the first time in the full light of day, upon my striped clothes. I am degraded to a beast! My first impression of a prisoner in stripes is painfully vivid: he resembled a dangerous brute. Some-how the idea is associated in my mind with a wild tigress,—and I, too, must now look like that.

The door of the rotunda swings open, admitting the tall, lank figure of the Deputy Warden.

"Hands up!"

The Deputy slowly passes along the line, examining a hand here and there. He separates the men into groups; then, pointing to the one in which I am included, he says in his feminine accents:

"None crippled. Officers, take them, hm, hm, to Number Seven. Turn them over to Mr. Hoods."

"Fall in! Forward, march!"

My resentment at the cattle-like treatment is merged into eager expectation. At last I am assigned to work! I speculate on the character of "Number Seven," and on the possibilities of escape from there. Flanked by guards, we cross the prison yard in close lockstep. The sentinels on the wall, their rifles resting loosely on

crooked arm, face the striped line winding snakelike
through the open space. The yard is spacious and clean,
the lawn well kept and inviting. The first breath of
fresh air in two weeks violently stimulates my longing
for liberty. Perhaps the shop will offer an opportunity
to escape. The thought quickens my observation.
Bounded north, east, and south by the stone wall, the
two blocks of the cell-house form a parallelogram, enclosing the shops, kitchen, hospital, and, on the extreme
south, the women's quarters.

"Break ranks!"

We enter Number Seven, a mat shop. With difficulty
I distinguish the objects in the dark, low-ceilinged room,
with its small, barred windows. The air is heavy with
dust; the rattling of the looms is deafening. An
atmosphere of noisy gloom pervades the place.

The officer in charge assigns me to a machine
occupied by a lanky prisoner in stripes. "Jim, show
him what to do."

Considerable time passes, without Jim taking the
least notice of me. Bent low over the machine, he
seems absorbed in the work, his hands deftly manipulat-
ing the shuttle, his foot on the treadle. Presently he
whispers, hoarsely:

"Fresh fish?"

"What did you say?"

"You bloke, long here?"

"Two weeks."

"Wotcher doin'?"

"Twenty-one years."

"Quitcher kiddin'."

"It's true."

"Honest? Holy gee!"

The shuttle flies to and fro. Jim is silent for a while,
then he demands, abruptly:

"Wat dey put you here for?"

"I don't know."

"Been kickin'?"

"No."

"Den you'se bugs."

"Why so?"

"Dis 'ere is crank shop. Dey never put a mug 'ere 'cept he's bugs, or else dey got it in for you."

"How do *you* happen to be here?"

"Me? De God damn —— got it in for me. See dis?" He points to a deep gash over his temple. "Had a scrap wid de screws. Almost knocked me glimmer out. It was dat big bull* dere, Pete Hoods. I'll get even wid *him,* all right, damn his rotten soul. I'll kill him. By God, I will. I'll croak 'ere, anyhow."

"Perhaps it isn't so bad," I try to encourage him.

"It ain't, eh? Wat d'*you* know 'bout it? I've got the con bad, spittin' blood every night. Dis dust's killin' me. Kill you, too, damn quick."

As if to emphasize his words, he is seized with a fit of coughing, prolonged and hollow.

The shuttle has in the meantime become entangled in the fringes of the matting. Recovering his breath, Jim snatches the knife at his side, and with a few deft strokes releases the metal. To and fro flies the gleaming thing, and Jim is again absorbed in his task.

"Don't bother me no more," he warns me, "I'm behind wid me work."

Every muscle tense, his long body almost stretched across the loom, in turn pulling and pushing, Jim bends every effort to hasten the completion of the day's task.

The guard approaches. "How's he doing?" he inquires, indicating me with a nod of the head.

---

* Guard.

"He's all right. But say, Hoods, dis 'ere is no place for de kid. He's got a twenty-one spot." *

"Shut your damned trap!" the officer retorts, angrily. The consumptive bends over his work, fearfully eyeing the keeper's measuring stick.

As the officer turns away, Jim pleads:

"Mr. Hoods, I lose time teachin'. Won't you please take off a bit? De task is more'n I can do, an' I'm sick."

"Nonsense. There's nothing the matter with you, Jim. You're just lazy, that's what you are. Don't be shamming, now. It don't go with *me*."

At noon the overseer calls me aside. "You are green here," he warns me, "pay no attention to Jim. He wanted to be bad, but we showed him different. He's all right *now*. You have a long time; see that you behave yourself. This is no playhouse, you understand?"

As I am about to resume my place in the line forming to march back to the cells for dinner, he recalls me:

"Say, Aleck, you'd better keep an eye on that fellow Jim. He is a little off, you know."

He points toward my head, with a significant rotary motion.

II

The mat shop is beginning to affect my health: the dust has inflamed my throat, and my eyesight is weakening in the constant dusk. The officer in charge has repeatedly expressed dissatisfaction with my slow progress in the work. "I'll give you another chance," he cautioned me yesterday, "and if you don't make a good mat by next week, down in the hole you go." He severely upbraided Jim for his inefficiency as instructor.

---

* Sentence.

As the consumptive was about to reply, he suffered an attack of coughing. The emaciated face turned greenish-yellow, but in a moment he seemed to recover, and continued working. Suddenly I saw him clutch at the frame, a look of terror spread over his face, he began panting for breath, and then a stream of dark blood gushed from his mouth, and Jim fell to the floor.

The steady whir of the looms continued. The prisoner at the neighboring machine cast a furtive look at the prostrate form, and bent lower over his work. Jim lay motionless, the blood dyeing the floor purple. I rushed to the officer.

"Mr. Hoods, Jim has—"

"Back to your place, damn you!" he shouted at me. "How dare you leave it without permission?"

"I just—"

"Get back, I tell you!" he roared, raising the heavy stick.

I returned to my place. Jim lay very still, his lips parted, his face ashen.

Slowly, with measured step, the officer approached.

"What's the matter here?"

I pointed at Jim. The guard glanced at the unconscious man, then lightly touched the bleeding face with his foot.

"Get up, Jim, get up!"

The nerveless head rolled to the side, striking the leg of the loom.

"Guess he isn't shamming," the officer muttered. Then he shook his finger at me, menacingly: "Don't you ever leave your place without orders. Remember, *you!*"

After a long delay, causing me to fear that Jim had been forgotten, the doctor arrived. It was Mr. Rankin, the senior prison physician, a short, stocky man of advanced middle age, with a humorous twinkle in his eye. He ordered the sick prisoner taken to the hospital. "Did any one see the man fall?" he inquired.

"This man did," the keeper replied, indicating me.

While I was explaining, the doctor eyed me curiously. Presently he asked my name. "Oh, the celebrated case," he smiled. "I know Mr. Frick quite well. Not such a bad man, at all. But you'll be treated well here, Mr. Berkman. This is a democratic institution, you know. By the way, what is the matter with your eyes? They are inflamed. Always that way?"

"Only since I am working in this shop."

"Oh, he is all right, Doctor," the officer interposed. "He's only been here a week."

Mr. Rankin cast a quizzical look at the guard.

"You want him here?"

"Y-e-s: we're short of men."

"Well, *I* am the doctor, Mr. Hoods." Then, turning to me, he added: "Report in the morning on sick list."

III

The doctor's examination has resulted in my removal to the hosiery department. The change has filled me with renewed hope. A disciplinary shop, to which are generally assigned the "hard cases"—inmates in the first stages of mental derangement, or exceptionally unruly prisoners—the mat shop is the point of special supervision and severest discipline. It is the best-guarded shop, from which escape is impossible. But in the hosiery department, a recent addition to the local industries, I may find the right opportunity. It will require time, of course; but my patience shall be equal to the great object. The working conditions, also, are more favorable: the room is light and airy, the discipline not so stringent. My near-sightedness has secured for me immunity from machine work. The Deputy at first insisted that my eyes were "good enough" to see the numerous needles of the hosiery machine. It is true, I could see them; but not with sufficient distinctness to insure the proper insertion of the initial threads. To admit partial ability would result, I knew, in being ordered to produce the task; and failure, or faulty work, would be severely punished. Necessity drove me to subterfuge: I pretended total inability to distinguish the needles. Repeated threats of punishment failing to change my determination, I have been assigned the comparatively easy work of "turning" the stockings. The occupation, though tedious, is not exacting. It consists in gathering the hosiery manufactured by the knitting machines, whence the product issues without soles. I carry the pile to the table provided with an iron post, about eighteen inches high, topped with a small inverted disk. On this instrument the stockings are turned "inside out" by slipping the article over the post, then quickly "undressing" it. The hosiery thus "turned" is forwarded to the looping machines, by which the product is finished and sent back to me, once more to be "turned," preparatory to sorting and shipment.

Monotonously the days and weeks pass by. Practice lends me great dexterity in the work, but the hours of drudgery drag with heavy heel. I seek to hasten time by forcing myself to take an interest in the task. I count the stockings I turn, the motions required by each operation, and the amount accomplished within a given time. But in spite of these efforts, my mind persistently reverts to unprofitable subjects: my friends and the propaganda; the terrible injustice of my excessive sentence; suicide and escape.

My nights are restless. Oppressed with a nameless weight, or tormented by dread, I awake with a start, breathless and affrighted, to experience the momentary relief of danger past. But the next instant I am overwhelmed by the consciousness of my surroundings, and plunged into rage and despair, powerless, hopeless.

Thus day succeeds night, and night succeeds day, in the ceaseless struggle of hope and discouragement, of life and death, amid the externally placid tenor of my Pennsylvania nightmare.

CHAPTER VI

MY FIRST LETTER

I

Direct to Box A 7,
Allegheny City, Pa.,
October 19th, 1892.

Dear Sister:*

It is just a month, a month to-day, since my coming here. I keep wondering, can such a world of misery and torture be compressed into one short month? . . . How I have longed for this opportunity! You will understand: a month's stay is required before we are permitted to write. But many, many long letters I have written to you—in my mind, dear Sonya. Where shall I begin now? My space is very limited, and I have so much to say to you and to the Twin.—I received your letters. You need not wait till you hear from me: keep on writing. I am allowed to receive all mail sent, "of moral contents," in the phraseology of the rules. And I shall write whenever I may.

Dear Sonya, I sense bitterness and disappointment in your letter. Why do you speak of failure? You, at least, you and Fedya, should not have your judgment obscured by the mere accident of physical results. Your lines pained and grieved me beyond words. Not because you should write thus; but that you, even you, should *think* thus. Need I enlarge? True morality deals with motives, not consequences. I cannot believe that we differ on this point.

I fully understand what a terrible blow the apostasy of Wurst† must have been to you. But however it may minimize

---

* The Girl; also referred to as Sonya, Musick, and Sailor.

† John Most.

Direct to Box A 7
Allegheny City, Pa.
October 19th, 1892.

Dear Sister,

It is just a month, a month today, since my coming
here. I keep wondering, can such a world of misery and torture
be compressed into one short month? How I have longed for this
opportunity! You will understand: a month's stay is required before
we are permitted to write. But many, many long letters I have
written to you—in my mind, dear Sonya. Where shall I begin now?
My space is very limited, and I have so much to say to you and to
the Twin.—I received your letters. You need not wait till you hear
from me: keep on writing. I will be are allowed to receive all
mail sent, "of moral contents", in the phraseology of the rules.
And I shall write whenever I may.

Dear Sonya, I sense bitterness and disappointment
in your letter. Why do you speak of failure? You, at least, you and
Fedya, should not have your judgment obscured by the mere
accident of physical results. Your lines pained and grieved
me beyond words. Not because you should write thus; but
that you, even you, should think thus. Need I enlarge? True
morality deals with motives, not consequences. I cannot
believe that we differ on this point.

I fully understand what a terrible blow the apostasy
of Wurst must have been to you. But however it may minimize
the effect, it cannot possibly alter the fact, or its
character. This you seem to have lost sight
of. In spite of Wurst, a great deal could have
been accomplished. I don't know whether it
has been done: your letter is very meagre on
this point. Yet it is of supreme interest to me. But

FACSIMILE OF PRISON LETTER, REDUCED ONE-THIRD

the effect, it cannot possibly alter the fact, or its character. This you seem to have lost sight of. In spite of Wurst, a great deal could have been accomplished. I don't know whether it has been done: your letter is very meagre on this point. Yet it is of supreme interest to me. But I know, Sonya,—of this one thing, at least, I am sure—you will do all that is in your power. Perhaps it is not much—but the Twin and part of Orchard Street* will be with you.

Why that note of disappointment, almost of resentment, as to Tolstogub's relation to the Darwinian theory?† You must consider that the layman cannot judge of the intricacies of scientific hypotheses. The scientist would justly object to such presumption.

I embrace you both. The future is dark; but, then, who knows? . . . Write often. Tell me about the movement, yourself and friends. It will help to keep me in touch with the outside world, which daily seems to recede further. I clutch desperately at the thread that still binds me to the living—it seems to unravel in my hands, the thin skeins are breaking, one by one. My hold is slackening. But the Sonya thread, I know, will remain taut and strong. I have always called you the Immutable.   **Alex.**

II

I posted the letter in the prisoners' mail-box when the line formed for work this morning. But the moment the missive left my hands, I was seized with a great longing. Oh, if some occult means would transform me into that slip of paper! I should now be hidden in that green box—with bated breath I'd flatten myself in the darkest recess, and wait for the Chaplain to collect the mail. . . .

---

* 54 Orchard Street—the hall in which the first Jewish Anarchist gatherings were held in New York. An allusion to the aid of the Jewish comrades.

† Tolstogub—the author's Russian nickname. The expression signifies the continued survival of the writer.

My heart beats tumultuously as the wild fancy flutters in my brain. I am oblivious of the forming lines, the sharp commands, the heavy tread. Automatically I turn the hosiery, counting one, two, one pair; three, four, two pair. Whose voice is it I hear? I surely know the man—there is something familiar about him. He bends over the looping machines and gathers the stockings. Now he is counting: one, two, one pair; three, four, two pair. Just like myself. Why, he looks like myself! And the men all seem to think it is I. Ha, ha, ha! the officer, also. I just heard him say, "Aleck, work a little faster, can't you? See the piles there, you're falling behind." He thinks it's I. What a clever substitution! And all the while the real "me" is snugly lying here in the green box, peeping through the keyhole, on the watch for the postman. S-sh! I hear a footstep. Perhaps it is the Chaplain: he will open the box with his quick, nervous hands, seize a handful of letters, and thrust them into the large pocket of his black serge coat. There are so many letters here—I'll slip among them into the large pocket—the Chaplain will not notice me. He'll think it's just a letter, ha, ha! He'll scrutinize every word, for it's the letter of a long-timer; his first one, too. But I am safe, I'm invisible; and when they call the roll, they will take that man there for me. He is counting nineteen, twenty, ten pair; twenty-one, twenty-two . . . What was that? Twenty-two—oh, yes, twenty-two, that's my sentence. The imbeciles, they think I am going to serve it. I'd kill myself first. But it will not be necessary, thank goodness! It was such a lucky thought, this going out in my letter. But what has become of the Chaplain? If he'd only come—why is he so long? They might miss me in the shop. No, no! that man is there—he is turning the stockings—they don't know I am here in the box. The Chaplain won't know it, either: I am invisible; he'll think it's a letter when he puts me in his pocket, and then he'll seal me in an envelope and address—I must flatten myself so his hand shouldn't feel—and he'll address me to Sonya. He'll not know whom he is sending to her—he doesn't know who she is, either—the *Deckadresse* is splendid—we must keep it up. Keep it up? Why? It will not be necessary: after he mails me, we don't need to write any more—it is well, too—I have so much to tell Sonya—and it wouldn't pass the censor. But it's all right now—they'll throw the letters into the mail-carrier's bag--there'll be many of them—this is general letter day. I'll hide in the pile, and they'll pass me through the post-office, on to New York. Dear, dear New York! I have been away so long. Only a month? Well, I must be patient—and not breathe so loud. When I get to New York, I shall not go at once into the house—Sonya might get frightened. I'll first peep in through the window—I wonder what she'll be doing—and who will be at home? Yes, Fedya will be there, and perhaps Claus and Sep. How surprised they'll all be! Sonya will embrace me—she'll throw her arms around my neck—they'll feel so soft and warm—

"Hey, there! Are you deaf? Fall in line!"

Dazed, bewildered, I see the angry face of the guard before me. The striped men pass me, enveloped in a mist. I grasp the "turner." The iron feels cold. Chills shake my frame, and the bundle of hosiery drops from my hand.

"Fall in line, I tell you!"

"Sucker!" some one hisses behind me. "Workin' after whistle. 'Fraid you won't get 'nough in yer twenty-two spot, eh? You sucker, you!"

CHAPTER VII

WINGIE

THE hours at work help to dull the acute consciousness of my environment. The hosiery department is
past the stage of experiment; the introduction of additional knitting machines has enlarged my task, necessi-
tating increased effort and more sedulous application.

The shop routine now demands all my attention. It
leaves little time for thinking or brooding. My physical
condition alarms me: the morning hours completely
exhaust me, and I am barely able to keep up with the
line returning to the cell-house for the noon meal. A
feeling of lassitude possesses me, my feet drag heavily,
and I experience great difficulty in mastering my
sleepiness.

I have grown indifferent to the meals; the odor of
food nauseates me. I am nervous and morbid: the sight
of a striped prisoner disgusts me; the proximity of a
guard enrages me. The shop officer has repeatedly
warned me against my disrespectful and surly manner.
But I am indifferent to consequences: what matter what
happens? My waning strength is a source of satisfaction:
perhaps it indicates the approach of death. The thought
pleases me in a quiet, impersonal way. There will be
no more suffering, no anguish. The world at large is
non-existent; it is centered in Me; and yet I myself stand
aloof, and see it falling into gradual peace and quiet, into
extinction.

. . . : . . . .

Back in my cell after the day's work, I leave the evening meal of bread and coffee untouched. My candle remains unlit. I sit listlessly in the gathering dusk, conscious only of the longing to hear the gong's deep bass,—the three bells tolling the order to retire. I welcome the blessed permission to fall into bed. The coarse straw mattress beckons invitingly; I yearn for sleep, for oblivion.

Occasional mail from friends rouses me from my apathy. But the awakening is brief: the tone of the letters is guarded, their contents too general in character, the matters that might kindle my interest are missing. The world and its problems are drifting from my horizon. I am cast into the darkness. No ray of sunshine holds out the promise of spring.

At times the realization of my fate is borne in upon me with the violence of a shock, and I am engulfed in despair, now threatening to break down the barriers of sanity, now affording melancholy satisfaction in the wild play of fancy. . . . Existence grows more and more unbearable with the contrast of dream and reality. Weary of the day's routine, I welcome the solitude of the cell, impatient even of the greeting of the passing convict. I shrink from the uninvited familiarity of these men, the horizontal gray and black constantly reviving the image of the tigress, with her stealthy, vicious cunning. They are not of *my* world. I would aid them, as in duty bound to the victims of social injustice. But I cannot be friends with them: they do not belong to the People, to whose service my life is consecrated. Unfortunates, indeed; yet parasites upon the producers, less in degree, but no less in kind than the rich exploiters. By virtue of my principles, rather than their deserts, I must give them my intellectual sympathy; they touch no chord in my heart.

Only Wingie seems different. There is a gentle note about his manner that breathes cheer and encouragement. Often I long for his presence, yet he seldom finds opportunity to talk with me, save Sundays during church service, when I remain in the cell. Perhaps I may see him to-day. He must be careful of the Block Captain, on his rounds of the galleries, counting the church delinquents.* The Captain is passing on the range now. I recognize the uncertain step, instantly ready to halt at the sight of a face behind the bars. Now he is at the cell. He pencils in his note-book the number on the wooden block over the door, A 7.

"Catholic?" he asks, mechanically. Then, looking up, he frowns on me.

"You're no Catholic, Berkman. What d'you stay in for?"

"I am an atheist."

"A what?"

"An atheist, a non-believer."

"Oh, an infidel, are you? You'll be damned, shore 'nough."

The wooden stairs creak beneath the officer's weight. He has turned the corner. Wingie will take advantage now. I hope he will come soon. Perhaps somebody is watching—

"Hello, Aleck! Want a piece of pie? Here, grab it!"

"Pie, Wingie?" I whisper wonderingly. "Where do you get such luxuries?"

"Swiped from the screw's poke, Cornbread Tom's

---

*Inmates of Catholic faith are excused from attending Protestant service, and *vice versa*.

dinner-basket, you know. The cheap guy saved it after breakfast. Rotten, ain't he?"

"Why so?"

"Why, you greenie, he's a stomach robber, that's what he is. It's *our* pie, Aleck, made here in the bakery. That's why our punk is stale, see; they steals the east* to make pies for th' screws. Are you next? How d' you like the grub, anyhow?"

"The bread is generally stale, Wingie. And the coffee tastes like tepid water."

"Coffee you call it? He, he, coffee hell. It ain't no damn coffee; 'tnever was near coffee. It's just bootleg, Aleck, bootleg. Know how't's made?"

"No."

"Well, I been three months in th' kitchen. You c'llect all the old punk that the cons dump out with their dinner pans. Only the crust's used, see. Like as not some syph coon spit on 't. Some's mean enough to do't, you know. Makes no diff, though. Orders is, cut off th' crusts an' burn 'em to a good black crisp. Then you pour boiling water over it an' dump it in th' kettle, inside a bag, you know, an' throw a little dirty chic'ry in—there's your *coffee*. I never touch th' rotten stuff. It rooins your stummick, that's what it does, Aleck. You oughtn't drink th' swill."

"I don't care if it kills me."

"Come, come, Aleck. Cheer up, old boy. You got a tough bit, I know, but don' take it so hard. Don' think of your time. Forget it. Oh, yes, you can; you jest take my word for't. Make some friends. Think who you wan' to see to-morrow, then try t' see 'm. That's what you wan' to do, Aleck. It'll keep you hustlin'. Best thing for the blues, kiddie."

---

* Yeast.

For a moment he pauses in his hurried whisper. The soft eyes are full of sympathy, the lips smile encouragingly. He leans the broom against the door, glances quickly around, hesitates an instant, and then deftly slips a slender, delicate hand between the bars, and gives my cheek a tender pat.

Involuntarily I step back, with the instinctive dislike of a man's caress. Yet I would not offend my kind friend. But Wingie must have noticed my annoyance: he eyes me critically, wonderingly. Presently picking up the broom, he says with a touch of diffidence:

"You are all right, Aleck. I like you for 't. Jest wanted t' try you, see?"

"How 'try me,' Wingie?"

"Oh, you ain't next? Well, you see—" he hesitates, a faint flush stealing over his prison pallor, "you see, Aleck, it's—oh, wait till I pipe th' screw."

Poor Wingie, the ruse is too transparent to hide his embarrassment. I can distinctly follow the step of the Block Captain on the upper galleries. He is the sole officer in the cell-house during church service. The unlocking of the yard door would apprise us of the entrance of a guard, before the latter could observe Wingie at my cell.

I ponder over the flimsy excuse. Why did Wingie leave me? His flushed face, the halting speech of the usually loquacious rangeman, the subterfuge employed to "sneak off,"—as he himself would characterize his hasty departure,—all seem very peculiar. What could he have meant by "trying" me? But before I have time to evolve a satisfactory explanation, I hear Wingie tiptoeing back.

"It's all right, Aleck. They won't come from the chapel for a good while yet."

"What did you mean by 'trying' me, Wingie?"

"Oh, well," he stammers, "never min', Aleck. You

are a good boy, all right. You don't belong here, that's what *I* say."

"Well, I *am* here; and the chances are I'll die here."

"Now, don't talk so foolish, boy. I 'lowed you looked down at the mouth. Now, don't you fill your head with such stuff an' nonsense. Croak here, hell! You ain't goin' t'do nothin' of the kind. Don't you go broodin', now. You listen t'me, Aleck, that's your friend talkin', see? You're so young, why, you're just a kid. Twenty-one, ain't you? An' talkin' about dyin'! Shame on you, shame!"

His manner is angry, but the tremor in his voice sends a ray of warmth to my heart. Impulsively I put my hand between the bars. His firm clasp assures me of returned appreciation.

"You must brace up, Aleck. Look at the lifers. You'd think they'd be black as night. Nit, my boy, the jolliest lot in th' dump. You seen old Henry? No? Well, you ought' see 'im. He's the oldest man here; in fifteen years. A lifer, an' hasn't a friend in th' woild, but he's happy as th' day's long. An' you got plenty friends; true blue, too. I know you have."

"I have, Wingie. But what could they do for me?"

"How you talk, Aleck. Could do anythin'. You got rich friends, I know. You was mixed up with Frick. Well, your friends are all right, ain't they?"

"Of course. What could they do, Wingie?"

"Get you pard'n, in two, three years may be, see? You must make a good record here."

"Oh, I don't care for a pardon."

"Wha-a-t? You're kiddin'."

"No, Wingie, quite seriously. I am opposed to it on principle."

"You're sure bugs. What you talkin' 'bout? Principle fiddlesticks. Want to get out o' here?"

"Of course I do."

"Well, then, quit your principle racket. What's principle got t' do with 't? Your principle's 'gainst gettin' out?"

"No, but against being pardoned."

"You're beyond me, Aleck. Guess you're joshin' me."

"Now listen, Wingie. You see, I wouldn't apply for a pardon, because it would be asking favors from the government, and I am against it, you understand? It would be of no use, anyhow, Wingie."

"An' if you could get a pard'n for the askin', you won't ask, Aleck. That's what you mean?"

"Yes."

"You're hot stuff, Aleck. What they call you, Narchist? Hot stuff, by gosh! Can't make you out, though. Seems daffy. Lis'n t' me, Aleck. If I was you, I'd take anythin' I could get, an' then tell 'em to go t'hell. That's what *I* would do, my boy."

He looks at me quizzically, searchingly. The faint echo of the Captain's step reaches us from a gallery on the opposite side. With a quick glance to right and left, Wingie leans over toward the door. His mouth between the bars, he whispers very low:

"Principles opposed to a get-a-way, Aleck?"

The sudden question bewilders me. The instinct of liberty, my revolutionary spirit, the misery of my existence, all flame into being, rousing a wild, tumultuous beating of my heart, pervading my whole being with hope, intense to the point of pain. I remain silent. Is it safe to trust him? He seems kind and sympathetic—

"You may trust me, Aleck," Wingie whispers, as if reading my thoughts. "I'm your friend."

"Yes, Wingie, I believe you. My principles are not opposed to an escape. I have been thinking about it, but so far—"

"S-sh! Easy. Walls have ears."

"Any chance here, Wingie?"

"Well, it's a damn tough dump, this 'ere is; but there's
many a star in heaven, Aleck, an' you may have a lucky
one. Hasn't been a get-a-way here since Paddy McGraw
sneaked over th' roof, that's—lemme see, six, seven years
ago, 'bout."

"How did he do it?" I ask, breathlessly.

"Jest Irish luck. They was finishin' the new block,
you know. Paddy was helpin' lay th' roof. When he got
good an' ready, he jest goes to work and slides down th'
roof. Swiped stuff in the mat shop an' spliced a rope together, see. They never got 'im, either."

"Was he in stripes, Wingie?"

"Sure he was. Only been in a few months."

"How did he manage to get away in stripes?
Wouldn't he be recognized as an escaped prisoner?"

"*That* bother you, Aleck? Why, it's easy. Get
planted till dark, then hold up th' first bloke you see an'
take 'is duds. Or you push in th' back door of a rag
joint; plenty of 'em in Allegheny."

"Is there any chance now through the roof?"

"Nit, my boy. Nothin' doin' *there*. But a feller's
got to be alive. Many ways to kill a cat, you know.
R'member the stiff* you got in them things, tow'l an'
soap?"

"You know about it, Wingie?" I ask, in amazement.

"Do I? He, he, you little—"

The click of steel sounds warning. Wingie disappears.

---

* Note.

CHAPTER VIII

TO THE GIRL

Direct to Box A 7,
Allegheny City, Pa.,
November 18, 1892.

My dear Sonya:

It seems an age since I wrote to you, yet it is only a month. But the monotony of my life weights down the heels of time,—the only break in the terrible sameness is afforded me by your dear, affectionate letters, and those of Fedya. When I return to the cell for the noon meal, my step is quickened by the eager expectation of finding mail from you. About eleven in the morning, the Chaplain makes his rounds; his practiced hand shoots the letter between the bars, toward the bed or on to the little table in the corner. But if the missive is light, it will flutter to the floor. As I reach the cell, the position of the little white object at once apprises me whether the letter is long or short. With closed eyes I sense its weight, like the warm pressure of your own dear hand, the touch reaching softly to my heart, till I feel myself lifted across the chasm into your presence. The bars fade, the walls disappear, and the air grows sweet with the aroma of fresh air and flowers,—I am again with you, walking in the bright July moonlight. . . . The touch of the *velikorussian* in your eyes and hair conjures up the Volga, our beautiful *bogatir*,* and the strains of the *dubinushka*,† trembling with suffering and yearning, float about me. . . . The meal remains untouched. I dream over your letter, and again I read it, slowly, slowly, lest I reach the end too quickly. The afternoon hours are hallowed by your touch and your presence, and I am conscious only of

---

* Brave knight—affectionately applied to the great river.
† Folk-song.

the longing for my cell,—in the quiet of the evening, freed from the nightmare of the immediate, I walk in the garden of our dreams.

And the following morning, at work in the shop, I pass in anxious wonder whether some cheering word from my own, my real world, is awaiting me in the cell. With a glow of emotion I think of the Chaplain: perhaps at the very moment your letter is in his hands. He is opening it, reading. Why should strange eyes . . . but the Chaplain seems kind and discreet. Now he is passing along the galleries, distributing the mail. The bundle grows meagre as the postman reaches the ground floor. Oh! if he does not come to my cell quickly, he may have no letters left. But the next moment I smile at the childish thought, —if there is a letter for me, no other prisoner will get it. Yet some error might happen. . . . No, it is impossible—my name and prison number, and the cell number marked by the Chaplain across the envelope, all insure the mail against any mistake in delivery. Now the dinner whistle blows. Eagerly I hasten to the cell. There is nothing on the floor! Perhaps on the bed, on the table. . . . I grow feverish with the dread of disappointment. Possibly the letter fell under the bed, or in that dark corner. No, none there,—but it can't be that there is no mail for me to-day! I must look again—it may have dropped among the blankets. . . . No, there is no letter!

Thus pass my days, dear friend. In thought I am ever with you and Fedya, in our old haunts and surroundings. I shall never get used to this life, nor find an interest in the reality of the moment. What will become of me, I don't know. I hardly care. We are revolutionists, dear: whatever sacrifices the Cause demands, though the individual perish, humanity will profit in the end. In that consciousness we must find our solace.

                                        ALEX.

Sub rosa,

Last Day of November, 1892.

Beloved Girl:

I thought I would not survive the agony of our meeting, but human capacity for suffering seems boundless. All my thoughts, all my yearnings, were centered in the one desire to see you, to look into your eyes, and there read the beautiful promise that has filled my days with strength and hope. . . . An embrace, a lingering kiss, and the gift of Lingg* would have been mine. To grasp your hand, to look down for a mute, immortal instant into your soul, and then die at your hands, Beloved, with the warm breath of your caress wafting me into peaceful eternity—oh, it were bliss supreme, the realization of our day dreams, when, in transports of ecstasy, we kissed the image of the Social Revolution. Do you remember that glorious face, so strong and tender, on the wall of our little Houston Street hallroom? How far, far in the past are those inspired moments! But they have filled my hours with hallowed thoughts, with exulting expectations. And then you came. A glance at your face, and I knew my doom to terrible life. I read it in the evil look of the guard. It was the Deputy himself. Perhaps you had been searched! He followed our every moment, like a famished cat that feigns indifference, yet is alert with every nerve to spring upon the victim. Oh, I know the calculated viciousness beneath that meek exterior. The accelerated movement of his drumming fingers, as he deliberately seated himself between us, warned me of the beast, hungry for prey. . . . The halo was dissipated. The words froze within me, and I could meet you only with a vapid smile, and on the instant it was mirrored in my soul as a leer, and I was filled with anger and resentment at everything about us—myself, the Deputy (I could have throttled him to death), and—at you, dear. Yes, Sonya, even at you: the quick come to bury the dead. . . . But the next moment, the unworthy throb of my agonized soul was stilled by the passionate pressure of my lips upon your hand. How it trembled! I held it between my own, and then, as I lifted my face to yours, the expression I beheld seemed to bereave me of my own self: it was you who were I! The

---

* Louis Lingg, one of the Chicago martyrs, who committed suicide with a dynamite cartridge in a cigar given him by a friend.

drawn face, the look of horror, your whole being the cry of torture—were *you* not the real prisoner? Or was it my visioned suffering that cemented the spiritual bond, annihilating all misunderstanding, all resentment, and lifting us above time and place in the afflatus of martyrdom?

Mutely I held your hand. There was no need for words. Only the prying eyes of the catlike presence disturbed the sacred moment. Then we spoke—mechanically, trivialities. . . . What though the cadaverous Deputy with brutal gaze timed the seconds, and forbade the sound of our dear Russian,—nor heaven nor earth could violate the sacrament sealed with our pain.

The echo accompanied my step as I passed through the rotunda on my way to the cell. All was quiet in the block. No whir of loom reached me from the shops. Thanksgiving Day: all activities were suspended. I felt at peace in the silence. But when the door was locked, and I found myself alone, all alone within the walls of the tomb, the full significance of your departure suddenly dawned on me. The quick had left the dead. . . . Terror of the reality seized me and I was swept by a paroxysm of anguish—

I must close. The friend who promised to have this letter mailed *sub rosa* is at the door. He is a kind unfortunate who has befriended me. May this letter reach you safely. In token of which, send me postal of indifferent contents, casually mentioning the arrival of news from my brother in Moscow. Remember to sign "Sister."

With a passionate embrace,

YOUR SASHA.

CHAPTER IX

PERSECUTION

I

SUFFERING and ever-present danger are quick teachers. In the three months of penitentiary life I have learned many things. I doubt whether the vague terrors pictured by my inexperience were more dreadful than the actuality of prison existence.

In one respect, especially, the reality is a source of bitterness and constant irritation. Notwithstanding all its terrors, perhaps because of them, I had always thought of prison as a place where, in a measure, nature comes into its own: social distinctions are abolished, artificial barriers destroyed; no need of hiding one's thoughts and emotions; one could be his real self, shedding all hypocrisy and artifice at the prison gates. But how different is this life! It is full of deceit, sham, and pharisaism—an aggravated counterpart of the outside world. The flatterer, the backbiter, the spy,—these find here a rich soil. The ill-will of a guard portends disaster, to be averted only by truckling and flattery, and servility fawns for the reward of an easier job. The dissembling soul in stripes whines his conversion into the pleased ears of the Christian ladies, taking care he be not surprised without tract or Bible,—and presently simulated piety secures a pardon, for the angels rejoice at the sinner's return to the fold. It sickens me to witness these scenes.

The officers make the alternative quickly apparent to the new inmate: to protest against injustice is unavailing and dangerous. Yesterday I witnessed in the shop a characteristic incident—a fight between Johnny Davis and Jack Bradford, both recent arrivals and mere boys. Johnny, a manly-looking fellow, works on a knitting machine, a few feet from my table. Opposite him is Jack, whose previous experience in a reformatory has "put him wise," as he expresses it. My three months' stay has taught me the art of conversing by an almost imperceptible motion of the lips. In this manner I learned from Johnny that Bradford is stealing his product, causing him repeated punishment for shortage in the task. Hoping to terminate the thefts, Johnny complained to the overseer, though without accusing Jack. But the guard ignored the complaint, and continued to report the youth. Finally Johnny was sent to the dungeon. Yesterday morning he returned to work. The change in the rosy-cheeked boy was startling: pale and hollow-eyed, he walked with a weak, halting step. As he took his place at the machine, I heard him say to the officer:

"Mr. Cosson, please put me somewhere else."

"Why so?" the guard asked.

"I can't make the task here. I'll make it on another machine, please, Mr. Cosson."

"Why can't you make it here?"

"I'm missing socks."

"Ho, ho, playing the old game, are you? Want to go to th' hole again, eh?"

"I couldn't stand the hole again, Mr. Cosson, swear to God, I couldn't. But my socks's missing here."

"Missing hell! Who's stealing your socks, eh? Don't come with no such bluff. Nobody can't steal your socks while I'm around. You go to work now, and you'd better make the task, understand?"

Late in the afternoon, when the count was taken, Johnny proved eighteen pairs short. Bradford was "over."

I saw Mr. Cosson approach Johnny.

"Eh, thirty, machine thirty," he shouted. "You won't make the task, eh? Put your coat and cap on."

Fatal words! They meant immediate report to the Deputy, and the inevitable sentence to the dungeon.

"Oh, Mr. Cosson," the youth pleaded, "it ain't my fault, so help me God, it isn't."

"It ain't, eh? Whose fault is it; mine?"

Johnny hesitated. His eyes sought the ground, then wandered toward Bradford, who studiously avoided the look.

"I can't squeal," he said, quietly.

"Oh, hell! You ain't got nothin' to squeal. Get your coat and cap."

Johnny passed the night in the dungeon. This morning he came up, his cheeks more sunken, his eyes more hollow. With desperate energy he worked. He toiled steadily, furiously, his gaze fastened upon the growing pile of hosiery. Occasionally he shot a glance at Bradford, who, confident of the officer's favor, met the look of hatred with a sly winking of the left eye.

Once Johnny, without pausing in the work, slightly turned his head in my direction. I smiled encouragingly, and at that same instant I saw Jack's hand slip across the table and quickly snatch a handful of Johnny's stockings. The next moment a piercing shriek threw the shop into commotion. With difficulty they tore away the infuriated boy from the prostrate Bradford. Both prisoners were taken to the Deputy for trial, with Senior Officer Cosson as the sole witness.

Impatiently I awaited the result. Through the open window I saw the overseer return. He entered the shop, a smile about the corners of his mouth. I resolved to speak to him when he passed by.

"Mr. Cosson," I said, with simulated respectfulness, "may I ask you a question?"

"Why, certainly, Burk, I won't eat you. Fire away!"

"What have they done with the boys?"

"Johnny got ten days in the hole. Pretty stiff, eh? You see, he started the fight, so he won't have to make the task. Oh, I'm next to *him* all right. They can't fool *me* so easy, can they, Burk?"

"Well, I should say not, Mr. Cosson. Did you see how the fight started?"

"No. But Johnny admitted he struck Bradford first. That's enough, you know. 'Brad' will be back in the shop to-morrow. I got 'im off easy, see; he's a good worker, always makes more than th' task. He'll jest lose his supper. Guess he can stand it. Ain't much to lose, is there, Burk?"

"No, not much," I assented. "But, Mr. Cosson, it was all Bradford's fault."

"How so?" the guard demanded.

"He has been stealing Johnny's socks."

"You didn't see him do 't."

"Yes, Mr. Cosson. I saw him this—"

"Look here, Burk. It's all right. Johnny is no good anyway; he's too fresh. You'd better say nothing about it, see? My word goes with the Deputy."

The terrible injustice preys on my mind. Poor Johnny is already the fourth day in the dreaded dungeon. His third time, too, and yet absolutely innocent. My blood boils at the thought of the damnable treatment and the officer's perfidy. It is my duty as a revolutionist

to take the part of the persecuted.   Yes, I will do so.
But how proceed in the matter?   Complaint against
Mr. Cosson would in all likelihood prove futile.   And
the officer, informed of my action, will make life miserable for me: his authority in the shop is absolute.

The several plans I revolve in my mind do not
prove, upon closer examination, feasible.   Considerations of personal interest struggle against my sense of
duty.   The vision of Johnny in the dungeon, his vacant
machine, and Bradford's smile of triumph, keep the
accusing conscience awake, till silence grows unbearable.
I determine to speak to the Deputy Warden at the first
opportunity.

Several days pass.   Often I am assailed by doubts:
is it advisable to mention the matter to the Deputy?
It cannot benefit Johnny; it will involve me in trouble.
But the next moment I feel ashamed of my weakness.
I call to mind the much-admired hero of my youth,
the celebrated Mishkin.   With an overpowering sense
of my own unworthiness, I review the brave deeds of
Hippolyte Nikitich.   What a man!   Single-handed he
essayed to liberate Chernishevsky from prison.   Ah, the
curse of poverty!   But for that, Mishkin would have
succeeded, and the great inspirer of the youth of Russia
would have been given back to the world.   I dwell
on the details of the almost successful escape, Mishkin's
fight with the pursuing Cossacks, his arrest, and his
remarkable speech in court.   Sentenced to ten years of
hard labor in the Siberian mines, he defied the Russian
tyrant by his funeral oration at the grave of Dmo-
khovsky, his boldness resulting in an additional fifteen
years of *kátorga*.*   Minutely I follow his repeated attempts to escape, the transfer of the redoubtable prisoner

---

* Hard labor in the mines.

to the Petropavloskaia fortress, and thence to the terrible Schlüsselburg prison, where Mishkin braved death by avenging the maltreatment of his comrades on a high government official. Ah! thus acts the revolutionist; and I—yes, I am decided. No danger shall seal my lips against outrage and injustice.

At last an opportunity is at hand. The Deputy enters the shop. Tall and gray, slightly stooping, with head carried forward, he resembles a wolf following the trail.

"Mr. McPane, one moment, please."

"Yes."

"I think Johnny Davis is being punished innocently."

"You think, hm, hm. And who is this innocent Johnny, hm, Davis?"

His fingers drum impatiently on the table; he measures me with mocking, suspicious eyes.

"Machine thirty, Deputy."

"Ah, yes; machine thirty; hm, hm, Reddy Davis. Hm, he had a fight."

"The other man stole his stockings. I saw it, Mr. McPane."

"So, so. And why, hm, hm, did you see it, my good man? You confess, then, hm, hm, you were not, hm, attending to your own work. That is bad, hm, very bad. Mr. Cosson!"

The guard hastens to him.

"Mr. Cosson, this man has made a, hm, hm, a charge against you. Prisoner, don't interrupt me. Hm, what is your number?"

"A 7."

"Mr. Cosson, A 7 makes a, hm, complaint against the officer, hm, in charge of this shop. Please, hm, hm, note it down."

Both draw aside, conversing in low tones. The words "kicker," "his kid," reach my ears. The Deputy nods at the overseer, his steely eyes fastened on me in hatred.

II

I feel helpless, friendless. The consolation of Wingie's cheerful spirit is missing. My poor friend is in trouble. From snatches of conversation in the shop I have pieced together the story. "Dutch" Adams, a third-timer and the Deputy's favorite stool pigeon, had lost his month's allowance of tobacco on a prize-fight bet. He demanded that Wingie, who was stakeholder, share the spoils with him. Infuriated by refusal, "Dutch" reported my friend for gambling. The unexpected search of Wingie's cell discovered the tobacco, thus apparently substantiating the charge. Wingie was sent to the dungeon. But after the expiration of five days my friend failed to return to his old cell, and I soon learned that he had been ordered into solitary confinement for refusing to betray the men who had trusted him.

The fate of Wingie preys on my mind. My poor kind friend is breaking down under the effects of the dreadful sentence. This morning, chancing to pass his cell, I hailed him, but he did not respond to my greeting. Perhaps he did not hear me, I thought. Impatiently I waited for the noon return to the block. "Hello, Wingie!" I called. He stood at the door, intently peering between the bars. He stared at me coldly, with blank, expressionless eyes. "Who are you?" he whimpered, brokenly. Then he began to babble. Suddenly the terrible truth dawned on me. My poor, poor friend, the first to speak a kind word to me,—he's gone mad!

CHAPTER X

THE YEGG

I

WEEKS and months pass without clarifying plans of escape. Every step, every movement, is so closely guarded, I seem to be hoping against hope. I am restive and nervous, in a constant state of excitement.

Conditions in the shop tend to aggravate my frame of mind. The task of the machine men has been increased; in consequence, I am falling behind in my work. My repeated requests for assistance have been ignored by the overseer, who improves every opportunity to insult and humiliate me. His feet wide apart, arms akimbo, belly disgustingly protruding, he measures me with narrow, fat eyes. "Oh, what's the matter with you," he drawls, "get a move on, won't you, Burk?" Then, changing his tone, he vociferates, "Don't stand there like a fool, d'ye hear? Nex' time I report you, to th' hole you go. That's *me* talkin', understand?"

Often I feel the spirit of Cain stirring within me. But for the hope of escape, I should not be able to bear this abuse and persecution. As it is, the guard is almost overstepping the limits of my endurance. His low cunning invents numerous occasions to mortify and harass me. The ceaseless dropping of the poison is making my days in the shop a constant torture. I seek relief—forgetfulness rather—in absorbing myself in the work: I bend my energies to outdo the efforts of the previous day; I compete with myself, and find melancholy pleasure in establishing and breaking high records for "turning." Again, I tax my ingenuity to perfect means of communication with Johnny Davis, my young neighbor. Apparently intent upon our task, we carry on a silent conversation with eyes, fingers, and an occasional motion of the lips. To facilitate the latter method, I am cultivating the habit of tobacco chewing. The practice also affords greater opportunity for exchanging impressions with my newly-acquired assistant, an old-timer, who introduced himself as "Boston Red." I owe this development to the return of the Warden from his vacation. Yesterday he visited the shop. A military-looking man, with benevolent white beard and stately carriage, he approached me, in company with the Superintendent of Prison Manufactures.

"Is this the celebrated prisoner?" he asked, a faint smile about the rather coarse mouth.

"Yes, Captain, that's Berkman, the man who shot Frick."

"I was in Naples at the time. I read about you in the English papers there, Berkman. How is his conduct, Superintendent?"

"Good."

"Well, he should have behaved outside."

But noticing the mountain of unturned hosiery, the Warden ordered the overseer to give me help, and thus "Boston Red" joined me at work the next day.

My assistant is taking great pleasure in perfecting me in the art of lipless conversation. A large quid of tobacco inflating his left cheek, mouth slightly open and curved, he delights in recounting "ghost stories," under the very eyes of the officers. "Red" is initiating me into the world of "de road," with its free life, so full of interest and adventure, its romance, joys and sorrows. An interesting character, indeed, who facetiously pretends to "look down upon the world from the sublime heights of applied cynicism."

"Why, Red, you can talk good English," I admonish him. "Why do you use so much slang? It's rather difficult for me to follow you."

"I'll learn you, pard. See, I should have said 'teach' you, not 'learn.' That's how they talk in school. Have I been there? Sure, boy. Gone through college. Went through it with a bucket of coal," he amplifies, with a sly wink. He turns to expectorate, sweeping the large shop with a quick, watchful eye. Head bent over the work, he continues in low, guttural tones:

"Don't care for your classic language. I can use it all right, all right. But give me the lingo, every time. You see, pard, I'm no gun;* don't need it in me biz. I'm a yegg."

"What's a yegg, Red?"

"A supercilious world of cheerful idiots applies to my kind the term 'tramp.'"

"A yegg, then, is a tramp. I am surprised that you should care for the life of a bum."

A flush suffuses the prison pallor of the assistant. "You are stoopid as the rest of 'em," he retorts, with considerable heat, and I notice his lips move as in ordinary conversation. But in a moment he has regained composure, and a good-humored twinkle plays about his eyes.

"Sir," he continues, with mock dignity, "to say the least, you are not discriminative in your terminology. No, sir, you are not. Now, lookee here, pard, you're a good boy, but your education has been sadly neglected.

---

* Professional thief.

Catch on? Don't call me that name again. It's offensive. It's an insult, entirely gratuitous, sir. Indeed, sir, I may say without fear of contradiction, that this insult is quite supervacaneous. Yes, sir, that's *me*. I ain't no bum, see; no such damn thing. Eliminate the disgraceful epithet from your vocabulary, sir, when you are addressing yours truly. I am a yagg, y—a— double g, sir, of the honorable clan of yaggmen. Some spell it y—e— double g, but I insist on the a, sir, as grammatically more correct, since the peerless word has no etymologic consanguinity with hen fruit, and should not be confounded by vulgar misspelling."

"What's the difference between a yegg and a bum?"

"All the diff in the world, pard. A bum is a low-down city bloke, whose intellectual horizon, sir, revolves around the back door, with a skinny hand-out as his center of gravity. He hasn't the nerve to forsake his native heath and roam the wide world, a free and independent gentleman. That's the yagg, me bye. He dares to be and do, all bulls notwithstanding. He lives, aye, he lives,—on the world of suckers, thank you, sir. Of them 'tis wisely said in the good Book, 'They shall increase and multiply like the sands of the seashore,' or words to that significant effect. A yagg's the salt of the earth, pard. A real, true-blood yagg will not deign to breathe the identical atmosphere with a city bum or gaycat. No, sirree."

I am about to ask for an explanation of the new term, when the quick, short coughs of "Red" warn me of danger. The guard is approaching with heavy, measured tread, head thrown back, hands clasped behind,—a sure indication of profound self-satisfaction.

"How are you, Reddie?" he greets the assistant.

"So, so."

"Ain't been out long, have you?"

"Two an' some."

"That's pretty long for you."

"Oh, I dunno. I've been out four years oncet."

"Yes, you have! Been in Columbus* then, I s'pose."

"Not on your life, Mr. Cosson. It was Sing Sing."

"Ha, ha! You're all right, Red. But you'd better hustle up, fellers. I'm putting in ten more machines, so look lively."

"When's the machines comin', Mr. Cosson?"

"Pretty soon, Red."

The officer passing on, "Red" whispers to me:

"Aleck, 'pretty soon' is jest the time I'll quit. Damn his work and the new machines. I ain't no gaycat to work. Think I'm a nigger, eh? No, sir, the world owes me a living, and I generally manage to get it, you bet you. Only mules and niggers work. I'm a free man; I can live on my wits, see? I don't never work outside; damme if I'll work here. I ain't no office-seeker. What d' I want to work for, eh? Can you tell me *that?*"

"Are you going to refuse work?"

"Refuse? Me? Nixie. That's a crude word, that. No, sir, I never refuse. They'll knock your damn block off, if you refuse. I merely avoid, sir, discriminately and with steadfast purpose. Work is a disease, me bye. One must exercise the utmost care to avoid contagion. It's a regular pest. *You* never worked, did you?"

The unexpected turn surprises me into a smile, which I quickly suppress, however, observing the angry frown on "Red's" face.

"You bloke," he hisses, "shut your face; the screw'll pipe you. You'll get us in th' hole for chewin' th' rag. Whatcher hehawin' about?" he demands, repeating the

---

* The penitentiary at Columbus, Ohio.

manoeuvre of pretended expectoration. "D'ye mean t' tell me you work?"

"I am a printer, a compositor," I inform him.

"Get off! You're an Anarchist. I read the papers, sir. You people don't believe in work. You want to divvy up. Well, it is all right, I'm with you. Rockefeller has no right to the whole world. He ain't satisfied with that, either; he wants a fence around it."

"The Anarchists don't want to 'divvy up,' Red. You got your misinformation—"

"Oh, never min', pard. I don' take stock in reforming the world. It's good enough for suckers, and as Holy Writ says, sir, 'Blessed be they that neither sow nor hog; all things shall be given unto them.' Them's wise words, me bye. Moreover, sir, neither you nor me will live to see a change, so why should I worry me nut about 't? It takes all my wits to dodge work. It's disgraceful to labor, and it keeps me industriously busy, sir, to retain my honor and self-respect. Why, you know, pard, or perhaps you don't, greenie, Columbus is a pretty tough dump; but d'ye think I worked the four-spot there? Not me; no, sirree!"

"Didn't you tell Cosson you were in Sing Sing, not in Columbus?"

"'Corse I did. What of it? Think I'd open my guts to my Lord Bighead? I've never been within thirty miles of the York pen. It was Hail Columbia all right, but that's between you an' I, savvy. Don' want th' screws to get next."

"Well, Red, how did you manage to keep away from work in Columbus?"

"Manage? That's right, sir. 'Tis a word of profound significance, quite adequately descriptive of my humble endeavors. Just what I did, buddy. I managed, with a capital M. To good purpose, too, me bye. Not

a stroke of work in a four-spot. How? I had Billie
with me, that's me kid, you know, an' a fine boy he
was, too. I had him put a jigger on me; kept it up
for four years. There's perseverance and industry for
you, sir."

"What's 'putting a jigger on'?"

"A jigger? Well, a jigger is—"

The noon whistle interrupts the explanation. With
a friendly wink in my direction, the assistant takes
his place in the line. In silence we march to the cell-
house, the measured footfall echoing a hollow threat
in the walled quadrangle of the prison yard.

II

Conversation with "Boston Red," Young Davis, and
occasional other prisoners helps to while away the
tedious hours at work. But in the solitude of the cell,
through the long winter evenings, my mind dwells in
the outside world. Friends, the movement, the growing
antagonisms, the bitter controversies between the
Mostianer and the defenders of my act, fill my thoughts
and dreams. By means of fictitious, but significant,
names, Russian and German words written backward,
and similar devices, the Girl keeps me informed of the
activities in our circles. I think admiringly, yet quite
impersonally, of her strenuous militancy in championing
my cause against all attacks. It is almost weak on my
part, as a terrorist of Russian traditions, to consider
her devotion deserving of particular commendation.
She is a revolutionist; it is her duty to our common
Cause. Courage, whole-souled zeal, is very rare, it is
true. The Girl, Fedya, and a few others,—hence the
sad lack of general opposition in the movement to
Most's attitude. . . . But communications from comrades

and unknown sympathizers germinate the hope of an approaching reaction against the campaign of denunciation. With great joy I trace the ascending revolutionary tendency in *Der Arme Teufel*. I have persuaded the Chaplain to procure the admission of the ingenious Robert Reitzel's publication. All the other periodicals addressed to me are regularly assigned to the waste basket, by orders of the Deputy. The latter refused to make an exception even in regard to the *Knights of Labor Journal*. "It is an incendiary Anarchist sheet," he persisted.

The arrival of the *Teufel* is a great event. What joy to catch sight of the paper snugly reposing between the legs of the cell table! Tenderly I pick it up, fondling the little visitor with quickened pulse. It is an animate, living thing, a ray of warmth in the dreary evenings. What cheering message does Reitzel bring me now? What beauties of his rich mind are hidden to-day in the quaint German type? Reverently I unfold the roll. The uncut sheet opens on the fourth page, and the stirring paean of Hope's prophecy greets my eye,—

Gruss an Alexander Berkman!

For days the music of the Dawn rings in my ears. Again and again recurs the refrain of faith and proud courage,

> Schon rüstet sich der Freiheit Schaar
> Zur heiligen Entscheidungsschlacht;
> Es enden „zweiundzwanzig" Jahr'
> Vielleicht in e i n e r Sturmesnacht!

But in the evening, when I return to the cell, reality lays its heavy hand upon my heart. The flickering of the candle accentuates the gloom, and I sit brooding over the interminable succession of miserable days and evenings and nights. . . . The darkness gathers around the candle, as I motionlessly watch its desperate struggle to be. Its dying agony, ineffectual and vain, presages my own doom, approaching, inevitable. Weaker and fainter grows the light, feebler, feebler—a last spasm, and all is utter blackness.

Three bells. "Lights out!"

Alas, mine did not last its permitted hour. . . .

The sun streaming into the many-windowed shop routs the night, and dispels the haze of the fire-spitting city. Perhaps my little candle with its bold defiance has shortened the reign of darkness,—who knows? Perhaps the brave, uneven struggle coaxed the sun out of his slumbers, and hastened the coming of Day. The fancy lures me with its warming embrace, when suddenly the assistant startles me:

"Say, pard, slept bad last night? You look boozy, me lad."

Surprised at my silence, he admonishes me:

"Young man, keep a stiff upper lip. Just look at me! Permit me to introduce to you, sir, a gentleman who has sounded the sharps and flats of life, and faced the most intricate network, sir, of iron bars between York and Frisco. Always acquitted himself with flying colors, sir, merely by being wise and preserving a stiff upper lip; see th' point?"

"What are you driving at, Red?"

"They'se goin' to move me down on your row,* now that I'm in this 'ere shop. Dunno how long I shall choose to remain, sir, in this magnificent hosiery establishment, but I see there's a vacant cell next yours, an' I'm goin' to try an' land there. Are you next, me bye? I'm goin' to learn you to be wise, sonny. I shall, so to

---

* Gallery.

speak, assume benevolent guardianship over you; over you and your morals, yes, sir, for you're my kid now, see?"

"How, your kid?"

"How? My kid, of course. That's just what I mean. Any objections, sir, as the learned gentlemen of the law say in the honorable courts of the blind goddess. You betcher life she's blind, blind as an owl on a sunny midsummer day. Not in your damn smoky city, though; sun's ashamed here. But 'way down in my Kentucky home, down by the Suanee River, Sua-a-nee-ee Riv—"

"Hold on, Red. You are romancing. You started to tell me about being your 'kid'. Now explain, what do you mean by it?"

"Really, you—" He holds the unturned stocking suspended over the post, gazing at me with half-closed, cynical eyes, in which doubt struggles with wonder. In his astonishment he has forgotten his wonted caution, and I warn him of the officer's watchful eye.

"Really, Alex; well, now, damme, I've seen something of this 'ere round globe, some mighty strange sights, too, and there ain't many things to surprise *me,* lemme tell you. But *you* do, Alex; yes, me lad, you do. Haven't had such a stunnin' blow since I first met Cigarette Jimmie in Oil City. Innocent? Well, I should snicker. He was, for sure. Never heard a ghost story; was fourteen, too. Well, I got 'im all right, all right. Now he's doin' a five-bit down in Kansas, poor kiddie. Well, he certainly was a surprise. But many tempestuous billows of life, sir, have since flown into the shoreless ocean of time, yes, sir, they have, but I never got such a stunner as you just gave me. Why, man, it's a body-blow, a reg'lar knockout to my knowledge of the world, sir, to my settled estimate of the world's supercilious righteousness. Well, damme, if I'd ever believe it. Say, how old are you, Alex?"

"I'm over twenty-two, Red. But what has all this to do with the question I asked you?"

"Everythin', me bye, everythin'. You're twenty-two and don't know what a kid is! Well, if it don't beat raw eggs, I don't know what does. Green? Well, sir, it would be hard to find an adequate analogy to your inconsistent immaturity of mind; aye, sir, I may well say, of soul, except to compare it with the virtuous condition of green corn in the early summer moon. You know what 'moon' is, don't you?" he asks, abruptly, with an evident effort to suppress a smile.

I am growing impatient of his continuous avoidance of a direct answer. Yet I cannot find it in my heart to be angry with him; the face expressive of a deep-felt conviction of universal wisdom, the eyes of humorous cynicism, and the ludicrous manner of mixing tramp slang with "classic" English, all disarm my irritation. Besides, his droll chatter helps to while away the tedious hours at work; perhaps I may also glean from this experienced old-timer some useful information regarding my plans of escape.

"Well, d'ye know a moon when you see 't?" "Red" inquires, chaffingly.

"I suppose I do."

"I'll bet you my corn dodger you don't. Sir, I can see by the tip of your olfactory organ that you are steeped in the slough of densest ignorance concerning the supreme science of moonology. Yes, sir, do not contradict me. I brook no sceptical attitude regarding my undoubted and proven perspicacity of human nature. How's that for classic style, eh? That'll hold you down a moment, kid. As I was about to say when you interrupted—eh, what? You didn't? Oh, what's the

matter with you? Don't yer go now an' rooin the
elegant flight of my rhetorical Pegasus with an insignificant interpolation of mere fact. None of your lip, now,
boy, an' lemme develop this sublime science of moonology before your wondering gaze. To begin with, sir,
moonology is an exclusively aristocratic science. Not
for the pretenders of Broad Street and Fifth Avenue.
Nixie. But for the only genuine aristocracy of de road,
sir, for the pink of humankind, for the yaggman, me lad,
for yours truly and his clan. Yes, sirree!"

"I don't know what you are talking about."

"I know you don't. That's why I'm goin' to chap-
eron you, kid. In plain English, sir, I shall endeavor
to generate within your postliminious comprehension a
discriminate conception of the subject at issue, sir, by
divesting my lingo of the least shadow of imperspicuity
or ambiguity. Moonology, my Marktwainian Innocent,
is the truly Christian science of loving your neighbor,
provided he be a nice little boy. Understand now?"

"How can you love a boy?"

"Are you really so dumb? You are not a ref boy,
I can see that."

"Red, if you'd drop your stilted language and talk
plainly, I'd understand better."

"Thought you liked the classic. But you ain't long
on lingo neither. How can a self-respecting gentleman
explain himself to you? But I'll try. You love a boy
as you love the poet-sung heifer, see? Ever read Billy
Shakespeare? Know the place, 'He's neither man nor
woman; he's punk.' Well, Billy knew. A punk's a boy
that'll . . ."

"What!"

"Yes, sir. Give himself to a man. Now we'se
talkin' plain. Savvy now, Innocent Abroad?"

"I don't believe what you are telling me, Red.

"You don't be-lie-ve? What th' devil—damn me
soul t' hell, what d' you mean, you don't b'lieve? Gee,
look out!"

The look of bewilderment on his face startles me.
In his excitement, he had raised his voice almost to a
shout, attracting the attention of the guard, who is now
hastening toward us.

"Who's talkin' here?" he demands, suspiciously
eyeing the knitters. "You, Davis?"

"No, sir."

"Who was, then?"

"Nobody here, Mr. Cosson."

"Yes, they was. I heard hollerin'."

"Oh, that was me," Davis replies, with a quick glance
at me. "I hit my elbow against the machine."

"Let me see 't."

The guard scrutinizes the bared arm.

"Wa-a-ll," he says, doubtfully, "it don't look sore."

"It hurt, and I hollered."

The officer turns to my assistant: "Has he been
talkin', Reddie?"

"I don't think he was, Cap'n."

Pleased with the title, Cosson smiles at "Red," and
passes on, with a final warning to the boy: "Don't you
let me catch you at it again, you hear!"

During the rest of the day the overseers exercise
particular vigilance over our end of the shop. But
emboldened by the increased din of the new knitting
machinery, "Red" soon takes up the conversation again.

"Screws can't hear us now," he whispers, " 'cept
they's close to us. But watch your lips, boy; the damn
bulls got sharp lamps. An' don' scare me again like
that. Why, you talk so foolish, you make me plumb
forget myself. Say, that kid is all to the good, ain't

he? What's his name, Johnny Davis? Yes, a wise kid all right. Just like me own Billie I tole you 'bout. He was no punk, either, an' don't you forget it. True as steel, he was; stuck to me through my four-spot like th' bark to a tree. Say, what's that you said, you don't believe what I endeavored so conscientiously, sir, to drive into your noodle? You was only kiddin' me, wasn't you?"

"No, Red, I meant it quite seriously. You're spinning ghost stories, or whatever you call it. I don't believe in this kid love."

"An' why don't you believe it?"

"Why—er—well, I don't think it possible."

"*What* isn't possible?"

"You know what I mean. I don't think there can be such intimacy between those of the same sex."

"Ho, ho! *That's* your point? Why, Alex, you're more of a damfool than the casual observer, sir, would be apt to postulate. You don't believe it possible, you don't, eh? Well, you jest gimme half a chance, and I'll show you."

"Red, don't you talk to me like that," I burst out, angrily. "If you—"

"Aisy, aisy, me bye," he interrupts, good-naturedly. "Don't get on your high horse. No harm meant, Alex. You're a good boy, but you jest rattle me with your crazy talk. Why, you're bugs to say it's impossible. Man alive, the dump's chuckful of punks. It's done in every prison, an' on th' road, everywhere. Lord, if I had a plunk for every time I got th' best of a kid, I'd rival Rockefeller, sir; I would, me bye."

"You actually confess to such terrible practices? You're disgusting. But I don't really believe it, Red."

"Confess hell! I confess nothin'. Terrible, disgusting! You talk like a man up a tree, you holy sky-pilot."

"Are there no women on the road?"

"Pshaw! Who cares for a heifer when you can get a kid? Women are no good. I wouldn't look at 'em when I can have my prushun.* Oh, it is quite evident, sir, you have not delved into the esoteric mysteries of moonology, nor tasted the mellifluous fruit on the forbidden tree of—"

"Oh, quit!"

"Well, you'll know better before *your* time's up, me virtuous sonny."

For several days my assistant fails to appear in the shop on account of illness. He has been "excused" by the doctor, the guard informs me. I miss his help at work; the hours drag heavier for lack of "Red's" companionship. Yet I am gratified by his absence. His cynical attitude toward woman and sex morality has roused in me a spirit of antagonism. The panegyrics of boy-love are deeply offensive to my instincts. The very thought of the unnatural practice revolts and disgusts me. But I find solace in the reflection that "Red's" insinuations are pure fabrication; no credence is to be given them. Man, a reasonable being, could not fall to such depths; he could not be guilty of such unspeakably vicious practices. Even the lowest outcast must not be credited with such perversion, such depravity. I should really take the matter more calmly. The assistant is a queer fellow; he is merely teasing me. These things are not credible; indeed, I don't believe they are possible. And even if they were, no human being would be capable of such iniquity. I must not suffer "Red's" chaffing to disturb me.

---

* A boy serving his apprenticeship with a full-fledged tramp.

CHAPTER XI

THE ROUTE SUB ROSA

March 4, 1893.

GIRL AND TWIN:

I am writing with despair in my heart. I was taken to Pittsburgh as a witness in the trial of Nold and Bauer. I had hoped for an opportunity—you understand, friends. It was a slender thread, but I clung to it desperately, prepared to stake everything on it. It proved a broken straw. Now I am back, and I may never leave this place alive.

I was bitterly disappointed not to find you in the courtroom. I yearned for the sight of your faces. But you were not there, nor any one else of our New York comrades. I knew what it meant: you are having a hard struggle to exist. Otherwise perhaps something could be done to establish friendly relations between Rakhmetov and Mr. Gebop.* It would require an outlay beyond the resources of our own circle; others cannot be approached in this matter. Nothing remains but the "inside" developments,—a terribly slow process.

This is all the hope I can hold out to you, dear friends. You will think it quite negligible; yet it is the sole ray that has again and again kindled life in moments of utmost darkness. . . . I did not realize the physical effects of my stay here (it is five months now) till my return from court. I suppose the excitement of being on the outside galvanized me for the nonce. . . . My head was awhirl; I could not collect my thoughts. The wild hope possessed me,—*pobeg!* The click of the steel, as I was handcuffed to the Deputy, struck my death-knell. . . . The unaccustomed noise of the streets, the people and loud voices in the courtroom, the scenes of the trial, all absorbed me in the moment. It seemed to me as if I were a spectator, interested, but personally unconcerned, in the sur-

---

* Reading backward, *pobeg;* Russian for "escape."

roundings; and these, too, were far away, of a strange world in which I had no part. Only when I found myself alone in the cell, the full significance of the lost occasion was borne in upon me with crushing force.

But why sadden you? There is perhaps a cheerier side, now that Nold and Bauer are here. I have not seen them yet, but their very presence, the circumstance that somewhere within these walls there are *comrades,* men who, like myself, suffer for an ideal—the thought holds a deep satisfaction for me. It brings me closer, in a measure, to the environment of political prisoners in Europe. Whatever the misery and torture of their daily existence, the politicals—even in Siberia—breathe the atmosphere of solidarity, of appreciation. What courage and strength there must be for them in the inspiration radiated by a common cause! Conditions here are entirely different. Both inmates and officers are at loss to "class" me. They have never known political prisoners. That one should sacrifice or risk his life with no apparent personal motives, is beyond their comprehension, almost beyond their belief. It is a desert of sordidness that constantly threatens to engulf one. I would gladly exchange places with our comrades in Siberia.

The former *podpoilnaya** was suspended, because of the great misfortune that befell my friend Wingie, of whom I wrote to you before. This dove will be flown by Mr. Tiuremshchick,† an old soldier who really sympathizes with Wingie. I believe they served in the same regiment. He is a kindly man, who hates his despicable work. But there is a family at home, a sick wife—you know the old, weak-kneed tale. I had a hint from him the other day: he is being spied upon; it is dangerous for him to be seen at my cell, and so forth. It is all quite true; but what he means is, that a little money would be welcome. You know how to manage the matter. Leave no traces.

I hear the felt-soled step. It's the soldier. I bid my birdie a hasty good-bye.   SASHA.

---

* *Sub rosa* route.   † Russian for "guard."

CHAPTER XII

"ZUCHTHAUSBLUETHEN"

I

A DENSE FOG rises from the broad bosom of the Ohio. It ensnares the river banks in its mysterious embrace, veils tree and rock with sombre mist, and mocks the sun with angry frown. Within the House of Death is felt the chilling breath, and all is quiet and silent in the iron cages.

Only an occasional knocking, as on metal, disturbs the stillness. I listen intently. Nearer and more audible seem the sounds, hesitating and apparently intentional. I am involuntarily reminded of the methods of communication practiced by Russian politicals, and I strive to detect some meaning in the tapping. It grows clearer as I approach the back wall of the cell, and instantly I am aware of a faint murmur in the privy. Is it fancy, or did I hear my name?

"Halloa!" I call into the pipe.

The knocking ceases abruptly. I hear a suppressed, hollow voice: "That you, Aleck?"

"Yes. Who is it?"

"Never min'. You must be deaf not to hear me callin' you all this time. Take that cott'n out o' your ears."

"I didn't know you could talk this way."

"You didn't? Well, you know now. Them's empty

pipes, no standin' water, see? Fine t' talk. Oh, dammit to—"

The words are lost in the gurgle of rushing water. Presently the flow subsides, and the knocking is resumed. I bend over the privy.

"Hello, hello! That you, Aleck?"

"Git off that line, ye jabberin' idiot!" some one shouts into the pipe.

"Lay down, there!"

"Take that trap out o' the hole."

"Quit your foolin', Horsethief."

"Hey, boys, stop that now. That's me, fellers. It's Bob, Horsethief Bob. I'm talkin' business. Keep quiet now, will you? Are you there, Aleck? Yes? Well, pay no 'tention to them dubs. 'Twas that crazy Southside Slim that turned th' water on—"

"Who you call crazy, damn you," a voice interrupts.

"Oh, lay down, Slim, will you? Who said you was crazy? Nay, nay, you're bugs. Hey, Aleck, you there?"

"Yes, Bob."

"Oh, got me name, have you? Yes, I'm Bob, Horsethief Bob. Make no mistake when you see me; I'm Big Bob, the Horsethief. Can you hear me? It's you, Aleck?"

"Yes, yes."

"Sure it's you? Got t' tell you somethin'. What's your number?"

"A 7."

"Right you are. What cell?"

"6 K."

"An' this is me, Big Bob, in—"

"Windbag Bob," a heavy bass comments from above.

"Shut up, Curley, I'm on th' line. I'm in 6 F, Aleck, top tier. Call me up any time I'm in, ha, ha! You see, pipe's runnin' up an' down, an' you can talk to any range

you want, but always to th' same cell as you're in, Cell
6, understand? Now if you wan' t' talk to Cell 14, to
Shorty, you know—"

"I don't want to talk to Shorty. I don't know him,
Bob."

"Yes, you do. You list'n what I tell you, Aleck, an'
you'll be all right. That's me talkin', Big Bob, see?
Now, I say if you'd like t' chew th' rag with Shorty, you
jest tell me. Tell Brother Bob, an' he'll connect you all
right. Are you on? Know who's Shorty?"

"No."

"Yo oughter. That's Carl, Carl Nold. Know *him*,
don't you?"

"What!" I cry in astonishment. "Is it true, Bob?
Is Nold up there on your gallery?"

"Sure thing. Cell 14."

"Why didn't you say so at once? You've been talking ten minutes now. Did you see him?"

"What's your hurry, Aleck? *You* can't see 'im; not
jest now, anyway. P'r'aps bimeby, mebbe. There's no
hurry, Aleck. *You* got plenty o' time. A few years,
rather, ha, ha, ha!"

"Hey, there, Horsethief, quit that!" I recognize
"Curley's" deep bass. "What do you want to make the
kid feel bad for?"

"No harm meant, Curley," Bob returns, "I was jest
joshin' him a bit."

"Well, quit it."

"You don' min' it, Aleck, do you?" I hear Bob again,
his tones softened, "I didn' mean t' hurt your feelin's.
I'm your friend, Aleck, you can bet your corn dodger
on that. Say, I've got somethin' for you from Shorty,
I mean Carl, you savvy?"

"What have you, Bob?"

"Nixie through th' hole, ain't safe. I'm coffee-boy

on this 'ere range. I'll sneak around to you in the
mornin', when I go t' fetch me can of bootleg. Now,
jiggaroo,* screw's comin'."

II

The presence of my comrades is investing existence
with interest and meaning. It has brought to me a
breeze from the atmosphere of my former environment;
it is stirring the graves, where lie my soul's dead, into
renewed life and hope.

The secret exchange of notes lends color to the
routine. It is like a fresh mountain streamlet joyfully
rippling through a stagnant swamp. At work in the
shop, my thoughts are engrossed with our correspondence. Again and again I review the arguments eluci-
dating to my comrades the significance of my *Attentat:*
they, too, are inclined to exaggerate the importance of
the purely physical result. The exchange of views gradually ripens our previously brief and superficial acquaintance into closer intimacy. There is something in Carl
Nold that especially attracts me: I sense in him a con-
genial spirit. His spontaneous frankness appeals to me;
my heart echoes his grief at the realization of Most's
unpardonable behavior. But the ill-concealed antagonism of Bauer is irritating. It reflects his desperate
clinging to the shattered idol. Presently, however, a
better understanding begins to manifest itself. The
big, jovial German has earned my respect; he braved
the anger of the judge by consistently refusing to betray
the man who aided him in the distribution of the Anarchist leaflet among the Homestead workers. On the
other hand, both Carl and Henry appreciate my efforts

* Look out.

on the witness stand, to exonerate them from complicity
in my act. Their condemnation, as acknowledged Anarchists, was, of course, a foregone conclusion, and I
am gratified to learn that neither of my comrades had
entertained any illusions concerning the fate that awaited
them. Indeed, both have expressed surprise that the
maximum revenge of the law was not visited upon them.
Their philosophical attitude exerts a soothing effect upon
me. Carl even voices satisfaction that the sentence of
five years will afford him a long-needed vacation from
many years of ceaseless factory toil. He is facetiously
anxious lest capitalist industry be handicapped by the
loss of such a splendid carpenter as Henry, whom he
good-naturedly chaffs on the separation from his newly
affianced.

The evening hours have ceased to drag: there is
pleasure and diversion in the correspondence. The
notes have grown into bulky letters, daily cementing
our friendship. We compare views, exchange impressions, and discuss prison gossip. I learn the history of
the movement in the twin cities, the personnel of Anarchist circles, and collect a fund of anecdotes about
Albrecht, the philosophic old shoemaker whose diminutive shop in Allegheny is the center of the radical
inteligenzia. With deep contrition Bauer confesses how
narrowly he escaped the rôle of my executioner. My
unexpected appearance in their midst, at the height of
the Homestead struggle, had waked suspicion among the
Allegheny comrades. They sent an inquiry to Most,
whose reply proved a warning against me. Unknown to
me, Bauer shared the room I occupied in Nold's house.
Through the long hours of the night he lay awake,
with revolver cocked. At the first sign of a suspicious
move on my part, he had determined to kill me.

The personal tenor of our correspondence is gradually broadening into the larger scope of socio-political theories, methods of agitation, and applied tactics. The discussions, prolonged and often heated, absorb our interest. The bulky notes necessitate greater circumspection; the difficulty of procuring writing materials assumes a serious aspect. Every available scrap of paper is exhausted; margins of stray newspapers and magazines have been penciled on, the contents repeatedly erased, and the frayed tatters microscopically covered with ink. Even an occasional fly-leaf from library books has been sacrilegiously forced to leave its covers, and every evidence of its previous association dexterously removed. The problem threatens to terminate our correspondence, and fills us with dismay. But the genius of our faithful postman, of proud horsethieving proclivities, proves equal to the occasion: Bob constitutes himself our commissary, designating the broom shop, in which he is employed, as the base of our future supplies.

The unexpected affluence fills us with joy. The big rolls requisitioned by "Horsethief" exclude the fear of famine; the smooth yellow wrapping paper affords the luxury of larger and more legible chirography. The pride of sudden wealth germinates ambitious projects. We speculate on the possibility of converting our correspondence into a magazinelet, and wax warm over the proposed list of readers. Before long the first issue of the *Zuchthausblüthen** is greeted with the encouraging approval of our sole subscriber, whose contribution surprises us in the form of a rather creditable poem on the blank last page of the publication. Elated at the happy acquisition, we unanimously crown him *Meistersinger,* with dominion over the department of poetry.

---

* Prison Blossoms.

Soon we plan more pretentious issues: the outward size of the publication is to remain the same, three by five inches, but the number of pages is to be enlarged; each issue to have a different editor, to ensure equality of opportunity; the readers to serve as contributing editors. The appearance of the *Blüthen* is to be regulated by the time required to complete the circle of readers, whose identity is to be masked with certain initials, to protect them against discovery. Henceforth Bauer, physically a giant, is to be known as "G"; because of my medium stature, I shall be designated with the letter "M"; and Nold, as the smallest, by "K."* The poet, his history somewhat shrouded in mystery, is christened "D" for *Dichter.* "M," "K," "G," are to act, in turn, as editor-in-chief, whose province it is to start the *Blüthen* on its way, each reader contributing to the issue till it is returned to the original editor, to enable him to read and comment upon his fellow-contributors. The publication, its contents growing in transit, is finally to reach the second contributor, upon whom will devolve the editorial management of the following issue.

The unique arrangement proves a source of much pleasure and recreation. The little magazine is rich in contents and varied in style. The diversity of handwriting heightens the interest, and stimulates speculation on the personality of our increasing readers-contributors. In the arena of the diminutive publication, there rages the conflict of contending social philosophies; here a political essay rubs elbows with a witty anecdote, and a dissertation on "The Nature of Things" is interspersed with prison small-talk and personal reminiscence. Flashes of unstudied humor and unconscious rivalry

---

* Initial of the German *klein,* small.

Special Spring Edition

of the

Z. Blüthen.

of orthography lend peculiar charm to the unconventional editorials, and waft a breath of Josh Billings into the manuscript pages.

But the success of the *Zuchthausblüthen* soon discovers itself a veritable Frankenstein, which threatens the original foundation and aims of the magazinelet. The popularity of joint editorship is growing at the cost of unity and tendency; the Bard's astonishing facility at versification, coupled with his Jules Vernian imagination, causes us grave anxiety lest his untamable Pegasus traverse the limits of our paper supply. The appalling warning of the commissary that the improvident drain upon his resources is about to force him on a strike, imperatively calls a halt. We are deliberating policies of retrenchment and economy, when unexpectedly the arrival of two Homestead men suggests an auspicious solution.

III

The presence of Hugh F. Dempsey and Robert J. Beatty, prominent in the Knights of Labor organization, offers opportunity for propaganda among workers representing the more radical element of American labor. Accused of poisoning the food served to the strikebreakers in the mills, Dempsey and Beatty appear to me men of unusual type. Be they innocent or guilty, the philosophy of their methods is in harmony with revolutionary tactics. Labor can never be unjust in its demands: is it not the creator of all the wealth in the world? Every weapon may be employed to return the despoiled People into its rightful ownership. Is not the terrorizing of scabbery, and ultimately of the capitalist exploiters, an effective means of aiding the struggle? Therefore Dempsey and Beatty deserve acclaim. Morally certain of their guilt, I respect them the more for it, though I am saddened by their denial of complicity in the scheme of wholesale extermination of the scabs. The blackleg is also human, it is true, and desires to live. But one should starve rather than turn traitor to the cause of his class. Moreover, the individual—or any number of them—cannot be weighed against the interests of humanity.

Infinite patience weaves the threads that bring us in contact with the imprisoned labor leaders. In the ceaseless duel of vital need against stupidity and malice, caution and wit are sharpened by danger. The least indiscretion, the most trifling negligence, means discovery, disaster. But perseverance and intelligent purpose conquer: by the aid of the faithful "Horsethief," communication with Dempsey and Beatty is established. With the aggressiveness of strong conviction I present to them my views, dwelling on the historic rôle of the *Attentäter* and the social significance of conscious individual protest. The discussion ramifies, the interest aroused soon transcending the limits of my paper supply. Presently I am involved in a correspondence with several men, whose questions and misinterpretations regarding my act I attempt to answer and correct with individual notes. But the method proves an impossible tax on our opportunities, and "KGM" finally decide to publish an English edition of the *Zuchthausblüthen*. The German magazinelet is suspended, and in its place appears the first issue of the *Prison Blossoms*.

CHAPTER XIII

THE JUDAS

"Ah, there, Sporty!" my assistant greets me in the shop. "Stand treat on this festive occasion?"

"Yes, Red. Have a chew," I reply with a smile, handing him my fresh plug of tobacco.

His eyes twinkle with mischievous humor as he scrutinizes my changed suit of dark gray. The larger part of the plug swelling out his cheek, he flings to me the remnant across the table, remarking:

"Don't care for't. Take back your choo, I'll keep me honor,—your plug, I mean, sonny. A gentleman of my eminence, sir, a natural-born navigator on the high seas of social life,—are you on, me bye?—a gentleman, I repeat, sir, whose canoe the mutations of all that is human have chucked on this here dry, thrice damned dry latitude, sir, this nocuous plague-spot of civilization,—say, kid, what t' hell am I talkin' about? Damn if I ain't clean forgot."

"I'm sure I don't know, Red."

"Like hell you don't! It's your glad duds, kid. Offerin' *me* a ch-aw tob-b-bac-co! Christ, I'm dyin' for a drop of booze. This magnificent occasion deserves a wetting, sir. And, say, Aleck, it won't hurt your beauty to stretch them sleeves of yours a bit. You look like a scarecrow in them high-water pants. Ain't old Sandy the king of skinners, though!"

"Whom do you mean, Red?"

"Who I mean, you idjot! Who but that skunk of a Warden, the Honorable Captain Edward S. Wright, if you please, sir. Captain of rotten old punks, that's what he is. You ask th' screws. He's never smelt powder; why, he's been *here* most o' his life. But some o' th' screws been here longer, borned here, damn 'em; couldn't pull 'em out o' here with a steam engine, you couldn't. They can tell you all 'bout the Cap, though. Old Sandy didn' have a plugged nickel to his name when he come 'ere, an' now the damn stomach-robber is rich. Reg'lar gold mine this dump's for 'im. Only gets a lousy five thousan' per year. Got big fam'ly an' keeps carriages an' servants, see, an' can 'ford t' go to Europe every year, an' got a big pile in th' bank to boot, all on a scurvy five thousan' a year. Good manager, ain't he? A reg'lar church member, too, damn his rotten soul to hell!"

"Is he as bad as all that, Red?"

"Is he? A hypocrite dyed in th' wool, that's what he is. Plays the humanitarian racket. He had a great deal t' say t' the papers why he didn't believe in the brutal way Iams was punished by that Homestead colonel—er—what's 'is name?"

"Colonel Streator, of the Tenth Pennsylvania."

"That's the cur. He hung up Private Iams by the thumbs till th' poor boy was almost dead. For nothin', too. Suppose you remember, don't you? Iams had called for 'three cheers for the man who shot Frick,' an' they pretty near killed 'im for 't, an' then drummed 'im out of th' regiment with 'is head half shaved."

"It was a most barbarous thing."

"An' that damn Sandy swore in th' papers he didn't believe in such things, an' all th' while th' lyin' murderer is doin' it himself. Not a day but some poor con is 'cuffed up' in th' hole. That's th' kind of humanitarian *he* is! It makes me wild t' think on 't. Why, kid, I even get a bit excited, and forget that you, young sir, are attuned to the dulcet symphonies of classic English. But whenever that skunk of a Warden is the subject of conversation, sir, even my usually imperturbable serenity of spirit and tranquil stoicism are not equal to 'Patience on a monument smiling at grief.' Watch me, sonny, that's yours truly spielin'. Why, look at them dingy rags of yours. I liked you better in th' striped duds. They give you the hand-me-downs of that nigger that went out yesterday, an' charge you on th' books with a bran' new suit. See where Sandy gets his slice, eh? An' say, kid, how long are you here?"

"About eight months, Red."

"They beat you out o' two months all right. Suppose they obey their own rules? Nit, sir. You are aware, my precious lamb, that you are entitled to discard your polychromic vestments of zebra hue after a sojourn of six months in this benevolent dump. I bet you that fresh fish at the loopin' machine there, came up 'ere some days ago, *he* won't be kept waitin' more'n six months for 'is black clothes."

I glance in the direction of the recent arrival. He is a slender man, with swarthy complexion and quick, shifting eye. The expression of guilty cunning is repelling.

"Who is that man?" I whisper to the assistant.

"Like 'im, don't you? Permit me, sir, to introduce to you the handiwork of his Maker, a mealy-mouthed, oily-lipped, scurvy gaycat, a yellow cur, a snivelling, fawning stool, a filthy, oozy sneak, a snake in the grass whose very presence, sir, is a mortal insult to a self-respecting member of my clan,—Mr. Patrick Gallagher, of the honorable Pinkerton family, sir."

"Gallagher?" I ask, in astonishment. "The informer, who denounced Dempsey and Beatty?"

"The very same. The dirty snitch that got those fellows railroaded here for seven years. Dempsey was a fool to bunch up with such vermin as Gallagher and Davidson. He was Master Workman of some district of the Knights of Labor. Why in hell didn't he get his own men to do th' job? Goes to work an' hires a brace of gaycats; sent 'em to the scab mills, you savvy, to sling hash for the blacklegs and keep 'im posted on the goings on, see? S'pose you have oriented yourself, sir, concerning the developments in the culinary experiment?"

"Yes. Croton oil is supposed to have been used to make the scabs sick with diarrhœa."

"Make 'em sick? Why, me bye, scores of 'em croaked. I am surprised, sir, at your use of such a vulgar term as diarrhœa. You offend my aestheticism. The learned gentlemen who delve deeply into the bowels of earth and man, sir, ascribed the sudden and phenomenal increase of unmentionable human obligations to nature, the mysterious and extravagant popularity of the houses of ill odor, sir, and the automatic obedience to their call, as due entirely to the dumping of a lot o' lousy bums, sir, into filthy quarters, or to impurities of the liquid supply, or to—pardon my frankness, sir— to intestinal effeminacy, which, in flaccid excitability, persisted in ill-timed relaxation unseemly in well-mannered Christians. Some future day, sir, there may arise a poet to glorify with beauteous epic the heroic days of the modern Bull Run—an' I kin tell you, laddie, **they run and kept runnin', top** and bottom—**or some** lyric bard may put to Hudibrastic verse—watch me climbin' th' Parnassus, kid—the poetic feet, the numbers, the assonance, and strain of the inspiring days when Croton Oil was King. Yes, sirree; but for yours truly, me hand ain't in such pies; and moreover, sir, I make it an invariable rule of gentlemanly behavior t' keep me snout out o' other people's biz."

"Dempsey may be innocent, Red."

"Well, th' joory didn't think so. But there's no tellin'. Honest t' God, Aleck, that rotten scab of a Gallagher has cast the pale hue of resolution, if I may borrow old Billy Shake's slang, sir, over me gener'ly settled convictions. You know, in the abundant plenitude of my heterogeneous experience with all sorts and conditions of rats and gaycats, sir, fortified by a natural genius of no mean order, of 1859 vintage, damme if I ever run across such an acute form of confessionitis as manifested by the lout on th' loopin' machine there. You know what he done yesterday?"

"What?"

"Sent for th' distric' attorney and made another confesh."

"Really? How do you know?"

"Night screw's a particular fren' o' mine, kid. I shtands in, see? The mick's a reg'lar Yahoo, can't hardly spell 'is own name. He daily requisitions upon my humble but abundant intelligence, sir, to make out his reports. Catch on, eh? I've never earned a hand-out with more dignified probity, sir. It's a cinch. Last night he gimme a great slice of corn dodger. It was A 1, I tell you, an' two hard boiled eggs and half a tomato, juicy and luscious, sir. Didn't I enjoy it, though! Makes your mouth water, eh, kid? Well, you be good t' me, an' you kin have what I got. I'll divvy up with you. We-ll! Don' stand there an' gape at me like a wooden Injun. Has the unexpected revelation of my magnanimous generosity deprived you of articulate utterance, sir?"

The sly wink with which he emphasizes the offer, and his suddenly serious manner, affect me unpleasantly. With pretended indifference, I decline to share his delicacies.

"You need those little extras for yourself, Red," I explain. "You told me you suffer from indigestion. A change of diet now and then will do you good. But you haven't finished telling me about the new confession of Gallagher."

"Oh, you're a sly one, Aleck; no flies on you. But it's all right, me bye, mebbe I can do somethin' for you some day. I'm your friend, Aleck; count on me. But that mutt of a Gallagher, yes, sirree, made another confession; damme if it ain't his third one. Ever hear such a thing? I got it straight from th' screw all right. I can't make the damn snitch out. Unreservedly I avow, sir, that the incomprehensible vacillations of the honorable gentleman puzzle me noodle, and are calculated to disturb the repose of a right-thinking yagg in the silken lap of Morpheus. What's 'is game, anyhow? Shall we diagnoze the peculiar mental menstruation as, er—er— what's your learned opinion, my illustrious colleague, eh? What you grinnin' for, Four Eyes? It's a serious matter, sir; a highly instructive phenomenon of intellectual vacuity, impregnated with the pernicious virus of Pinkertonism, sir, and transmuted in the alembic of Carnegie alchemy. A judicious injection of persuasive germs by the sagacious jurisconsults of the House of Dempsey, and lo! three brand-new confessions, mutually contradictory and exclusive. Does that strike you in th' right spot, sonny?"

"In the second confession he retracted his accusations against Dempsey. What is the third about, Red?"

"Retracts his retraction, me bye. Guess why, Aleck."

"I suppose he was paid to reaffirm his original charges."

"You're not far off. After that beauty of a Judas cleared the man, Sandy notified Reed and Knox. Them's smart guys, all right; the attorneys of the Carnegie Company to interpret Madame Justicia, sir, in a manner—"

"I know, Red," I interrupt him, "they are the lawyers who prosecuted me. Even in court they were giving directions to the district attorney, and openly whispering to him questions to be asked the witnesses. He was just a figurehead and a tool for them, and it sounded so ridiculous when he told the jury that he was not in the service of any individual or corporation, but that he acted solely as an officer of the commonwealth, charged with the sacred duty of protecting its interests in my prosecution. And all the time he was the mouthpiece of Frick's lawyers."

"Hold on, kid. I don't get a chance to squeeze a word in edgewise when you start jawin'. Think you're on th' platform haranguing the long-haired crowd? You can't convert *me*, so save your breath, man."

"I shouldn't want to convert you, Red. You are intelligent, but a hopeless case. You are not the kind that could be useful to the Cause."

"Glad you're next. Got me sized up all right, eh? Well, me saintly bye, I'm Johnny-on-the-spot to serve the cause, all right, all right, and the cause is Me, with a big M, see? A fellow's a fool not t' look out for number one. I give it t' you straight, Aleck. What's them high-flown notions of yours—oppressed humanity and suffering people—fiddlesticks! There you go and shove your damn neck into th' noose for the strikers, but what did them fellows ever done for you, eh? Tell me that! They won't do a darned thing fer you. Catch *me* swinging for the peo-pul! The cattle don't deserve any better than they get, that's what *I* say."

"I don't want to discuss these questions with you, Red. You'll never understand, anyhow."

"Git off, now. You voice a sentiment, sir, that my adequate appreciation of myself would prompt me to resent on the field of honor, sir. But the unworthy spirit of acerbity is totally foreign to my nature, sir, and I shall preserve the blessed meekness so becoming the true Christian, and shall follow the bidding of the Master by humbly offering the other cheek for that chaw of th' weed I gave you. Dig down into your poke, kid."

I hand him the remnant of my tobacco, remarking:

"You've lost the thread of our conversation, as usual, Red. You said the Warden sent for the Carnegie lawyers after Gallagher had recanted his original confession. Well, what did they do?"

"Don't know what *they* done, but I tole you that the muttonhead sent for th' district attorney the same day, an' signed a third confesh. Why, Dempsey was tickled to death, 'cause—"

He ceases abruptly. His quick, short coughs warn me of danger. Accompanied by the Deputy and the shop officer, the Warden is making the rounds of the machines, pausing here and there to examine the work, and listen to the request of a prisoner. The youthfully sparkling eyes present a striking contrast to the sedate manner and seamed features framed in grayish-white. Approaching the table, he greets us with a benign smile:

"Good morning, boys."

Casting a glance at my assistant, the Warden inquires: "Your time must be up soon, Red?"

"Been out and back again, Cap'n," the officer laughs.

"Yes, he is, hm, hm, back home." The thin feminine accents of the Deputy sound sarcastic.

"Didn't like it outside, Red?" the Warden sneers.

A flush darkens the face of the assistant. "There's more skunks out than in," he retorts.

The Captain frowns. The Deputy lifts a warning finger, but the Warden laughs lightly, and continues on his rounds.

We work in silence for a while. "Red" looks restive, his eyes stealthily following the departing officials. Presently he whispers:

"See me hand it to 'im, Aleck? He knows I'm on to 'im, all right. Didn't he look mad, though? Thought he'd burst. Sobered 'im up a bit. Pipe 'is lamps, kid?"

"Yes. Very bright eyes."

"Bright eyes your grandmother! Dope, that's what's th' matter. Think I'd get off as easy if he wasn't chuck full of th' stuff? I knowed it the minute I laid me eyes on 'im. I kin tell by them shinin' glimmers and that sick smile of his, when he's feelin' good; know th' signals, all right. Always feelin' fine when he's hit th' pipe. That's th' time you kin get anythin' you wan' of 'im. Nex' time you see that smirk on 'im, hit 'im for some one t' give us a hand here; we's goin' t' be drowned in them socks, first thing you know."

"Yes, we need more help. Why didn't *you* ask him?"

"Me? Me ask a favor o' the damn swine? Not on your tintype! You don' catch me to vouchsafe the high and mighty, sir, the opportunity—"

"All right, Red. I won't ask him, either."

"I don't give a damn. For all I care, Aleck, and —well, confidentially speaking, sir, they may ensconce

their precious hosiery in the infundibular dehiscence of
his Nibs, which, if I may venture my humble opinion,
young sir, is sufficiently generous in its expansiveness
to disregard the rugosity of a stocking turned inside
out, sir. Do you follow the argument, me bye?"

"With difficulty, Red," I reply, with a smile. "What
are you really talking about? I do wish you'd speak
plainer."

"You do, do you? An' mebbe you don't. Got to
train you right; gradual, so to speak. It's me dooty
to a prushun. But we'se got t' get help here. I ain't
goin' t' kill meself workin' like a nigger. I'll quit first.
D' you think—s-s-ss!"

The shop officer is returning. "Damn your impudence, Red," he shouts at the assistant. "Why don't you
keep that tongue of yours in check?"

"Why, Mr. Cosson, what's th' trouble?"

"You know damn well what's the trouble. You made
the old man mad clean through. You ought t' know
better'n that. He was nice as pie till you opened that
big trap of yourn. Everythin' went wrong then. He
gave me th' dickens about that pile you got lyin' aroun'
here. Why don't you take it over to th' loopers, Burk?"

"They have not been turned yet," I reply.

"What d' you say? Not turned!" he bristles. "What
in hell are you fellows doin', I'd like t' know."

"We're doin' more'n we should," "Red" retorts,
defiantly.

"Shut up now, an' get a move on you."

"On that rotten grub they feed us?" the assistant
persists.

"You better shut up, Red."

"Then give us some help."

"I will like hell!"

The whistle sounds the dinner hour.

CHAPTER XIV

THE DIP

FOR a week "Boston Red" is absent from work. My best efforts seem ineffectual in the face of the increasing mountain of unturned hosiery, and the officer grows more irritable and insistent. But the fear of clogging the industrial wheel presently forces him to give me assistance, and a dapper young man, keen-eyed and nervous, takes the vacant place.

"He's a dip,"* Johnny Davis whispers to me. "A top-notcher," he adds, admiringly.

I experience a tinge of resentment at the equality implied by the forced association. I have never before come in personal contact with a professional thief, and I entertain the vaguest ideas concerning his class. But they are not producers; hence parasites who deliberately prey upon society, upon the poor, mostly. There can be nothing in common between me and this man.

The new helper's conscious superiority is provoking. His distant manner piques my curiosity. How unlike his scornful mien and proudly independent bearing is my youthful impression of a thief! Vividly I remember the red-headed Kolya, as he was taken from the class-room by a fierce gendarme. The boys had been missing their lunches, and Kolya confessed the theft. We ran

* Pickpocket.

after the prisoner, and he hung his head and looked frightened, and so pale I could count each freckle on his face. He did not return to school, and I wondered what had become of him. The terror in his eyes haunted my dreams, the brown spots on his forehead shaping themselves into fiery letters, spelling the fearful word *vor*.*

"That's a snap," the helper's voice breaks in on my reverie. He speaks in well-modulated tones, the accents nasal and decided. "You needn't be afraid to talk," he adds, patronizingly.

"I am not afraid," I impatiently resent the insinuation. "Why should I be afraid of you?"

"Not of me; of the officer, I meant."

"I am not afraid of him, either."

"Well, then, let's talk about something. It will help while away the time, you know."

His cheerful friendliness smooths my ruffled temper. The correct English, in striking contrast with the peculiar language of my former assistant, surprises me.

"I am sorry," he continues, "they gave you such a long sentence, Mr. Berkman, but—"

"How do you know my name?" I interrupt. "You have just arrived."

"They call me 'Lightning Al'," he replies, with a tinge of pride. "I'm here only three days, but a fellow in my line can learn a great deal in that time. I had you pointed out to me."

"What do you call your line? What are you here for?"

For a moment he is silent. With surprise I watch his face blush darkly.

---

* Thief.

"You're a dead give-away. Oh, excuse me, Mr. Berkman," he corrects himself, "I sometimes lapse into lingo, under provocation, you know. I meant to say, it's easy to see that you are not next to the way—not familiar, I mean, with such things. You should never ask a man what he is in for."

"Why not?"

"Well, er—"

"You are ashamed."

"Not a bit of it. Ashamed to fall, perhaps,—I mean, to be caught at it—it's no credit to a gun's rep, his reputation, you understand. But I'm proud of the jobs I've done. I'm pretty slick, you know."

"But you don't like to be asked why you were sent here."

"Well, it's not good manners to ask such questions."

"Against the ethics of the trade, I suppose?"

"How sarcastic we can be, Mr. Berkman. But it's true, it's not the ethics. And it isn't a trade, either; it's a profession. Oh, you may smile, but I'd rather be a gun, a professional, I mean, than one of your stupid factory hands."

"They are honest, though. Honest producers, while you are a thief."

"Oh, there's no sting in that word for *me*. I take pride in being a thief, and what's more, I *am* an A number one gun, you see the point? The best dip in the States."

"A pickpocket? Stealing nickels off passengers on the street cars, and—"

"Me? A hell of a lot *you* know about it. Take me for such small fry, do you? I work only on race tracks."

"You call it work?"

"Sure. Damned hard work, too. Takes more brains than a whole shopful of your honest producers can show."

"And you prefer that to being honest?"

"Do I? I spend more on gloves than a bricklayer makes in a year. Think I'm so dumb I have to slave all week for a few dollars?"

"But you spend most of your life in prison."

"Not by a long shot. A real good gun's always got his fall money planted,—I mean some ready coin in case of trouble,—and a smart lawyer will spring you most every time; beat the case, you know. I've never seen the fly-cop you couldn't fix if you got enough dough; and most judges, too. Of course, now and then, the best of us may fall; but it don't happen very often, and it's all in the game. This whole life is a game, Mr. Berkman, and every one's got his graft."

"Do you mean there are no honest men?" I ask, angrily.

"Pshaw! I'm just as honest as Rockefeller or Carnegie, only they got the law with them. And I work harder than they, I'll bet you on that. I've got to eat, haven't I? Of course," he adds, thoughtfully, "if I could be sure of my bread and butter, perhaps—"

The passing overseer smiles at the noted pickpocket, inquiring pleasantly:

"How're you doin', Al?"

"Tip-top, Mr. Cosson. Hope you are feeling good to-day."

"Never better, Al."

"A friend of mine often spoke to me about you, Mr. Cosson."

"Who was that?"

"Barney. Jack Barney."

"Jack Barney! Why, he worked for me in the broom shop."

"Yes, he did a three-spot. He often said to me, 'Al, if you ever land in Riverside,' he says, 'be sure you don't forget to give my best to Mr. Cosson, Mr. Ed. Cosson,' he says, 'he's a good fellow.'"

The officer looks pleased. "Yes, I treated him white, all right," he remarks, continuing on his rounds.

"I knew he'd swallow it," the assistant sneers after him. "Always good to get on the right side of them," he adds, with a wink. "Barney told me about him all right. Said he's the rottenest sneak in the dump, a swell-head yap. You see, Mr. Berkman,—may I call you Aleck? It's shorter. Well, you see, Aleck, I make it a point to find things out. It's wise to know the ropes. I'm next to the whole bunch here. That Jimmy McPane, the Deputy, he's a regular brute. Killed his man, all right. Barney told me all about it; he was doing his bit, then,—I mean serving his sentence. You see, Aleck," he lowers his voice, confidentially, "I don't like to use slang; it grows on one, and every fly-cop can spot you as a crook. It's necessary in my business to present a fine front and use good English, so I must not get the lingo habit. Well, I was speaking of Barney telling me about the Deputy. He killed a con in cold blood. The fellow was bughouse, D. T., you know; saw snakes. He ran out of his cell one morning, swinging a chair and hollering 'Murder! Kill 'em!' The Deputy was just passing along, and he out with his gat—I mean his revolver, you know—and bangs away. He pumped the poor loony fellow full of holes; he did, the murderer. Killed him dead. Never was tried, either. Warden told the newspapers it was done in self-defence. A damn lie. Sandy knew better; everybody in the dump knew it was a cold-blooded murder, with no provocation at all. It's a regular ring, you see, and that old Warden is the biggest grafter of them all; and that sky-pilot, too, is an A 1 fakir. Did you hear about the kid born here? Before your time. A big scandal. Since then the holy man's got to have a screw with him at Sunday service for the females, and I tell you he needs watching all right."

The whistle terminates the conversation.

CHAPTER XV

THE URGE OF SEX

SUNDAY night: my new cell on the upper gallery is hot and stuffy; I cannot sleep.   Through the bars, I gaze upon the Ohio.   The full moon hangs above the river, bathing the waters in mellow light.   The strains of a sweet lullaby wander through the woods, and the banks are merry with laughter.   A girlish cadence rings like a silvery bell, and voices call in the distance.   Life is joyous and near, terribly, tantalizingly near,—but all is silent and dead around me.

For days the feminine voice keeps ringing in my ears.   It sounded so youthful and buoyant, so fondly alluring.   A beautiful girl, no doubt.   What joy to feast my eyes on her!   I have not beheld a woman for many months: I long to hear the soft accents, feel the tender touch.   My mind persistently reverts to the voice on the river, the sweet strains in the woods; and fancy wreathes sad-toned fugues upon the merry carol, paints vision and image, as I pace the floor in agitation.   They live, they breathe!   I see the slender figure with the swelling bosom, the delicate white throat, the babyish face with large, wistful eyes.   Why, it is Luba!   My blood tingles violently, passionately, as I live over again the rapturous wonder at the first touch of her maiden breast.   How temptingly innocent sounded the immodest invitation on the velvety lips, how exquisite the suddenness of it all!   We were in New Haven then.   One by one we had gathered, till the little New York commune was complete. The Girl joined me first, for I felt lonely in the strange city, drudging as compositor on a country weekly, the evenings cold and cheerless in the midst of a conservative household. But the Girl brought light and sunshine, and then came the Twin and Manya. Luba remained in New York; but Manya, devoted little soul, yearned for her sister, and presently the three girls worked side by side in the corset factory. All seemed happy in the free atmosphere, and Luba was blooming into beautiful womanhood. There was a vague something about her that now and then roused in me a fond longing, a rapturous desire. Once—it was in New York, a year before—I had experienced a sudden impulse toward her. It seized me unheralded, unaccountably. I had called to try a game of chess with her father, when he informed me that Luba had been ill. She was recovering now, and would be pleased to see me. I sat at the bedside, conversing in low tones, when I noticed the pillows slipping from under the girl's head. Bending over, I involuntarily touched her hair, loosely hanging down the side. The soft, dark chestnut thrilled me, and the next instant I stooped and stealthily pressed the silken waves to my lips. The momentary sense of shame was lost in the feeling of reverence for the girl with the beautiful hair, that bewildered and fascinated me, and a deep yearning suddenly possessed me, as she lay in exquisite disarray, full of grace and beauty. And all the while we talked, my eyes feasted on her ravishing form, and I felt envious of her future lover, and hated the desecration. But when I left her bedside, all trace of desire disappeared, and the inspiration of the moment faded like a vision affrighted by the dawn. Only a transient, vague inquietude remained, as of something unattainable.

Then came that unforgettable moment of undreamed

bliss. We had just returned from the performance of *Tosca*, with Sarah Bernhardt in her inimitable rôle. I had to pass through Luba's room on my way to the attic, in the little house occupied by the commune. She had already retired, but was still awake. I sat down on the edge of the bed, and we talked of the play. She glowed with the inspiration of the great tragedienne; then, somehow, she alluded to the *décolleté* of the actresses.

"I don't mind a fine bust exposed on the stage," I remarked. "But I had a powerful opera glass: their breasts looked fleshy and flabby. It was disgusting."

"Do you think—mine nice?" she asked, suddenly.

For a second I was bewildered. But the question sounded so enchantingly unpremeditated, so innocently eager.

"I never— Let me see them," I said, impulsively.

"No, no!" she cried, in aroused modesty; "I can't, I can't!"

"I won't look, Luba. See, I close my eyes. Just a touch."

"Oh, I can't, I'm ashamed! Only over the blanket, please, Sasha," she pleaded, as my hand softly stole under the covers. She gripped the sheet tightly, and my arm rested on her side. The touch of the firm, round breast thrilled me with passionate ecstasy. In fear of arousing her maidenly resistance, I strove to hide my exultation, while cautiously and tenderly I released the coverlet.

"They are very beautiful, Luba," I said, controlling the tremor of my voice.

"You—like them, really, Sasha?" The large eyes looked lustrous and happy.

"They are Greek, dear," and snatching the last covering aside, I kissed her between the breasts.

"I'm so glad I came here," she spoke dreamily.

"Were you very lonesome in New York?"

"It was terrible, Sasha."

"You like the change?"

"Oh, you silly boy! Don't you know?"

"What, Luba?"

"I wanted *you,* dear." Her arms twined softly about me.

I felt appalled. The Girl, my revolutionary plans, flitted through my mind, chilling me with self-reproach. The pale hue of the attained cast its shadow across the spell, and I lay cold and quiet on Luba's breast. The coverlet was slipping down, and, reaching for it, my hand inadvertently touched her knee.

"Sasha, how *can* you!" she cried in alarm, sitting up with terrified eyes.

"I didn't mean to, Luba. How could you *think* that of me?" I was deeply mortified.

My hand relaxed on her breast. We lay in silent embarrassment.

"It is getting late, Sasha." She tenderly drew my head to her bosom.

"A little while yet, dear," and again the enchantment of the virgin breasts was upon me, and I showered wild kisses on them, and pressed them passionately, madly, till she cried out in pain.

"You must go now, dear."

"Good night, Luba."

"Good night, dearest. You haven't kissed me, Sashenka."

I felt her detaining lips, as I left.

.   .   .   .

IN the wakeful hours of the night, the urge of sex grows more and more insistent. Scenes from the past live in my thoughts; the cell is peopled with familiar faces. Episodes long dead to memory rise animated before me; they emerge from the darkest chambers of my soul, and move with intense reality, like the portraits of my sires come to life in the dark, fearful nights of my childhood. Pert Masha smiles at me from her window across the street, and a bevy of girls pass me demurely, with modestly averted gaze, and then call back saucily, in thinly disguised voices. Again I am with my playmates, trailing the schoolgirls on their way to the river, and we chuckle gleefully at their affright and confusion, as they discover the eyes glued to the peep-holes we had cut in the booth. Inwardly I resent Nadya's bathing in her shirt, and in revenge dive beneath the boards, rising to the surface in the midst of the girls, who run to cover in shame and terror. But I grow indignant at Vainka who badgers the girls with "Tsiba,* tsiba, ba-aa!" and I soundly thrash Kolya for shouting nasty epithets across the school yard at little Nunya, whom I secretly adore.

But the note of later days returns again and again, and the scenes of youth recede into their dim frames. Clearer and more frequently appear Sonya and Luba, and the little sweetheart of my first months in America. What a goose she was! She would not embrace me, because it's a great sin, unless one is married. But how slyly she managed to arrange kissing games at the Sunday gatherings at her home, and always lose to me! She must be quite a woman now, with a husband, children . . . Quickly she flits by, the recollection even of her name lost in the glow of Anarchist emotionalism and the fervent enthusiasm of my Orchard Street days. There flames the light that irradiates the vague long-

---

* Goat: derisively applied to schoolgirls.

ings of my Russian youth, and gives rapt interpretation to obscurely pulsating idealism. It sheds the halo of illuminating justification upon my blindly rebellious spirit, and visualizes my dreams on the sunlit mountains. The sordid misery of my "greenhorn" days assumes a new aspect. Ah, the wretchedness of those first years in America! . . . . And still Time's woof and warp unroll the tapestry of life in the New World, its joys and heart-throbs. I stand a lone stranger, bewildered by the flurry of Castle Garden, yet strong with hope and courage to carve my fate in freedom. The Tsar is far away, and the fear of his hated Cossacks is past. How inspiring is liberty! The very air breathes enthusiasm and strength, and with confident ardor I embrace the new life. I join the ranks of the world's producers, and glory in the full manhood conferred by the dignity of labor. I resent the derision of my adopted country on the part of my family abroad,—resent it hotly. I feel wronged by the charge of having disgraced my parents' respected name by turning "a low, dirty workingman." I combat their snobbishness vehemently, and revenge the indignity to labor by challenging comparison between the Old and the New World. Behold the glory of liberty and prosperity, the handiwork of a nation that honors labor! . . . The loom of Time keeps weaving. Lone and friendless, I struggle in the new land. Life in the tenements is sordid, the fate of the worker dreary. There is no "dignity of labor." Sweatshop bread is bitter. Oppression guards the golden promise, and servile brutality is the only earnest of success. Then like a clarion note in the desert sounds the call of the Ideal. Strong and rousing rolls the battle-cry of Revolution. Like a flash in the night, it illumines my groping. My life becomes full of new meaning and interest, translated into the struggle of a world's emancipa-

tion. Fedya joins me, and together we are absorbed in
the music of the new humanity.

It is all far, far—yet every detail is sharply etched
upon my memory. Swiftly pass before me the years of
complete consecration to the movement, the self-im-
posed poverty and sacrifices, the feverish tide of agitation in the wake of the Chicago martyrdom, the evenings of spirited debate, the nights of diligent study.
And over all loom the Fridays in the little dingy hall
in the Ghetto, where the handful of Russian refugees
gather; where bold imprecations are thundered against
the tyranny and injustice of the existing, and winged
words prophesy the near approach of a glorious Dawn.
Beshawled women, and men, long-coated and piously
bearded, steal into the hall after synagogue prayers, and
listen with wondering eyes, vainly striving to grasp the
strange Jewish, so perplexedly interspersed with the
alien words of the new evangel. How our hearts rejoice, as, with exaggerated deference, we eagerly encourage the diffident questioner, "Do you really mean—
may the good Lord forgive me—there is no one in
heaven above?" . . . Late in the evening the meeting
resolves into small groups, heatedly contending over
the speaker's utterances, the select circle finally adjourn-
ing to "the corner." The obscure little tea room resounds with the joust of learning and wit. Fascinating is the feast of reason, impassioned the flow of soul,
as the passage-at-arms grows more heated with the
advance of the night. The alert-eyed host diplomatically
pacifies the belligerent factions, "Gentlemen, gentlemen,
s-sh! The police station is just across the street." There
is a lull in the combat. The angry opponents frown at
each other, and in the interim the Austrian Student in his
mellow voice begins an interminable story of personal

reminiscence, apropos of nothing and starting nowhere, but intensely absorbing. With sparkling eyes he holds us spellbound, relating the wonderful journey, taking us through the Nevsky in St. Petersburg, thence to the Caucasus, to engage in the blood-feuds of the Tcherkessi; or, enmeshed in a perilous flirtation with an Albanian beauty in a Moslem harem, he descants on the philosophy of Mohammed, imperceptibly shifting the scene to the Nile to hunt the hippopotamus, and suddenly interrupting the amazing adventures by introducing an acquaintance of the evening, "My excellent friend, the coming great Italian virtuoso, from Odessa, gentlemen.   He will entertain us with an aria from *Trovatore*."   But the circle is not in a musical mood: some one challenges the Student's familiarity with the Moslem philosophy, and the Twin hints at the gossiped intimacy of the Austrian with Christian missionaries.   There are protestations, and loud clamor for an explanation.   The Student smilingly assents, and presently he is launched upon the Chinese sea, in the midst of a strange caravan, trading tea at Yachta, and aiding a political to escape to Vladivostok. . . . The night pales before the waking sun, the Twin yawns, and I am drowsy with—

"Cof-fee? Want coffee? Hey, git up there! Didn't you hear th' bell?"

CHAPTER XVI

THE WARDEN'S THREAT

I

THE dying sun grows pale with haze and fog. Slowly the dark-gray line undulates across the shop, and draws its sinuous length along the gloaming yard. The shadowy waves cleave the thickening mist, vibrate ghostlike, and are swallowed in the yawning blackness of the cell-house.

"Aleck, Aleck!" I hear an excited whisper behind me, "quick, plant it. The screw's goin' t' frisk* me."

Something small and hard is thrust into my coat pocket. The guard in front stops short, suspiciously scanning the passing men.

"Break ranks!"

The overseer approaches me. "You are wanted in the office, Berk."

The Warden, blear-eyed and sallow, frowns as I am led in.

"What have you got on you?" he demands, abruptly.

"I don't understand you."

"Yes, you do. Have you money on you?"

"I have not."

"Who sends clandestine mail for you?"

"What mail?"

---

* Search.

"The letter published in the Anarchist sheet in New York."

I feel greatly relieved. The letter in question passed through official channels.

"It went through the Chaplain's hands," I reply, boldly.

"It isn't true. Such a letter could never pass Mr. Milligan. Mr. Cosson," he turns to the guard, "fetch the newspaper from my desk."

The Warden's hands tremble as he points to the marked item. "Here it is! You talk of revolution, and comrades, and Anarchism. Mr. Milligan never saw *that*, I'm sure. It's a nice thing for the papers to say that you are editing—from the prison, mind you—editing an Anarchist sheet in New York."

"You can't believe everything the papers say," I protest.

"Hm, this time the papers, hm, hm, may be right," the Deputy interposes. "They surely didn't make the story, hm, hm, out of whole cloth."

"They often do," I retort. "Didn't they write that I tried to jump over the wall—it's about thirty feet high—and that the guard shot me in the leg?"

A smile flits across the Warden's face. Impulsively I blurt out:

"Was the story inspired, perhaps?"

"Silence!" the Warden thunders. "You are not to speak, unless addressed, remember. Mr. McPane, please search him."

The long, bony fingers slowly creep over my neck and shoulders, down my arms and body, pressing in my armpits, gripping my legs, covering every spot, and immersing me in an atmosphere of clamminess. The loathsome touch sickens me, but I rejoice in the thought of my security: I have nothing incriminating about me.

Suddenly the snakelike hand dips into my coat pocket.

"Hm, what's this?" He unwraps a small, round object. "A knife, Captain."

"Let me see!" I cry in amazement.

"Stand back!" the Warden commands. "This knife has been stolen from the shoe shop. On whom did you mean to use it?"

"Warden, I didn't even know I had it. A fellow dropped it into my pocket as we—"

"That'll do. You're not so clever as you think."

"It's a conspiracy!" I cry.

He lounges calmly in the armchair, a peculiar smile dancing in his eyes.

"Well, what have you got to say?"

"It's a put-up job."

"Explain yourself."

"Some one threw this thing into my pocket as we were coming—"

"Oh, we've already heard that. It's too fishy."

"You searched me for money and secret letters—"

"That will do now. Mr. McPane, what is the sentence for the possession of a dangerous weapon?"

"Warden," I interrupt, "it's no weapon. The blade is only half an inch, and—"

"Silence! I spoke to Mr. McPane."

"Hm, three days, Captain."

"Take him down."

In the storeroom I am stripped of my suit of dark gray, and again clad in the hateful stripes. Coatless and shoeless, I am led through hallways and corridors, down a steep flight of stairs, and thrown into the dungeon.

.   .   .   .

Total darkness. The blackness is massive, palpable,—

I feel its hand upon my head, my face. I dare not move, lest a misstep thrust me into the abyss. I hold my hand close to my eyes—I feel the touch of my lashes upon it, but I cannot see its outline. Motionless I stand on one spot, devoid of all sense of direction. The silence is sinister; it seems to me I can hear it. Only now and then the hasty scrambling of nimble feet suddenly rends the stillness, and the gnawing of invisible river rats haunts the fearful solitude.

Slowly the blackness pales. It ebbs and melts; out of the sombre gray, a wall looms above; the silhouette of a door rises dimly before me, sloping upward and growing compact and impenetrable.

The hours drag in unbroken sameness. Not a sound reaches me from the cell-house. In the maddening quiet and darkness I am bereft of all consciousness of time, save once a day when the heavy rattle of keys apprises me of the morning: the dungeon is unlocked, and the silent guards hand me a slice of bread and a cup of water. The double doors fall heavily to, the steps grow fainter and die in the distance, and all is dark again in the dungeon.

The numbness of death steals upon my soul. The floor is cold and clammy, the gnawing grows louder and nearer, and I am filled with dread lest the starving rats attack my bare feet. I snatch a few unconscious moments leaning against the door; and then again I pace the cell, striving to keep awake, wondering whether it be night or day, yearning for the sound of a human voice.

Utterly forsaken! Cast into the stony bowels of the underground, the world of man receding, leaving no trace behind. . . . Eagerly I strain my ear—only the ceaseless, fearful gnawing. I clutch the bars in despera-

tion—a hollow echo mocks the clanking iron. My hands
tear violently at the door—"Ho, there! Any one here?"
All is silent. Nameless terrors quiver in my mind, weaving nightmares of mortal dread and despair. Fear shapes
convulsive thoughts: they rage in wild tempest, then
calm, and again rush through time and space in a rapid
succession of strangely familiar scenes, wakened in my
slumbering consciousness.

Exhausted and weary I droop against the wall. A
slimy creeping on my face startles me in horror, and
again I pace the cell. I feel cold and hungry. Am I
forgotten? Three days must have passed, and more.
Have they forgotten me? . . .

The clank of keys sends a thrill of joy to my heart.
My tomb will open—oh, to see the light, and breathe the
air again. . . .

"Officer, isn't my time up yet?"

"What's your hurry? You've only been here one
day."

The doors fall to. Ravenously I devour the bread,
so small and thin, just a bite. Only *one* day! Despair
enfolds me like a pall. Faint with anguish, I sink to the
floor.

II

The change from the dungeon to the ordinary cell
is a veritable transformation. The sight of the human
form fills me with delight, the sound of voices is sweet
music. I feel as if I had been torn from the grip of
death when all hope had fled me,—caught on the very
brink, as it were, and restored to the world of the living.
How bright the sun, how balmy the air! In keen
sensuousness I stretch out on the bed. The tick is soiled,
the straw protrudes in places, but it is luxury to rest,

secure from the vicious river rats and the fierce vermin. It is almost liberty, freedom!

But in the morning I awake in great agony. My eyes throb with pain; every joint of my body is on the rack. The blankets had been removed from the dungeon; three days and nights I lay on the bare stone. It is unnecessarily cruel to deprive me of my spectacles, in pretended anxiety lest I commit suicide with them. It is very touching, this solicitude for my safety, in view of the flimsy pretext to punish me. Some hidden motive must be actuating the Warden. But what can it be? Probably they will not keep me long in the cell. When I am returned to work, I shall learn the truth.

The days pass in vain expectation. The continuous confinement is becoming distressing. I miss the little comforts I have lost by the removal to the "single" cell, considerably smaller than my previous quarters. My library, also, has disappeared, and the pictures I had so patiently collected for the decoration of the walls. The cell is bare and cheerless, the large card of ugly-printed rules affording no relief from the irritating whitewash. The narrow space makes exercise difficult: the necessity of turning at every second and third step transforms walking into a series of contortions. But some means must be devised to while away the time. I pace the floor, counting the seconds required to make ten turns. I recollect having heard that five miles constitutes a healthy day's walk. At that rate I should make 3,771 turns, the cell measuring seven feet in length. I divide the exercise into three parts, adding a few extra laps to make sure of five miles. Carefully I count, and am overcome by a sense of calamity when the peal of the gong confuses my numbers. I must begin over again.

The change of location has interrupted communication with my comrades. I am apprehensive of the fate of the *Prison Blossoms:* strict surveillance makes the prospect of restoring connections doubtful. I am assigned to the ground floor, my cell being but a few feet distant from the officers' desk at the yard door. Watchful eyes are constantly upon me; it is impossible for any prisoner to converse with me. The rangeman alone could aid me in reaching my friends, but I have been warned against him: he is a "stool" who has earned his position as trusty by spying upon the inmates. I can expect no help from him; but perhaps the coffee-boy may prove of service.

I am planning to approach the man, when I am informed that prisoners from the hosiery department are locked up on the upper gallery. By means of the waste pipe, I learn of the developments during my stay in the dungeon. The discontent of the shop employees with the insufficient rations was intensified by the arrival of a wagon-load of bad meat. The stench permeated the yard, and several men were punished for passing uncomplimentary remarks about the food. The situation was aggravated by an additional increase of the task. The knitters and loopers were on the verge of rebellion. Twice within the month had the task been enlarged. They sent to the Warden a request for a reduction; in reply came the appalling order for a further increase. Then a score of men struck. They remained in the cells, refusing to return to the shop unless the demand for better food and less work was complied with. With the aid of informers, the Warden conducted a quiet investigation. One by one the refractory prisoners were forced to submit. By a process of elimination the authorities sifted the situation, and now it is whispered about that a decision has been reached, placing responsibility for the unique episode of a strike in the prison.

An air of mystery hangs about the guards. Repeatedly I attempt to engage them in conversation, but the least reference to the strike seals their lips. I wonder at the peculiar looks they regard me with, when unexpectedly the cause is revealed.

III

It is Sunday noon. The rangeman pushes the dinner wagon along the tier. I stand at the door, ready to receive the meal. The overseer glances at me, then motions to the prisoner. The cart rolls past my cell.

"Officer," I call out, "you missed me."

"Smell the pot-pie, do you?"

"Where's my dinner?"

"You get none."

The odor of the steaming delicacy, so keenly looked forward to every second Sunday, reaches my nostrils and sharpens my hunger. I have eaten sparingly all week in expectation of the treat, and now— I am humiliated and enraged by being so unceremoniously deprived of the rare dinner. Angrily I rap the cup across the door; again and again I strike the tin against it, the successive falls from bar to bar producing a sharp, piercing clatter.

A guard hastens along. "Stop that damn racket," he commands. "What's the matter with you?"

"I didn't get dinner."

"Yes, you did."

"I did not."

"Well, I s'pose you don't deserve it."

As he turns to leave, my can crashes against the door—one, two, three—

"What t'hell do you want, eh?"

"I want to see the Warden."

"You can't see 'im. You better keep quiet now."

"I demand to see the Warden. He is supposed to visit us every day. He hasn't been around for weeks. I must see him now."

"If you don't shut up, I'll—

The Captain of the Block approaches.

"What do you want, Berkman?"

"I want to see the Warden."

"Can't see him. It's Sunday."

"Captain," I retort, pointing to the rules on the wall of the cell, "there is an excerpt here from the statutes of Pennsylvania, directing the Warden to visit each prisoner every day—"

"Never mind, now," he interrupts. "What do you want to see the Warden about?"

"I want to know why I got no dinner."

"Your name is off the list for the next four Sundays."

"What for?"

"That you'll have to ask the boss. I'll tell him you want to see him."

Presently the overseer returns, informing me in a confidential manner that he has induced "his Nibs" to grant me an audience. Admitted to the inner office, I find the Warden at the desk, his face flushed with anger.

"You are reported for disturbing the peace," he shouts at me.

"There is also, hm, hm, another charge against him," the Deputy interposes.

"Two charges," the Warden continues. "Disturbing the peace and making demands. How dare you demand?" he roars. "Do you know where you are?"

"I wanted to see you."

"It is not a question of what you want or don't want. Understand that clearly. You are to obey the rules implicitly."

"The rules direct you to visit—"

"Silence! What is your request?"

"I want to know why I am deprived of dinner."

"It is not, hm, for *you* to know. It is enough, hm, hm, that *we* know," the Deputy retorts.

"Mr. McPane," the Warden interposes, "I am going to speak plainly to him. From this day on," he turns to me, "you are on 'Pennsylvania diet' for four weeks. During that time no papers or books are permitted you. It will give you leisure to think over your behavior. I have investigated your conduct in the shop, and I am satisfied it was you who instigated the trouble there. You shall not have another chance to incite the men, even if you live as long as your sentence. But," he pauses an instant, then adds, threateningly, "but you may as well understand it now as later—your life is not worth the trouble you give us. Mark you well, whatever the cost, it will be at *your* expense. For the present you'll remain in solitary, where you cannot exert your pernicious influence. Officers, remove him to the 'basket.' "

CHAPTER XVII

THE "BASKET" CELL

Four weeks of "Pennsylvania diet" have reduced me almost to a skeleton. A slice of wheat bread with a cup of unsweetened black coffee is my sole meal, with twice a week dinner of vegetable soup, from which every trace of meat has been removed. Every Saturday I am conducted to the office, to be examined by the physician and weighed. The whole week I look forward to the brief respite from the terrible "basket" cell. The sight of the striped men scouring the floor, the friendly smile on a stealthily raised face as I pass through the hall, the strange blue of the sky, the sweet-scented aroma of the April morning—how quickly it is all over! But the seven deep breaths I slowly inhale on the way to the office, and the eager ten on my return, set my blood aglow with renewed life. For an instant my brain reels with the sudden rush of exquisite intoxication, and then—I am in the tomb again.

. . . .

The torture of the "basket" is maddening; the constant dusk is driving me blind. Almost no light or air reaches me through the close wire netting covering the barred door. The foul odor is stifling; it grips my throat with deathly hold. The walls hem me in; daily they press closer upon me, till the cell seems to contract, and I feel crushed in the coffin of stone. From every point the whitewashed sides glare at me, unyielding, inexorable, in confident assurance of their prey.

The darkness of despondency gathers day by day; the hand of despair weighs heavier. At night the screeching of a crow across the river ominously voices the black raven keeping vigil in my heart. The windows in the hallway quake and tremble in the furious wind. Bleak and desolate wakes the day—another day, then another—

Weak and apathetic I lie on the bed. Ever further recedes the world of the living. Still day follows night, and life is in the making, but I have no part in the pain and travail. Like a spark from the glowing furnace, flashing through the gloom, and swallowed in the darkness, I have been cast upon the shores of the forgotten. No sound reaches me from the island prison where beats the fervent heart of the Girl, no ray of hope falls across the bars of desolation. But on the threshold of Nirvana life recoils; in the very bowels of torment it cries out *to be!* Persecution feeds the fires of defiance, and nerves my resolution. Were I an ordinary prisoner, I should not care to suffer all these agonies. To what purpose, with my impossible sentence? But my Anarchist ideals and traditions rise in revolt against the vampire gloating over its prey. No, I shall not disgrace the Cause, I shall not grieve my comrades by weak surrender! I will fight and struggle, and not be daunted by threat or torture.

.   .   .   .

With difficulty I walk to the office for the weekly weighing. My step falters as I approach the scales, and I sway dizzily. As through a mist I see the doctor bending over me, his head pressing against my body. Somehow I reach the "basket," mildly wondering why I did not feel the cold air. Perhaps they did not take me through the yard— Is it the Block Captain's voice? "What did you say?"

"Return to your old cell. You're on full diet now."

CHAPTER XVIII

THE SOLITARY

I

Direct to Box A 7,
Allegheny City, Pa.
March 25, 1894.

DEAR FEDYA:

This letter is somewhat delayed: for certain reasons I missed mail-day last month. Prison life, too, has its ups and downs, and just now I am on the down side. We are cautioned to refrain from referring to local affairs; therefore I can tell you only that I am in solitary, without work. I don't know how long I am to be kept "locked up." It may be a month, or a year, but I hope it will not be the latter.

I was not permitted to receive the magazines and delicacies you sent. . . . We may subscribe for the daily papers, and you can easily imagine how religiously I read them from headline to the last ad: they keep me in touch, to some extent, with the living. . . . Blessed be the shades of Guttenberg! Hugo and Zola, even Gogol and Turgenev, are in the library. It is like meeting an old friend in a strange land to find our own Bazarov discoursing—in English. . . . . Page after page unfolds the past— the solitary is forgotten, the walls melt away, and again I roam with Leather Stocking in the primitive forest, or sorrow with poor Oliver Twist. But the "Captain's Daughter" irritates me, and Pugatchev, the rebellious soul, has turned a caricature in the awkward hands of the translator. And now comes Tarass Bulba—is it our own Tarass, the fearless warrior, the scourge of Turk and Tartar? How grotesque is the brave old hetman storming maledictions against the hated Moslems—in long-winded German periods! Exasperated and offended, I turn my back upon the desecration, and open a book of poems. But instead of the requested Robert Burns, I find a volume of Wordsworth. Posies bloom on his pages, and rosebuds scent his rhymes, but the pains of the world's labor wake no chord in his soul. . . . Science and romance, history and travel, religion and philosophy— all come trooping into the cell in irrelevant sequence, for the allowance of only one book at a time limits my choice. The variety of reading affords rich material for reflection, and helps to perfect my English. But some passage in the "Starry Heavens" suddenly brings me to earth, and the present is illumined with the direct perception of despair, and the anguished question surges through my mind, What is the use of all this study and learning? And then—but why harrow you with this tenor.

I did not mean to say all this when I began. It cannot be undone: the sheet must be accounted for. Therefore it will be mailed to you. But I know, dear friend, you also are not bedded on roses. And the poor Sailor?

My space is all.

ALEX.

II

The lengthening chain of days in the solitary drags its heavy links through every change of misery. The cell is suffocating with the summer heat; rarely does the fresh breeze from the river steal a caress upon my face. On the pretext of a "draught" the unfriendly guard has closed the hall windows opposite my cell. Not a breath of air is stirring. The leaden hours of the night are insufferable with the foul odor of the perspiration and excrement of a thousand bodies. Sleepless, I toss on the withered mattress. The ravages of time and the weight of many inmates have demoralized it out of all semblance of a bedtick. But the Block Captain persistently ignores my request for new straw, directing me to "shake it up a bit." I am fearful of repeating the experiment: the clouds of dust almost strangled me; for days the cell remained hazy with the powdered filth. Impatiently I await the morning: the yard door will open before the marching lines, and the fresh air be wafted past my cell. I shall stand ready to receive the precious tonic that is to give me life this day.

And when the block has belched forth its striped prey, and silence mounts its vigil, I may improve a favorable moment to exchange a greeting with Johnny Davis. The young prisoner is in solitary on the tier above me. Thrice his request for a "high gear" machine has been refused, and the tall youth forced to work doubled over a low table. Unable to exert his best efforts in the cramped position, Johnny has repeatedly been punished with the dungeon. Last week he suffered a hemorrhage; all through the night resounds his hollow cough. Desperate with the dread of consumption, Johnny has refused to return to work. The Warden, relenting in a kindly mood, permitted him to resume his original high machine. But the boy has grown obdurate: he is determined not to go back to the shop whose officer caused him so much trouble. The prison discipline takes no cognizance of the situation. Regularly every Monday the torture is repeated: the youth is called before the Deputy, and assigned to the hosiery department; the unvarying refusal is followed by the dungeon, and then Johnny is placed in the solitary, to be cited again before the Warden the ensuing Monday. I chafe at my helplessness to aid the boy. His course is suicidal, but the least suggestion of yielding enrages him. "I'll die before I give in," he told me.

From whispered talks through the waste pipe I learn the sad story of his young life. He is nineteen, with a sentence of five years before him. His father, a brakeman, was killed in a railroad collision. The suit for damages was dragged through years of litigation, leaving the widow destitute. Since the age of fourteen young Johnny had to support the whole family. Lately he was employed as the driver of a delivery wagon, associating with a rough element that gradually drew him into gambling. One day a shortage of twelve dollars was discovered in the boy's accounts: the mills of justice began to grind, and Johnny was speedily clad in stripes.

In vain I strive to absorb myself in the library book. The shoddy heroes of Laura Jean wake no response in my heart; the superior beings of Corelli, communing with mysterious heavenly circles, stalk by, strange and unhuman. Here, in the cell above me, cries and moans the terrible tragedy of Reality. What a monstrous thing it is that the whole power of the commonwealth, all the machinery of government, is concentrated to crush this unfortunate atom! Innocently guilty, too, the poor boy is. Ensnared by the gaming spirit of the time, the feeble creature of vitiating environment, his fate is sealed by a moment of weakness. Yet his deviation from the path of established ethics is but a faint reflectioı of the lives of the men that decreed his doom. The hypocrisy of organized Society! The very foundation of its existence rests upon the negation and defiance of every professed principle of right and justice. Every feature of its face is a caricature, a travesty upon the semblance of truth; the whole life of humanity a mockery of the very name. Political mastery based on violence and jesuitry; industry gathering the harvest of human blood; commerce ascendant on the ruins of manhod—such is the morality of civilization. And over the edifice of this stupendous perversion the Law sits enthroned, and Religion weaves the spell of awe, and varnishes right and puzzles wrong, and bids the cowering helot intone, "Thy will be done!"

Devoutly Johnny goes to Church, and prays forgiveness for his "sins." The prosecutor was "very

hard" on him, he told me. The blind mole perceives
only the immediate, and is embittered against the persons directly responsible for his long imprisonment.
But greater minds have failed fully to grasp the
iniquity of the established. My beloved Burns, even,
seems inadequate, powerfully as he moves my spirit
with his deep sympathy for the poor, the oppressed.
But "man's inhumanity to man" is not the last word.
The truth lies deeper. It is economic slavery, the
savage struggle for a crumb, that has converted
mankind into wolves and sheep. In liberty and com-
munism, none would have the will or the power "to make
countless thousands mourn." Verily, it is the system,
rather than individuals, that is the source of pollution
and degradation. My prison-house environment is
but another manifestation of the Midas-hand, whose
cursed touch turns everything to the brutal service of
Mammon. Dullness fawns upon cruelty for advancement; with savage joy the shop foreman cracks his whip,
for his meed of the gold-transmuted blood. The famished bodies in stripes, the agonized brains reeling
in the dungeon night, the men buried in "basket" and
solitary,—what human hand would turn the key upon
a soul in utter darkness, but for the dread of a like fate,
and the shadow it casts before? This nightmare is but
an intensified replica of the world beyond, the larger
prison locked with the levers of Greed, guarded by the
spawn of Hunger.

My mind reverts insistently to the life outside. It
is a Herculean task to rouse Apathy to the sordidness
of its misery. Yet if the People would but realize the
depths of their degradation and be informed of the
means of deliverance, how joyously they would embrace
Anarchy! Quick and decisive would be the victory of

the workers against the handful of their despoilers. An hour of sanity, freed from prejudice and superstition, and the torch of liberty would flame 'round the world, and the banner of equality and brotherhood be planted upon the hills of a regenerated humanity. Ah, if the world would but pause for one short while, and understand, and become free!

Involuntarily I am reminded of the old rabbinical lore: only one instant of righteousness, and Messiah would come upon earth. The beautiful promise had strongly appealed to me in the days of childhood. The merciful God requires so little of us, I had often pondered. Why will we not abstain from sin and evil, for just "the twinkling of an eye-lash"? For weeks I went about weighed down with the grief of impenitent Israel refusing to be saved, my eager brain pregnant with projects of hastening the deliverance. Like a divine inspiration came the solution: at the stroke of the noon hour, on a preconcerted day, all the men and women of the Jewry throughout the world should bow in prayer. For a single stroke of time, all at once—behold the Messiah come! In agonizing perplexity I gazed at my Hebrew tutor shaking his head. How his kindly smile quivered dismay into my thrilling heart! The children of Israel could not be saved thus,—he spoke sadly. Nay, not even in the most circumspect manner, affording our people in the farthest corners of the earth time to prepare for the solemn moment. The Messiah will come, the good tutor kindly consoled me. It had been promised. "But the hour hath not arrived," he quoted; "no man hath the power to hasten the steps of the Deliverer."

With a sense of sobering sadness, I think of the new hope, the revolutionary Messiah. Truly the old rabbi was wise beyond his ken: it hath been given to no man to

hasten the march of delivery. Out of the People's need,
from the womb of their suffering, must be born the hour
of redemption. Necessity, Necessity alone, with its iron
heel, will spur numb Misery to effort, and waken the
living dead. The process is tortuously slow, but the
gestation of a new humanity cannot be hurried by impatience. We must bide our time, meanwhile preparing the
workers for the great upheaval. The errors of the past
are to be guarded against: always has apparent victory
been divested of its fruits, and paralyzed into defeat,
because the People were fettered by their respect for
property, by the superstitious awe of authority, and by
reliance upon leaders. These ghosts must be cast out,
and the torch of reason lighted in the darkness of men's
minds, ere blind rebellion can rend the midway clouds
of defeat, and sight the glory of the Social Revolution,
and the beyond.

III

A heavy nightmare oppresses my sleep. Confused
sounds ring in my ears, and beat upon my head. I wake
in nameless dread. The cell-house is raging with uproar:
crash after crash booms through the hall; it thunders
against the walls of the cell, then rolls like some
monstrous drum along the galleries, and abruptly ceases.
In terror I cower on the bed. All is deathly still.
Timidly I look around. The cell is in darkness, and only
a faint gas light flickers unsteadily in the corridor.
Suddenly a cry cuts the silence, shrill and unearthly,
bursting into wild laughter. And again the fearful
thunder, now bellowing from the cell above, now muttering menacingly in the distance, then dying with a growl.
And all is hushed again, and only the unearthly laughter
rings through the hall.

"Johnny, Johnny!" I call in alarm. "Johnny!"

"Th' kid's in th' hole," comes hoarsely through the privy. "This is Horsethief. Is that you, Aleck?"

"Yes. What *is* it, Bob?"

"Some one breakin' up housekeepin'."

"Who?"

"Can't tell. May be Smithy."

"What Smithy, Bob?"

"Crazy Smith, on crank row. Look out now, they're comin'."

The heavy doors of the rotunda groan on their hinges. Shadowlike, giant figures glide past my cell. They walk inaudibly, felt-soled and portentous, the long riot clubs rigid at their sides. Behind them others, and then the Warden, a large revolver gleaming in his hand. With bated breath I listen, conscious of the presence of other men at the doors. Suddenly wailing and wild laughter pierce the night: there is the rattling of iron, violent scuffling, the sickening thud of a falling body, and all is quiet. Noiselessly the bread cart flits by, the huge shadows bending over the body stretched on the boards.

.   .   .   .

The gong booms the rising hour. The morning sun glints a ray upon the bloody trail in the hall, and hides behind the gathering mist. A squad of men in gray and black is marched from the yard. They kneel on the floor, and with sand and water scour the crimson flag-stones.

With great relief I learn that "Crazy Smithy" is not dead. He will recover, the rangeman assures me. The doctor bandaged the man's wounds, and then the prisoner, still unconscious, was dragged to the dungeon. Little by little I glean his story from my informant. Smith has been insane, at times violently, ever since his imprisonment, about four years ago. His "partner," Burns, has also become deranged through worry over his sentence of twenty-five years. His madness assumed such revolting expression that the authorities caused his commitment to the insane asylum. But Smith remains on "crank row," the Warden insisting that he is shamming to gain an opportunity to escape.

IV

The rare snatches of conversation with the old range-man are events in the monotony of the solitary. Owing to the illness of Bob, communication with my friends is almost entirely suspended. In the forced idleness the hours grow heavy and languid, the days drag in unvarying sameness. By violent efforts of will I strangle the recurring thought of my long sentence, and seek forgetfulness in reading. Volume after volume passes through my hands, till my brain is steeped with the printed word. Page by page I recite the history of the Holy Church, the lives of the Fathers and the Saints, or read aloud, to hear a human voice, the mythology of Greece and India, mingling with it, for the sake of variety, a few chapters from Mill and Spencer. But in the midst of an intricate passage in the "Unknowable," or in the heart of a difficult mathematical problem, I suddenly become aware of my pencil drawing familiar figures on the library slate: $22 \times 12 = 264$. What is this, I wonder. And immediately I proceed, in semiconscious manner, to finish the calculation:

$$264 \times 30 = 7,920 \text{ days.}$$
$$7,920 \times 24 = 190,080 \text{ hours.}$$
$$190,080 \times 60 = 11,404,800 \text{ minutes.}$$
$$11,404,800 \times 60 = 684,288,000 \text{ seconds.}$$

But the next moment I am aghast at the realization

that my computation allows only 30 days per month, whereas the year consists of 365, sometimes even of 366 days. And again I repeat the process, multiplying 22 by 365, and am startled to find that I have almost 700,000,000 seconds to pass in the solitary. From the official calendar alongside of the rules the cheering promise faces me, Good conduct shortens time. But I have been repeatedly reported and punished—they will surely deprive me of the commutation. With great care I figure out my allowance: one month on the first year, one on the second; two on the third and fourth; three on the fifth, sixth, seventh, eighth, and ninth; four months' "good time" on each succeeding year. I shall therefore have to serve fifteen years and three months in this place, and then eleven months in the workhouse. I have been here now two years. It still leaves me 14 years and 2 months, or more than 5,170 days. Appalled by the figures, I pace the cell in agitation. It is hopeless! It is folly to expect to survive such a sentence, especially in view of the Warden's persecution, and the petty tyranny of the keepers.

Thoughts of suicide and escape, wild fancies of unforeseen developments in the world at large that will somehow result in my liberation, all struggle in confusion, leaving me faint and miserable. My absolute isolation holds no promise of deliverance; the days of illness and suffering fill me with anguish. With a sharp pang I observe the thinning of my hair. The evidence of physical decay rouses the fear of mental collapse, insanity. . . . I shudder at the terrible suggestion, and lash myself into a fever of irritation with myself, the rangeman, and every passing convict, my heart seething with hatred of the Warden, the guards, the judge, and that unembodied, shapeless, but inexorable and merciless, thing—the world. In the moments of reacting calm I apply myself to philosophy and science, determinedly, with the desperation born of horror. But the dread ghost is ever before me; it follows me up and down the cell, mocks me with the wild laughter of "Crazy Smith" in the stillness of the night, and with the moaning and wailing of my neighbor suddenly gone mad.

CHAPTER XIX

MEMORY-GUESTS

OFTEN the Chaplain pauses at my door, and speaks words of encouragement. I feel deeply moved by his sympathy, but my revolutionary traditions forbid the expression of my emotions: a cog in the machinery of oppression, he might mistake my gratitude for the obsequiousness of the fawning convict. But I hope he feels my appreciation in the simple "thank you." It is kind of him to lend me books from his private library, and occasionally also permit me an extra sheet of writing paper. Correspondence with the Girl and the Twin, and the unfrequent exchange of notes with my comrades, are the only links that still bind me to the living. I feel weary and life-worn, indifferent to the trivial incidents of existence that seem to hold such exciting interest for the other inmates. "Old Sammy," the rangeman, grown nervous with the approach of liberty, invents a hundred opportunities to unburden his heart. All day long he limps from cell to cell, pretending to scrub the doorsills or dust the bars, meanwhile chattering volubly to the solitaries. Listlessly I suffer the oft-repeated recital of the "news," elaborately discussed and commented upon with impassioned earnestness. He interrupts his anathemas upon the "rotten food" and the "thieving murderers," to launch into enthusiastic details of the meal he will enjoy on the day of release, the imprisoned friends he will remember with towels and

handkerchiefs. But he grows pensive at the mention of
the folks at home: the "old woman" died of a broken
heart, the boys have not written a line in three years.
He fears they have sold the little farmhouse, and flown
to the city. But the joy of coming freedom drives away
the sad thought, and he mumbles hopefully, "I'll see,
I'll see," and rejoices in being "alive and still good for
a while," and then abruptly changes the conversation, and
relates minutely how "that poor, crazy Dick" was yesterday found hanging in the cell, and he the first to discover
him, and to help the guards cut him down. And last
week he was present when the physician tried to revive
"the little dago," and if the doctor had only returned
quicker from the theatre, poor Joe might have been
saved. He "took a fit" and "the screws jest let 'im lay;
'waitin' for the doc,' they says. Hope they don't kill *me*
yet," he comments, hobbling away.

The presence of death daunts the thought of self-
destruction. Ever stronger asserts itself the love of life;
the will to be roots deeper. But the hope of escape
recedes with the ebbing of my vitality. The constant
harassing has forced the discontinuation of the *Blossoms*.
The eccentric Warden seems to have conceived a great
fear of an Anarchist conspiracy: special orders have
been issued, placing the trio under extraordinary
surveillance. Suspecting our clandestine correspondence,
yet unable to trace it, the authorities have decided to
separate us in a manner excluding all possibility of communication. Apparently I am to be continued in the
solitary indefinitely, while Nold is located in the South
Wing, and Bauer removed to the furthest cell on an
upper gallery in the North Block. The precious magazine is suspended, and only the daring of the faithful
"Horsethief" enables us to exchange an occasional note.

Amid the fantastic shapes cast by the dim candle light, I pass the long winter evenings. The prison day between 7 A. M. and 9 P. M. I divide into three parts, devoting four hours each to exercise, English, and reading, the remaining two hours occupied with meals and "cleaning up." Surrounded by grammars and dictionaries, borrowed from the Chaplain, I absorb myself in a sentence of Shakespeare, dissecting each word, studying origin and derivation, analyzing prefix and suffix. I find moments of exquisite pleasure in tracing some simple expression through all the vicissitudes of its existence, to its Latin or Greek source. In the history of the corresponding epoch, I seek the people's joys and tragedies, contemporary with the fortunes of the word. Philology, with the background of history, leads me into the pastures of mythology and comparative religion, through the mazes of metaphysics and warring philosophies, to rationalism and evolutionary science.

Oblivious of my environment, I walk with the disciples of Socrates, flee Athens with the persecuted Diagoras, "the Atheist," and listen in ecstasy to the sweet-voiced lute of Arion; or with Suetonius I pass in review the Twelve Caesars, and weep with the hostages swelling the triumph of the Eternal City. But on the very threshold of Cleopatra's boudoir, about to enter with the intrepid Mark Antony, I am met by three giant slaves with the command:

"A 7, hands up! Step out to be searched!"

For days my enfeebled nerves quiver with the shock. With difficulty I force myself to pick up the thread of my life amid the spirits of the past. The placid waters have been disturbed, and all the miasma of the quagmire seethes toward the surface, and fills my cup with the bitterness of death.

The release of "Old Sammy" stirs me to the very depths. Many prisoners have come and gone during my stay; with some I merely touched hands as they passed in the darkness and disappeared, leaving no trace in my existence. But the old rangeman, with his smiling eyes and fervid optimism, has grown dear to me. He shared with me his hopes and fears, divided his extra slice of cornbread, and strove to cheer me in his own homely manner. I miss his genial presence. Something has gone out of my life with him, leaving a void, saddening, gnawing. In thought I follow my friend through the gates of the prison, out into the free, the alluring "outside," the charmed circle that holds the promise of life and joy and liberty. Like a horrible nightmare the sombre walls fade away, and only a dark shadow vibrates in my memory, like a hidden menace, faint, yet ever-present and terrible. The sun glows brilliant in the heavens, shell-like wavelets float upon the azure, and sweet odors are everywhere about me. All the longing of my soul wells up with violent passion, and in a sudden transport of joy I fling myself upon the earth, and weep and kiss it in prayerful bliss. . . . .

The candle sputters, hisses, and dies. I sit in the dark. Silently lifts the veil of time. The little New York flat rises before me. The Girl is returning home, the roses of youth grown pallid amid the shadows of death. Only her eyes glow firmer and deeper, a look of challenge in her saddened face. As on an open page, I read the suffering of her prison experience, the sharper lines of steadfast purpose. . . . The joys and sorrows of our mutual past unfold before me, and again I live in the old surroundings. The memorable scene of our first meeting, in the little café at Sachs', projects

clearly. The room is chilly in the November dusk, as
I return from work and secure my accustomed place.
One by one the old habitués drop in, and presently I am
in a heated discussion with two Russian refugees at the
table opposite. The door opens, and a young woman
enters. Well-knit, with the ruddy vigor of youth, she
diffuses an atmosphere of strength and vitality. I
wonder who the newcomer may be. Two years in the
movement have familiarized me with the personnel of
the revolutionary circles of the metropolis. This girl
is evidently a stranger; I am quite sure I have never
met her at our gatherings. I motion to the passing
proprietor. He smiles, anticipating my question. "You
want to know who the young lady is?" he whispers;
"I'll see, I'll see."—Somehow I find myself at her table.
Without constraint, we soon converse like old acquaintances, and I learn that she left her home in Rochester
to escape the stifling provincial atmosphere. She is
a dressmaker, and hopes to find work in New York.
I like her simple, frank confidence; the "comrade" on her
lips thrills me. She is one of us, then. With a sense
of pride in the movement, I enlarge upon the activities
of our circle. There are important meetings she ought
to attend, many people to meet; Hasselmann is conducting a course in sociology; Schultze is giving splendid
lectures. "Have you heard Most?" I ask suddenly.
"No? You must hear our Grand Old Man. He speaks
to-morrow; will you come with me?"—Eagerly I look
forward to the next evening, and hasten to the café.
It is frosty outdoors as I walk the narrow, dark streets
in animated discussion with "Comrade Rochester." The
ancient sidewalks are uneven and cracked, in spots
crusted with filth. As we cross Delancey Street, the girl
slips and almost falls, when I catch her in my arms just
in time to prevent her head striking the curbstone. "You

have saved my life," she smiles at me, her eyes dancing
vivaciously. . . . . With great pride I introduce my new
friend to the *inteligentzia* of the Ghetto, among the
exiles of the colony. Ah, the exaltation, the joy of
being! . . . . The whole history of revolutionary Russia
is mirrored in our circles; every shade of temperamental
Nihilism and political view is harbored there. I see
Hartman, surrounded by the halo of conspirative mystery; at his side is the *velikorussian*, with flowing beard
and powerful frame, of the older generation of the
narodovoiltzy; and there is Schewitsch, big and broad of
feature, the typical *dvoryanin* who has cast in his lot
with the proletariat. The line of contending faiths is
not drawn sharply in the colony: Cahan is among us,
stentorian of voice and bristling with aggressive vitality;
Solotaroff, his pale student face peculiarly luminous;
Miller, poetically eloquent, and his strangely-named
brother Brandes, looking consumptive from his experience in the Odessa prison. Timmermann and
Aleinikoff, Rinke and Weinstein—all are united in
enthusiasm for the common cause. Types from Turgenev and Chernishevski, from Dostoyevski and Ne-
krassov, mingle in the seeming confusion of reality, in-
dividualized with varying shade and light. And other
elements are in the colony, the splashed quivers of the
simmering waters of Tsardom. Shapes in the making,
still being kneaded in the mold of old tradition and
new environment. Who knows what shall be the amal-
gam, some day to be recast by the master hand of a
new Turgenev? . . .

Often the solitary hours are illumined by scenes of
the past. With infinite detail I live again through the
years of the inspiring friendship that held the Girl, the
Twin, and myself in the closest bonds of revolutionary

aspiration and personal intimacy. How full of interest and rich promise was life in those days, so far away, when after the hours of humiliating drudgery in the factory I would hasten to the little room in Suffolk Street! Small and narrow, with its diminutive table and solitary chair, the cage-like bedroom would be transfigured into the sanctified chamber of fate, holding the balance of the world's weal. Only two could sit on the little cot, the third on the rickety chair. And if somebody else called, we would stand around the room, filling the air with the glowing hope of our young hearts, in the firm consciousness that we were hastening the steps of progress, advancing the glorious Dawn.

The memory of the life "outside" intensifies the misery of the solitary. I brood over the uselessness of my suffering. My mission in life terminated with the *Attentat*. What good can my continued survival do? My propagandistic value as a living example of class injustice and political persecution is not of sufficient importance to impose upon me the duty of existence. And even if it were, the almost three years of my imprisonment have served the purpose. Escape is out of consideration, so long as I remain constantly under lock and key, the subject of special surveillance. Communication with Nold and Bauer, too, is daily growing more difficult. My health is fast failing; I am barely able to walk. What is the use of all this misery and torture? What is the use? . . . .

In such moments, I stand on the brink of eternity. Is it sheer apathy and languor that hold the weak thread of life, or nature's law and the inherent spirit of resistance? Were I not in the enemy's power, I should unhesitatingly cross the barrier. But as a pioneer of the Cause, I must live and struggle. Yet life without activity or interest is terrifying. . . . I long for sympathy and affection. With an aching heart I remember my comrades and friends, and the Girl. More and more my mind dwells upon tender memories. I wake at night with a passionate desire for the sight of a sweet face, the touch of a soft hand. A wild yearning fills me for the women I have known, as they pass in my mind's eye from the time of my early youth to the last kiss of feminine lips. With a thrill I recall each bright look and tender accent. My heart beats tumultuously as I meet little Nadya, on the way to school, pretending I do not see her. I turn around to admire the golden locks floating in the breeze, when I surprise her stealthily watching me. I adore her secretly, but proudly decline my chum's offer to introduce me. How foolish of me! But I know no timid shrinking as I wait, on a cold winter evening, for our neighbor's servant girl to cross the yard; and how unceremoniously I embrace her! She is not a *barishnya;* I need not mask my feelings. And she is so primitive; she accuses me of knowing things "not fit for a boy" of my age. But she kisses me again, and passion wakes at the caress of the large, coarse hand. . . . My Eldridge Street platonic sweetheart stands before me, and I tingle with every sensual emotion of my first years in New York. . . . Out of the New Haven days rises the image of Luba, sweeping me with unutterable longing for the unattained. And again I live through the experiences of the past, passionately visualizing every detail with images that flatter my erotic palate and weave exquisite allurement about the urge of sex.

CHAPTER XX

A DAY IN THE CELL-HOUSE

I

To K. & G.

Good news! I was let out of the cell this morning. The coffee-boy on my range went home yesterday, and I was put in his place.

It's lucky the old Deputy died—he was determined to keep me in solitary. In the absence of the Warden, Benny Greaves, the new Deputy, told me he will "risk" giving me a job. But he has issued strict orders I should not be permitted to step into the yard. I'll therefore still be under special surveillance, and I shall not be able to see you. But I am in touch with our "Faithful," and we can now resume a more regular correspondence.

Over a year in solitary. It's almost like liberty to be out of the cell!

M.

II

My position as coffee-boy affords many opportunities for closer contact with the prisoners. I assist the range-man in taking care of a row of sixty-four cells situated on the ground floor, and lettered K. Above it are, successively, I, H, G, and F, located on the yard side of the cell-house. On the opposite side, facing the river, the ranges are labelled A, B, C, D, and E. The galleries form parallelograms about each double cell-row; bridged at the centre, they permit easy access to the several

240

CELL RANGES—SOUTH BLOCK

ranges. The ten tiers, with a total of six hundred and
forty cells, are contained within the outer stone building, and comprise the North Block of the penitentiary.
It connects with the South Wing by means of the
rotunda.

The bottom tiers A and K serve as "receiving"
ranges. Here every new arrival is temporarily "celled,"
before he is assigned to work and transferred to the gallery occupied by his shop-fellows. On these ranges are
also located the men undergoing special punishment in
basket and solitary. The lower end of the two ranges
is designated "bughouse row." It contains the "cranks,"
among whom are classed inmates in different stages of
mental aberration.

My various duties of sweeping the hall, dusting the
cell doors, and assisting at feeding, enable me to become
acquainted and to form friendships. I marvel at the
inadequacy of my previous notions of "the criminal."
I resent the presumption of "science" that pretends to
evolve the intricate convolutions of a living human brain
out of the shape of a digit cut from a dead hand, and
labels it "criminal type." Daily association dispels the
myth of the "species," and reveals the individual. Growing intimacy discovers the humanity beneath fibers coars-
ened by lack of opportunity, and brutalized by misery and
fear. There is "Reddie" Butch, a rosy-cheeked young
fellow of twenty-one, as frank-spoken a boy as ever
honored a striped suit. A jolly criminal is Butch, with
his irrepressible smile and gay song. He was "just dying
to take his girl for a ride," he relates to me. But he
couldn't afford it; he earned only seven dollars per week,
as butcher's boy. He always gave his mother every
penny he made, but the girl kept taunting him because
he couldn't spend anything on her. "And I goes to work
and swipes a rig, and say, Aleck, you ought to see me

drive to me girl's house, big-like. In I goes. 'Put on
your glad duds, Kate,' I says, says I, 'I'll give you the
drive of your life.' And I did; you bet your sweet life,
I did, ha, ha, ha!" But when he returned the rig to its
owner, Butch was arrested. "'Just a prank, Your
Honor,' I says to the Judge. And what d' you think,
Aleck? Thought I'd die when he said three years. I was
foolish, of course; but there's no use crying over spilt
milk, ha, ha, ha! But you know, the worst of it is, me
girl went back on me. Wouldn't that jar you, eh? Well,
I'll try hard to forget th' minx. She's a sweet girl,
though, you bet, ha, ha, ha!"

And there is Young Rush, the descendant of the
celebrated family of the great American physician. The
delicate features, radiant with spirituality, bear a striking resemblance to Shelley; the limping gait recalls the
tragedy of Byron. He is in for murder! He sits at the
door, an open book in his hands,—the page is moist with
the tears silently trickling down his face. He smiles at
my approach, and his expressive eyes light up the dark-
ened cell, like a glimpse of the sun breaking through
the clouds. He was wooing a girl on a Summer night;
the skiff suddenly upturned, "right opposite here,"—he
points to the river,—"near McKees Rocks." He was
dragged out, unconscious. They told him the girl was
dead, and that he was her murderer! He reaches for
the photograph on his table, and bursts into sobs.

Daily I sweep the length of the hall, advancing from
cell to cell with deliberate stroke, all the while watching
for an opportunity to exchange a greeting. with the
prisoners. My mind reverts to poor Wingie. How he
cheered me in the first days of misery; how kind he
was! In gentler tones I speak to the unfortunates, and

encourage the new arrivals, or indulge some demented prisoner in a harmless whim. The dry sweeping of the hallway raises a cloud of dust, and loud coughing follows in my wake. Taking advantage of the old Block Captain's "cold in the head," I cautiously hint at the danger of germs lurking in the dust-laden atmosphere. "A little wet sawdust on the floor, Mr. Mitchell, and you wouldn't catch colds so often." A capital idea, he thinks, and thereafter I guard the precious supply under the bed in my cell.

In little ways I seek to help the men in solitary. Every trifle means so much. "Long Joe," the rangeman, whose duty it is to attend to their needs, is engrossed with his own troubles. The poor fellow is serving twenty-five years, and he is much worried by "Wild Bill" and "Bighead" Wilson. They are constantly demanding to see the Warden. It is remarkable that they are never refused. The guards seem to stand in fear of them. "Wild Bill" is a self-confessed invert, and there are peculiar rumors concerning his intimacy with the Warden. Recently Bill complained of indigestion, and a guard sent me to deliver some delicacies to him. "From the Warden's table," he remarked, with a sly wink. And Wilson is jocularly referred to as "the Deputy," even by the officers. He is still in stripes, but he seems to wield some powerful influence over the new Deputy; he openly defies the rules, upbraids the guards, and issues orders. He is the Warden's "runner," clad with the authority of his master. The prisoners regard Bill and Wilson as stools, and cordially hate them; but none dare offend them. Poor Joe is constantly harassed by "Deputy" Wilson; there seems to be bitter enmity between the two on account of a young prisoner who prefers the friendship of Joe. Worried by the complex intrigues of life in the block, the rangeman is indifferent

to the unfortunates in the cells.   Butch is devoured by
bedbugs, and "Praying" Andy's mattress is flattened into
a pancake.   The simple-minded life-timer is being neglected: he has not yet recovered from the assault by
Johnny Smith, who hit him on the head with a hammer.
I urge the rangeman to report to the Captain the need
of "bedbugging" Butch's cell, of supplying Andy with a
new mattress, and of notifying the doctor of the increasing signs of insanity among the solitaries.

III

Breakfast is over; the lines form in lockstep, and
march to the shops.   Broom in hand, rangemen and
assistants step upon the galleries, and commence to
sweep the floors.   Officers pass along the tiers, closely
scrutinizing each cell.   Now and then they pause, facing
a "delinquent."   They note his number, unlock the door,
and the prisoner joins the "sick line" on the ground floor.

One by one the men augment the row; they walk
slowly, bent and coughing, painfully limping down the
steep flights.   From every range they come; the old and
decrepit, the young consumptives, the lame and asthmatic, a tottering old negro, an idiotic white boy.   All
look withered and dejected,—a ghastly line, palsied and
blear-eyed, blanched in the valley of death.

The rotunda door opens noisily, and the doctor enters, accompanied by Deputy Warden Greaves and
Assistant Deputy Hopkins.   Behind them is a prisoner,
dressed in dark gray and carrying a medicine box.   Dr.
Boyce glances at the long line, and knits his brows.   He
looks at his watch, and the frown deepens.   He has
much to do.   Since the death of the senior doctor, the
young graduate is the sole physician of the big prison.
He must make the rounds of the shops before noon,

and visit the patients in the hospital before the Warden or the Deputy drops in.

Mr. Greaves sits down at the officers' desk, near the hall entrance. The Assistant Deputy, pad in hand, places himself at the head of the sick line. The doctor leans against the door of the rotunda, facing the Deputy. The block officers stand within call, at respectful distances.

"Two-fifty-five!" the Assistant Deputy calls out.

A slender young man leaves the line and approaches the doctor. He is tall and well featured, the large eyes lustrous in the pale face. He speaks in a hoarse voice:

"Doctor, there is something the matter with my side. I have pains, and I cough bad at night, and in the morning—"

"All right," the doctor interrupts, without looking up from his note book. "Give him some salts," he adds, with a nod to his assistant.

"Next!" the Deputy calls.

"Will you please excuse me from the shop for a few days?" the sick prisoner pleads, a tremor in his voice.

The physician glances questioningly at the Deputy. The latter cries, impatiently, "Next, next man!" striking the desk twice, in quick succession, with the knuckles of his hand.

"Return to the shop," the doctor says to the prisoner.

"Next!" the Deputy calls, spurting a stream of tobacco juice in the direction of the cuspidor. It strikes sidewise, and splashes over the foot of the approaching new patient, a young negro, his neck covered with bulging tumors.

"Number?" the doctor inquires.

"One-thirty-seven, A one-thirty-seven!" the Deputy mumbles, his head thrown back to receive a fresh handful of "scrap" tobacco.

"Guess Ah's got de big neck, Ah is, Mistah Boyce,"
the negro says hoarsely.

"Salts. Return to work. Next!"

"A one-twenty-six!"

A young man with parchment-like face, sere and
yellow, walks painfully from the line.

"Doctor, I seem to be gettin' worser, and I'm
afraid—"

"What's the trouble?"

"Pains in the stomach. Gettin' so turrible, I—"

"Give him a plaster. Next!"

"Plaster hell!" the prisoner breaks out in a fury, his
face growing livid. "Look at this, will you?" With a
quick motion he pulls his shirt up to his head. His chest
and back are entirely covered with porous plasters; not
an inch of skin is visible. "Damn yer plasters," he cries
with sudden sobs, "I ain't got no more room for plasters.
I'm putty near dyin', an' you won't do nothin' fer me."

The guards pounce upon the man, and drag him
into the rotunda.

One by one the sick prisoners approach the doctor.
He stands, head bent, penciling, rarely glancing up. The
elongated ascetic face wears a preoccupied look; he
drawls mechanically, in monosyllables, "Next! Numb'r?
Salts! Plaster! Salts! Next!" Occasionally he glances
at his watch; his brows knit closer, the heavy furrow
deepens, and the austere face grows more severe and
rigid. Now and then he turns his eyes upon the Deputy
Warden, sitting opposite, his jaws incessantly working,
a thin stream of tobacco trickling down his chin, and
heavily streaking the gray beard. Cheeks protruding,
mouth full of juice, the Deputy mumbles unintelligently,
turns to expectorate, suddenly shouts "Next!" and gives
two quick knocks on the desk, signaling to the physician

to order the man to work. Only the withered and the lame are temporarily excused, the Deputy striking the desk thrice to convey the permission to the doctor.

Dejected and forlorn, the sick line is conducted to the shops, coughing, wheezing, and moaning, only to repeat the ordeal the following morning. Quite often, breaking down at the machine or fainting at the task, the men are carried on a stretcher to the hospital, to receive a respite from the killing toil,—a short intermission, or a happier, eternal reprieve.

The lame and the feeble, too withered to be useful in the shops, are sent back to their quarters, and locked up for the day. Only these, the permitted delinquents, the insane, the men in solitary, and the sweepers, remain within the inner walls during working hours. The pall of silence descends upon the House of Death.

IV

The guards creep stealthily along the tiers. Officer George Dean, lank and tall, tiptoes past the cells, his sharply hooked nose in advance, his evil-looking eyes peering through the bars, scrutinizing every inmate. Suddenly the heavy jaws snap. "Hey, you, Eleven-thirty-nine! On the bed again! Wha-at? Sick, hell! No din-ner!" Noisily he pretends to return to the desk "in front," quietly steals into the niche of a cell door, and stands motionless, alertly listening. A suppressed murmur proceeds from the upper galleries. Cautiously the guard advances, hastily passes several cells, pauses a moment, and then quickly steps into the center of the hall, shouting: "Cells forty-seven K, I, H! Talking through the pipe! Got you this time, all right." He grins broadly as he returns to the desk, and reports to the Block Captain. The guards ascend the galleries.

Levers are pulled, doors opened with a bang, and the three prisoners are marched to the office. For days their cells remain vacant: the men are in the dungeon.

Gaunt and cadaverous, Guard Hughes makes the rounds of the tiers, on a tour of inspection. With bleary eyes, sunk deep in his head, he gazes intently through the bars. The men are out at work. Leisurely he walks along, stepping from cell to cell, here tearing a picture off the wall, there gathering a few scraps of paper. As I pass along the hall, he slams a door on the range above, and appears upon the gallery. His pockets bulge with confiscated goods. He glances around, as the Deputy enters from the yard. "Hey, Jasper!" the guard calls. The colored trusty scampers up the stairs. "Take this to the front." The officer hands him a dilapidated magazine, two pieces of cornbread, a little square of cheese, and several candles that some weak-eyed prisoner had saved up by sitting in the dark for weeks. "Show 't to the Deputy," the officer says, in an undertone. "I'm doing business, all right!" The trusty laughs boisterously, "Yassah, yassah, dat yo sure am."

The guard steps into the next cell, throwing a quick look to the front. The Deputy is disappearing through the rotunda door. The officer casts his eye about the cell. The table is littered with magazines and papers. A piece of matting, stolen from the shops, is on the floor. On the bed are some bananas and a bunch of grapes,—forbidden fruit. The guard steps back to the gallery, a faint smile on his thin lips. He reaches for the heart-shaped wooden block hanging above the cell. It bears the legend, painted in black, A 480. On the reverse side the officer reads, "Collins Hamilton, dated ——." His watery eyes strain to decipher the penciled marks paled by the damp, whitewashed wall. "Jasper!"

he calls, "come up here." The trusty hastens to him.

"You know who this man is, Jasper? A four-eighty."

"Ah sure knows. Dat am Hamilton, de bank 'bez-leh."

"Where's he working?"

"Wat *he* wan' teh work foh? He am de Cap'n's clerk. In de awfice, *he* am."

"All right, Jasper." The guard carefully closes the clerk's door, and enters the adjoining cell. It looks clean and orderly. The stone floor is bare, the bedding smooth; the library book, tin can, and plate, are neatly arranged on the table. The officer ransacks the bed, throws the blankets on the floor, and stamps his feet upon the pillow in search of secreted contraband. He reaches up to the wooden shelf on the wall, and takes down the little bag of scrap tobacco,—the weekly allowance of the prisoners. He empties a goodly part into his hand, shakes it up, and thrusts it into his mouth. He produces a prison "plug" from his pocket, bites off a piece, spits in the direction of the privy, and yawns; looks at his watch, deliberates a moment, spurts a stream of juice into the corner, and cautiously steps out on the gallery. He surveys the field, leans over the railing, and squints at the front. The chairs at the officers' desk are vacant. The guard retreats into the cell, yawns and stretches, and looks at his watch again. It is only nine o'clock. He picks up the library book, listlessly examines the cover, flings the book on the shelf, spits disgustedly, then takes another chew, and sprawls down on the bed.

V

At the head of the hall, Senior Officer Woods and Assistant Deputy Hopkins sit at the desk. Of superb physique and glowing vitality, Mr. Woods wears his new honors as Captain of the Block with aggressive self-importance. He has recently been promoted from the shop to the charge of the North Wing, on the morning shift, from 5 A. M. to 1 P. M. Every now and then he leaves his chair, walks majestically down the hallway, crosses the open centre, and returns past the opposite cell-row.

With studied dignity he resumes his seat and addresses his superior, the Assistant Deputy, in measured, low tones. The latter listens gravely, his head slightly bent, his sharp gray eyes restless above the heavy-rimmed spectacles. As Mr. Hopkins, angular and stoop-shouldered, rises to expectorate into the nearby sink, he espies the shining face of Jasper on an upper gallery. The Assistant Deputy smiles, produces a large apple from his pocket, and, holding it up to view, asks:

"How does this strike you, Jasper?"

"Looks teh dis niggah like a watahmelon, Cunnel."

Woods struggles to suppress a smile. Hopkins laughs, and motions to the negro. The trusty joins them at the desk.

"I'll bet the coon could get away with this apple in two bites," the Assistant Deputy says to Woods.

"Hardly possible," the latter remarks, doubtfully.

"You don't know this darky, Scot," Hopkins rejoins. "I know him for the last—let me see—fifteen, eighteen, twenty years. That's when you first came here, eh, Jasper?"

"Yassah, 'bout dat."

"In the old prison, then?" Woods inquires.

"Yes, of course. You was there, Jasper, when 'Shoebox' Miller got out, wasn't you?"

"Yo 'member good, Cunnel. Dat Ah was, sure 'nuf.

En mighty slick it was, bress me, teh hab imsef nailed in dat shoebox, en mek his get-away."

"Yes, yes. And this is your fourth time since then, I believe."

"No, sah, no, sah; dere yo am wrong, Cunnel. Youh remnishent am bad. Dis jus' free times, jus' free."

"Come off, it's four."

"Free, Cunnel, no moah."

"Do you think, Mr. Hopkins, Jasper could eat the apple in two bites?" Woods reminds him.

"I'm sure he can. There's nothing in the eating line this coon couldn't do. Here, Jasper, you get the apple if you make it in two bites. Don't disgrace me, now."

The negro grins. "Putty big, Cunnel, but Ah'm a gwine teh try powful hard."

With a heroic effort he stretches his mouth, till his face looks like a veritable cavern, reaching from ear to ear, and edged by large, shimmering tusks. With both hands he inserts the big apple, and his sharp teeth come down with a loud snap. He chews quickly, swallows, repeats the performance, and then holds up his hands. The apple has disappeared.

The Assistant Deputy roars with laughter. "What did I tell you, eh, Scot? What did I tell you, ho, ho, ho!" The tears glisten in his eye.

They amuse themselves with the negro trusty by the hour. He relates his experiences, tells humorous anecdotes, and the officers are merry. Now and then Deputy Warden Greaves drops in. Woods rises.

"Have a seat, Mr. Greaves."

"That's all right, that's all right, Scot," the Deputy mumbles, his eye searching for the cuspidor. "Sit down, Scot; I'm as young as any of you."

With mincing step he walks into the first cell, reserved for the guards, pulls a bottle from his hip pocket, takes several quick gulps, wabbles back to the desk, and sinks heavily into Woods's seat.

"Jasper, go bring me a chew," he turns to the trusty.

"Yassah. Scrap, Dep'ty?"

"Yah. A nip of plug, too."

"Yassah, yassah, immejitly."

"What are you men doing here?" the Deputy blusters at the two subordinates.

Woods frowns, squares his shoulders, glances at the Deputy, and then relaxes into a dignified smile. Assistant Hopkins looks sternly at the Deputy Warden from above his glasses. "That's all right, Greaves," he says, familiarly, a touch of scorn in his voice. "Say, you should have seen that nigger Jasper swallow a great, big apple in two bites; as big as your head, I'll swear."

"That sho?" the Deputy nods sleepily.

The negro comes running up with a paper of scrap in one hand, a plug in the other. The Deputy slowly opens his eyes. He walks unsteadily to the cell, remains there a few minutes, and returns with both hands fumbling at his hip pocket. He spits viciously at the sink, sits down, fills his mouth with tobacco, glances at the floor, and demands, hoarsely:

"Where's all them spittoons, eh, you men?"

"Just being cleaned, Mr. Greaves," Woods replies.

"Cleaned, always th' shame shtory. I ordered—ya—ordered—hey, bring shpittoon, Jasper." He wags his head drowsily.

"He means he ordered spittoons by the wagonload," Hopkins says, with a wink at Woods. "It was the very first order he gave when he became Deputy after Jimmie McPane died. I tell you, Scot, we won't see so soon another Deputy like old Jimmie. He was Deputy all right, every inch of him. Wouldn't stand for the old man, the Warden, interfering with him, either. Not like this here," he points contemptuously at the snoring Greaves. "Here, Benny," he raises his voice and slaps the Deputy on the knee, "here's Jasper with your spittoon."

Greaves wakes with a start, and gazes stupidly about; presently, noticing the trusty with the large cuspidor, he spurts a long jet at it.

"Say, Jasper," Hopkins calls to the retiring negro, "the Deputy wants to hear that story you told us a while ago, about how you got the left hind foot of a she-rabbit, on a moonlit night in a graveyard."

"Who shaid I want to hear 't?" the Deputy bristles, suddenly wide awake.

"Yes, you do, Greaves," Hopkins asserts. "The rabbit foot brings good luck, you know. This coon here wears it on his neck. Show it to the Deputy, Jasper."

Prisoner Wilson, the Warden's favorite messenger, enters from the yard. With quick, energetic step he passes the officers at the desk, entirely ignoring their presence, and walks nonchalantly down the hall, his unnaturally large head set close upon the heavy, almost neckless shoulders.

"Hey, you, Wilson, what are you after?" the Deputy shouts after him.

Without replying, Wilson continues on his way.

"Dep'ty Wilson," the negro jeers, with a look of hatred and envy.

Assistant Deputy Hopkins rises in his seat. "Wilson," he calls with quiet sternness, "Mr. Greaves is speaking to you. Come back at once."

His face purple with anger, Wilson retraces his steps. "What do you want, Deputy?" he demands, savagely.

The Deputy looks uneasy and fidgets in his chair,

but catching the severe eye of Hopkins, he shouts vehemently: "What do you want in the block?"

"On Captain Edward S. Wright's business," Wilson replies with a sneer.

"Well, go ahead. But next time I call you, you better come back."

"The Warden told me to hurry. I'll report to him that you detained me with an idle question," Wilson snarls back.

"That'll do, Wilson," the Assistant Deputy warns him.

"Wait till I see the Captain," Wilson growls, as he departs.

"If I had my way, I'd knock his damn block off," the Assistant mutters.

"Such impudence in a convict cannot be tolerated," Woods comments.

"The Cap'n won't hear a word against Wilson," the Deputy says meekly.

Hopkins frowns. They sit in silence. The negro busies himself, wiping the yellow-stained floor around the cuspidor. The Deputy ambles stiffly to the open cell. Woods rises, steps back to the wall, and looks up to the top galleries. No one is about. He crosses to the other side, and scans the bottom range. Long and dismal stretches the hall, in melancholy white and gray, the gloomy cell-building brooding in the centre, like some monstrous hunchback, without life or motion. Woods resumes his seat.

"Quiet as a church," he remarks with evident satisfaction.

"You're doing well, Scot," the Deputy mumbles. "Doing well."

A faint metallic sound breaks upon the stillness. The officers prick up their ears. The rasping continues and grows louder. The negro trusty tiptoes up the tiers.

"It's somebody with his spoon on the door," the Assistant Deputy remarks, indifferently.

The Block Captain motions to me. "See who's rapping there, will you?"

I walk quickly along the hall. By keeping close to the wall, I can see up to the doors of the third gallery. Here and there a nose protrudes in the air, the bleached face glued to the bars, the eyes glassy. The rapping grows louder as I advance.

"Who is it?" I call.

"Up here, 18 C."

"Is that you, Ed?"

"Yes. Got a bad hemorrhage. Tell th' screw I must see the doctor."

I run to the desk. "Mr. Woods," I report, "18 C got a hemorrhage. Can't stop it. He needs the doctor."

"Let him wait," the Deputy growls.

"Doctor hour is over. He should have reported in the morning," the Assistant Deputy flares up.

"What shall I tell him, Mr. Woods?" I ask.

"Nothing! Get back to your cell."

"Perhaps you'd better go up and take a look, Scot," the Deputy suggests.

Mr. Woods strides along the gallery, pauses a moment at 18 C, and returns.

"Nothing much. A bit of blood. I ordered him to report on sick list in the morning."

A middle-aged prisoner, with confident bearing and polished manner, enters from the yard. It is the "French Count," one of the clerks in the "front office."

"Good morning, gentlemen," he greets the officers. He leans familiarly over the Deputy's chair, remarking:

"I've been hunting half an hour for you. The Captain is a bit ruffled this morning. He is looking for you."

The Deputy hurriedly rises. "Where is he?" he asks anxiously.

"In the office, Mr. Greaves. You know what's about?"

"What? Quick, now."

"They caught Wild Bill right in the act. Out in the yard there, back of the shed."

The Deputy stumps heavily out into the yard.

"Who's the kid?" the Assistant Deputy inquires, an amused twinkle in his eye.

"Bobby."

"Who? That boy on the whitewash gang?"

"Yes, Fatty Bobby."

The clatter on the upper tier grows loud and violent. The sick man is striking his tin can on the bars, and shaking the door. Woods hastens to C 18.

"You stop that, you hear!" he commands angrily.

"I'm sick. I want th' doctor."

"This isn't doctor hour. You'll see him in the morning."

"I may be dead in the morning. I want him now."

"You won't see him, that's all. You keep quiet there."

Furiously the prisoner raps on the door. The hall reverberates with hollow booming.

The Block Captain returns to the desk, his face crimson. He whispers to the Assistant Deputy. The latter nods his head. Woods claps his hands, deliberately, slowly—one, two, three. Guards hurriedly descend from the galleries, and advance to the desk. The rangemen appear at their doors.

"Everybody to his cell. Officers, lock 'em in!" Woods commands.

"You can stay here, Jasper," the Assistant Deputy remarks to the trusty.

The rangemen step into their cells. The levers are pulled, the doors locked. I hear the tread of many feet on the third gallery. Now they cease, and all is quiet.

"C 18, step out here!"

The door slams, there is noisy shuffling and stamping, and the dull, heavy thuds of striking clubs. A loud cry and a moan. They drag the prisoner along the range, and down the stairway. The rotunda door creaks, and the clamor dies away.

A few minutes elapse in silence. Now some one whispers through the pipes; insane solitaries bark and crow. Loud coughing drowns the noises, and then the rotunda door opens with a plaintive screech.

The rangemen are unlocked. I stand at the open door of my cell. The negro trusty dusts and brushes the officers, their backs and arms covered with whitewash, as if they had been rubbed against the wall.

Their clothes cleaned and smoothed, the guards loll in the chairs, and sit on the desk. They look somewhat ruffled and flustered. Jasper enlarges upon the piquant gossip. "Wild Bill," notorious invert and protégé of the Warden, he relates, had been hanging around the kids from the stocking shop; he has been after "Fatty Bobby" for quite a while, and he's forever pestering "Lady Sally," and Young Davis, too. The guards are astir with curiosity; they ply the negro with questions. He responds eagerly, raises his voice, and gesticulates excitedly. There is merriment and laughter at the officers' desk.

VI

Dinner hour is approaching. Officer Gerst, in charge of the kitchen squad, enters the cell-house. Behind him, a score of prisoners carry large wooden tubs filled with steaming liquid. The negro trusty, his nostrils expanded and eyes glistening, sniffs the air, and announces with a grin: "Dooke's mixchoor foh dinneh teh day!"

The scene becomes animated at the front. Tables are noisily moved about, the tinplate rattles, and men talk and shout. With a large ladle the soup is dished out from the tubs, and the pans, bent and rusty, stacked up in long rows. The Deputy Warden flounces in, splutters some orders that remain ignored, and looks critically at the dinner pans. He produces a pocket knife, and ambles along the tables, spearing a potato here, a bit of floating vegetable there. Guard Hughes, his inspection of the cells completed, saunters along, casting greedy eyes at the food. He hovers about, waiting for the Deputy to leave. The latter stands, hands dug into his pockets, short legs wide apart, scraggy beard keeping time with the moving jaws. Guard Hughes winks at one of the kitchen men, and slinks into an open cell. The prisoner fusses about, pretends to move the empty tubs out of the way, and then quickly snatches a pan of soup, and passes it to the guard. Negro Jasper, alert and watchful, strolls by Woods, surreptitiously whispering. The officer walks to the open cell and surprises the guard, his head thrown back, the large pan covering his face. Woods smiles disdainfully, the prisoners giggle and chuckle.

"Chief Jim," the head cook, a Pittsburgh saloonkeeper serving twelve years for murder, promenades down the range. Large-bellied and whitecapped, he wears an air of prosperity and independence. With swelling chest,

stomach protruding, and hand wrapped in his dirty
apron, the Chief walks leisurely along the cells, nodding
and exchanging greetings. He pauses at a door: it's
Cell 9 A,—the "Fat Kid." Jim leans against the wall,
his back toward the dinner tables; presently his hand
steals between the bars. Now and then he glances
toward the front, and steps closer to the door. He draws
a large bundle from his bosom, hastily tears it open, and
produces a piece of cooked meat, several raw onions,
some cakes. One by one he passes the delicacies to the
young prisoner, forcing them through the narrow open-
ings between the bars. He lifts his apron, fans the
door sill, and carefully wipes the ironwork; then he
smiles, casts a searching look to the front, grips the bars
with both hands, and vanishes into the deep niche.

As suddenly he appears to view again, takes several
quick steps, then pauses at another cell. Standing away
from the door, he speaks loudly and laughs boisterously,
his hands fumbling beneath the apron. Soon he leaves,
advancing to the dinner tables. He approaches the
rangeman, lifts his eyebrows questioningly, and winks.
The man nods affirmatively, and retreats into his cell.
The Chief dives into the bosom of his shirt, and flings
a bundle through the open door. He holds out his hand,
whispering: "Two bits. Broke now? Be sure you pay
me to-morrow. That steak there's worth a plunk."

The gong tolls the dinner hour. The negro trusty
snatches two pans, and hastens away. The guards unlock the prisoners, excepting the men in solitary who are
deprived of the sole meal of the day. The line forms
in single file, and advances slowly to the tables; then,
pan in hand, the men circle the block to the centre,
ascend the galleries, and are locked in their cells.

The loud tempo of many feet, marching in step,

sounds from the yard. The shop workers enter, receive the pan of soup, and walk to the cells. Some sniff the air, make a wry face, and pass on, empty-handed. There is much suppressed murmuring and whispering.

Gradually the sounds die away. It is the noon hour. Every prisoner is counted and locked in. Only the trusties are about.

VII

The afternoon brings a breath of relief. "Old Jimmie" Mitchell, rough-spoken and kind, heads the second shift of officers, on duty from 1 till 9 P. M. The venerable Captain of the Block trudges past the cells, stroking his flowing white beard, and profusely swearing at the men. But the prisoners love him: he frowns upon clubbing, and discourages trouble-seeking guards.

Head downward, he thumps heavily along the hall, on his first round of the bottom ranges. Presently a voice hails him: "Oh, Mr. Mitchell! Come here, please."

"Damn your soul t' hell," the officer rages, "don't you know better than to bother me when I'm counting, eh? Shut up now, God damn you. You've mixed me all up."

He returns to the front, and begins to count again, pointing his finger at each occupied cell. This duty over, and his report filed, he returns to the offending prisoner.

"What t' hell do you want, Butch?"

"Mr. Mitchell, my shoes are on th' bum. I am walking on my socks."

"Where th' devil d' you think you're going, anyhow? To a ball?"

"Papa Mitchell, be good now, won't you?" the youth coaxes.

"Go an' take a—thump to yourself, will you?"

The officer walks off, heavy-browed and thoughtful, but pauses a short distance from the cell, to hear Butch mumbling discontentedly. The Block Captain retraces his steps, and, facing the boy, storms at him:

"What did you say? 'Damn the old skunk!' that's what you said, eh? You come on out of there!"

With much show of violence he inserts the key into the lock, pulls the door open with a bang, and hails a passing guard:

"Mr. Kelly, quick, take this loafer out and give 'im— er—give 'im a pair of shoes."

He starts down the range, when some one calls from an upper tier:

"Jimmy, Jimmy! Come on up here!"

"I'll jimmy your damn carcass for you," the old man bellows, angrily. "Where th' hell are you?"

"Here, on B, 20 B. Right over you."

The officer steps back to the wall, and looks up toward the second gallery.

"What in th' name of Jesus Christ do you want, Slim?"

"Awful cramps in me stomach. Get me some cramp mixture, Jim."

"Cramps in yer head, that's what you've got, you big bum you. Where in hell did you get your cramp mixture, when you was spilling around in a freight car, eh?"

"I got booze then," the prisoner retorts.

"Like hell you did! You were damn lucky to get a louzy hand-out at the back door, you ornery pimple on God's good earth."

"Th' hell you say! The hand-out was a damn sight better'n th' rotten slush I get here. I wouldn't have a belly-ache, if it wasn't for th' hogwash they gave us to-day."

"Lay down now! You talk like a horse's rosette."

It's the old man's favorite expression, in his rich vocabulary of picturesque metaphor and simile. But there is no sting in the brusque speech, no rancor in the scowling eyes. On the way to the desk he pauses to whisper to the block trusty:

"John, you better run down to the dispensary, an' get that big stiff some cramp mixture."

Happening to glance into a cell, Mitchell notices a new arrival, a bald-headed man, his back against the door, reading.

"Hey you!" the Block Captain shouts at him, startling the green prisoner off his chair, "take that bald thing out of there, or I'll run you in for indecent exposure."

He chuckles at the man's fright, like a boy pleased with a naughty prank, and ascends the upper tiers.

Duster in hand, I walk along the range. The guards are engaged on the galleries, examining cells, overseeing the moving of the newly-graded inmates to the South Wing, or chatting with the trusties. The chairs at the officers' desk are vacant. Keeping alert watch on the rotunda doors, I walk from cell to cell, whiling away the afternoon hours in conversation. Johnny, the friendly runner, loiters at the desk, now and then glancing into the yard, and giving me "the office" by sharply snapping his fingers, to warn me of danger. I ply the duster diligently, while the Deputy and his assistants linger about, surrounded by the trusties imparting information gathered during the day. Gradually they disperse, called into a shop where a fight is in progress, or nosing about the kitchen and assiduously killing time. The "coast is clear," and I return to pick up the thread of interrupted conversation.

But the subjects of common interest are soon exhausted. The oft-repeated tirade against the "rotten grub," the "stale punk," and the "hogwash"; vehement cursing of the brutal "screws," the "stomach-robber of a Warden" and the unreliability of his promises; the exchange of gossip, and then back again to berating the food and the treatment. Within the narrow circle runs the interminable tale, colored by individual temperament, intensified by the length of sentence. The whole is dominated by a deep sense of unmerited suffering and bitter resentment, often breathing dire vengeance against those whom they consider responsible for their misfortune, including the police, the prosecutor, the informer, the witnesses, and, in rare instances, the trial judge. But as the longed-for release approaches, the note of hope and liberty rings clearer, stronger, with the swelling undercurrent of frank and irrepressible sex desire.

CHAPTER XXI

THE DEEDS OF THE GOOD TO THE EVIL

THE new arrivals are forlorn and dejected, a look of fear and despair in their eyes. The long-timers among them seem dazed, as if with some terrible shock, and fall upon the bed in stupor-like sleep. The boys from the reformatories, some mere children in their teens, weep and moan, and tremble at the officer's footstep. Only the "repeaters" and old-timers preserve their composure, scoff at the "fresh fish," nod at old acquaintances, and exchange vulgar pleasantries with the guards. But all soon grow nervous and irritable, and stand at the door, leaning against the bars, an expression of bewildered hopelessness or anxious expectancy on their faces. They yearn for companionship, and are pathetically eager to talk, to hear the sound of a voice, to unbosom their heavy hearts.

I am minutely familiar with every detail of their "case," their life-history, their hopes and fears. Through the endless weeks and months on the range, their tragedies are the sole subject of conversation. A glance into the mournful faces, pressed close against the bars, and the panorama of misery rises before me,—the cell-house grows more desolate, bleaker, the air gloomier and more depressing.

There is Joe Zappe, his bright eyes lighting up with a faint smile as I pause at his door. "Hello, Alick," he greets me in his sweet, sad voice. He knows me from the jail. His father and elder brother have been executed, and he commuted to life because of youth. He is barely eighteen, but his hair has turned white. He has been acting queerly of late: at night I often hear him muttering and walking, walking incessantly and muttering. There is a peculiar look about his eyes, restless, roving.

"Alick," he says, suddenly, "me wanna tell you sometink. You no tell nobody, yes?"

Assured I'll keep his confidence, he begins to talk quickly, excitedly:

"Nobody dere, Alick? No scroo? S-sh! Lassa night me see ma broder. Yes, see Gianni. Jesu Cristo, me see ma poor broder in da cella 'ere, an' den me fader he come. Broder and fader day stay der, on da floor, an so quieta, lika dead, an' den dey come an lay downa in ma bed. Oh, Jesu Christo, me so fraida, me cry an' pray. You not know wat it mean? No-o-o? Me tell you. It mean me die, me die soon."

His eyes glow with a sombre fire, a hectic flush on his face. He knits his brows, as I essay to calm him, and continues hurriedly:

"S-sh! Waita till me tell you all. You know watta for ma fader an' Gianni come outa da grave? Me tell you. Dey calla for ravange, 'cause dey innocente. Me tell you trut. See, we all worka in da mine, da coal mine, me an' my fader an' Gianni. All worka hard an' mek one dollar, maybe dollar quater da day. An' bigga American man, him come an' boder ma fader. Ma fader him no wanna trouble; him old man, no boder nobody. An' da American man him maka two dollars an mebbe two fifty da day an' him boder my fader, all da time, boder 'im an' kick 'im to da legs, an' steal ma broder's shovel, an' hide fader's hat, an' maka trouble for ma countrymen, an' call us 'dirty dagoes.' An' one day him an' two Arish dey all drunk, an' smash ma fader, an'

American man an Arish holler, 'Dago s—— b—— fraida
fight,' an' da American man him take a bigga pickax
an' wanna hit ma fader, an' ma fader him run, an' me
an' ma broder an' friend we fight, an' American man
him fall, an' we all go way home. Den p'lice come an'
arresta me an' fader an' broder, an' say we killa American man. Me an' ma broder no use knife, mebbe ma
friend do. Me no know; him no arresta; him go home in
Italia. Ma fader an' broder dey save nineda-sev'n dollar, an' me save twenda-fife, an' gotta laiyer. Him no
good, an' no talk much in court. We poor men, no can
take case in oder court, an' fader him hang, an' Gianni
hang, an' me get life. Ma fader an' broder dey come
lassa night from da grave, cause dey innocente an' wanna
ravange, an' me gotta mek ravange, me no rest, gotta—"

The sharp snapping of Johnny, the runner, warns
me of danger, and I hastily leave.

The melancholy figures line the doors as I walk up
and down the hall. The blanched faces peer wistfully
through the bars, or lean dejectedly against the wall, a
vacant stare in the dim eyes. Each calls to mind the
stories of misery and distress, the scenes of brutality
and torture I witness in the prison house. Like ghastly
nightmares, the shadows pass before me. There is
"Silent Nick," restlessly pacing his cage, never ceasing,
his lips sealed in brutish muteness. For three years he
has not left the cell, nor uttered a word. The stolid
features are cut and bleeding. Last night he had attempted suicide, and the guards beat him, and left him
unconscious on the floor.

There is "Crazy Hunkie," the Austrian. Every
morning, as the officer unlocks his door to hand in
the loaf of bread, he makes a wild dash for the yard,
shouting, "Me wife! Where's me wife?" He rushes

toward the front, and desperately grabs the door handle. The double iron gate is securely locked. A look of blank amazement on his face, he slowly returns to the cell. The guards await him with malicious smile. Suddenly they rush upon him, blackjacks in hand. "Me wife, me seen her!" the Austrian cries. The blood gushing from his mouth and nose, they kick him into the cell. "Me wife waiting in de yard," he moans.

In the next cell is Tommy Wellman; adjoining him, Jim Grant. They are boys recently transferred from the reformatory. They cower in the corner, in terror of the scene. With tearful eyes, they relate their story. Orphans in the slums of Allegheny, they had been sent to the reform school at Morganza, for snatching fruit off a corner stand. Maltreated and beaten, they sought to escape. Childishly they set fire to the dormitory, almost in sight of the keepers. "I says to me chum, says I," Tommy narrates with boyish glee, "'Kid,' says I, 'let's fire de louzy joint; dere'll be lots of fun, and we'll make our get-away in de' 'citement.'" They were taken to court, and the good judge sentenced them to five years to the penitentiary. "Glad to get out of dat dump," Tommy comments; "it was jest fierce. Dey paddled an' starved us someting' turrible."

In the basket cell, a young colored man grovels on the floor. It is Lancaster, Number 8523. He was serving seven years, and working every day in the mat shop. Slowly the days passed, and at last the longed-for hour of release arrived. But Lancaster was not discharged. He was kept at his task, the Warden informing him that he had lost six months of his "good time" for defective work. The light-hearted negro grew sullen and morose. Often the silence of the cell-house was pierced by his anguished cry in the night, "My time's up, time's up. I want to go home." The guards would take him from the cell, and place him in the dungeon. One morning, in a fit of frenzy, he attacked Captain McVey, the officer of the shop. The Captain received a slight scratch on the neck, and Lancaster was kept chained to the wall of the dungeon for ten days. He returned to the cell, a driveling imbecile. The next day they dressed him in his citizen clothes, Lancaster mumbling, "Going home, going home." The Warden and several officers accompanied him to court, on the way coaching the poor idiot to answer "yes" to the question, "Do you plead guilty?" He received seven years, the extreme penalty of the law, for the "attempted murder of a keeper." They brought him back to the prison, and locked him up in a basket cell, the barred door covered with a wire screen that almost entirely excludes light and air. He receives no medical attention, and is fed on a bread-and-water diet.

The witless negro crawls on the floor, unwashed and unkempt, scratching with his nails fantastic shapes on the stone, and babbling stupidly, "Going, Jesus going to Jerusalem. See, he rides the holy ass; he's going to his father's home. Going home, going home." As I pass he looks up, perplexed wonder on his face; his brows meet in a painful attempt to collect his wandering thoughts, and he drawls with pathetic sing-song, "Going home, going home; Jesus going to father's home." The guards raise their hands to their nostrils as they approach the cell: the poor imbecile evacuates on the table, the chair, and the floor. Twice a month he is taken to the bathroom, his clothes are stripped, and the hose is turned on the crazy negro.

The cell of "Little Sammy" is vacant. He was Number 9521, a young man from Altoona. I knew him quite well. He was a kind boy and a diligent worker; but now and then he would fall into a fit of melancholy. He would then sit motionless on the chair, a blank stare on his face, neglecting food and work. These spells generally lasted two or three days, Sammy refusing to leave the cell. Old Jimmy McPane, the dead Deputy, on such occasions commanded the prisoner to the shop, while Sammy sat and stared in a daze. McPane would order the "stubborn kid" to the dungeon, and every time Sammy got his "head workin'," he was dragged, silent and motionless, to the cellar. The new Deputy has followed the established practice, and last evening, at "music hour," while the men were scraping their instruments, "Little Sammy" was found on the floor of the cell, his throat hacked from ear to ear.

At the Coroner's inquest the Warden testified that the boy was considered mentally defective; that he was therefore excused from work, and never punished.

Returning to my cell in the evening, my gaze meets the printed rules on the wall:

"The prison authorities desire to treat every prisoner in their charge with humanity and kindness. * * * The aim of all prison discipline is, by enforcing the law, to restrain the evil and to protect the innocent from further harm; to so apply the law upon the criminal as to produce a cure from his moral infirmities, by calling out the better principles of his nature."

CHAPTER XXII

THE GRIST OF THE PRISON-MILL

I

THE comparative freedom of the range familiarizes me with the workings of the institution, and brings me in close contact with the authorities. The personnel of the guards is of very inferior character. I find their average intelligence considerably lower than that of the inmates. Especially does the element recruited from the police and the detective service lack sympathy with the unfortunates in their charge. They are mostly men discharged from city employment because of habitual drunkenness, or flagrant brutality and corruption. Their attitude toward the prisoners is summed up in coercion and suppression. They look upon the men as will-less objects of iron-handed discipline, exact unquestioning obedience and absolute submissiveness to peremptory whims, and harbor personal animosity toward the less pliant. The more intelligent among the officers scorn inferior duties, and crave advancement. The authority and remuneration of a Deputy Wardenship is alluring to them, and every keeper considers himself the fittest for the vacancy. But the coveted prize is awarded to the guard most feared by the inmates, and most subservient to the Warden,—a direct incitement to brutality, on the one hand, to sycophancy, on the other.

A number of the officers are veterans of the Civil

War; several among them had suffered incarceration in
Libby Prison. These often manifest a more sympathetic spirit. The great majority of the keepers, however, have been employed in the penitentiary from fifteen
to twenty-five years; some even for a longer period, like
Officer Stewart, who has been a guard for forty years.
This element is unspeakably callous and cruel. The
prisoners discuss among themselves the ages of the old
guards, and speculate on the days allotted them. The
death of one of them is hailed with joy: seldom they
are discharged; still more seldom do they resign.

The appearance of a new officer sheds hope into the
dismal lives. New guards—unless drafted from the
police bureau—are almost without exception lenient and
forbearing, often exceedingly humane. The inmates vie
with each other in showing complaisance to the "can-
didate." It is a point of honor in their unwritten ethics
to "treat him white." They frown upon the fellow-con-
vict who seeks to take advantage of the "green screw,"
by misusing his kindness or exploiting his ignorance of
the prison rules. But the older officers secretly resent
the infusion of new blood. They strive to discourage
the applicant by exaggerating the dangers of the position, and depreciating its financial desirability for an
ambitious young man; they impress upon him the Warden's unfairness to the guards, and the lack of opportunity for advancement. Often they dissuade the new
man, and he disappears from the prison horizon. But if
he persists in remaining, the old keepers expostulate
with him, in pretended friendliness, upon his leniency,
chide him for a "soft-hearted tenderfoot," and improve
every opportunity to initiate him into the practices of
brutality. The system is known in the prison as "breaking in": the new man is constantly drafted in the "clubbing squad," the older officers setting the example of

cruelty. Refusal to participate signifies insubordination to his superiors and the shirking of routine duty, and results in immediate discharge. But such instances are extremely rare. Within the memory of the oldest officer, Mr. Stewart, it happened only once, and the man was sickly.

Slowly the poison is instilled into the new guard. Within a short time the prisoners notice the first signs of change: he grows less tolerant and chummy, more irritated and distant. Presently he feels himself the object of espionage by the favorite trusties of his fellow-officers. In some mysterious manner, the Warden is aware of his every step, berating him for speaking unduly long to this prisoner, or for giving another half a banana,—the remnant of his lunch. In a moment of commiseration and pity, the officer is moved by the tearful pleadings of misery to carry a message to the sick wife or child of a prisoner. The latter confides the secret to some friend, or carelessly brags of his intimacy with the guard, and soon the keeper faces the Warden "on charges," and is deprived of a month's pay. Repeated misplacement of confidence, occasional betrayal by a prisoner seeking the good graces of the Warden, and the new officer grows embittered against the species "convict." The instinct of self-preservation, harassed and menaced on every side, becomes more assertive, and the guard is soon drawn into the vortex of the "system."

II

Daily I behold the machinery at work, grinding and pulverizing, brutalizing the officers, dehumanizing the inmates. Far removed from the strife and struggle of the larger world, I yet witness its miniature replica, more agonizing and merciless within the walls. A perfected model it is, this prison life, with its apparent uniformity and dull passivity. But beneath the torpid surface smolder the fires of being, now crackling faintly under a dun smothering smoke, now blazing forth with the ruthlessness of despair. Hidden by the veil of discipline rages the struggle of fiercely contending wills, and intricate meshes are woven in the quagmire of darkness and suppression.

Intrigue and counter plot, violence and corruption, are rampant in cell-house and shop. The prisoners spy upon each other, and in turn upon the officers. The latter encourage the trusties in unearthing the secret doings of the inmates, and the stools enviously compete with each other in supplying information to the keepers. Often they deliberately inveigle the trustful prisoner into a fake plot to escape, help and encourage him in the preparations, and at the critical moment denounce him to the authorities. The luckless man is severely punished, usually remaining in utter ignorance of the intrigue. The *provocateur* is rewarded with greater liberty and special privileges. Frequently his treachery proves the stepping-stone to freedom, aided by the Warden's official recommendation of the "model prisoner" to the State Board of Pardons.

The stools and the trusties are an essential element in the government of the prison. With rare exception, every officer has one or more on his staff. They assist him in his duties, perform most of his work, and make out the reports for the illiterate guards. Occasionally they are even called upon to help the "clubbing squad." The more intelligent stools enjoy the confidence of the Deputy and his assistants, and thence advance to the favor of the Warden. The latter places more reliance upon his favorite trusties than upon the guards. "I have about a hundred paid officers to keep watch over the prisoners," the Warden informs new applicants, "and two hundred volunteers to watch both." The "volunteers" are vested with unofficial authority, often exceeding that of the inferior officers. They invariably secure the sinecures of the prison, involving little work and affording opportunity for espionage. They are "runners," "messengers," yard and office men.

Other desirable positions, clerkships and the like, are awarded to influential prisoners, such as bankers, embezzlers, and boodlers. These are known in the institution as holding "political jobs." Together with the stools they are scorned by the initiated prisoners as "the pets."

The professional craftiness of the "con man" stands him in good stead in the prison. A shrewd judge of human nature, quick-witted and self-confident, he applies the practiced cunning of his vocation to secure whatever privileges and perquisites the institution affords. His evident intelligence and aplomb powerfully impress the guards; his well-affected deference to authority flatters them. They are awed by his wonderful facility of expression, and great attainments in the mysterious world of baccarat and confidence games. At heart they envy the high priest of "easy money," and are proud to befriend him in his need. The officers exert themselves to please him, secure light work for him, and surreptitiously favor him with delicacies and even money. His game is won. The "con" has now secured the friendship and confidence of his keepers, and will continue to exploit them by pretended warm interest in their physical complaints, their family troubles, and their whispered ambition of promotion and fear of the Warden's discrimination.

The more intelligent officers are the easiest victims of his wiles. But even the higher officials, more difficult to approach, do not escape the confidence man. His "business" has perfected his sense of orientation; he quickly rends the veil of appearance, and scans the undercurrents. He frets at his imprisonment, and hints at high social connections. His real identity is a great secret: he wishes to save his wealthy relatives from public disgrace. A careless slip of the tongue betrays his college education. With a deprecating nod he confesses that his father is a State Senator; he is the only black sheep in his family; yet they are "good" to him, and will not disown him. But he must not bring notoriety upon them.

Eager for special privileges and the liberty of the trusties, or fearful of punishment, the "con man" matures his campaign. He writes a note to a fellow-prisoner. With much detail and thorough knowledge of prison conditions, he exposes all the "ins and outs" of the institution. In elegant English he criticizes the management, dwells upon the ignorance and brutality of the guards, and charges the Warden and the Board of Prison Inspectors with graft, individually and collectively. He denounces the Warden as a stomach-robber of poor unfortunates: the counties pay from twenty-five to thirty cents per day for each inmate; the Federal Government, for its quota of men, fifty cents per person. Why are the prisoners given qualitatively and quantitatively inadequate food? he demands. Does not the State appropriate thousands of dollars for the support of the penitentiary, besides the money received from the counties?—With keen scalpel the "con man" dissects the anatomy of the institution. One by one he analyzes the industries, showing the most intimate knowledge. The hosiery department produces so and so many dozen of stockings per day. They are not stamped "convict-made," as the law requires. The labels attached are misleading, and calculated to decoy the innocent buyer. The character of the product in the several mat shops is similarly an infraction of the statutes of the great State of Pennsylvania for the protection of free labor. The broom shop is leased by contract to a firm of manufacturers known as Lang Brothers: the law expressly forbids contract labor in prisons. The stamp "convict-made" on the brooms is pasted over with a label, concealing the source of manufacture.

Thus the "con man" runs on in his note. With much show of secrecy he entrusts it to a notorious stool, for delivery to a friend. Soon the writer is called before the Warden. In the latter's hands is the note. The offender smiles complacently. He is aware the authorities are terrorized by the disclosure of such intimate familiarity with the secrets of the prison house, in the possession of an intelligent, possibly well-connected man. He must be propitiated at all cost. The "'con man" joins the "politicians."

The ingenuity of imprisoned intelligence treads devious paths, all leading to the highway of enlarged liberty and privilege. The "old-timer," veteran of oft-repeated experience, easily avoids hard labor. He has many friends in the prison, is familiar with the keepers, and is welcomed by them like a prodigal coming home. The officers are glad to renew the old acquaintance and talk over old times. It brings interest into their tedious existence, often as gray and monotonous as the prisoner's.

The seasoned "yeggman," constitutionally and on principle opposed to toil, rarely works. Generally suffering a comparatively short sentence, he looks upon his imprisonment as, in a measure, a rest-cure from the wear and tear of tramp life. Above average intelligence, he scorns work in general, prison labor in particular. He avoids it with unstinted expense of energy and effort. As a last resort, he plays the "jigger" card, producing an artificial wound on leg or arm, having every appearance of syphilitic excrescence. He pretends to be frightened by the infection, and prevails upon the physician to examine him. The doctor wonders at the wound, closely resembling the dreaded disease. "Ever had syphilis?" he demands. The prisoner protests indignantly. "Perhaps in the family?" the medicus suggests. The patient looks diffident, blushes, cries, "No, never!" and assumes a guilty look. The doctor is now convinced the prisoner is a victim of syphilis. The man is "excused" from work, indefinitely.

The wily yegg, now a patient, secures a "snap" in the yard, and adapts prison conditions to his habits of life. He sedulously courts the friendship of some young inmate, and wins his admiration by "ghost stories" of great daring and cunning. He puts the boy "next to de ropes," and constitutes himself his protector against the abuse of the guards and the advances of other prisoners. He guides the youth's steps through the maze of conflicting rules, and finally initiates him into the "higher wisdom" of "de road."

The path of the "gun" is smoothed by his colleagues in the prison. Even before his arrival, the *esprit de corps* of the "profession" is at work, securing a soft berth for the expected friend. If noted for success and skill, he enjoys the respect of the officers, and the admiration of a retinue of aspiring young crooks, of lesser experience and reputation. With conscious superiority he

instructs them in the finesse of his trade, practices them
in nimble-fingered "touches," and imbues them with the
philosophy of the plenitude of "suckers," whom the
good God has put upon the earth to afford the thief an
"honest living." His sentence nearing completion, the
"gun" grows thoughtful, carefully scans the papers,
forms plans for his first "job," arranges dates with his
"partners," and gathers messages for their "moll buz-
zers."* He is gravely concerned with the somewhat
roughened condition of his hands, and the possible dull-
ing of his sensitive fingers. He maneuvers, generally
successfully, for lighter work, to "limber up a bit," "jol-
lies" the officers and cajoles the Warden for new shoes,
made to measure in the local shops, and insists on the
ten-dollar allowance to prisoners received from counties
outside of Allegheny.† He argues the need of money
"to leave the State." Often he does leave. More frequently a number of charges against the man are held
in reserve by the police, and he is arrested at the gate
by detectives who have been previously notified by the
prison authorities.

The great bulk of the inmates, accidental and occasional offenders direct from the field, factory, and mine,
plod along in the shops, in sullen misery and dread. Day
in, day out, year after year, they drudge at the monotonous work, dully wondering at the numerous trusties
idling about, while their own heavy tasks are constantly
increased. From cell to shop and back again, always
under the stern eyes of the guards, their days drag in
deadening toil. In mute bewilderment they receive con-

---

* Women thieves.

† Upon their discharge, prisoners tried and convicted in the
County of Allegheny—in which the Western Penitentiary is
located—receive only five dollars.

tradictory orders, unaware of the secret antagonisms
between the officials. They are surprised at the new
rule making attendance at religious service obligatory;
and again at the succeeding order (the desired appropriation for a new chapel having been secured) making
church-going optional. They are astonished at the sudden disappearance of the considerate and gentle guard,
Byers, and anxiously hope for his return, not knowing
that the officer who discouraged the underhand methods
of the trusties fell a victim to their cabal.

III

Occasionally a bolder spirit grumbles at the exasper-
ating partiality. Released from punishment, he patiently
awaits an opportunity to complain to the Warden of
his unjust treatment. Weeks pass. At last the Captain
visits the shop. A propitious moment! The carefully
trimmed beard frames the stern face in benevolent white,
mellowing the hard features and lending dignity to his
appearance. His eyes brighten with peculiar brilliancy
as he slowly begins to stroke his chin, and then, almost
imperceptibly, presses his fingers to his lips. As he
passes through the shop, the prisoner raises his hand.
"What is it?" the Warden inquires, a pleasant smile on
his face. The man relates his grievance with nervous
eagerness. "Oh, well," the Captain claps him on the
shoulder, "perhaps a mistake; an unfortunate mistake.
But, then, you might have done something at another
time, and not been punished." He laughs merrily at
his witticism. "It's so long ago, anyhow; we'll forget
it," and he passes on.

But if the Captain is in a different mood, his features
harden, the stern eyes scowl, and he says in his clear,
sharp tones: "State your grievance in writing, on the

printed slip which the officer will give you." The written complaint, deposited in the mail-box, finally reaches the Chaplain, and is forwarded by him to the Warden's office. There the Deputy and the Assistant Deputy read and classify the slips, placing some on the Captain's file and throwing others into the waste basket, according as the accusation is directed against a friendly or an unfriendly brother officer. Months pass before the prisoner is called for "a hearing." By that time he very likely has a more serious charge against the guard, who now persecutes the "kicker." But the new complaint has not yet been "filed," and therefore the hearing is postponed. Not infrequently men are called for a hearing, who have been discharged, or died since making the complaint.

The persevering prisoner, however, unable to receive satisfaction from the Warden, sends a written complaint to some member of the highest authority in the penitentiary—the Board of Inspectors. These are supposed to meet monthly to consider the affairs of the institution, visit the inmates, and minister to their moral needs. The complainant waits, mails several more slips, and wonders why he receives no audience with the Inspectors. But the latter remain invisible, some not visiting the penitentiary within a year. Only the Secretary of the Board, Mr. Reed, a wealthy jeweler of Pittsburgh, occasionally puts in an appearance. Tall and lean, immaculate and trim, he exhales an atmosphere of sanctimoniousness. He walks leisurely through the block, passes a cell with a lithograph of Christ on the wall, and pauses. His hands folded, eyes turned upwards, lips slightly parted in silent prayer, he inquires of the rangeman:

"Whose cell is this?"

"A 1108, Mr. Reed," the prisoner informs him.

It is the cell of Jasper, the colored trusty, chief stool of the prison.

"He is a good man, a good man, God bless him," the Inspector says, a quaver in his voice.

He steps into the cell, puts on his gloves, and carefully adjusts the little looking-glass and the rules, hanging awry on the wall. "It offends my eye," he smiles at the attending rangeman, "they don't hang straight."

Young Tommy, in the adjoining cell, calls out: "Mr. Officer, please."

The Inspector steps forward. "This is Inspector Reed," he corrects the boy. "What is it you wish?"

"Oh, Mr. Inspector, I've been askin' t' see you a long time. I wanted—"

"You should have sent me a slip. Have you a copy of the rules in the cell, my man?"

"Yes, sir."

"Can you read?"

"No, sir."

"Poor boy, did you never go to school?"

"No, sir. Me moder died when I was a kid. Dey put me in de orphan an' den in de ref."

"And your father?"

"I had no fader. Moder always said he ran away before I was born'd."

"They have schools in the orphan asylum. Also in the reformatory, I believe."

"Yep. But dey keeps me most o' de time in punishment. I didn' care fer de school, nohow."

"You were a bad boy. How old are you now?"

"Sev'nteen."

"What is your name?"

"Tommy Wellman."

"From Pittsburgh?"

282 PRISON MEMOIRS OF AN ANARCHIST

"Allegheny. Me moder use'ter live on de hill, near dis 'ere dump."

"What did you wish to see me about?"

"I can't stand de cell, Mr. Inspector. Please let me have some work."

"Are you locked up 'for cause'?"

"I smashed a guy in de jaw fer callin' me names."

"Don't you know it's wrong to fight, my little man?"

"He said me moder was a bitch, God damn his—"

"Don't! Don't swear! Never take the holy name in vain. It's a great sin. You should have reported the man to your officer, instead of fighting."

"I ain't no snitch. Will you get me out of de cell, Mr. Inspector?"

"You are in the hands of the Warden. He is very kind, and he will do what is best for you."

"Oh, hell! I'm locked up five months now. Dat's de best *he's* doin' fer me."

"Don't talk like that to me," the Inspector upbraids him, severely. "You are a bad boy. You must pray; the good Lord will take care of you."

"You get out o' here!" the boy bursts out in sudden fury, cursing and swearing.

Mr. Reed hurriedly steps back. His face, momentarily paling, turns red with shame and anger. He motions to the Captain of the Block.

"Mr. Woods, report this man for impudence to an Inspector," he orders, stalking out into the yard.

The boy is removed to the dungeon.

Oppressed and weary with the scenes of misery and torture, I welcome the relief of solitude, as I am locked in the cell for the night.

IV

Reading and study occupy the hours of the evening. I spend considerable time corresponding with Nold and Bauer: our letters are bulky—ten, fifteen, and twenty pages long. There is much to say! We discuss events in the world at large, incidents of the local life, the maltreatment of the inmates, the frequent clubbings and suicides, the unwholesome food. I share with my comrades my experiences on the range; they, in turn, keep me informed of occurrences in the shops. Their paths run smoother, less eventful than mine, yet not without much heartache and bitterness of spirit. They, too, are objects of prejudice and persecution. The officer of the shop where Nold is employed has been severely reprimanded for "neglect of duty": the Warden had noticed Carl, in the company of several other prisoners, passing through the yard with a load of mattings. He ordered the guard never to allow Nold out of his sight. Bauer has also felt the hand of petty tyranny. He has been deprived of his dark clothes, and reduced to the stripes for "disrespectful behavior." Now he is removed to the North Wing, where my cell also is located, while Nold is in the South Wing, in a "double" cell, enjoying the luxury of a window. Fortunately, though, our friend, the "Horsethief," is still coffee-boy on Bauer's range, thus enabling me to reach the big German. The latter, after reading my notes, returns them to our trusted carrier, who works in the same shop with Carl. Our mail connections are therefore complete, each of us exercising utmost care not to be trapped during the frequent surprises of searching our cells and persons.

Again the *Prison Blossoms* is revived. Most of the readers of the previous year, however, are missing. Dempsey and Beatty, the Knights of Labor men, have

been pardoned, thanks to the multiplied and conflicting
confessions of the informer, Gallagher, who still remains
in prison. "D," our poet laureate, has also been released,
his short term having expired. His identity remains a
mystery, he having merely hinted that he was a "scientist
of the old school, an alchemist," from which we inferred
that he was a counterfeiter. Gradually we recruit our
reading public from the more intelligent and trustworthy
element: the Duquesne strikers renew their "subscrip-
tions" by contributing paper material; with them join
Frank Shay, the philosophic "second-story man"; George,
the prison librarian; "Billy" Ryan, professional gambler
and confidence man; "Yale," a specialist in the art of safe
blowing, and former university student; the "Attorney-
General," a sharp lawyer; "Magazine Alvin," writer and
novelist; "Jim," from whose ingenuity no lock is secure,
and others. "M" and "K" act as alternate editors; the
rest as contributors. The several departments of the
little magazinelet are ornamented with pen and ink
drawings, one picturing Dante visiting the Inferno, another sketching a "pete man," with mask and dark lantern, in the act of boring a safe, while a third bears the
inscription:

> I sometimes hold it half a sin
> To put in words the grief I feel,—
> For words, like nature, half reveal
> And half conceal the soul within.

The editorials are short, pithy comments on local
events, interspersed with humorous sketches and cari-
catures of the officials; the balance of the *Blossoms* consists of articles and essays of a more serious character,
embracing religion and philosophy, labor and politics,
with now and then a personal reminiscence by the "second-story man," or some sex experience by "Magazine
Alvin." One of the associate editors lampoons "Billy-

goat Benny," the Deputy Warden; "K" sketches the
"Shop Screw" and "The Trusted Prisoner"; and "G"
relates the story of the recent strike in his shop, the
men's demand for clear pump water instead of the liquid
mud tapped from the river, and the breaking of the
strike by the exile of a score of "rioters" to the dungeon.
In the next issue the incident is paralleled with the
Pullman Car Strike, and the punished prisoners eulogized
for their courageous stand, some one dedicating an ultra-
original poem to the "Noble Sons of Eugene Debs."

But the vicissitudes of our existence, the change
of location of several readers, the illness and death of
two contributors, badly disarrange the route. During
the winter, "K" produces a little booklet of German
poems, while I elaborate the short "Story of Luba,"
written the previous year, into a novelette, dealing with
life in New York and revolutionary circles. Presently
"G" suggests that the manuscripts might prove of interest to a larger public, and should be preserved. We
discuss the unique plan, wondering how the intellectual
contraband could be smuggled into the light of day. In
our perplexity we finally take counsel with Bob, the
faithful commissary. He cuts the Gordian knot with
astonishing levity: "Youse fellows jest go ahead an'
write, an' don't bother about nothin'. Think I can walk
off all right with a team of horses, but ain't got brains
enough to get away with a bit of scribbling, eh? Jest
leave that to th' Horsethief, an' write till you bust th'
paper works, see?" Thus encouraged, with entire confidence in our resourceful friend, we give the matter
serious thought, and before long we form the ambitious
project of publishing a book by "MKG"!

In high elation, with new interest in life, we set to
work. The little magazine is suspended, and we devote
all our spare time, as well as every available scrap of

writing material, to the larger purpose. We decide to
honor the approaching day, so pregnant with revolutionary inspiration, and as the sun bursts in brilliant splendor
on the eastern skies, the *First of May, 1895,* he steals a
blushing beam upon the heading of the first chapter—
"The Homestead Strike."

CHAPTER XXIII

THE SCALES OF JUSTICE

I

THE summer fades into days of dull gray; the fog thickens on the Ohio; the prison house is dim and damp. The river sirens sound sharp and shrill, and the cells echo with coughing and wheezing. The sick line stretches longer, the men looking more forlorn and dejected. The prisoner in charge of tier "K" suffers a hemorrhage, and is carried to the hospital. From assistant, I am advanced to his position on the range.

But one morning the levers are pulled, the cells unlocked, and the men fed, while I remain under key. I wonder at the peculiar oversight, and rap on the bars for the officers. The Block Captain orders me to desist. I request to see the Warden, but am gruffly told that he cannot be disturbed in the morning. In vain I rack my brain to fathom the cause of my punishment. I review the incidents of the past weeks, ponder over each detail, but the mystery remains unsolved. Perhaps I have unwittingly offended some trusty, or I may be the object of the secret enmity of a spy.

The Chaplain, on his daily rounds, hands me a letter from the Girl, and glances in surprise at the closed door.

"Not feeling well, m' boy?" he asks.

"I'm locked up, Chaplain."

"What have you done?"

287

"Nothing that I know of."

"Oh, well, you'll be out soon. Don't fret, m' boy."

But the days pass, and I remain in the cell. The guards look worried, and vent their ill-humor in profuse vulgarity. The Deputy tries to appear mysterious, wobbles comically along the range, and splutters at me: "Nothin'. Shtay where you are." Jasper, the colored trusty, flits up and down the hall, tremendously busy, his black face more lustrous than ever. Numerous stools nose about the galleries, stop here and there in confidential conversation with officers and prisoners, and whisper excitedly at the front desk. Assistant Deputy Hopkins goes in and out of the block, repeatedly calls Jasper to the office, and hovers in the neighborhood of my cell. The rangemen talk in suppressed tones. An air of mystery pervades the cell-house.

Finally I am called to the Warden. With unconcealed annoyance, he demands:

"What did you want?"

"The officers locked me up—"

"Who said you're locked up?" he interrupts, angrily. "You're merely locked *in*."

"Where's the difference?" I ask.

"One is locked up 'for cause.' You're just kept in for the present."

"On what charge?"

"No charge. None whatever. Take him back, Officers."

.   .   .   .

Close confinement becomes increasingly more dismal and dreary. By contrast with the spacious hall, the cell grows smaller and narrower, oppressing me with a sense of suffocation. My sudden isolation remains unexplained. Notwithstanding the Chaplain's promise to intercede in my behalf, I remain locked "in," and again return the days of solitary, with all their gloom and anguish of heart.

II

A ray of light is shed from New York. The Girl writes in a hopeful vein about the progress of the movement, and the intense interest in my case among radical circles. She refers to Comrade Merlino, now on a tour of agitation, and is enthusiastic about the favorable labor sentiment toward me, manifested in the cities he had visited. Finally she informs me of a plan on foot to secure a reduction of my sentence, and the promising outlook for the collection of the necessary funds. From Merlino I receive a sum of money already contributed for the purpose, together with a letter of appreciation and encouragement, concluding: "Good cheer, dear Comrade; the last word has not yet been spoken."

My mind dwells among my friends. The breath from the world of the living fans the smoldering fires of longing; the tone of my comrades revibrates in my heart with trembling hope. But the revision of my sentence involves recourse to the courts! The sudden realization fills me with dismay. I cannot be guilty of a sacrifice of principle to gain freedom; the mere suggestion rouses the violent protest of my revolutionary traditions. In bitterness of soul, I resent my friends' ill-advised waking of the shades. I shall never leave the house of death. . . .

And yet mail from my friends, full of expectation and confidence, arrives more frequently. Prominent lawyers have been consulted; their unanimous opinion augurs well: the multiplication of my sentences was illegal; according to the statutes of Pennsylvania, the maximum penalty should not have exceeded seven years; the Supreme Court would undoubtedly reverse the judgment of the lower tribunal, specifically the conviction on charges not constituting a crime under the laws of the State. And so forth.

I am assailed by doubts. Is it consequent in me to decline liberty, apparently within reach? John Most appealed his case to the Supreme Court, and the Girl also took advantage of a legal defence. Considerable propaganda resulted from it. Should I refuse the opportunity which would offer such a splendid field for agitation? Would it not be folly to afford the enemy the triumph of my gradual annihilation? I would without hesitation reject freedom at the price of my convictions; but it involves no denial of my faith to rob the vampire of its prey. We must, if necessary, fight the beast of oppression with its own methods, scourge the law in its own tracks, as it were. Of course, the Supreme Court is but another weapon in the hands of authority, a pretence of impartial right. It decided against Most, sustaining the prejudiced verdict of the trial jury. They may do the same in my case. But that very circumstance will serve to confirm our arraignment of class justice. I shall therefore endorse the efforts of my friends.

But before long I am informed that an application to the higher court is not permitted. The attorneys, upon examination of the records of the trial, discovered a fatal obstacle, they said. The defendant, not being legally represented, neglected to "take exceptions" to rulings of the court prejudicial to the accused. Because of the technical omission, there exists no basis for an appeal. They therefore advise an application to the Board of Pardons, on the ground that the punishment in my case is excessive. They are confident that the Board will act favorably, in view of the obvious unconstitutionality of the compounded sentences,—the five minor indictments being indispensible parts of the major charge and, as such, not constituting separate offences.

The unexpected development disquiets me: the sound of "pardon" is detestable. What bitter irony that the noblest intentions, the most unselfish motives, need seek pardon! Aye, of the very source that misinterprets and perverts them! For days the implied humiliation keeps agitating me; I recoil from the thought of personally affixing my name to the meek supplication of the printed form, and finally decide to refuse.

An accidental conversation with the "Attorney General" disturbs my resolution. I learn that in Pennsylvania the applicant's signature is not required by the Pardon Board. A sense of guilty hope steals over me. Yet—I reflect—the pardon of the Chicago Anarchists had contributed much to the dissemination of our ideas. The impartial analysis of the trial-evidence by Governor Altgeld completely exonerated our comrades from responsibility for the Haymarket tragedy, and exposed the heinous conspiracy to destroy the most devoted and able representatives of the labor movement. May not a similar purpose be served by my application for a pardon?

I write to my comrades, signifying my consent. We arrange for a personal interview, to discuss the details of the work. Unfortunately, the Girl, a *persona non grata,* cannot visit me. But a mutual friend, Miss Garrison, is to call on me within two months. At my request, the Chaplain forwards to her the necessary permission, and I impatiently await the first friendly face in two years.

III

As unaccountably as my punishment in the solitary, comes the relief at the expiration of three weeks. The "K" hall-boy is still in the hospital, and I resume the duties of rangeman. The guards eye me with suspicion and greater vigilance, but I soon unravel the tangled skein, and learn the details of the abortive escape that caused my temporary retirement.

The lock of my neighbor, Johnny Smith, had been tampered with. The youth, in solitary at the time, necessarily had the aid of another, it being impossible to reach the keyhole from the inside of the cell. The suspicion of the Warden centered upon me, but investigation by the stools discovered the men actually concerned, and "Dutch" Adams, Spencer, Smith, and Jim Grant were chastised in the dungeon, and are now locked up "for cause," on my range.

By degrees Johnny confides to me the true story of the frustrated plan. "Dutch," a repeater serving his fifth "bit," and favorite of Hopkins, procured a piece of old iron, and had it fashioned into a key in the machine shop, where he was employed. He entrusted the rude instrument to Grant, a young reformatory boy, for a preliminary trial. The guileless youth easily walked into the trap, and the makeshift key was broken in the lock—with disastrous results.

The tricked boys now swear vengeance upon the *provocateur,* but "Dutch" is missing from the range. He has been removed to an upper gallery, and is assigned to a coveted position in the shops.

The newspapers print vivid stories of the desperate attempt to escape from Riverside, and compliment Captain Wright and the officers for so successfully protecting the community. The Warden is deeply affected, and orders the additional punishment of the offenders with a bread-and-water diet. The Deputy walks with inflated chest; Hopkins issues orders curtailing the privileges of the inmates, and inflicting greater hardships. The tone of the guards sounds haughtier, more peremptory; Jasper's face wears a blissful smile. The trusties look pleased and cheerful, but sullen gloom shrouds the prison.

IV

I am standing at my cell, when the door of the rotunda slowly opens, and the Warden approaches me.

"A lady just called; Miss Garrison, from New York. Do you know her?"

"She is one of my friends."

"I dismissed her. You can't see her."

"Why? The rules entitle me to a visit every three months. I have had none in two years. I want to see her."

"You can't. She needs a permit."

"The Chaplain sent her one at my request."

"A member of the Board of Inspectors rescinded it by telegraph."

"What Inspector?"

"You can't question me. Your visitor has been refused admittance."

"Will you tell me the reason, Warden?"

"No reason, no reason whatever."

He turns on his heel, when I detain him: "Warden, it's two years since I've been in the dungeon. I am in the first grade now," I point to the recently earned dark suit. "I am entitled to all the privileges. Why am I deprived of visits?"

"Not another word."

He disappears through the yard door. From the galleries I hear the jeering of a trusty. A guard near by brings his thumb to his nose, and wriggles his fingers in my direction. Humiliated and angry, I return to the cell, to find the monthly letter-sheet on my table. I pour out all the bitterness of my heart to the Girl, dwell on the Warden's discrimination against me, and repeat our conversation and his refusal to admit my visitor. In conclusion, I direct her to have a Pittsburgh lawyer apply to the courts, to force the prison authorities to restore to me the privileges allowed by the law to the ordinary prisoner. I drop the letter in the mail-box, hoping that my outburst and the threat of the law will induce the Warden to retreat from his position. The Girl will, of course, understand the significance of the epistle, aware that my reference to a court process is a diplomatic subterfuge for effect, and not meant to be acted upon.

But the next day the Chaplain returns the letter to me. "Not so rash, my boy," he warns me, not unkindly. "Be patient; I'll see what I can do for you."

"But the letter, Chaplain?"

"You've wasted your paper, Aleck. I can't pass this letter. But just keep quiet, and I'll look into the matter."

Weeks pass in evasive replies. Finally the Chaplain advises a personal interview with the Warden. The latter refers me to the Inspectors. To each member of the Board I address a request for a few minutes' conversation, but a month goes by without word from the high officials. The friendly runner, "Southside" Johnny, offers to give me an opportunity to speak to an Inspector, on the payment of ten plugs of tobacco. Unfortunately, I cannot spare my small allowance, but I tender him a dollar bill of the money the Girl had sent me artfully concealed in the buckle of a pair of suspenders. The runner is highly elated, and assures me of success, directing me to keep careful watch on the yard door.

Several days later, passing along the range engaged in my duties, I notice "Southside" entering from the yard, in friendly conversation with a strange gentleman in citizen clothes. For a moment I do not realize the situation, but the next instant I am aware of Johnny's violent efforts to attract my attention. He pretends to show the man some fancy work made by the inmates, all the while drawing him closer to my door, with surreptitious nods at me. I approach my cell.

"This is Berkman, Mr. Nevin, the man who shot Frick," Johnny remarks.

The gentleman turns to me with a look of interest.

"Good morning, Berkman," he says pleasantly. "How long are you doing?"

"Twenty-two years."

"I'm sorry to hear that. It's rather a long sentence. You know who I am?"

"Inspector Nevin, I believe."

"Yes. You have never seen me before?"

"No. I sent a request to see you recently."

"When was that?"

"A month ago."

"Strange. I was in the office three weeks ago. There was no note from you on my file. Are you sure you sent one?"

"Quite sure. I sent a request to each Inspector."

"What's the trouble?"

I inform him briefly that I have been deprived of visiting privileges. Somewhat surprised, he glances at my dark clothes, and remarks:

"You are in the first grade, and therefore entitled to visits. When did you have your last visitor?"

"Two years ago."

"Two years?" he asks, almost incredulously.   "Did the lady from New York have a permit?"

The Warden hurriedly enters from the yard.

"Mr. Nevin," he calls out anxiously, "I've been looking for you."

"Berkman was just telling me about his visitor being sent away, Captain," the Inspector remarks.

"Yes, yes," the Warden smiles, forcedly, " 'for cause.' "

"Oh!" the face of Mr. Nevin assumes a grave look. "Berkman," he turns to me, "you'll have to apply to the Secretary of the Board, Mr. Reed.   I am not familiar with the internal affairs."

The Warden links his arm with the Inspector, and they walk toward the yard door.   At the entrance they are met by "Dutch" Adams, the shop messenger.

"Good morning, Mr. Nevin," the trusty greets him. "Won't you issue me a special visit?   My mother is sick; she wants to see me."

The Warden grins at the ready fiction.

"When did you have your last visit?" the Inspector inquires.

"Two weeks ago."

"You are entitled to one only every three months."

"That is why I asked you for an extra, Mr. Inspector," "Dutch" retorts boldly.   "I know you are a kind man."

Mr. Nevin smiles good-naturedly and glances at the Warden.

"Dutch is all right," the Captain nods.

The Inspector draws his visiting card, pencils on it, and hands it to the prisoner.

CHAPTER XXIV

THOUGHTS THAT STOLE OUT OF PRISON

April 12, 1896.

My Dear Girl:

I have craved for a long, long time to have a free talk with you, but this is the first opportunity. A good friend, a "lover of horseflesh," promised to see this "birdie" through. I hope it will reach you safely.

In my local correspondence you have been christened the "Immutable." I realize how difficult it is to keep up letter-writing through the endless years, the points of mutual interest gradually waning. It is one of the tragedies in the existence of a prisoner. "K" and "G" have almost ceased to expect mail. But I am more fortunate. The Twin writes very seldom nowadays; the correspondence of other friends is fitful. But you are never disappointing. It is not so much the contents that matter: these increasingly sound like the language of a strange world, with its bewildering flurry and ferment, disturbing the calm of cell-life. But the very arrival of a letter is momentous. It brings a glow into the prisoner's heart to feel that he is remembered, actively, with that intimate interest which alone can support a regular correspondence. And then your letters are so vital, so palpitating with the throb of our common cause. I have greatly enjoyed your communications from Paris and Vienna, the accounts of the movement and of our European comrades. Your letters are so much part of yourself, they bring me nearer to you and to life.

The newspaper clippings you have referred to on various occasions, have been withheld from me. Nor are any radical publications permitted. I especially regret to miss *Solidarity*. I have not seen a single copy since its resurrection two years ago. I have followed the activities of Chas. W. Mowbray and the recent tour of John Turner, so far as the press accounts arc concerned. I hope you'll write more about our English comrades.

I need not say much of the local life, dear. That you know from my official mail, and you can read between the lines. The action of the Pardon Board was a bitter disappointment to me. No less to you also, I suppose. Not that I was very enthusiastic as to a favorable decision. But that they should so cynically evade the issue,—I was hardly prepared for *that*. I had hoped they would at least consider the case. But evidently they were averse to going on record, one way or another. The lawyers informed me that they were not even allowed an opportunity to present their arguments. The Board ruled that "the wrong complained of is not actual"; that is, that I am not yet serving the sentence we want remitted. A lawyer's quibble. It means that I must serve the first sentence of seven years, before applying for the remission of the other indictments. Discounting commutation time, I still have about a year to complete the first sentence. I doubt whether it is advisable to try again. Little justice can be expected from those quarters. But I want to submit another proposition to you; consult with our friends regarding it. It is this: there is a prisoner here who has just been pardoned by the Board, whose president, the Lieutenant-Governor, is indebted to the prisoner's lawyer for certain political services. The attorney's name is K—— D—— of Pittsburgh. He has intimated to his client that he will guarantee my release for $1,000.00, the sum to be deposited in safe hands and to be paid *only* in case of success. Of course, we cannot afford such a large fee. And I cannot say whether the offer is worth considering; still, you know that almost anything can be bought from politicians. I leave the matter in your hands.

The question of my visits seems tacitly settled; I can procure no permit for my friends to see me. For some obscure reason, the Warden has conceived a great fear of an Anarchist plot against the prison. The local "trio" is under special surveillance and constantly discriminated against, though "K" and "G" are permitted to receive visits. You will smile at the infantile terror of the authorities: it is bruited about that a "certain Anarchist lady" (meaning you, I presume; in reality it was Henry's sweetheart, a jolly devil-may-care girl) made a threat against the prison. The gossips have it that she visited Inspector Reed at his business place, and requested to see me. The Inspector refusing, she burst out: "We'll blow your dirty walls down." I could not determine whether there is any foundation for the story, but it is circulated here, and the prisoners firmly believe it explains my deprivation of visits.

That is a characteristic instance of local conditions. Involuntarily I smile at Kennan's naïve indignation with the brutalities he thinks possible only in Russian and Siberian prisons. He would find it almost impossible to learn the true conditions in the American prisons: he would be conducted the rounds of the "show" cells, always neat and clean for the purpose; he would not see the basket cell, nor the bull rings in the dungeon, where men are chained for days; nor would he be permitted to converse for hours, or whole evenings, with the prisoners, as he did with the exiles in Siberia. Yet if he succeeded in learning even half the truth, he would be forced to revise his views of American penal institutions, as he did in regard to Russian politicals. He would be horrified to witness the brutality that is practised here as a matter of routine, the abuse of the insane, the petty persecution. Inhumanity is the keynote of stupidity in power.

Your soul must have been harrowed by the reports of the terrible tortures in Montjuich. What is all indignation and lamenting, in the face of the revival of the Inquisition? Is there no Nemesis in Spain?

CHAPTER XXV

HOW SHALL THE DEPTHS CRY?

I

THE change of seasons varies the tone of the prison. A cheerier atmosphere pervades the shops and the cell-house in the summer. The block is airier and lighter; the guards relax their stern look, in anticipation of their vacations; the men hopefully count the hours till their approaching freedom, and the gates open daily to release some one going back to the world.

But heavy gloom broods over the prison in winter. The windows are closed and nailed; the vitiated air, artificially heated, is suffocating with dryness. Smoke darkens the shops, and the cells are in constant dusk. Tasks grow heavier, the punishments more severe. The officers look sullen; the men are morose and discontented. The ravings of the insane become wilder, suicides more frequent; despair and hopelessness oppress every heart.

The undercurrent of rebellion, swelling with mute suffering and repression, turbulently sweeps the barriers. The severity of the authorities increases, methods of penalizing are more drastic; the prisoners fret, wax more querulous, and turn desperate with blind, spasmodic defiance.

But among the more intelligent inmates, dissatisfaction manifests more coherent expression. The Lexow investigation in New York has awakened an echo in the prison. A movement is quietly initiated among the solitaries, looking toward an investigation of Riverside.

I keep busy helping the men exchange notes maturing the project. Great care must be exercised to guard
against treachery: only men of proved reliability may
be entrusted with the secret, and precautions taken that
no officer or stool scent our design. The details of the
campaign are planned on "K" range, with Billy Ryan,
Butch, Sloane, and Jimmie Grant, as the most trustworthy, in command. It is decided that the attack upon
the management of the penitentiary is to be initiated
from the "outside." A released prisoner is to inform
the press of the abuses, graft, and immorality rampant
in Riverside. The public will demand an investigation.
The "cabal" on the range will supply the investigators
with data and facts that will rouse the conscience of the
community, and cause the dismissal of the Warden and
the introduction of reforms.

A prisoner, about to be discharged, is selected for the
important mission of enlightening the press. In great
anxiety and expectation we await the newspapers, the
day following his liberation; we scan the pages closely.
Not a word of the penitentiary! Probably the released
man has not yet had an opportunity to visit the editors.
In the joy of freedom, he may have looked too deeply
into the cup that cheers. He will surely interview the
papers the next day.

But the days pass into weeks, without any reference
in the press to the prison. The trusted man has failed
us! The revelation of the life at Riverside is of a nature
not to be ignored by the press. The discharged inmate
has proved false to his promise. Bitterly the solitaries
denounce him, and resolve to select a more reliable man
among the first candidates for liberty.

One after another, a score of men are entrusted with
the mission to the press. But the papers remain silent
Anxiously, though every day less hopefully, we search

their columns. Ryan cynically derides the faithlessness of convict promises; Butch rages and swears at the traitors. But Sloane is sternly confident in his own probity, and cheers me as I pause at his cell:

"Never min' them rats, Aleck. You jest wait till *I* go out. Here's the boy that'll keep his promise all right. What I won't do to old Sandy ain't worth mentionin'."

"Why, you still have two years, Ed," I remind him.

"Not on your tintype, Aleck. Only one and a stump."

"How big is the stump?"

"Wa-a-ll," he chuckles, looking somewhat diffident, "it's one year, elev'n months, an' twenty-sev'n days. It ain't no two years, though, see?"

Jimmy Grant grows peculiarly reserved, evidently disinclined to talk. He seeks to avoid me. The treachery of the released men fills him with resentment and suspicion of every one. He is impatient of my suggestion that the fault may lie with a servile press. At the mention of our plans, he bursts out savagely:

"Forget it! You're no good, none of you. Let me be!" He turns his back to me, and angrily paces the cell.

His actions fill me with concern. The youth seems strangely changed. Fortunately, his time is almost served.

II

Like wildfire the news circles the prison. "The papers are giving Sandy hell!" The air in the block trembles with suppressed excitement. Jimmy Grant, recently released, had sent a communication to the State Board of Charities, bringing serious charges against the management of Riverside. The press publishes startlingly significant excerpts from Grant's letter. Editorially, however, the indictment is ignored by the majority of the Pittsburgh papers. One writer comments ambiguously, in guarded language, suggesting the improbability of the horrible practices alleged by Grant. Another eulogizes Warden Wright as an intelligent and humane man, who has the interest of the prisoners at heart. The detailed accusations are briefly dismissed as unworthy of notice, because coming from a disgruntled criminal who had not found prison life to his liking. Only the *Leader* and the *Dispatch* consider the matter seriously, refer to the numerous complaints from discharged prisoners, and suggest the advisability of an investigation; they urge upon the Warden the necessity of disproving, once for all, the derogatory statements regarding his management.

Within a few days the President of the Board of Charities announces his decision to "look over" the penitentiary. December is on the wane, and the Board is expected to visit Riverside after the holidays.

III

K. & G.:

Of course, neither of you has any more faith in alleged investigations than myself. The Lexow investigation, which shocked the whole country with its exposé of police corruption, has resulted in practically nothing. One or two subordinates have been "scapegoated"; those "higher up" went unscathed, as usual; the "system" itself remains in *statu quo*. The one who has mostly profited by the spasm of morality is Goff, to whom the vice crusade afforded an opportunity to rise from obscurity into the national limelight. Parkhurst also has subsided, probably content with the enlarged size of his flock and—salary. To give the devil his due, however, I admired his perseverance and courage in face of the storm of ridicule and scorn that met his initial accusations against the glorious police department of the metropolis. But though every charge has been proved in the most absolute manner, the situation, as a whole, remains unchanged.

It is the history of all investigations. As the Germans say, you can't convict the devil in the court of his mother-in-law.

It has again been demonstrated by the Congressional "inquiry" into the Carnegie blow-hole armor plate; in the terrible revelations regarding Superintendent Brockway, of the Elmira Reformatory—a veritable den for maiming and killing; and in numerous other instances. Warden Wright also was investigated, about ten years ago; a double set of books was then found, disclosing peculation of appropriations and theft of the prison product; brutality and murder were uncovered—yet Sandy has remained in his position.

We can, therefore, expect nothing from the proposed investigation by the Board of Charities. I have no doubt it will be a whitewash. But I think that we—the Anarchist trio—should show our solidarity, and aid the inmates with our best efforts; we must prevent the investigation resulting in a farce, so far as evidence against the management is concerned. We should leave the Board no loophole, no excuse of a lack of witnesses or proofs to support Grant's charges. I am confident you will agree with me in this. I am collecting data for presentation to the investigators; I am also preparing a list of volunteer witnesses. I have seventeen numbers on my range, and others from various parts of this block and from the shops. They all seem anxious to testify, though I am sure some will weaken when the critical moment arrives. Several have already notified me to erase their names. But we shall have a sufficient number of witnesses; we want preferably such men as have personally suffered a clubbing, the bull ring, hanging by the wrists, or other punishment forbidden by the law.

I have already notified the Warden that I wish to testify before the Investigation Committee. My purpose was to anticipate his objection that there are already enough witnesses. I am the first on the list now. The completeness of the case against the authorities will surprise you. Fortunately, my position as rangeman has enabled me to gather whatever information I needed. I will send you to-morrow duplicates of the evidence (to insure greater safety for our material). For the present I append a partial list of our "exhibits":

(1) Cigarettes and outside tobacco; bottle of whiskey and "dope"; dice, playing cards, cash money, several knives, two razors, postage stamps, outside mail, and other contraband. (These are for the purpose of proving the Warden a liar in denying

to the press the existence of gambling in the prison, the selling of bakery and kitchen provisions for cash, the possession of weapons, and the possibility of underground communication.)

(2) Prison-made beer. A demonstration of the staleness of our bread and the absence of potatoes in the soup. (The beer is made from fermented yeast stolen by the trusties from the bakery; also from potatoes.)

(3) Favoritism; special privileges of trusties; political jobs; the system of stool espionage.

(4) Pennsylvania diet; basket; dungeon; cuffing and chaining up; neglect of the sick; punishment of the insane.

(5) Names and numbers of men maltreated and clubbed.

(6) Data of assaults and cutting affrays in connection with "kid-business," the existence of which the Warden absolutely denies.

(7) Special case of A 444, who attacked the Warden in church, because of jealousy of "Lady Goldie."

(8) Graft:

(a) Hosiery department: fake labels, fictitious names of manufacture, false book entries.

(b) Broom shop: convict labor hired out, contrary to law, to Lang Bros., broom manufacturers, of Allegheny, Pa. Goods sold to the United States Government, through sham middleman. Labels bear legend, "Union Broom." Sample enclosed.

(*c*) Mats, mattings, mops—product not stamped.

(*d*) Shoe and tailor shops: prison materials used for the private needs of the Warden, the officers, and their families.

(*e*) $75,000, appropriated by the State (1893) for a new chapel. The bricks of the old building used for the new, except one outside layer. All the work done by prisoners. Architect, Mr. A. Wright, the Warden's son. Actual cost of chapel, $7,000. The inmates *forced* to attend services to overcrowd the old church; after the desired appropriation was secured, attendance became optional.

(*f*) Library: the 25c. tax, exacted from every unofficial visitor, is supposed to go to the book fund. About 50 visitors per day, the year round. No new books added to the library in 10 years. Old duplicates donated by the public libraries of Pittsburgh are catalogued as purchased new books.

(*g*) Robbing the prisoners of remuneration for their labor. See copy of Act of 1883, P. L. 112.

LAW ON PRISON LABOR AND WAGES OF CONVICTS
(Act of 1883, June 13th, P. L. 112)

Section 1—At the expiration of existing contracts, Wardens are directed to employ the convicts under their control for and in behalf of the State.

Section 2—No labor shall be hired out by contract.

Section 4—All convicts under the control of the State and county officers, and all inmates of reformatory institutions engaged in the manufacture of articles for general consumption, shall receive quarterly wages equal to the amount of their earnings, to be fixed from time to time by the authorities of the institution, from which board, lodging, clothing, and costs of trial shall be deducted, and the balance paid to their families or dependents; in case none such appear, the amount shall be paid to the convict at the expiration of his term of imprisonment.

The prisoners receive no payment whatever, even for overtime work, except occasionally a slice of pork for supper.

K. G., plant this and other material I'll send you, in a safe place.

M.

CHAPTER XXVI

HIDING THE EVIDENCE

I

I⊤ is New Year's eve. An air of pleasant anticipation fills the prison; to-morrow's feast is the exciting subject of conversation. Roast beef will be served for dinner, with a goodly loaf of currant bread, and two cigars for dessert. Extra men have been drafted for the kitchen; they flit from block to yard, looking busy and important, yet halting every passer-by to whisper with secretive mien, "Don't say I told you. Sweet potatoes to-morrow!" The younger inmates seem skeptical, and strive to appear indifferent, the while they hover about the yard door, nostrils expanded, sniffing the appetizing wafts from the kitchen. Here and there an old-timer grumbles: we should have had sweet "murphies" for Christmas. " 'Too high-priced,' Sandy said," they sneer in ill humor. The new arrivals grow uneasy; perhaps they are still too expensive? Some study the market quotations on the delicacy. But the chief cook drops in to visit "his" boy, and confides to the rangeman that the sweet potatoes are a "sure thing," just arrived and counted. The happy news is whispered about, with confident assurance, yet tinged with anxiety. There is great rejoicing among the men. Only Sol, the lifer, is querulous: he doesn't care a snap about the "extra feed"—stomach still sour from the Christmas dinner—and, anyhow, it only makes the week-a-day "grub" more disgusting.

308 PRISON MEMOIRS OF AN ANARCHIST

The rules are somewhat relaxed. The hallmen converse freely; the yard gangs lounge about and cluster
in little groups, that separate at the approach of a
superior officer. Men from the bakery and kitchen run
in and out of the block, their pockets bulging suspiciously.
"What are you after?" the doorkeeper halts them. "Oh,
just to my cell; forgot my handkerchief." The guard
answers the sly wink with an indulgent smile. "All
right; go ahead, but don't be long." If "Papa" Mitchell
is about, he thunders at the chief cook, his bosom swelling with packages: "Wotch 'er got there, eh? Big
family of kids *you* have, Jim. First thing you know,
you'll swipe the hinges off th' kitchen door." The envied
bakery and kitchen employees supply their friends with
extra holiday tidbits, and the solitaries dance in glee at
the sight of the savory dainty, the fresh brown bread
generously dotted with sweet currants. It is the prelude
of the promised culinary symphony.

The evening is cheerful with mirth and jollity. The
prisoners at first converse in whispers, then become
bolder, and talk louder through the bars. As night
approaches, the cell-house rings with unreserved hilarity
and animation,—light-hearted chaff mingled with coarse
jests and droll humor. A wag on the upper tier banters
the passing guards, his quips and sallies setting the
adjoining cells in a roar, and inspiring imitation.

Slowly the babel of tongues subsides, as the gong
sounds the order to retire. Some one shouts to a distant
friend, "Hey, Bill, are you there? Ye-es? Stay there!"
It grows quiet, when suddenly my neighbor on the left
sing-songs, "Fellers, who's goin' to sit up with me to
greet New Year's?" A dozen voices yell their accept-
ance. "Little Frenchy," the spirited grayhead on the

top tier, vociferates shrilly, "Me, too, boys. I'm viz you all right."

All is still in the cell-house, save for a wild Indian whoop now and then by the vigil-keeping boys. The block breathes in heavy sleep; loud snoring sounds from the gallery above. Only the irregular tread of the felt-soled guards falls muffled in the silence.

.   .   .   .

The clock in the upper rotunda strikes the midnight hour. A siren on the Ohio intones its deep-chested bass. Another joins it, then another. Shrill factory whistles pierce the boom of cannon; the sweet chimes of a near-by church ring in joyful melody between. Instantly the prison is astir. Tin cans rattle against iron bars, doors shake in fury, beds and chairs squeak and screech, pans slam on the floor, shoes crash against the walls with a dull thud, and rebound noisily on the stone. Unearthly yelling, shouting, and whistling rend the air; an inventive prisoner beats a wild tattoo with a tin pan on the table— a veritable Bedlam of frenzy has broken loose in both wings. The prisoners are celebrating the advent of the New Year.

.   .   .   .

The voices grow hoarse and feeble. The tin clanks languidly against the iron, the grating of the doors sounds weaker. The men are exhausted with the unwonted effort. The guards stumbled up the galleries, their forms swaying unsteadily in the faint flicker of the gaslight. In maudlin tones they command silence, and bid the men retire to bed. The younger, more daring, challenge the order with husky howls and catcalls,—a defiant shout, a groan, and all is quiet.

Daybreak wakes the turmoil and uproar. For twenty-four hours the long-repressed animal spirits are rampant. No music or recreation honors the New Year; the day is passed in the cell. The prisoners, securely barred and locked, are permitted to vent their pain and sorrow, their yearnings and hopes, in a Saturnalia of tumult.

II

The month of January brings sedulous activity. Shops and block are overhauled, every nook and corner is scoured, and a special squad detailed to whitewash the cells. The yearly clean-up not being due till spring, I conclude from the unusual preparations that the expected visit of the Board of Charities is approaching.

The prisoners are agog with the coming investigation. The solitaries and prospective witnesses are on the *qui vive*, anxious lines on their faces. Some manifest fear of the ill will of the Warden, as the probable result of their testimony. I seek to encourage them by promising to assume full responsibility, but several men withdraw their previous consent. The safety of my data causes me grave concern, in view of the increasing frequency of searches. Deliberation finally resolves itself into the bold plan of secreting my most valuable material in the cell set aside for the use of the officers. It is the first cell on the range; it is never locked, and is ignored at searches because it is not occupied by prisoners. The little bundle, protected with a piece of oilskin procured from the dispensary, soon reposes in the depths of the waste pipe. A stout cord secures it from being washed away by the rush of water, when the privy is in use. I call Officer Mitchell's attention to the dusty condition of the cell, and offer to sweep it every morning and afternoon. He accedes in an offhand manner, and twice daily I surreptitiously examine the tension of the water-soaked cord, renewing the string repeatedly.

Other material and copies of my "exhibits" are deposited with several trustworthy friends on the range. Everything is ready for the investigation, and we confidently await the coming of the Board of Charities.

III

The cell-house rejoices at the absence of Scot Woods. The Block Captain of the morning has been "reduced to the ranks." The disgrace is signalized by his appearance on the wall, pacing the narrow path in the chilly winter blasts. The guards look upon the assignment as "punishment duty" for incurring the displeasure of the Warden. The keepers smile at the indiscreet Scot interfering with the self-granted privileges of "Southside" Johnny, one of the Warden's favorites. The runner who afforded me an opportunity to see Inspector Nevin, came out victorious in the struggle with Woods. The latter was upbraided by Captain Wright in the presence of Johnny, who is now officially authorized in his perquisites. Sufficient time was allowed to elapse, to avoid comment, whereupon the officer was withdrawn from the block.

I regret his absence. A severe disciplinarian, Woods was yet very exceptional among the guards, in that he sought to discourage the spying of prisoners on each other. He frowned upon the trusties, and strove to treat the men impartially.

Mitchell has been changed to the morning shift, to fill the vacancy made by the transfer of Woods. The charge of the block in the afternoon devolves upon Offi-

cer McIlvaine, a very corpulent man, with sharp, steely
eyes. He is considerably above the average warder in
intelligence, but extremely fond of Jasper, who now acts
as his assistant, the obese turnkey rarely leaving his seat
at the front desk.

Changes of keepers, transfers from the shops to the
two cell-houses are frequent; the new guards are alert
and active. Almost daily the Warden visits the ranges,
leaving in his wake more stringent discipline. Rarely
do I find a chance to pause at the cells; I keep in touch
with the men through the medium of notes. But one
day, several fights breaking out in the shops, the block
officers are requisitioned to assist in placing the combatants in the punishment cells. The front is deserted,
and I improve the opportunity to talk to the solitaries.
Jasper, "Southside," and Bob Runyon, the "politicians,"
also converse at the doors, Bob standing suspiciously
close to the bars. Suddenly Officer McIlvaine appears
in the yard door. His face is flushed, his eyes filling with
wrath as they fasten on the men at the cells.

"Hey, you fellows, get away from there!" he shouts.
"Confound you all, the 'Old Man' just gave me the
deuce; too much talking in the block. I won't stand
for it, that's all," he adds, petulantly.

Within half an hour I am haled before the Warden.
He looks worried, deep lines of anxiety about his mouth.

"You are reported for standing at the doors," he
snarls at me. "What are you always telling the men?"

"It's the first time the officer—"

"Nothing of the kind," he interrupts; "you're always
talking to the prisoners. They are in punishment, and
you have no business with them."

"Why was *I* picked out? Others talk, too."

"Ye-e-s?" he drawls sarcastically; then, turning to

the keeper, he says: "How is that, Officer? The man is charging you with neglect of duty."

"I am not charging—"

"Silence! What have you to say, Mr. McIlvaine?"

The guard reddens with suppressed rage. "It isn't true, Captain," he replies; "there was no one except Berkman."

"You hear what the officer says? You are always breaking the rules. You're plotting; I know you,— pulling a dozen wires. You are inimical to the management of the institution. But I will break your connections. Officer, take him directly to the South Wing, you understand? He is not to return to his cell. Have it searched at once, thoroughly. Lock him up."

"Warden, what for?" I demand. "I have not done anything to lose my position. Talking is not such a serious charge."

"Very serious, very serious. You're too dangerous on the range. I'll spoil your infernal schemes by removing you from the North Block. You've been there too long."

"I want to remain there."

"The more reason to take you away. That will do now."

"No, it won't," I burst out. "I'll stay where I am."

"Remove him, Mr. McIlvaine."

I am taken to the South Wing and locked up in a vacant cell, neglected and ill-smelling. It is Number 2, Range M—the first gallery, facing the yard; a "double" cell, somewhat larger than those of the North Block, and containing a small window. The walls are damp and bare, save for the cardboard of printed rules and the prison calendar. It is the 27th of February, 1896, but the calendar is of last year, indicating that the cell has not been occupied since the previous November. It contains the usual furnishings: bedstead and soiled straw mattress, a small table and a chair. It feels cold and dreary.

In thought I picture the guards ransacking my former cell. They will not discover anything: my material is well hidden. The Warden evidently suspects my plans: he fears my testimony before the investigation committee. My removal is to sever my connections, and now it is impossible for me to reach my data. I must return to the North Block; otherwise all our plans are doomed to fail. I can't leave my friends on the range in the lurch: some of them have already signified to the Chaplain their desire to testify; their statements will remain unsupported in the absence of my proofs. I must rejoin them. I have told the Warden that I shall remain where I was, but he probably ignored it as an empty boast.

I consider the situation, and resolve to "break up housekeeping." It is the sole means of being transferred to the other cell-house. It will involve the loss of the grade, and a trip to the dungeon; perhaps even a fight with the keepers: the guards, fearing the broken furniture will be used for defence, generally rush the prisoner with blackjacks. But my return to the North Wing will be assured,—no man in stripes can remain in the South Wing.

Alert for an approaching step, I untie my shoes, producing a scrap of paper, a pencil, and a knife. I write a hurried note to "K," briefly informing him of the new developments, and intimating that our data are safe. Guardedly I attract the attention of the runner on the floor beneath; it is Bill Say, through whom Carl occasionally communicates with "G." The note rolled into a little ball, I shoot between the bars to the waiting prisoner. Now everything is prepared.

It is near supper time; the men are coming back from work. It would be advisable to wait till everybody is locked in, and the shop officers depart home. There will then be only three guards on duty in the block. But I am in a fever of indignation and anger. Furiously snatching up the chair, I start "breaking up."

CHAPTER XXVII

LOVE'S DUNGEON FLOWER

THE dungeon smells foul and musty; the darkness is almost visible, the silence oppressive; but the terror of my former experience has abated. I shall probably be kept in the underground cell for a longer time than on the previous occasion,—my offence is considered very grave. Three charges have been entered against me: destroying State property, having possession of a knife, and uttering a threat against the Warden. When I saw the officers gathering at my back, while I was facing the Captain, I realized its significance. They were preparing to assault me. Quickly advancing to the Warden, I shook my fist in his face, crying:

"If they touch me, I'll hold you personally responsible."

He turned pale. Trying to steady his voice, he demanded:

"What do you mean? How dare you?"

"I mean just what I say. I won't be clubbed. My friends will avenge me, too."

He glanced at the guards standing rigid, in ominous silence. One by one they retired, only two remaining, and I was taken quietly to the dungeon.

.   .   .   .

The stillness is broken by a low, muffled sound. I listen intently. It is some one pacing the cell at the further end of the passage.

316

"Halloo! Who's there?" I shout.

No reply. The pacing continues. It must be "Silent Nick"; he never talks.

I prepare to pass the night on the floor. It is bare; there is no bed or blanket, and I have been deprived of my coat and shoes. It is freezing in the cell; my feet grow numb, hands cold, as I huddle in the corner, my head leaning against the reeking wall, my body on the stone floor. I try to think, but my thoughts are wandering, my brain frigid.

.   .   .   .

The rattling of keys wakes me from my stupor. Guards are descending into the dungeon. I wonder whether it is morning, but they pass my cell: it is not yet breakfast time. Now they pause and whisper. I recognize the mumbling speech of Deputy Greaves, as he calls out to the silent prisoner:

"Want a drink?"

The double doors open noisily.

"Here!"

"Give me the cup," the hoarse bass resembles that of "Crazy Smithy." His stentorian voice sounds cracked since he was shot in the neck by Officer Dean.

"You can't have th' cup," the Deputy fumes.

"I won't drink out of your hand, God damn you. Think I'm a cur, do you?" Smithy swears and curses savagely.

The doors are slammed and locked. The steps grow faint, and all is silent, save the quickened footfall of Smith, who will not talk to any prisoner.

I pass the long night in drowsy stupor, rousing at times to strain my ear for every sound from the rotunda above, wondering whether day is breaking. The minutes drag in dismal darkness. . . .

The loud clanking of the keys tingles in my ears like sweet music. It is morning! The guards hand me the day's allowance—two ounces of white bread and a quart of water. The wheat tastes sweet; it seems to me I've never eaten anything so delectable. But the liquid is insipid, and nauseates me. At almost one bite I swallow the slice, so small and thin. It whets my appetite, and I feel ravenously hungry.

At Smith's door the scene of the previous evening is repeated. The Deputy insists that the man drink out of the cup held by a guard. The prisoner refuses, with a profuse flow of profanity. Suddenly there is a splash, followed by a startled cry, and the thud of the cell bucket on the floor. Smith has emptied the contents of his privy upon the officers. In confusion they rush out of the dungeon.

Presently I hear the clatter of many feet in the cellar. There is a hubbub of suppressed voices. I recognize the rasping whisper of Hopkins, the tones of Woods, McIlvaine, and others. I catch the words, "Both sides at once." Several cells in the dungeon are provided with double entrances, front and back, to facilitate attacks upon obstreperous prisoners. Smith is always assigned to one of these cells. I shudder as I realize that the officers are preparing to club the demented man. He has been weakened by years of unbroken solitary confinement, and his throat still bleeds occasionally from the bullet wound. Almost half his time he has been kept in the dungeon, and now he has been missing from the range twelve days. It is . . . . Involuntarily I shut my eyes at the fearful thud of the riot clubs.

.   .   .   .

The hours drag on. The monotony is broken by the keepers bringing another prisoner to the dungeon. I hear his violent sobbing from the depth of the cavern.

"Who is there?" I hail him. I call repeatedly, without receiving an answer. Perhaps the new arrival is afraid of listening guards.

"Ho, man!" I sing out, "the screws have gone. Who are you? This is Aleck, Aleck Berkman."

"Is that you, Aleck? This is Johnny." There is a familiar ring about the young voice, broken by piteous moans. But I fail to identify it.

"What Johnny?"

"Johnny Davis—you know—stocking shop. I've just —killed a man."

In bewilderment I listen to the story, told with bursts of weeping. Johnny had returned to the shop; he thought he would try again: he wanted to earn his "good" time. Things went well for a while, till "Dutch" Adams became shop runner. He is the stool who got Grant and Johnny Smith in trouble with the fake key, and Davis would have nothing to do with him. But "Dutch" persisted, pestering him all the time; and then—

"Well, you know, Aleck," the boy seems diffident, "he lied about me like hell: he told the fellows he *used* me. Christ, my mother might hear about it! I couldn't stand it, Aleck; honest to God, I couldn't. I—I killed the lying cur, an' now—now I'll—I'll swing for it," he sobs as if his heart would break.

A touch of tenderness for the poor boy is in my voice, as I strive to condole with him and utter the hope that it may not be so bad, after all. Perhaps Adams will not die. He is a powerful man, big and strong; he may survive.

Johnny eagerly clutches at the straw. He grows more cheerful, and we talk of the coming investigation and local affairs. Perhaps the Board will even clear him, he suggests. But suddenly seized with fear, he weeps and moans again.

More men are cast into the dungeon. They bring news from the world above. An epidemic of fighting seems to have broken out in the wake of recent orders. The total inhibition of talking is resulting in more serious offences. "Kid Tommy" is enlarging upon his trouble. "You see, fellers," he cries in a treble, "dat skunk of a Pete he pushes me in de line, and I turns round t' give 'im hell, but de screw pipes me. Got no chance t' choo, so I turns an' biffs him on de jaw, see?" But he is sure, he says, to be let out at night, or in the morning, at most. "Them fellers that was scrappin' yesterday in de yard didn't go to de hole. Dey jest put 'em in de cell. Sandy knows de committee 's comin' all right."

Johnny interrupts the loquacious boy to inquire anxiously about "Dutch" Adams, and I share his joy at hearing that the man's wound is not serious. He was cut about the shoulders, but was able to walk unassisted to the hospital. Johnny overflows with quiet happiness; the others dance and sing. I recite a poem from Nekras-sov; the boys don't understand a word, but the sorrow-laden tones appeal to them, and they request more Russian "pieces." But Tommy is more interested in politics, and is bristling with the latest news from the Magee camp. He is a great admirer of Quay,—"dere's a smart guy fer you, fellers; owns de whole Keystone shebang all right, all right. He's Boss Quay, you bet you." He dives into national issues, rails at Bryan, "16 to 1 Bill, you jest list'n to 'm, he'll give sixteen dollars to every one; he will, nit!" and the boys are soon involved in a heated discussion of the respective merits of the two political parties, Tommy staunchly siding with the Republican. "Me gran'fader and me fader was Republicans," he vociferates, "an' all me broders vote de ticket. Me fer de Gran' Ole Party, ev'ry time." Some one twits him on his political wisdom, challenging the boy to explain the difference in the money standards. Tommy boldly appeals to me to corroborate him; but before I have an opportunity to speak, he launches upon other issues, berating Spain for her atrocities in Cuba, and insisting that this free country cannot tolerate slavery at its doors. Every topic is discussed, with Tommy orating at top speed, and continually broaching new subjects. Unexpectedly he reverts to local affairs, waxes reminiscent over former days, and loudly smacks his lips at the "great feeds" he enjoyed on the rare occasions when he was free to roam the back streets of Smoky City. "Say, Aleck, my boy," he calls to me familiarly, "many a penny I made on *you,* all right. How? Why, peddlin' extras, of course! Say, dem was fine days, all right; easy money; papers went like hot cakes off the griddle. Wish you'd do it agin, Aleck."

Invisible to each other, we chat, exchange stories and anecdotes, the boys talking incessantly, as if fearful of silence. But every now and then there is a lull; we become quiet, each absorbed in his own thoughts. The pauses lengthen—lengthen into silence. Only the faint steps of "Crazy Smith" disturb the deep stillness.

.   .   .   .

Late in the evening the young prisoners are relieved. But Johnny remains, and his apprehensions reawaken. Repeatedly during the night he rouses me from my drowsy torpor to be reassured that he is not in danger of the gallows, and that he will not be tried for his assault. I allay his fears by dwelling on the Warden's aversion to giving publicity to the sex practices in the prison, and remind the boy of the Captain's official denial of their existence. These things happen almost every week, yet no one has ever been taken to court from Riverside on such charges.

Johnny grows more tranquil, and we converse about his family history, talking in a frank, confidential manner. With a glow of pleasure, I become aware of the note of tenderness in his voice. Presently he surprises me by asking:

"Friend Aleck, what do they call you in Russian?"

He prefers the fond "Sashenka," enunciating the strange word with quaint endearment, then diffidently confesses dislike for his own name, and relates the story he had recently read of a poor castaway Cuban youth; Felipe was his name, and he was just like himself.

"Shall I call you Felipe?" I offer.

"Yes, please do, Aleck, dear; no, Sashenka."

The springs of affection well up within me, as I lie huddled on the stone floor, cold and hungry. With closed eyes, I picture the boy before me, with his delicate face, and sensitive, girlish lips.

"Good night, dear Sashenka," he calls.

"Good night, little Felipe."

In the morning we are served with a slice of bread and water. I am tormented by thirst and hunger, and the small ration fails to assuage my sharp pangs. Smithy still refuses to drink out of the Deputy's hand; his doors remain unopened. With tremulous anxiety Johnny begs the Deputy Warden to tell him how much longer he will remain in the dungeon, but Greaves curtly commands silence, applying a vile epithet to the boy.

"Deputy," I call, boiling over with indignation, "he asked you a respectful question. I'd give him a decent answer."

"You mind your own business, you hear?" he retorts.

But I persist in defending my young friend, and

berate the Deputy for his language. He hastens away in a towering passion, menacing me with "what Smithy got."

Johnny is distressed at being the innocent cause of the trouble. The threat of the Deputy disquiets him, and he warns me to prepare. My cell is provided with a double entrance, and I am apprehensive of a sudden attack. But the hours pass without the Deputy returning, and our fears are allayed. The boy rejoices on my account, and brims over with appreciation of my intercession.

The incident cements our intimacy; our first diffidence disappears, and we become openly tender and affectionate. The conversation lags: we feel weak and worn. But every little while we hail each other with words of encouragement. Smithy incessantly paces the cell; the gnawing of the river rats reaches our ears; the silence is frequently pierced by the wild yells of the insane man, startling us with dread foreboding. The quiet grows unbearable, and Johnny calls again:

"What are you doing, Sashenka?"

"Oh, nothing. Just thinking, Felipe."

"Am I in your thoughts, dear?"

"Yes, kiddie, you are."

"Sasha, dear, I've been thinking, too."

"What, Felipe?"

"You are the only one I care for. ·I haven't a friend in the whole place."

"Do you care much for me, Felipe?"

"Will you promise not to laugh at me, Sashenka?"

"I wouldn't laugh at you."

"Cross your hand over your heart. Got it, Sasha?"

"Yes."

"Well, I'll tell you. I was thinking—how shall I tell

you? I was thinking, Sashenka—if you were here with me—I would like to kiss you."

An unaccountable sense of joy glows in my heart, and I muse in silence.

"What's the matter, Sashenka? Why don't you say something? Are you angry with me?"

"No, Felipe, you foolish little boy."

"You are laughing at me."

"No, dear; I feel just as you do."

"Really?"

"Yes."

"Oh, I am so glad, Sashenka."

In the evening the guards descend to relieve Johnny; he is to be transferred to the basket, they inform him. On the way past my cell, he whispers: "Hope I'll see you soon, Sashenka." A friendly officer knocks on the outer blind door of my cell. "That you thar, Berkman? You want to b'have to th' Dep'ty. He's put you down for two more days for sassin' him."

I feel more lonesome at the boy's departure. The silence grows more oppressive, the hours of darkness heavier.

Seven days I remain in the dungeon. At the expiration of the week, feeling stiff and feeble, I totter behind the guards, on the way to the bathroom. My body looks strangely emaciated, reduced almost to a skeleton. The pangs of hunger revive sharply with the shock of the cold shower, and the craving for tobacco is overpowering at the sight of the chewing officers. I look forward to being placed in a cell, quietly exulting at my victory as I am led to the North Wing. But, in the cell-house, the Deputy Warden assigns me to the lower end of Range A, insane department. Exasperated by the terrible suggestion, my nerves on edge with the dungeon experience, I storm in furious protest, demanding to be returned to "the hole." The Deputy, startled by my violence, attempts to soothe me, and finally yields. I am placed in Number 35, the "crank row" beginning several cells further.

Upon the heels of the departing officers, the rangeman is at my door, bursting with the latest news. The investigation is over, the Warden whitewashed! For an instant I am aghast, failing to grasp the astounding situation. Slowly its full significance dawns on me, as Bill excitedly relates the story. It's the talk of the prison. The Board of Charities had chosen its Secretary, J. Francis Torrance, an intimate friend of the Warden, to conduct the investigation. As a precautionary measure, I was kept several additional days in the dungeon. Mr. Torrance has privately interviewed "Dutch" Adams, Young Smithy, and Bob Runyon, promising them their full commutation time, notwithstanding their bad records, and irrespective of their future behavior. They were instructed by the Secretary to corroborate the management, placing all blame upon me! No other witnesses were heard. The "investigation" was over within an hour, the committee of one retiring for dinner to the adjoining residence of the Warden.

Several friendly prisoners linger at my cell during the afternoon, corroborating the story of the rangeman, and completing the details. The cell-house itself bears out the situation; the change in the personnel of the men is amazing. "Dutch" Adams has been promoted to messenger for the "front office," the most privileged "political" job in the prison. Bob Runyon, a third-timer and notorious "kid man," has been appointed a trusty in the shops. But the most significant cue is the advancement

of Young Smithy to the position of rangeman. He has
but recently been sentenced to a year's solitary for the
broken key discovered in the lock of his door. His
record is of the worst. He is a young convict of extremely violent temper, who has repeatedly attacked
fellow-prisoners with dangerous weapons. Since his
murderous assault upon the inoffensive "Praying Andy,"
Smithy was never permitted out of his cell without the
escort of two guards. And now this irresponsible man
is in charge of a range!

At supper, Young Smithy steals up to my cell, bringing a slice of cornbread. I refuse the peace offering, and
charge him with treachery. At first he stoutly protests
his innocence, but gradually weakens and pleads his
dire straits in mitigation. Torrance had persuaded him
to testify, but he avoided incriminating me. That was
done by the other two witnesses; he merely exonerated
the Warden from the charges preferred by James Grant.
He had been clubbed four times, but he denied to the
committee that the guards practice violence; and he
supported the Warden in his statement that the officers
are not permittted to carry clubs or blackjacks. He
feels that an injustice has been done me, and now that
he occupies my former position, he will be able to repay
the little favors I did him when he was in solitary.

Indignantly I spurn his offer. He pleads his youth,
the torture of the cell, and begs my forgiveness; but I am
bitter at his treachery, and bid him go.

Officer McIlvaine pauses at my door. "Oh, what
a change, what an awful change!" he exclaims, pityingly.
I don't know whether he refers to my appearance, or to
the loss of range liberty; but I resent his tone of commiseration; it was he who had selected me as a victim, to

be reported for talking. Angrily I turn my back to him, refusing to talk.

Somebody stealthily pushes a bundle of newspapers between the bars. Whole columns detail the report of the "investigation," completely exonerating Warden Edward S. Wright. The base charges against the management of the penitentiary were the underhand work of Anarchist Berkman, Mr. Torrance assured the press. One of the papers contains a lengthy interview with Wright, accusing me of fostering discontent and insubordination among the men. The Captain expresses grave fear for the safety of the community, should the Pardon Board reduce my sentence, in view of the circumstance that my lawyers are preparing to renew the application at the next session.

In great agitation I pace the cell. The statement of the Warden is fatal to the hope of a pardon. My life in the prison will now be made still more unbearable. I shall again be locked in solitary. With despair I think of my fate in the hands of the enemy, and the sense of my utter helplessness overpowers me.

CHAPTER XXVIII

FOR SAFETY

DEAR K.:

I know you must have been worried about me. Give no credence to the reports you hear. I did not try to suicide. I was very nervous and excited over the things that happened while I was in the dungeon. I saw the papers after I came up —you know what they said. I couldn't sleep; I kept pacing the floor. The screws were hanging about my cell, but I paid no attention to them. They spoke to me, but I wouldn't answer: I was in no mood for talking. They must have thought something wrong with me. The doctor came, and felt my pulse, and they took me to the hospital. The Warden rushed in and ordered me into a strait-jacket. "For safety," he said.

You know Officer Erwin; he put the jacket on me. He's a pretty decent chap; I saw he hated to do it. But the evening screw is a rat. He called three times during the night, and every time he'd tighten the straps. I thought he'd cut my hands off; but I wouldn't cry for mercy, and that made him wild. They put me in the "full size" jacket that winds all around you, the arms folded. They laid me, tied in the canvas, on the bed, bound me to it feet and chest, with straps provided with padlocks. I was suffocating in the hot ward; could hardly breathe. In the morning they unbound me. My legs were paralyzed, and I could not stand up. The doctor ordered some medicine for me. The head nurse (he's in for murder, and he's rotten) taunted me with the "black bottle." Every time he passed my bed, he'd say: "You still alive? Wait till I fix something up for you." I refused the medicine, and then they took me down to the dispensary, lashed me to a chair, and used the pump on me. You can imagine how I felt. That went on for a week; every night in the strait-jacket, every morning the pump. Now I am back in the block, in 6 A. A peculiar

328

coincidence,—it's the same cell I occupied when I first came here.

Don't trust Bill Say. The Warden told me he knew about the note I sent you just before I smashed up. If you got it, Bill must have read it and told Sandy. Only dear old Horsethief can be relied upon.

How near the boundary of joy is misery! I shall never forget the first morning in the jacket. I passed a restless night, but just as it began to dawn I must have lost consciousness. Suddenly I awoke with the most exquisite music in my ears. It seemed to me as if the heavens had opened in a burst of ecstasy. . . . It was only a little sparrow, but never before in my life did I hear such sweet melody. I felt murder in my heart when the convict nurse drove the poor birdie from the window ledge.

A.

CHAPTER XXIX

DREAMS OF FREEDOM

I

LIKE an endless *miserere* are the days in the solitary. No glimmer of light cheers the to-morrows. In the depths of suffering, existence becomes intolerable; and as of old, I seek refuge in the past. The stages of my life reappear as the acts of a drama which I cannot bring myself to cut short. The possibilities of the dark motive compel the imagination, and halt the thought of destruction. Misery magnifies the estimate of self; the vehemence of revolt strengthens to endure. Despair engenders obstinate resistance; in its spirit hope is trembling. Slowly it assumes more definite shape: escape is the sole salvation. The world of the living is dim and unreal with distance; its voice reaches me like the pale echo of fantasy; the thought of its turbulent vitality is strange with apprehension. But the present is bitter with wretchedness, and gasps desperately for relief.

The efforts of my friends bring a glow of warmth into my life. The indefatigable Girl has succeeded in interesting various circles: she is gathering funds for my application for a rehearing before the Pardon Board in the spring of '98, when my first sentence of seven years will have expired. With a touch of old-time tenderness, I think of her loyalty, her indomitable perseverance in my behalf. It is she, almost she alone, who has kept my memory green throughout the long years. Even Fedya, my constant chum, has been swirled into the vortex of narrow ambition and self-indulgence, the plaything of commonplace fate.

Resentment at being thus lightly forgotten tinges my thoughts of the erstwhile twin brother of our ideal-kissed youth. By contrast, the Girl is silhouetted on my horizon as the sole personification of revolutionary persistence, the earnest of its realization. Beyond, all is darkness—the mystic world of falsehood and sham, that will hate and persecute me even as its brutal high priests in the prison. Here and there the gloom is rent: an unknown sympathizer, or comrade, sends a greeting; I pore eagerly over the chirography, and from the clear, decisive signature, "Voltairine de Cleyre," strive to mold the character and shape the features of the writer. To the Girl I apply to verify my "reading," and rejoice in the warm interest of the convent-educated American, a friend of my much-admired Comrade Dyer D. Lum, who is aiding the Girl in my behalf.

But the efforts for a rehearing wake no hope in my heart. My comrades, far from the prison world, do not comprehend the full significance of the situation resulting from the investigation. My underground connections are paralyzed; I cannot enlighten the Girl. But Nold and Bauer are on the threshold of liberty. Within two months Carl will carry my message to New York. I can fully rely on his discretion and devotion; we have grown very intimate through common suffering. He will inform the Girl that nothing is to be expected from legal procedure; instead, he will explain to her the plan I have evolved.

My position as rangeman nas served me to good advantage. I have thoroughly familiarized myself with the institution; I have gathered information and explored every part of the cell-house offering the least likelihood of an escape. The prison is almost impregnable; Tom's attempt to scale the wall proved disastrous, in spite of his exceptional opportunities as kitchen employee, and the thick fog of the early morning. Several other attempts also were doomed to failure, the great number of guards and their vigilance precluding success. No escape has taken place since the days of Paddy McGraw, before the completion of the prison. Entirely new methods must be tried: the road to freedom leads underground! But digging *out* of the prison is impracticable in the modern structure of steel and rock. We must force a passage *into* the prison: the tunnel is to be dug from the outside! A house is to be rented in the neighborhood of the penitentiary, and the underground passage excavated beneath the eastern wall, toward the adjacent bath-house. No officers frequent the place save at certain hours, and I shall find an opportunity to disappear into the hidden opening on the regular biweekly occasions when the solitaries are permitted to bathe.

The project will require careful preparation and considerable expense. Skilled comrades will have to be entrusted with the secret work, the greater part of which must be carried on at night. Determination and courage will make the plan feasible, successful. Such things have been done before. Not in this country, it is true. But the act will receive added significance from the circumstance that the liberation of the first American political prisoner has been accomplished by means similar to those practised by our comrades in Russia. Who knows? It may prove the symbol and precursor of Russian idealism on American soil. And what tremendous impression the consummation of the bold plan will make! What a stimulus to our propaganda, as a demonstration of Anarchist initiative and ability! I glow with the excitement of its great possibilities, and enthuse Carl with my hopes. If the preparatory work is hastened, the execution of the plan will be facilitated by the renewed agitation within the prison. Rumors of a legislative investigation are afloat, diverting the thoughts of the administration into different channels. I shall foster the ferment to afford my comrades greater safety in the work.

During the long years of my penitentiary life I have formed many friendships. I have earned the reputation of a "square man" and a "good fellow," have received many proofs of confidence, and appreciation of my uncompromising attitude toward the generally execrated management. Most of my friends observe the unwritten ethics of informing me of their approaching release, and offer to smuggle out messages or to provide me with little comforts. I invariably request them to visit the newspapers and to relate their experiences in Riverside. Some express fear of the Warden's enmity, of the fatal consequences in case of their return to the penitentiary. But the bolder spirits and the accidental offenders, who confidently bid me a final good-bye, unafraid of return, call directly from the prison on the Pittsburgh editors.

Presently the *Leader* and the *Dispatch* begin to voice their censure of the hurried whitewash by the State Board of Charities. The attitude of the press encourages the guards to manifest their discontent with the humiliating eccentricities of the senile Warden. They protest against the whim subjecting them to military drill to improve their appearance, and resent Captain Wright's insistence that they patronize his private tailor, high-priced and incompetent. Serious friction has also arisen between the management and Mr. Sawhill, Superintendent of local industries. The prisoners rejoice at the growing irascibility of the Warden, and the deeper lines on his face, interpreting them as signs of worry and fear. Expectation of a new investigation is at high pitch as Judge Gordon, of Philadelphia, severely censures the administration of the Eastern Penitentiary, charging inhuman treatment, abuse of the insane, and graft. The labor bodies of the State demand the abolition of convict competition, and the press becomes more assertive in urging an investigation of both penitentiaries. The air is charged with rumors of legislative action.

II

The breath of spring is in the cell-house. My two comrades are jubilant. The sweet odor of May wafts the resurrection! But the threshold of life is guarded by the throes of new birth. A tone of nervous excitement permeates their correspondence. Anxiety tortures the sleepless nights; the approaching return to the living is tinged with the disquietude of the unknown, the dread of the renewed struggle for existence. But the joy of coming emancipation, the wine of sunshine and liberty tingles in every fiber, and hope flutters its disused wings.

Our plans are complete. Carl is to visit the Girl, explain my project, and serve as the medium of communication by means of our prearranged system, investing apparently innocent official letters with *sub rosa* meaning. The initial steps will require time. Meanwhile "K" and "G" are to make the necessary arrangements for the publication of our book. The security of our manuscripts is a source of deep satisfaction and much merriment at the expense of the administration. The repeated searches have failed to unearth them. With characteristic daring, the faithful Bob had secreted them in a hole in the floor of his shop, almost under the very seat of the guard. One by one they have been smuggled outside by a friendly officer, whom we have christened "Schraube."* By degrees Nold has gained the confidence of the former mill-worker, with the result that sixty precious booklets now repose safely with a comrade in Allegheny. I am to supply the final chapters of the book through Mr. Schraube, whose friendship Carl is about to bequeath to me.

The month of May is on the wane. The last note is exchanged with my comrades. Dear Bob was not able to reach me in the morning, and now I read the lines quivering with the last pangs of release, while Nold and Bauer are already beyond the walls. How I yearned for a glance at Carl, to touch hands, even in silence! But the customary privilege was refused us. Only once in the long years of our common suffering have I looked into the eyes of my devoted friend, and stealthily pressed his hand, like a thief in the night. No last greeting was vouchsafed me to-day. The loneliness seems heavier, the void more painful.

The routine is violently disturbed. Reading and study are burdensome: my thoughts will not be compelled. They revert obstinately to my comrades, and storm against my steel cage, trying to pierce the distance, to commune with the absent. I seek diversion in the manufacture of prison "fancy work," ornamental little fruit baskets, diminutive articles of furniture, picture frames, and the like. The little mementos, constructed of tissue-paper rolls of various designs, I send to the Girl, and am elated at her admiration

---

* German for "screw."

of the beautiful workmanship and attractive color effects. But presently she laments the wrecked condition of the goods, and upon investigation I learn from the runner that the most dilapidated cardboard boxes are selected for my product. The rotunda turnkey, in charge of the shipments, is hostile, and I appeal to the Chaplain. But his well-meant intercession results in an order from the Warden, interdicting the expressage of my work, on the ground of probable notes being secreted therein. I protest against the discrimination, suggesting the dismembering of every piece to disprove the charge. But the Captain derisively remarks that he is indisposed to "take chances," and I am forced to resort to the subterfuge of having my articles transferred to a friendly prisoner and addressed by him to his mother in Beaver, Pa., thence to be forwarded to New York. At the same time the rotunda keeper detains a valuable piece of ivory sent to me by the Girl for the manufacture of ornamental toothpicks. The local ware, made of kitchen bones bleached in lime, turns yellow in a short time. My request for the ivory is refused on the plea of submitting the matter to the Warden's decision, who rules against me. I direct the return of it to my friend, but am informed that the ivory has been mislaid and cannot be found. Exasperated, I charge the guard with the theft, and serve notice that I shall demand the ivory at the expiration of my time. The turnkey jeers at the wild impossibility, and I am placed for a week on "Pennsylvania diet" for insulting an officer.

CHAPTER XXX

WHITEWASHED AGAIN

MY DEAR CARL: CHRISTMAS, 1897.

I have been despairing of reaching you *sub rosa,* but the holidays brought the usual transfers, and at last friend Schraube is with me. Dear Carolus, I am worn out with the misery of the months since you left, and the many disappointments. Your official letters were not convincing. I fail to understand why the plan is not practicable. Of course, you can't write openly, but you have means of giving a hint as to the "impossibilities" you speak of. You say that I have become too estranged from the outside, and so forth—which may be true. Yet I think the matter chiefly concerns the inside, and of that I am the best judge. I do not see the force of your argument when you dwell upon the application at the next session of the Pardon Board. You mean that the other plan would jeopardize the success of the legal attempt. But there is not much hope of favorable action by the Board. We have talked all this over before, but you seem to have a different view now. Why?

Only in a very small measure do your letters replace in my life the heart-to-heart talks we used to have here, though they were only on paper. But I am much interested in your activities. It seems strange that you, so long the companion of my silence, should now be in the very Niagara of life, of our movement. It gives me great satisfaction to know that your experience here has matured you, and helped to strengthen and deepen your convictions. It has had a similar effect upon me. You know what a voluminous reader I am. I have read—in fact, studied —every volume in the library here, and now the Chaplain supplies me with books from his. But whether it be philosophy, travel, or contemporary life that falls into my hands, it invariably distils into my mind the falsity of dominant ideas, and the beauty, the inevitability of Anarchism. But I do not want to enlarge upon this subject now; we can discuss it through official channels.

You know that Tony and his nephew are here. We are just
getting acquainted. He works in the shop; but as he is also
coffee-boy, we have an opportunity to exchange notes. It is
fortunate that his identity is not known; otherwise he would
fall under special surveillance. I have my eyes on Tony,—he
may prove valuable.

I am still in solitary, with no prospect of relief. You know
the policy of the Warden to use me as a scapegoat for everything that happens here. It has become a mania with him.
Think of it, he blames me for Johnny Davis' cutting "Dutch."
He laid everything at my door when the legislative investigation
took place. It was a worse sham than the previous whitewash.
Several members called to see me at the cell,—unofficially, they
said. They got a hint of the evidence I was prepared to give,
and one of them suggested to me that it is not advisable for
one in my position to antagonize the Warden. I replied that
I was no toady. He hinted that the authorities of the prison
might help me to procure freedom, if I would act "discreetly."
I insisted that I wanted to be heard by the committee. They
departed, promising to call me as a witness. One Senator remarked, as he left: "You are too intelligent a man to be at
large."

When the hearing opened, several officers were the first to
take the stand. The testimony was not entirely favorable to the
Warden. Then Mr. Sawhill was called. You know him; he is
an independent sort of man, with an eye upon the wardenship.
His evidence came like a bomb: he charged the management
with corruption and fraud, and so forth. The investigators took
fright. They closed the sessions and departed for Harrisburg,
announcing through the press that they would visit Moyamensing*
and then return to Riverside. But they did not return. The
report they submitted to the Governor exonerated the Warden.

The men were gloomy over the state of affairs. A hundred
prisoners were prepared to testify, and much was expected from
the committee. I had all my facts on hand: Bob had fished
out for me the bundle of material from its hiding place. It
was in good condition, in spite of the long soaking. (I am enclosing some new data in this letter, for use in our book.)

Now that he is "cleared," the Warden has grown even more
arrogant and despotic. Yet *some* good the agitation in the

* The Eastern Penitentiary at Philadelphia, Pa.

press has accomplished: clubbings are less frequent, and the bull ring is temporarily abolished. But his hatred of me has grown venomous. He holds us responsible (together with Dempsey and Beatty) for organizing the opposition to convict labor, which has culminated in the Muehlbronner law. It is to take effect on the first of the year. The prison administration is very bitter, because the statute, which permits only thirty-five per cent. of the inmates to be employed in productive labor, will considerably minimize opportunities for graft. But the men are rejoicing: the terrible slavery in the shops has driven many to insanity and death. The law is one of the rare instances of rational legislation. Its benefit to labor in general is nullified, however, by limiting convict competition only within the State. The Inspectors are already seeking a market for the prison products in other States, while the convict manufactures of New York, Ohio, Illinois, etc., are disposed of in Pennsylvania. The irony of beneficent legislation! On the other hand, the inmates need not suffer for lack of employment. The new law allows the unlimited manufacture, within the prison, of products for local consumption. If the whine of the management regarding the "detrimental effect of idleness on the convict" is sincere, they could employ five times the population of the prison in the production of articles for our own needs.

At present all the requirements of the penitentiary are supplied from the outside. The purchase of a farm, following the example set by the workhouse, would alone afford work for a considerable number of men. I have suggested, in a letter to the Inspectors, various methods by which every inmate of the institution could be employed,—among them the publication of a prison paper. Of course, they have ignored me. But what can you expect of a body of philanthropists who have the interest of the convict so much at heart that they delegated the President of the Board, George A. Kelly, to oppose the parole bill, a measure certainly along advanced lines of modern criminology. Owing to the influence of Inspector Kelly, the bill was shelved at the last session of the legislature, though the prisoners have been praying for it for years. It has robbed the moneyless life-timers of their last hope: a clause in the parole bill held out to them the promise of release after 20 years of good behavior.

Dark days are in store for the men. Apparently the cam-

paign of the Inspectors consists in forcing the repeal of the
Muehlbronner law, by raising the hue and cry of insanity and
sickness. They are actually causing both by keeping half the
population locked up. You know how quickly the solitary drives
certain classes of prisoners insane. Especially the more ignorant
element, whose mental horizon is circumscribed by their personal
troubles and pain, speedily fall victims. Think of men, who
cannot even read, put *incommunicado* for months at a time,
for years even! Most of the colored prisoners, and those accustomed to outdoor life, such as farmers and the like, quickly
develop the germs of consumption in close confinement. Now,
this wilful murder—for it is nothing else—is absolutely unnecessary. The yard is big and well protected by the thirty-foot wall,
with armed guards patrolling it. Why not give the unemployed
men air and exercise, since the management is determined to
keep them idle? I suggested the idea to the Warden, but he
berated me for my "habitual interference" in matters that do
not concern me. I often wonder at the enigma of human
nature. There's the Captain, a man 72 years old. He should
bethink himself of death, of "meeting his Maker," since he
pretends to believe in religion. Instead, he is bending all his
energies to increase insanity and disease among the convicts, in
order to force the repeal of the law that has lessened the flow
of blood money. It is almost beyond belief; but you have
yourself witnessed the effect of a brutal atmosphere upon new
officers. Wright has been Warden for thirty years: he has
come to regard the prison as his undisputed dominion; and
now he is furious at the legislative curtailment of his absolute
control.

This letter will remind you of our bulky notes in the "good"
old days when "KG" were here. I miss our correspondence.
There are some intelligent men on the range, but they are not
interested in the thoughts that seethe within me and call for
expression. Just now the chief topic of local interest (after, of
course, the usual discussion of the grub, women, kids, and their
health and troubles) is the Spanish War and the new dining-
room, in which the shop employees are to be fed *en masse,* out
of chinaware, think of it! Some of the men are tremendously
patriotic; others welcome the war as a sinecure affording easy
money and plenty of excitement. You remember Young Butch
and his partners, Murtha, Tommy, etc. They have recently been

released, too wasted and broken in health to be fit for manual labor. All of them have signified their intention of joining the insurrection; some are enrolling in the regular army for the war. Butch is already in Cuba. I had a letter from him. There is a passage in it that is tragically characteristic. He refers to a skirmish he participated in. "We shot a lot of Spaniards, mostly from ambush," he writes; "it was great sport." It is the attitude of the military adventurer, to whom a sacred cause like the Cuban uprising unfortunately affords the opportunity to satisfy his lust for blood. Butch was a very gentle boy when he entered the prison. But he has witnessed much heartlessness and cruelty during his term of three years.

Letter growing rather long. Good night.

A.

CHAPTER XXXI

"AND BY ALL FORGOT, WE ROT AND ROT"

I

A YEAR of solitary has wasted my strength, and left me feeble and languid. My expectations of relief from complete isolation have been disappointed. Existence is grim with despair, as day by day I feel my vitality ebbing; the long nights are tortured with insomnia; my body is racked with constant pains. All my heart is dark.

A glimmer of light breaks through the clouds, as the session of the Pardon Board approaches. I clutch desperately at the faint hope of a favorable decision. With feverish excitement I pore over the letters of the Girl, breathing cheer and encouraging news. My application is supported by numerous labor bodies, she writes. Comrade Harry Kelly has been tireless in my behalf; the success of his efforts to arouse public sympathy augurs well for the application. The United Labor League of Pennsylvania, representing over a hundred thousand toilers, has passed a resolution favoring my release. Together with other similar expressions, individual and collective, it will be laid before the Pardon Board, and it is confidently expected that the authorities will not ignore the voice of organized labor. In a ferment of anxiety and hope I count the days and hours, irritable with impatience and apprehension as I near the fateful moment. Visions of liberty flutter before me, glorified by the meeting with the Girl and my former companions, and I thrill with the return to the world, as I restlessly pace the cell in the silence of the night.

The thought of my prison friends obtrudes upon my visions. With the tenderness born of common misery I think of their fate, resolving to brighten their lives with little comforts and letters, that mean so much to every prisoner. My first act in liberty shall be in memory of the men grown close to me with the kinship of suffering, the unfortunates endeared by awakened sympathy and understanding. For so many years I have shared with them the sorrows and the few joys of penitentiary life, I feel almost guilty to leave them. But henceforth their cause shall be mine, a vital part of the larger, social cause. It will be my constant endeavor to ameliorate their condition, and I shall strain every effort for my little friend Felipe; I must secure his release. How happy the boy will be to join me in liberty! . . . The flash of the dark lantern dispels my fantasies, and again I walk the cell in vehement misgiving and fervent hope of to-morrow's verdict.

At noon I am called to the Warden. He must have received word from the Board,—I reflect on the way. The Captain lounges in the armchair, his eyes glistening, his seamed face yellow and worried. With an effort I control my impatience as he offers me a seat. He bids the guard depart, and a wild hope trembles in me. He is not afraid,—perhaps good news!

"Sit down, Berkman," he speaks with unwonted affability. "I have just received a message from Harrisburg. Your attorney requests me to inform you that the Pardon Board has now reached your case. It is probably under consideration at this moment."

PRISON MEMOIRS OF AN ANARCHIST

I remain silent. The Warden scans me closely.

"You would return to New York, if released?" he inquires.

"Yes."

"What are your plans?"

"Well, I have not formed any yet."

"You would go back to your Anarchist friends?"

"Certainly."

"You have not changed your views?"

"By no means."

A turnkey enters. "Captain, on official business," he reports.

"Wait here a moment, Berkman," the Warden remarks, withdrawing. The officer remains.

In a few minutes the Warden returns, motioning to the guard to leave.

"I have just been informed that the Board has refused you a hearing."

I feel the cold perspiration running down my back. The prison rumors of the Warden's interference flash through my mind. The Board promised a rehearing at the previous application,—why this refusal?

"Warden," I exclaim, "you objected to my pardon!"

"Such action lies with the Inspectors," he replies evasively. The peculiar intonation strengthens my suspicions.

A feeling of hopelessness possesses me. I sense the Warden's gaze fastened on me, and I strive to control my emotion.

"How much time have you yet?" he asks.

"Over eleven years."

"How long have you been locked up this time?"

"Sixteen months."

"There is a vacancy on your range. The assistant

hallman is going home to-morrow. You would like the position?" he eyes me curiously.

"Yes."

"I'll consider it."

I rise weakly, but he detains me: "By the way, Berkman, look at this."

He holds up a small wooden box, disclosing several casts of plaster of paris. I wonder at the strange proceeding.

"You know what they are?" he inquires.

"Plaster casts, I think."

"Of what? For what purpose? Look at them well, now."

I glance indifferently at the molds bearing the clear impression of an eagle.

"It's the cast of a silver dollar, I believe."

"I am glad you speak truthfully. I had no doubt you would know. I examined your library record and found that you have drawn books on metallurgy."

"Oh, you suspect me of this?" I flare up.

"No, not this time," he smiles in a suggestive manner. "You have drawn practically every book from the library. I had a talk with the Chaplain, and he is positive that you would not be guilty of counterfeiting, because it would be robbing poor people."

"The reading of my letters must have familiarized the Chaplain with Anarchist ideas."

"Yes, Mr. Milligan thinks highly of you. You might antagonize the management, but he assures me you would not abet such a crime."

"I am glad to hear it."

"You would protect the Federal Government, then?"

"I don't understand you."

"You would protect the people from being cheated by counterfeit money?"

346 PRISON MEMOIRS OF AN ANARCHIST

"The government and the people are not synonymous."

Flushing slightly, and frowning, he asks: "But you would protect the poor?"

"Yes, certainly."

His face brightens. "Oh, quite so, quite so," he smiles reassuringly. "These molds were found hidden in the North Block. No; not in a cell, but in the hall. We suspect a certain man. It's Ed Sloane; he is located two tiers above you. Now, Berkman, the management is very anxious to get to the bottom of this matter. It's a crime against the people. You may have heard Sloane speaking to his neighbors about this."

"No. I am sure you suspect an innocent person."

"How so?"

"Sloane is a very sick man. It's the last thing he'd think of."

"Well, we have certain reasons for suspecting him. If you should happen to hear anything, just rap on the door and inform the officers you are ill. They will be instructed to send for me at once."

"I can't do it, Warden."

"Why not?" he demands.

"I am not a spy."

"Why, certainly not, Berkman. I should not ask you to be. But you have friends on the range, you may learn something. Well, think the matter over," he adds, dismissing me.

Bitter disappointment at the action of the Board, indignation at the Warden's suggestion, struggle within me as I reach my cell. The guard is about to lock me in, when the Deputy Warden struts into the block.

"Officer, unlock him," he commands. "Berkman, the

Captain says you are to be assistant rangeman. **Report to Mr. McIlvaine for a broom."**

II

The unexpected relief strengthens the hope of liberty. Legal methods are of no avail, but now my opportunities for escape are more favorable. Considerable changes have taken place during my solitary, and the first necessity is to orient myself. Some of my confidants have been released; others were transferred during the investigation period to the South Wing, to disrupt my connections. New men are about the cellhouse, and I miss many of my chums. The lower half of the bottom ranges A and K is now exclusively occupied by the insane, their numbers greatly augmented. Poor Wingie has disappeared. Grown violently insane, he was repeatedly lodged in the dungeon, and finally sent to an asylum. There my unfortunate friend had died after two months. His cell is now occupied by "Irish Mike," a good-natured boy, turned imbecile by solitary. He hops about on all fours, bleating: "Baah, baah, see the goat. I'm the goat, baah, baah." I shudder at the fate I have escaped, as I look at the familiar faces that were so bright with intelligence and youth, now staring at me from the "crank row," wild-eyed and corpse-like, their minds shattered, their bodies wasted to a shadow. My heart bleeds as I realize that Sid and Nick fail to recognize me, their memory a total blank; and Patsy, the Pittsburgh bootblack, stands at the door, motionless, his eyes glassy, lips frozen in an inane smile.

From cell to cell I pass the graveyard of the living dead, the silence broken only by intermittent savage yells and the piteous bleating of Mike. The whole day these men are locked in, deprived of exercise and recreation, their rations reduced because of "delinquency." New "bughouse cases" are continually added from the ranks of the prisoners forced to remain idle and kept in solitary. The sight of the terrible misery almost gives a touch of consolation to my grief over Johnny Davis. My young friend had grown ill in the foul basket. He begged to be taken to the hospital; but his condition did not warrant it, the physician said. Moreover, he was "in punishment." Poor boy, how he must have suffered! They found him dead on the floor of his cell.

My body renews its strength with the exercise and greater liberty of the range. The subtle hope of the Warden to corrupt me has turned to my advantage. I smile with scorn at his miserable estimate of human nature, determined by a lifetime of corruption and hypocrisy. How saddening is the shallowness of popular opinion! Warden Wright is hailed as a progressive man, a deep student of criminology, who has introduced modern methods in the treatment of prisoners. As an expression of respect and appreciation, the National Prison Association has selected Captain Wright as its delegate to the International Congress at Brussels, which is to take place in 1900. And all the time the Warden is designing new forms of torture, denying the pleadings of the idle men for exercise, and exerting his utmost efforts to increase sickness and insanity, in the attempt to force the repeal of the "convict labor" law. The puerility of his judgment fills me with contempt: public sentiment in regard to convict competition with outside labor has swept the State; the efforts of the Warden, disastrous though they be to the inmates, are doomed to failure. No less fatuous is the conceit of his boasted experience of thirty years. The so confidently uttered suspicion of Ed Sloane in regard to the counterfeiting charge, has proved mere lip-wisdom. The real culprit is Bob Runyon, the trusty basking in the Warden's special graces. His intimate friend, John Smith, the witness and protégé of Torrance, has confided to me the whole story, in a final effort to "set himself straight." He even exhibited to me the coins made by Runyon, together with the original molds, cast in the trusty's cell. And poor Sloane, still under surveillance, is slowly dying of neglect, the doctor charging him with eating soap to produce symptoms of illness.

III

The year passes in a variety of interests. The Girl and several newly-won correspondents hold the thread of outside life. The Twin has gradually withdrawn from our New York circles, and is now entirely obscured on my horizon. But the Girl is staunch and devoted, and I keenly anticipate her regular mail. She keeps me informed of events in the international labor movement, news of which is almost entirely lacking in the daily press. We discuss the revolutionary expressions of the times, and I learn more about Pallas and Luccheni, whose acts of the previous winter had thrown Europe into a ferment of agitation. I hunger for news of the agitation against the tortures in Montjuich, the revival of the Inquisition rousing in me the spirit of retribution and deep compassion for my persecuted comrades in the Spanish bastille. Beneath the suppressed tone of her letters, I read the Girl's suffering and pain, and feel the heart pangs of her unuttered personal sorrows.

Presently I am apprised that some prominent persons interested in my case are endeavoring to secure

Carnegie's signature for a renewed application to the
Board of Pardons. The Girl conveys the information
guardedly; the absence of comment discovers to me
the anguish of soul the step has caused her. What
terrible despair had given birth to the suggestion, I
wonder. If the project of the underground escape
had been put in operation, we should not have had
to suffer such humiliation. Why have my friends
ignored the detailed plan I had submitted to them
through Carl? I am confident of its feasibility and
success, if we can muster the necessary skill and outlay.
The animosity of the prison authorities precludes the
thought of legal release. The underground route, very
difficult and expensive though it be, is the sole hope.
It must be realized. My *sub rosa* communications suspended during the temporary absence of Mr. Schraube,
I hint these thoughts in official mail to the Girl, but
refrain from objecting to the Carnegie idea.

Other matters of interest I learn from correspondence with friends in Philadelphia and Pittsburgh. The
frequent letters of Carl, still reminiscent of his sojourn
at Riverside, thrill with the joy of active propaganda
and of his success as public speaker. Voltairine de
Cleyre and Sarah Patton lend color to my existence by
discursive epistles of great charm and rebellious thought.
Often I pause to wonder at the miracle of my mail passing the censorial eyes. But the Chaplain is a busy man;
careful perusal of every letter would involve too great a
demand upon his time. The correspondence with Mattie
I turn over to my neighbor Pasquale, a young Italian
serving sixteen years, who has developed a violent passion for the pretty face on the photograph. The roguish
eyes and sweet lips exert but a passing impression upon
me. My thoughts turn to Johnny, my young friend in
the convict grave. Deep snow is on the ground; it must

be cold beneath the sod. The white shroud is pressing, pressing heavily upon the lone boy, like the suffocating night of the basket cell. But in the spring little blades of green will sprout, and perhaps a rosebud will timidly burst and flower, all white, and perfume the air, and shed its autumn tears upon the convict grave of Johnny.

CHAPTER XXXII

THE DEVIOUSNESS OF REFORM LAW APPLIED

February 14, 1899.

Dear Carolus:

The Greeks thought the gods spiteful creatures. When things begin to look brighter for man, they grow envious. You'll be surprised,—Mr. Schraube has turned into an enemy. Mostly my own fault; that's the sting of it. It will explain to you the failure of the former *sub rosa* route. The present one is safe, but very temporary.

It happened last fall. From assistant I was advanced to hallman, having charge of the "crank row," on Range A. A new order curtailed the rations of the insane,—no cornbread, cheese, or hash; only bread and coffee. As rangeman, I help to "feed," and generally have "extras" left on the wagon,—some one sick, or refusing food, etc. I used to distribute the extras, "on the q. t.," among the men deprived of them. One day, just before Christmas, an officer happened to notice Patsy chewing a piece of cheese. The poor fellow is quite an imbecile; he did not know enough to hide what I gave him. Well, you are aware that "Cornbread Tom" does not love me. He reported me. I admitted the charge to the Warden, and tried to tell him how hungry the men were. He wouldn't hear of it, saying that the insane should not "overload" their stomachs. I was ordered locked up. Within a month I was out again, but imagine my surprise when Schraube refused even to talk to me. At first I could not fathom the mystery; later I learned that he was reprimanded, losing ten days' pay for "allowing" me to feed the demented. He knew nothing about it, of course, but he was at the time in special charge of "crank row." The Schraube has been telling my friends that I got him in trouble wilfully. He seems to nurse his grievance with much bitterness; he apparently hates me now with the hatred we often feel toward

352

those who know our secrets. But he realizes he has nothing to fear from me.

Many changes have taken place since you left. You would hardly recognize the block if you returned (better stay out, though). No more talking through the waste pipes; the new privies have standing water. Electricity is gradually taking the place of candles. The garish light is almost driving me blind, and the innovation has created a new problem: how to light our pipes. We are given the same monthly allowance of matches, each package supposed to contain 30, but usually having 27; and last month I received only 25. I made a kick, but it was in vain. The worst of it is, fully a third of the matches are damp and don't light. While we used candles we managed somehow, borrowing a few matches occasionally from non-smokers. But now that candles are abolished, the difficulty is very serious. I split each match into four; sometimes I succeed in making six. There is a man on the range who is an artist at it: he can make eight cuts out of a match; all serviceable, too. Even at that, there is a famine, and I have been forced to return to the stone age: with flint and tinder I draw the fire of Prometheus.

The mess-room is in full blast. The sight of a thousand men, bent over their food in complete silence, officers flanking each table, is by no means appetizing. But during the Spanish war, the place resembled the cell-house on New Year's eve. The patriotic Warden daily read to the diners the latest news, and such cheering and wild yelling you have never heard. Especially did the Hobson exploit fire the spirit of jingoism. But the enthusiasm suddenly cooled when the men realized that they were wasting precious minutes hurrahing, and then leaving the table hungry when the bell terminated the meal. Some tried to pocket the uneaten beans and rice, but the guards detected them, and after that the Warden's war reports were accompanied only with loud munching and champing.

Another innovation is exercise. Your interviews with the reporters, and those of other released prisoners, have at last forced the Warden to allow the idle men an hour's recreation. In inclement weather, they walk in the cell-house; on fine days, in the yard. The reform was instituted last autumn, and the improvement in health is remarkable. The doctor is enthusiastically in favor of the privilege; the sick-line has been so considerably reduced that he estimates his time-saving at two hours daily. Some of the boys tell me they have almost entirely ceased masturbating. The shop employees envy the "idlers" now; many have purposely precipitated trouble in order to be put in solitary, and thus enjoy an hour in the open. But Sandy "got next," and now those locked up "for cause" are excluded from exercise.

Here are some data for our book. The population at the end of last year was 956—the lowest point in over a decade. The Warden admits that the war has decreased crime; the Inspectors' report refers to the improved economic conditions, as compared with the panicky times of the opening years in the 90's. But the authorities do not appear very happy over the reduction in the Riverside population. You understand the reason: the smaller the total, the less men may be exploited in the industries. I am not prepared to say whether there is collusion between the judges and the administration of the prison, but it is very significant that the class of offenders formerly sent to the workhouse are being increasingly sentenced to the penitentiary, and an unusual number are transferred here from the Reformatory at Huntington and the Reform School of Morganza. The old-timers joke about the Warden telephoning to the Criminal Court, to notify the judges how many men are "wanted" for the stocking shop.

The unions might be interested in the methods of nullifying the convict labor law. In every shop twice as many are employed as the statute allows; the "illegal" are carried on the books as men working on "State account"; that is, as cleaners and clerks, not as producers. Thus it happens that in the mat shop, for instance, more men are booked as clerks and sweepers than are employed on the looms! In the broom shop there are 30 supposed clerks and 15 cleaners, to a total of 53 producers legally permitted. This is the way the legislation works on which the labor bodies have expended such tremendous efforts. The broom shop is still contracted to Lang Bros., with their own foreman in charge, and his son a guard in the prison.

Enough for to-day. When I hear of the safe arrival of this letter, I may have more intimate things to discuss.   A.

CHAPTER XXXIII

THE TUNNEL

I

THE adverse decision of the Board of Pardons terminates all hope of release by legal means. Had the
Board refused to commute my sentence after hearing
the argument, another attempt could be made later on.
But the refusal to grant a rehearing, the crafty stratagem to circumvent even the presentation of my case,
reveals the duplicity of the previous promise and the
guilty consciousness of the illegality of my multiplied
sentences. The authorities are determined that I should
remain in the prison, confident that it will prove my
tomb. Realizing this fires my defiance, and all the stubborn resistance of my being. There is no hope of surviving my term. At best, even with the full benefit of
the commutation time—which will hardly be granted
me, in view of the attitude of the prison management—
I still have over nine years to serve. But existence is
becoming increasingly more unbearable; long confinement and the solitary have drained my vitality. To endure the nine years is almost a physical impossibility. I
must therefore concentrate all my energy and efforts
upon escape.

My position as rangeman is of utmost advantage. I
have access to every part of the cell-house, excepting the

"crank row." The incident of feeding the insane has put an embargo upon my communication with them, a special hallboy having been assigned to care for the deranged. But within my area on the range are the recent arrivals and the sane solitaries; the division of my duties with the new man merely facilitates my task, and affords me more leisure.

The longing for liberty constantly besets my mind, suggesting various projects. The idea of escape daily strengthens into the determination born of despair. It possesses me with an exclusive passion, shaping every thought, molding every action. By degrees I curtail correspondence with my prison chums, that I may devote the solitude of the evening to the development of my plans. The underground tunnel masters my mind with the boldness of its conception, its tremendous possibilities. But the execution! Why do my friends regard the matter so indifferently? Their tepidity irritates me. Often I lash myself into wild anger with Carl for having failed to impress my comrades with the feasibility of the plan, to fire them with the enthusiasm of activity. My *sub rosa* route is sporadic and uncertain. Repeatedly I have hinted to my friends the bitter surprise I feel at their provoking indifference; but my reproaches have been studiously ignored. I cannot believe that conditions in the movement preclude the realization of my suggestion. These things have been accomplished in Russia. Why not in America? The attempt should be made, if only for its propagandistic effect. True, the project will require considerable outlay, and the work of skilled and trustworthy men. Have we no such in our ranks? In Parsons and Lum, this country has produced her Zheliabovs; is the genius of America not equal to a Hartman?* The tacit skepticism of my correspondents pains me, and rouses my resentment. They evidently lack faith in the judgment of "one who has been so long separated" from their world, from the interests and struggles of the living. The consciousness of my helplessness without aid from the outside gnaws at me, filling my days with bitterness. But I will persevere: I will compel their attention and their activity; aye, their enthusiasm!

With utmost zeal I cultivate the acquaintance of Tony. The months of frequent correspondence and occasional personal meetings have developed a spirit of congeniality and good will. I exert my ingenuity to create opportunities for stolen interviews and closer comradeship. Through the aid of a friendly officer, I procure for Tony the privilege of assisting his rangeman after shop hours, thus enabling him to communicate with me to greater advantage. Gradually we become intimate, and I learn the story of his life, rich in adventure and experience. An Alsatian, small and wiry, Tony is a man of quick wit, with a considerable dash of the Frenchman about him. He is intelligent and daring—the very man to carry out my plan.

For days I debate in my mind the momentous question: shall I confide the project to Tony? It would be placing myself in his power, jeopardizing the sole hope of my life. Yet it is the only way; I must rely on my intuition of the man's worth. My nights are sleepless, excruciating with the agony of indecision. But my friend's sentence is nearing completion. We shall need time for discussion and preparation, for thorough con-

---

* Hartman engineered the tunnel beneath the Moscow railway, undermined in an unsuccessful attempt to kill Alexander II., in 1880.

sideration of every detail. At last I resolve to take the
decisive step, and next day I reveal the secret to Tony.

His manner allays apprehension. Serene and self-
possessed, he listens gravely to my plan, smiles with apparent satisfaction, and briefly announces that it shall
be done. Only the shining eyes of my reticent comrade
betray his elation at the bold scheme, and his joy in the
adventure. He is confident that the idea is feasible, suggesting the careful elaboration of details, and the inven-
tion of a cipher to insure greater safety for our correspondence. The precaution is necessary; it will prove
of inestimable value upon his release.

With great circumspection the cryptogram is prepared, based on a discarded system of German short-
hand, but somewhat altered, and further involved by the
use of words of our own coinage. The cipher, thus
perfected, will defy the skill of the most expert.

But developments within the prison necessitate
changes in the project. The building operations near
the bathhouse destroy the serviceability of the latter
for my purpose. We consider several new routes,
but soon realize that lack of familiarity with the
construction of the penitentiary gas and sewer sys-
tems may defeat our success. There are no means
of procuring the necessary information: Tony is confined to the shop, while I am never permitted out of
the cell-house. In vain I strive to solve the difficulty;
weeks pass without bringing light.

My Providence comes unexpectedly, in the guise
of a fight in the yard. The combatants are locked
up on my range. One of them proves to be "Mac,"
an aged prisoner serving a third term. During his
previous confinement, he had filled the position of
fireman, one of his duties consisting in the weekly
flushing of the sewers. He is thoroughly familiar

with the underground piping of the yard, but his reputation among the inmates is tinged with the odor of sycophancy. He is, however, the only means of solving my difficulty, and I diligently set myself to gain his friendship. I lighten his solitary by numerous expressions of my sympathy, often secretly supplying him with little extras procured from my kitchen friends. The loquacious old man is glad of an opportunity to converse, and I devote every propitious moment to listening to his long-winded stories of the "great jobs" he had accomplished in "his" time, the celebrated "guns" with whom he had associated, the "great hauls" he had made and "blowed in with th' fellers." I suffer his chatter patiently, encouraging the recital of his prison experiences, and leading him on to dwell upon his last "bit." He becomes reminiscent of his friends in Riverside, bewails the early graves of some, others "gone bugs," and rejoices over his good chum Patty McGraw managing to escape. The ever-interesting subject gives "Mac" a new start, and he waxes enthusiastic over the ingenuity of Patty, while I express surprise that he himself had never attempted to take French leave. "What!" he bristles up, "think I'm such a dummy?" and with great detail he discloses his plan, " 'way in th' 80's" to swim through the sewer. I scoff at his folly. "You must have been a chump, Mac, to think it could be done," I remark. "I was, was I? What do you know about the piping, eh? Now, let me tell you. Just wait," and, snatching up his library slate, he draws a complete diagram of the prison sewerage. In the extreme southwest corner of the yard he indicates a blind underground alley.

"What's this?" I ask, in surprise.

"Nev'r knew *that,* did yer? It's a little tunn'l, con-

nectin' th' cellar with th' females, see? Not a dozen
men in th' dump know 't; not ev'n a good many screws.
Passage ain't been used fer a long time."

In amazement I scan the diagram. I had noticed
a little trap door at the very point in the yard indicated
in the drawing, and I had often wondered what purpose it might serve. My heart dances with joy at the
happy solution of my difficulty. The "blind alley" will
greatly facilitate our work. It is within fifteen feet,
or twenty at most, of the southwestern wall. Its situation is very favorable: there are no shops in the vicinity;
the place is never visited by guards or prisoners.

The happy discovery quickly matures the details of
my plan: a house is to be rented opposite the southern wall, on Sterling Street. Preferably it is to be
situated very near to the point where the wall
adjoins the cell-house building. Dug in a direct line
across the street, and underneath the south wall, the
tunnel will connect with the "blind alley." I shall
manage the rest.

II

Slowly the autumn wanes. The crisp days of the
Indian summer linger, as if unwilling to depart. But
I am impatient with anxiety, and long for the winter.
Another month, and Tony will be free. Time lags
with tardy step, but at last the weeks dwarf into
days, and with joyful heart we count the last hours.

To-morrow my friend will greet the sunshine. He
will at once communicate with my comrades, and urge
the immediate realization of the great plan. His self-
confidence and faith will carry conviction, and stir
them with enthusiasm for the undertaking. A house

is to be bought or rented without loss of time, and the environs inspected. Perhaps operations could not begin till spring; meanwhile funds are to be collected to further the work. Unfortunately, the Girl, a splendid organizer, is absent from the country. But my friends will carefully follow the directions I have entrusted to Tony, and through him I shall keep in touch with the developments. I have little opportunity for *sub rosa* mail; by means of our cipher, however, we can correspond officially, without risk of the censor's understanding, or even suspecting, the innocent-looking flourishes scattered through the page.

With the trusted Tony my thoughts walk beyond the gates, and again and again I rehearse every step in the project, and study every detail. My mind dwells in the outside. In silent preoccupation I perform my duties on the range. More rarely I converse with the prisoners: I must take care to comply with the rules, and to retain my position. To lose it would be disastrous to all my hopes of escape.

As I pass the vacant cell, in which I had spent the last year of my solitary, the piteous chirping of a sparrow breaks in upon my thoughts. The little visitor, almost frozen, hops on the bar above. My assistant swings the duster to drive it away, but the sparrow hovers about the door, and suddenly flutters to my shoulder. In surprise I pet the bird; it seems quite tame. "Why, it's Dick!" the assistant exclaims. "Think of him coming back!" My hands tremble as I examine the little bird. With great joy I discover the faint marks of blue ink I had smeared under its wings last summer, when the Warden had ordered my little companion thrown out of the window. How wonderful that it should return and recognize the old friend and the cell! Tenderly I warm and feed the bird. What strange sights my little pet must have seen since he was driven out into the world! what struggles and sorrows has he suffered! The bright eyes look cheerily into mine, speaking mute confidence and joy, while he pecks from my hand crumbs of bread and sugar. Foolish birdie, to return to prison for shelter and food! Cold and cruel must be the world, my little Dick; or is it friendship, that is stronger than even love of liberty?

So may it be. Almost daily I see men pass through the gates and soon return again, driven back by the world—even like you, little Dick. Yet others there are who would rather go cold and hungry in freedom, than be warm and fed in prison—even like me, little Dick. And still others there be who would risk life and liberty for the sake of their friendship —even like you and, I hope, Tony, little Dick.

CHAPTER XXXIV

THE DEATH OF DICK

Sub Rosa,
Jan. 15, 1900.

TONY:

I write in an agony of despair. I am locked up again. It was all on account of my bird. You remember my feathered pet, Dick. Last summer the Warden ordered him put out, but when cold weather set in, Dick returned. Would you believe it? He came back to my old cell, and recognized me when I passed by. I kept him, and he grew as tame as before—he had become a bit wild in the life outside. On Christmas day, as Dick was playing near my cell, Bob Runyon—the stool, you know—came by and deliberately kicked the bird. When I saw Dick turn over on his side, his little eyes rolling in the throes of death, I rushed at Runyon and knocked him down. He was not hurt much, and everything could have passed off quietly, as no screw was about. But the stool reported me to the Deputy, and I was locked up.

Mitchell has just been talking to me. The good old fellow was fond of Dick, and he promises to get me back on the range. He is keeping the position vacant for me, he says; he put a man in my place who has only a few more weeks to serve. Then I'm to take charge again.

I am not disappointed at your information that "the work" will have to wait till spring. It's unavoidable, but I am happy that preparations have been started. How about those revolvers, though? You haven't changed your mind, I hope. In one of your letters you seem to hint that the matter has been attended to. How can that be? Jim, the plumber—you know he can be trusted—has been on the lookout for a week. He assures me that nothing came, so far. Why do you delay? I hope you didn't throw the package through the cellar window when Jim wasn't at his post. Hardly probable. But if you did, what the devil could have become of it? I see no sign here of the things being discovered: there would surely be a terrible hubbub. Look to it, and write at once. A.

CHAPTER XXXV

AN ALLIANCE WITH THE BIRDS

I

The disappearance of the revolvers is shrouded in mystery. In vain I rack my brain to fathom the precarious situation; it defies comprehension and torments me with misgivings. Jim's certainty that the weapons did not pass between the bars of the cellar, momentarily allays my dread. But Tony's vehement insistence that he had delivered the package, throws me into a panic of fear. My firm faith in the two confidants distracts me with uncertainty and suspense. It is incredible that Tony should seek to deceive me. Yet Jim has kept constant vigil at the point of delivery; there is little probability of his having missed the package. But supposing he has, what has become of it? Perhaps it fell into some dark corner of the cellar. The place must be searched at once.

Desperate with anxiety, I resort to the most reckless means to afford Jim an opportunity to visit the cellar. I ransack the cell-house for old papers and rags; with miserly hand I gather all odds and ends, broken tools, pieces of wood, a bucketful of sawdust. Trembling with fear of discovery, I empty the treasure into the sewer at the end of the hall, and tightly jam the elbow of the waste pipe. The smell of excrement fills the block, the cell privies overrun, and inundate the hall. The stench is overpowering; steadily the water rises, threatening to flood the cell-house. The place is in a turmoil: the solitaries shout and rattle on the bars, the guards rush about in confusion. The Block Captain yells, "Hey, Jasper, hurry! Call the plumber; get Jim. Quick!"

But repeated investigation of the cellar fails to disclose the weapons. In constant dread of dire possibilities, I tremble at every step, fancying lurking suspicion, sudden discovery, and disaster. But the days pass; the calm of the prison routine is undisturbed, giving no indication of untoward happening or agitation. By degrees my fears subside. The inexplicable disappearance of the revolvers is fraught with danger; the mystery is disquieting, but it has fortunately brought no results, and must apparently remain unsolved.

Unexpectedly my fears are rearoused. Called to the desk by Officer Mitchell for the distribution of the monthly allowance of matches, I casually glance out of the yard door. At the extreme northwestern end, Assistant Deputy Hopkins loiters near the wall, slowly walking on the grass. The unusual presence of the overseer at the abandoned gate wakes my suspicion. The singular idling of the energetic guard, his furtive eyeing of the ground, strengthens my worst apprehensions. Something must have happened. Are they suspecting the tunnel? But work has not been commenced; besides, it is to terminate at the very opposite point of the yard, fully a thousand feet distant. In perplexity I wonder at the peculiar actions of Hopkins. Had the weapons been found, every inmate would immediately be subjected to a search, and shops and cell-house ransacked.

In anxious speculation I pass a sleepless night; morning dawns without bringing a solution. But after breakfast the cell-house becomes strangely quiet; the shop employees remain locked in. The rangemen are ordered to their cells, and guards from the yard and shops march into the block, and noisily ascend the galleries. The Deputy and Hopkins scurry about the hall; the rotunda door is thrown open with a clang, and the sharp command of the Warden resounds through the cell-house, "General search!"

I glance hurriedly over my table and shelf. Surprises of suspected prisoners are frequent, and I am always prepared. But some contraband is on hand. Quickly I snatch my writing material from the womb of the bedtick. In the very act of destroying several sketches of the previous year, a bright thought flashes across my mind. There is nothing dangerous about them, save the theft of the paper. "Prison Types," "In the Streets of New York," "Parkhurst and the Prostitute," "Libertas—a Study in Philology," "The Slavery of Tradition"—harmless products of evening leisure. Let them find the booklets! I'll be severely reprimanded for appropriating material from the shops, but my sketches will serve to divert suspicion: the Warden will secretly rejoice that my mind is not busy with more dangerous activities. But the sudden search signifies grave developments. General overhaulings, involving temporary suspension of the industries and consequent financial loss, are rare. The search of the entire prison is not due till spring. Its precipitancy confirms my worst fears: the weapons have undoubtedly been found! Jim's failure to get possession of them assumes a peculiar aspect. It is possible, of course, that some guard, unexpectedly passing through the cellar, discovered the bundle between the bars, and

appropriated it without attracting Jim's notice. Yet the
latter's confident assertion of his presence at the window at the appointed moment indicates another probability. The thought is painful, disquieting. But who
knows? In an atmosphere of fear and distrust and
almost universal espionage, the best friendships are
tinged with suspicion. It may be that Jim, afraid
of consequences, surrendered the weapons to the
Warden. He would have no difficulty in explaining
the discovery, without further betrayal of my confidence. Yet Jim, a "pete man"* of international re-
nown, enjoys the reputation of a thoroughly "square
man" and loyal friend. He has given me repeated
proof of his confidence, and I am disinclined to
accuse a possibly innocent man. It is fortunate, however,
that his information is limited to the weapons. No
doubt he suspects some sort of escape; but I have
left him in ignorance of my real plans. With these
Tony alone is entrusted.

The reflection is reassuring. Even if indiscretion
on Tony's part is responsible for the accident, he has
demonstrated his friendship. Realizing the danger of
his mission, he may have thrown in the weapons
between the cellar bars, ignoring my directions of previously ascertaining the presence of Jim at his post.
But the discovery of the revolvers vindicates the
veracity of Tony, and strengthens my confidence in
him. My fate rests in the hands of a loyal comrade,
a friend who has already dared great peril for my
sake.

The general search is over, bringing to light quan-
tities of various contraband. The counterfeit outfit,

---

* Safe blower.

whose product has been circulating beyond the walls of the prison, is discovered, resulting in a secret investigation by Federal officials. In the general excitement, the sketches among my effects have been ignored, and left in my possession. But no clew has been found in connection with the weapons. The authorities are still further mystified by the discovery that the lock on the trapdoor in the roof of the cell-house building had been tampered with. With an effort I suppress a smile at the puzzled bewilderment of the kindly old Mitchell, as, with much secrecy, he confides to me the information. I marvel at the official stupidity that failed to make the discovery the previous year, when, by the aid of Jim and my young friend Russell, I had climbed to the top of the cell-house, while the inmates were at church, and wrenched off the lock of the trapdoor, leaving in its place an apparent counterpart, provided by Jim. With the key in our possession, we watched for an opportunity to reach the outside roof, when certain changes in the block created insurmountable obstacles, forcing the abandonment of the project. Russell was unhappy over the discovery, the impulsive young prisoner steadfastly refusing to be reconciled to the failure. His time, however, being short, I have been urging him to accept the inevitable. The constant dwelling upon escape makes imprisonment more unbearable; the passing of his remaining two years would be hastened by the determination to serve out his sentence.

The boy listens quietly to my advice, his blue eyes dancing with merriment, a sly smile on the delicate lips. "You are right, Aleck," he replies, gravely, "but say, last night I thought out a scheme; it's great, and we're sure to make our get-a-way." With minute detail he pictures the impossible plan of sawing through the bars of the cell at night, "holding up" the guards, binding and gagging them, and "then the road would be clear." The innocent boy, for all his back-country reputation of "bad man," is not aware that "then" is the very threshold of difficulties. I seek to explain to him that, the guards being disposed of, we should find ourselves trapped in the cell-house. The solid steel double doors leading to the yard are securely locked, the key in the sole possession of the Captain of the night watch, who cannot be reached except through the well-guarded rotunda. But the boy is not to be daunted. "We'll have to storm the rotunda, then," he remarks, calmly, and at once proceeds to map out a plan of campaign. He smiles incredulously at my refusal to participate in the wild scheme. "Oh, yes, you will, Aleck. I don't believe a word you say. I know you're keen to make a get-a-way." His confidence somewhat shaken by my resolution, he announces that he will "go it alone."

The declaration fills me with trepidation: the reckless youth will throw away his life; his attempt may frustrate my own success. But it is in vain to dissuade him by direct means. I know the determination of the boy. The smiling face veils the boundless self-assurance of exuberant youth, combined with indomitable courage. The redundance of animal vitality and the rebellious spirit have violently disturbed the inertia of his rural home, aggravating its staid descendants of Dutch forbears. The taunt of "ne'er-do-well" has dripped bitter poison into the innocent pranks of Russell, stamping the brand of desperado upon the good-natured boy.

I tax my ingenuity to delay the carrying out of his project. He has secreted the saws I had procured from the Girl for the attempt of the previous year, and his determination is impatient to make the dash for liberty. Only his devotion to me and respect for my wishes still hold the impetuous boy in leash. But each day his restlessness increases; more insistently he urges my participation and a definite explanation of my attitude.

At a loss to invent new objections, I almost despair of dissuading Russell from his desperate purpose. From day to day I secure his solemn promise to await my final decision, the while I vaguely hope for some development that would force the abandonment of his plan. But nothing disturbs the routine, and I grow nervous with dread lest the boy, reckless with impatience, thwart my great project.

II

THE weather is moderating; the window sashes in the hall are being lowered: the signs of approaching spring multiply. I chafe at the lack of news from Tony, who had departed on his mission to New York. With greedy eyes I follow the Chaplain on his rounds of mail delivery. Impatient of his constant pauses on the galleries, I hasten along the range to meet the postman.

"Any letters for me, Mr. Milligan?" I ask, with an effort to steady my voice.

"No, m' boy."

My eyes devour the mail in his hand. "None to-day, Aleck," he adds; "this is for your neighbor Pasquale."

I feel apprehensive at Tony's silence. Another twenty-four hours must elapse before the Chaplain returns. Perhaps there will be no mail for me to-morrow, either. What can be the matter with my friend? So many dangers menace his every step—he might be sick—some accident . . . Anxious days pass without

mail. Russell is becoming more insistent, threatening
a "break." The solitaries murmur at my neglect. I am
nervous and irritable. For two weeks I have not heard
from Tony; something terrible must have happened.
In a ferment of dread, I keep watch on the upper
rotunda. The noon hour is approaching: the Chaplain
fumbles with his keys; the door opens, and he trips
along the ranges. Stealthily I follow him under the
galleries, pretending to dust the bars. He descends to
the hall.

"Good morning, Chaplain," I seek to attract his
attention, wistfully peering at the mail in his hand.

"Good morning, m' boy. Feeling good to-day?"

"Thank you; pretty fair." My voice trembles at
his delay, but I fear betraying my anxiety by renewed
questioning.

He passes me, and I feel sick with disappointment.
Now he pauses. "Aleck," he calls, "I mislaid a letter
for you yesterday. Here it is."

With shaking hand I unfold the sheet. In a
fever of hope and fear, I pore over it in the solitude of the cell. My heart palpitates violently as I
scan each word and letter, seeking hidden meaning,
analyzing every flourish and dash, carefully distilling
the minute lines, fusing the significant dots into the structure of meaning. Glorious! A house has been rented
—28 Sterling Street—almost opposite the gate of the
south wall. Funds are on hand, work is to begin at
once!

With nimble step I walk the range. The river
wafts sweet fragrance to my cell, the joy of spring is
in my heart. Every hour brings me nearer to liberty:
the faithful comrades are steadily working underground. Perhaps within a month, or two at most, the
tunnel will be completed. I count the days, crossing

off each morning the date on my calendar. The news from Tony is cheerful, encouraging: the work is progressing smoothly, the prospects of success are splendid. I grow merry at the efforts of uninitiated friends in New York to carry out the suggestions of the attorneys to apply to the Superior Court of the State for a writ, on the ground of the unconstitutionality of my sentence. I consult gravely with Mr. Milligan upon the advisability of the step, the amiable Chaplain affording me the opportunity of an extra allowance of letter paper. I thank my comrades for their efforts, and urge the necessity of collecting funds for the appeal to the upper court. Repeatedly I ask the advice of the Chaplain in the legal matter, confident that my apparent enthusiasm will reach the ears of the Warden: the artifice will mask my secret project and lull suspicion. My official letters breathe assurance of success, and with much show of confidence I impress upon the trusties my sanguine expectation of release. I discuss the subject with officers and stools, till presently the prison is agog with the prospective liberation of its fourth oldest inmate. The solitaries charge me with messages to friends, and the Deputy Warden offers advice on behavior beyond the walls. The moment is propitious for a bold stroke. Confined to the cell-house, I shall be unable to reach the tunnel. The privilege of the yard is imperative.

It is June. Unfledged birdies frequently fall from their nests, and I induce the kindly runner, "Southside" Johnny, to procure for me a brace of sparlings. I christen the little orphans Dick and Sis, and the memory of my previous birds is revived among inmates and officers. Old Mitchell is in ecstasy over the intelligence and adaptability of my new feathered friends. But the birds languish and waste in the close air of the block; they need sunshine and gravel, and the dusty street to bathe in. Gradually I enlist the sympathies of the new doctor by the curious performances of my pets. One day the Warden strolls in, and joins in admiration of the wonderful birds.

"Who trained them?" he inquires.

"This man," the physician indicates me. A slight frown flits over the Warden's face. Old Mitchell winks at me, encouragingly.

"Captain," I approach the Warden, "the birds are sickly for lack of air. Will you permit me to give them an airing in the yard?"

"Why don't you let them go? You have no permission to keep them."

"Oh, it would be a pity to throw them out," the doctor intercedes. "They are too tame to take care of themselves."

"Well, then," the Warden decides, "let Jasper take them out every day."

"They will not go with any one except myself," I inform him. "They follow me everywhere."

The Warden hesitates.

"Why not let Berkman go out with them for a few moments," the doctor suggests. "I hear you expect to be free soon," he remarks to me casually. "Your case is up for revision?"

"Yes."

"Well, Berkman," the Warden motions to me, "I will permit you ten minutes in the yard, after your sweeping is done. What time are you through with it?"

"At 9.30 A. M."

"Mr. Mitchell, every morning, at 9.30, you will pass Berkman through the doors. For ten minutes, on the watch." Then turning to me, he adds: "You are to stay near the greenhouse; there is plenty of sand there. If you cross the dead line of the sidewalk, or exceed your time a single minute, you will be punished."

CHAPTER XXXVI

THE UNDERGROUND

May 10, 1900.

MY DEAR TONY:

Your letters intoxicate me with hope and joy. No sooner have I sipped the rich aroma than I am athirst for more nectar. Write often, dear friend; it is the only solace of suspense.

Do not worry about this end of the line. All is well. By stratagem I have at last procured the privilege of the yard. Only for a few minutes every morning, but I am judiciously extending my prescribed time and area. The prospects are bright here; every one talks of my application to the Superior Court, and peace reigns—you understand.

A pity I cannot write directly to my dear, faithful comrades, your coworkers. You shall be the medium. Transmit to them my deepest appreciation. Tell "Yankee" and "Ibsen" and our Italian comrades what I feel—I know I need not explain it further to you. No one realizes better than myself the terrible risks they are taking, the fearful toil in silence and darkness, almost within hearing of the guards. The danger, the heroic self-sacrifice—what money could buy such devotion? I grow faint with the thought of their peril. I could almost cry at the beautiful demonstration of solidarity and friendship. Dear comrades, I feel proud of you, and proud of the great truth of Anarchism that can produce such disciples, such spirit. I embrace you, my noble comrades, and may you speed the day that will make me happy with the sight of your faces, the touch of your hands.

A.

June 5.

Dear Tony:

Your silence was unbearable. The suspense is terrible.
Was it really necessary to halt operations so long? I
am surprised you did not foresee the shortage of air and
the lack of light. You would have saved so much time.
It is a great relief to know that the work is progressing
again, and very fortunate indeed that "Yankee" understands
electricity. It must be hellish work to pump air into the
shaft. Take precautions against the whir of the machinery.
The piano idea is great Keep her playing and singing as
much as possible, and be sure you have all windows open.
The beasts on the wall will be soothed by the music, and
it will drown the noises underground. Have an electric but-
ton connected from the piano to the shaft; when the player
sees anything suspicious on the street or the guards on the
wall, she can at once notify the comrades to stop work.

I am enclosing the wall and yard measurements you
asked. But why do you need them? Don't bother with
unnecessary things. From house beneath the street, directly
toward the southwestern wall. For that you can procure
measurements outside. On the inside you require none.
Go under wall, about 20-30 feet, till you strike wall of
blind alley. Cut into it, and all will be complete. Write
of progress without delay. Greetings to all.

A.

June 20.

Tony:

Your letters bewilder me. Why has the route been
changed? You were to go to southwest, yet you say now
you are near the east wall. It's simply incredible, Tony.
Your explanation is not convincing. If you found a gas
main near the gate, you could have gone around it; besides,
the gate is out of your way anyhow. Why did you take
that direction at all? I wish, Tony, you would follow my
instructions and the original plan. Your failure to report the
change immediately, may prove fatal. I could have informed
you—once you were near the southeastern gate—to go

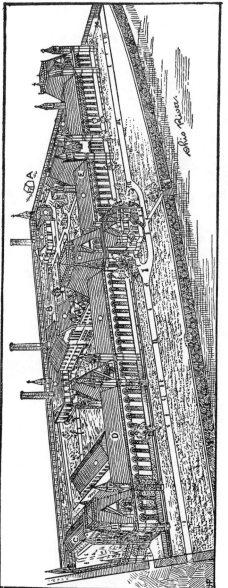

A—House on Sterling Street from which the Tunnel started. B—Point at which the Tunnel entered under the east wall. C—Mat Shop, near which the Author was permitted to take his birds for ten minutes every day, for exercise. D—North Block, where the Author was confined at the time of the Tunnel episode. E—South Block.

directly underneath; then you would have saved digging under the wall; there is no stone foundation, of course, beneath the gate. Now that you have turned the southeast corner, you will have to come under the wall there, and it is the worst possible place, because that particular part used to be a swamp, and I have learned that it was filled with extra masonry. Another point; an old abandoned natural-gas well is somewhere under the east wall, about 300 feet from the gate. Tell our friends to be on the lookout for fumes; it is a very dangerous place; special precautions must be taken.

Do not mind my brusqueness, dear Tony. My nerves are on edge, the suspense is driving me mad. And I must mask my feelings, and smile and look indifferent. But I haven't a moment's peace. I imagine the most terrible things when you fail to write. Please be more punctual. I know you have your hands full; but I fear I'll go insane before this thing is over. Tell me especially how far you intend going along the east wall, and where you'll come out. This complicates the matter. You have already gone a longer distance than would have been necessary per original plan. It was a grave mistake, and if you were not such a devoted friend, I'd feel very cross with you. Write at once. I am arranging a new *sub rosa* route. They are building in the yard; many outside drivers, you understand.

A.

DEAR TONY:

I'm in great haste to send this. You know the shed opposite the east wall. It has only a wooden floor and is not frequented much by officers. A few cons are there, from the stone pile. I'll attend to them. Make directly for that shed. It's a short distance from wall. I enclose measurements.

A.

TONY:

You distract me beyond words. What has become of your caution, your judgment? A hole in the grass *will not do*. I am absolutely opposed to it. There are a score of men on the stone pile and several screws. It is sure to be discovered. And even if you leave the upper crust intact for a foot or two, how am I to dive into the hole in the presence of so many? You don't seem to have considered that. There is only *one* way, the one I explained in my last. Go to the shed; it's only a little more work, 30-40 feet, no more. Tell the comrades the grass idea is impossible. A little more effort, friends, and all will be well. Answer at once.

A.

DEAR TONY:

Why do you insist on the hole in the ground? I tell you again it will not do. I won't consider it for a moment. I am on the inside—you must let me decide what can or cannot be done here. I am prepared to risk everything for liberty, would risk my life a thousand times. I am too desperate now for any one to block my escape; I'd break through a wall of guards, if necessary. But I still have a little judgment, though I am almost insane with the suspense and anxiety. If you insist on the hole, I'll make the break, though there is not one chance in a hundred for success. I beg of you, Tony, the thing must be dug to the shed; it's only a little way. After such a tremendous effort, can we jeopardize it all so lightly? I assure you, the success of the hole plan is unthinkable. They'd all see me go down into it; I'd be followed at once—what's the use talking.

Besides, you know I have no revolvers. Of course I'll have a weapon, but it will not help the escape. Another thing, your change of plans has forced me to get an assistant. The man is reliable, and I have only confided to him parts of the project. I need him to investigate around the shed, take measurements, etc. I am not permitted anywhere near the wall. But you need not trouble about this; I'll be responsible for my friend. But I tell you about it, so that you prepare two pair of overalls instead of one. Also leave two revolvers in the house, money, and cipher directions for us where to go. None of our comrades is to wait

for us. Let them all leave as soon as everything is ready.
But be sure you don't stop at the hole. Go to the shed,
absolutely.

A.

TONY:

The hole will not do. The more I think of it, the more
impossible I find it. I am sending an urgent call for money
to the Editor. You know whom I mean. Get in communication with him at once. Use the money to continue work
to shed.

A.

Direct to Box A 7,
Allegheny City, Pa.,
June 25, 1900.

DEAR COMRADE:

The Chaplain was very kind to permit me an extra sheet of
paper, on urgent business. I write to you in a very great extremity. You are aware of the efforts of my friends to appeal
my case. Read carefully, please. I have lost faith in their attorneys. I have engaged my *own* "lawyers." Lawyers in quota-
tion marks—a prison joke, you see. I have utmost confidence
in *these* lawyers. They will, absolutely, procure my release,
even if it is not a pardon, you understand. I mean, we'll go to
the Superior Court, different from a Pardon Board—another
prison joke.

My friends are short of money. We need some *at once*.
The work is started, but cannot be finished for lack of funds.
Mark well what I say: *I'll not be responsible for anything*—the
worst may happen—unless money is procured *at once*. You
have influence. I rely on you to understand and to act promptly.

Your comrade,

ALEXANDER BERKMAN.

MY POOR TONY:

I can see how this thing has gone on your nerves. To think that you, you the cautious Tony, should be so reckless—to send me a telegram. You could have ruined the whole thing. I had trouble explaining to the Chaplain, but it's all right now. Of course, if it must be the hole, it can't be helped. I understood the meaning of your wire: from the seventh bar on the east wall, ten feet to west. We'll be there on the minute—3 P. M. But July 4th won't do. It's a holiday: no work; my friend will be locked up. Can't leave him in the lurch. It will have to be next day, July 5th. It's only three days more. I wish it was over; I can't bear the worry and suspense any more. May it be my Independence Day!

                                                                    A.

                                                           July 6.

TONY:

It's terrible. It's all over. Couldn't make it. Went there on time, but found a big pile of stone and brick right on top of the spot. Impossible to do anything. I warned you they were building near there. I was seen at the wall—am now strictly forbidden to leave the cell-house. But my friend has been there a dozen times since—the hole can't be reached: a mountain of stone hides it. It won't be discovered for a little while. Telegraph at once to New York for more money. You must continue to the shed. I can force my way there, if need be. It's the only hope. Don't lose a minute.

                                                                    A.

                                                           July 13.

TONY:

A hundred dollars was sent to the office for me from New York. I told Chaplain it is for my appeal. I am sending the money to you. Have work continued at once. There is still hope. Nothing suspected. But the wire that you pushed through the grass to indicate the spot, was not found by my friend. Too much stone over it. Go to shed at once.

A.

July 16.

Tunnel discovered. Lose no time. Leave the city immediately. I am locked up on suspicion.

A.

CHAPTER XXXVII

ANXIOUS DAYS

THE discovery of the tunnel overwhelms me with the violence of an avalanche. The plan of continuing the work, the trembling hope of escape, of liberty, life —all is suddenly terminated. My nerves, tense with the months of suspense and anxiety, relax abruptly. With torpid brain I wonder, "Is it possible, is it really possible?"

An air of uneasiness, as of lurking danger, fills the prison. Vague rumors are afloat: a wholesale jail delivery had been planned, the walls were to be dynamited, the guards killed. An escape has actually taken place, it is whispered about. The Warden wears a look of bewilderment and fear; the officers are alert with suspicion. The inmates manifest disappointment and nervous impatience. The routine is violently disturbed: the shops are closed, the men locked in the cells.

The discovery of the tunnel mystifies the prison and the city authorities. Some children, at play on the street, had accidentally wandered into the yard of the deserted house opposite the prison gates. The piles of freshly dug soil attracted their attention; a boy, stumbling into the cellar, was frightened by the sight of the deep cavern; his mother notified the agent of the house, who, by a peculiar coincidence, proved to be an officer of the penitentiary. But in vain are the efforts of the prison authorities to discover any sign of the tunnel within the walls. Days pass in the fruitless investigation of the yard—the outlet of the

tunnel within the prison cannot be found. Perhaps the
underground passage does not extend to the penitentiary? The Warden voices his firm conviction that
the walls have not been penetrated. Evidently it was
not the prison, he argues, which was the objective
point of the diggers. The authorities of the City of
Allegheny decide to investigate the passage from the
house on Sterling Street. But the men that essay to
crawl through the narrow tunnel are forced to abandon
their mission, driven back by the fumes of escaping
gas. It is suggested that the unknown diggers, whatever their purpose, have been trapped in the abandoned gas well and perished before the arrival of aid.
The fearful stench no doubt indicates the decomposition of human bodies; the terrible accident has forced
the inmates of 28 Sterling Street to suspend their
efforts before completing the work. The condition
of the house—the half-eaten meal on the table, the
clothing scattered about the rooms, the general dis-
order—all seem to point to precipitate flight.

The persistence of the assertion of a fatal accident disquiets me, in spite of my knowledge to the
contrary. Yet, perhaps the reckless Tony, in his
endeavor to force the wire signal through the upper
crust, perished in the well. The thought unnerves me
with horror, till it is announced that a negro, whom
the police had induced to crawl the length of the
tunnel, brought positive assurance that no life was
sacrificed in the underground work. Still the prison
authorities are unable to find the objective point, and
it is finally decided to tear up the streets beneath
which the tunnel winds its mysterious way.

The undermined place inside the walls at last being
discovered after a week of digging at various points in

the yard, the Warden reluctantly admits the apparent
purpose of the tunnel, at the same time informing
the press that the evident design was the liberation of
the Anarchist prisoner. He corroborates his view by
the circumstance that I had been reported for unper-
mitted presence at the east wall, pretending to collect
gravel for my birds. Assistant Deputy Warden Hopkins further asserts having seen and talked with Carl
Nold near the "criminal" house, a short time before the
discovery of the tunnel. The developments, fraught
with danger to my friends, greatly alarm me. Fortunately, no clew can be found in the house, save a note
in cipher which apparently defies the skill of experts.
The Warden, on his Sunday rounds, passes my cell,
then turns as if suddenly recollecting something. "Here,
Berkman," he says blandly, producing a paper, "the
press is offering a considerable reward to any one
who will decipher the note found in the Sterling Street
house. It's reproduced here. See if you can't make
it out." I scan the paper carefully, quickly reading
Tony's directions for my movements after the escape.
Then, returning the paper, I remark indifferently,
"I can read several languages, Captain, but this is beyond me."

The police and detective bureaus of the twin cities
make the announcement that a thorough investigation
conclusively demonstrates that the tunnel was intended
for William Boyd, a prisoner serving twelve years for
a series of daring forgeries. His "pals" had succeeded
in clearing fifty thousand dollars on forged bonds, and
it is they who did the wonderful feat underground,
to secure the liberty of the valuable penman. The
controversy between the authorities of Allegheny and
the management of the prison is full of animosity
and bitterness. Wardens of prisons, chiefs of police,

and detective departments of various cities are consulted upon the mystery of the ingenious diggers, and the discussion in the press waxes warm and antagonistic. Presently the chief of police of Allegheny suffers a change of heart, and sides with the Warden, as against his personal enemy, the head of the Pittsburgh detective bureau. The confusion of published views, and my persistent denial of complicity in the tunnel, cause the much-worried Warden to fluctuate. A number of men are made the victims of his mental uncertainty. Following my exile into solitary, Pat McGraw is locked up as a possible beneficiary of the planned escape. In 1890 he had slipped through the roof of the prison, the Warden argues, and it is therefore reasonable to assume that the man is meditating another delivery. Jack Robinson, Cronin, "Nan," and a score of others, are in turn suspected by Captain Wright, and ordered locked up during the preliminary investigation. But because of absolute lack of clews the prisoners are presently returned to work, and the number of "suspects" is reduced to myself and Boyd, the Warden having discovered that the latter had recently made an attempt to escape by forcing an entry into the cupola of the shop he was employed in, only to find the place useless for his purpose.

A process of elimination and the espionage of the trusties gradually center exclusive suspicion upon myself. In surprise I learn that young Russell has been cited before the Captain. The fear of indiscretion on the part of the boy startles me from my torpor. I must employ every device to confound the authorities and save my friends. Fortunately none of the tunnelers have yet been arrested, the controversy between the city officials and the prison management having favored inaction. My comrades cannot be jeopardized by Rus-

sell. His information is limited to the mere knowledge
of the specific person for whom the tunnel was intended; the names of my friends are entirely unfamiliar
to him. My heart goes out to the young prisoner,
as I reflect that never once had he manifested curiosity concerning the men at the secret work. Desperate with confinement, and passionately yearning for
liberty though he was, he had yet offered to sacrifice his
longings to aid my escape. How transported with
joy was the generous youth when I resolved to share
my opportunity with him! He had given faithful
service in attempting to locate the tunnel entrance; the
poor boy had been quite distracted at our failure to
find the spot. I feel confident Russell will not betray
the secret in his keeping. Yet the persistent questioning by the Warden and Inspectors is perceptibly working on the boy's mind. He is so young and inexperienced—barely nineteen; a slip of the tongue, an
inadvertent remark, might convert suspicion into conviction.

Every day Russell is called to the office, causing
me torments of apprehension and dread, till a glance
at the returning prisoner, smiling encouragingly as he
passes my cell, informs me that the danger is past for
the day. With a deep pang, I observe the increasing
pallor of his face, the growing restlessness in his eyes,
the languid step. The continuous inquisition is breaking him down. With quivering voice he whispers as
he passes, "Aleck, I'm afraid of them." The Warden
has threatened him, he informs me, if he persists in
his pretended ignorance of the tunnel. His friendship
for me is well known, the Warden reasons; we have
often been seen together in the cell-house and yard;
I must surely have confided to Russell my plans of
escape. The big, strapping youth is dwindling to a

shadow under the terrible strain. Dear, faithful friend! How guilty I feel toward you, how torn in my inmost heart to have suspected your devotion, even for that brief instant when, in a panic of fear, you had denied to the Warden all knowledge of the slip of paper found in your cell. It cast suspicion upon me as the writer of the strange Jewish scrawl. The Warden scorned my explanation that Russell's desire to learn Hebrew was the sole reason for my writing the alphabet for him. The mutual denial seemed to point to some secret; the scrawl was similar to the cipher note found in the Sterling Street house, the Warden insisted. How strange that I should have so successfully confounded the Inspectors with the contradictory testimony regarding the tunnel, that they returned me to my position on the range. And yet the insignificant incident of Russell's hieroglyphic imitation of the Hebrew alphabet should have given the Warden a pretext to order me into solitary! How distracted and bitter I must have felt to charge the boy with treachery! His very reticence strengthened my suspicion, and all the while the tears welled into his throat, choking the innocent lad beyond speech. How little I suspected the terrible wound my hasty imputation had caused my devoted friend! In silence he suffered for months, without opportunity to explain, when at last, by mere accident, I learned the fatal mistake.

In vain I strive to direct my thoughts into different channels. My misunderstanding of Russell plagues me with recurring persistence; the unjust accusation torments my sleepless nights. It was a moment of intense joy that I experienced as I humbly begged his pardon to-day, when I met him in the Captain's office. A deep sense of relief, almost of peace, filled me at his unhesitating, "Oh, never mind, Aleck, it's all right; we were both excited." I was overcome by thankfulness and admiration of the noble boy, and the next instant the sight of his wan face, his wasted form, pierced me as with a knife-thrust. With the earnest conviction of strong faith I sought to explain to the Board of Inspectors the unfortunate error regarding the Jewish writing. But they smiled doubtfully. It was too late: their opinion of a prearranged agreement with Russell was settled. But the testimony of Assistant Deputy Hopkins that he had seen and conversed with Nold a few weeks before the discovery of the tunnel, and that he saw him enter the "criminal" house, afforded me an opportunity to divide the views among the Inspectors. I experienced little difficulty in convincing two members of the Board that Nold could not possibly have been connected with the tunnel, because for almost a year previously, and since, he had been in the employ of a St. Louis firm. They accepted my offer to prove by the official time-tables of the company that Nold was in St. Louis on the very day that Hopkins claimed to have spoken with him. The fortunate and very natural error of Hopkins in mistaking the similar appearance of Tony for that of Carl, enabled me to discredit the chief link connecting my friends with the tunnel. The diverging views of the police officials of the twin cities still further confounded the Inspectors, and I was gravely informed by them that the charge of attempted escape against me had not been conclusively substantiated. They ordered my reinstatement as rangeman, but the Captain, on learning the verdict, at once charged me before the Board with conducting a secret correspondence with Russell. On the pretext of the alleged Hebrew note, the Inspectors confirmed the Warden's judgment, and I was sentenced to the solitary and immediately locked up in the South Wing.

CHAPTER XXXVIII

"HOW MEN THEIR BROTHERS MAIM"

I

THE solitary is stifling with the August heat. The hall windows, high above the floor, cast a sickly light, shrouding the bottom range in darksome gloom. At every point, my gaze meets the irritating white of the walls, in spots yellow with damp. The long days are oppressive with silence; the stone cage echoes my languid footsteps mournfully.

Once more I feel cast into the night, torn from the midst of the living. The failure of the tunnel forever excludes the hope of liberty. Terrified by the possibilities of the planned escape, the Warden's determination dooms my fate. I shall end my days in strictest seclusion, he has informed me. Severe punishment is visited upon any one daring to converse with me; even officers are forbidden to pause at my cell. Old Evans, the night guard, is afraid even to answer my greeting, since he was disciplined with the loss of ten days' pay for being seen at my door. It was not his fault, poor old man. The night was sultry; the sashes of the hall window opposite my cell were tightly closed. Almost suffocated with the foul air, I requested the passing Evans to raise the window. It had been ordered shut by the Warden, he informed me. As he turned to leave, three sharp raps on the bars of the upper rotunda almost rooted him to the spot with amazement. It was 2 A. M. No one was supposed to be there at night. "Come here, Evans!" I recognized the curt tones of the Warden. "What business have you at that man's door?" I could distinctly hear each word, cutting the stillness of the night. In vain the frightened officer sought to explain: he had merely answered a question, he had stopped but a moment. "I've been watching you there for half an hour," the irate Warden insisted. "Report to me in the morning."

Since then the guards on their rounds merely glance between the bars, and pass on in silence. I have been removed within closer observation of the nightly prowling Captain, and am now located near the rotunda, in the second cell on the ground floor, Range Y. The stringent orders of exceptional surveillance have so terrorized my friends that they do not venture to look in my direction. A special officer has been assigned to the vicinity of my door, his sole duty to keep me under observation. I feel buried alive. Communication with my comrades has been interrupted, the Warden detaining my mail. I am deprived of books and papers, all my privileges curtailed. If only I had my birds! The company of my little pets would give me consolation. But they have been taken from me, and I fear the guards have killed them. Deprived of work and exercise I pass the days in the solitary, monotonous, interminable.

II

By degrees anxiety over my friends is allayed. The mystery of the tunnel remains unsolved. The Warden reiterates his moral certainty that the underground passage was intended for the liberation of the

Anarchist prisoner. The views of the police and detective officials of the twin cities are hopelessly divergent. Each side asserts thorough familiarity with the case, and positive conviction regarding the guilty parties. But the alleged clews proving misleading, the matter is finally abandoned. The passage has been filled with cement, and the official investigation is terminated.

The safety of my comrades sheds a ray of light into the darkness of my existence. It is consoling to reflect that, disastrous as the failure is to myself, my friends will not be made victims of my longing for liberty. At no time since the discovery of the tunnel has suspicion been directed to the right persons. The narrow official horizon does not extend beyond the familiar names of the Girl, Nold, and Bauer. These have been pointed at by the accusing finger repeatedly, but the men actually concerned in the secret attempt have not even been mentioned. No danger threatens them from the failure of my plans. In a communication to a local newspaper, Nold has incontrovertibly proved his continuous residence in St. Louis for a period covering a year previous to the tunnel and afterwards. Bauer has recently married; at no time have the police been in ignorance of his whereabouts, and they are aware that my former fellow-prisoner is to be discounted as a participator in the attempted escape. Indeed, the prison officials must have learned from my mail that the big German is regarded by my friends as an ex-comrade merely. But the suspicion of the authorities directed toward the Girl—with a pang of bitterness, I think of her unfortunate absence from the country during the momentous period of the underground work. With resentment I reflect that but for that I might now be at liberty! Her skill as an organizer, her growing influence in the movement, her energy and devotion, would have assured the success of the undertaking. But Tony's unaccountable delay had resulted in her departure without learning of my plans. It is to him, to his obstinacy and conceit, that the failure of the project is mostly due, staunch and faithful though he is.

In turn I lay the responsibility at the door of this friend and that, lashing myself into furious rage at the renegade who had appropriated a considerable sum of the money intended for the continuation of the underground work. Yet the outbursts of passion spent, I strive to find consolation in the correctness of the intuitive judgment that prompted the selection of my "lawyers," the devoted comrades who so heroically toiled for my sake in the bowels of the earth. Half-naked they had labored through the weary days and nights, stretched at full length in the narrow passage, their bodies perspiring and chilled in turn, their hands bleeding with the terrible toil. And through the weeks and months of nerve-racking work and confinement in the tunnel, of constant dread of detection and anxiety over the result, my comrades had uttered no word of doubt or fear, in full reliance upon their invisible friend. What self-sacrifice in behalf of one whom some of you had never even known! Dear, beloved comrades, had you succeeded, my life could never repay your almost superhuman efforts and love. Only the future years of active devotion to our great common Cause could in a measure express my thankfulness and pride in you, whoever, wherever you are. Nor were your heroism, your skill and indomitable perseverance, without avail. You have given an invaluable demonstration of the elemental reality of the Ideal, of the marvelous strength and courage born of solidaric purpose, of the heights devotion to a great Cause can ascend. And the lesson has not been lost. Almost unanimous is the voice of the press—only Anarchists could have achieved the wonderful feat!

The subject of the tunnel fascinates my mind. How little thought I had given to my comrades, toiling underground, in the anxious days of my own apprehension and suspense! With increasing vividness I visualize their trepidation, the constant fear of discovery, the herculean efforts in spite of ever-present danger. How terrible must have been *their* despair at the inability to continue the work to a successful termination! . . .

My reflections fill me with renewed strength. I must live! I must live to meet those heroic men, to take them by the hand, and with silent lips pour my heart into their eyes. I shall be proud of their comradeship, and strive to be worthy of it.

III

The lines form in the hallway, and silently march to the shops. I peer through the bars, for the sight of a familiar face brings cheer, and the memory of the days on the range. Many friends, unseen for years, pass by my cell. How Big Jack has wasted! The deep chest is sunk in, the face drawn and yellow, with reddish spots about the cheekbones. Poor Jack, so strong and energetic, how languid and weak his step is now! And Jimmy is all broken up with rheumatism, and hops on crutches. With difficulty I recognize Harry Fisher. The two years have completely changed the young Morganza boy. He looks old at seventeen, the rosy cheeks a ghastly white, the delicate features immobile, hard, the large bright eyes dull and glassy. Vividly my friends stand before me in the youth and strength of

their first arrival.   How changed their appearance! My
poor chums, readers of the *Prison Blossoms,* helpers in
our investigation efforts, what wrecks the torture of hell
has made of you! I recall with sadness the first years
of my imprisonment, and my coldly impersonal valuation
of social victims.   There is Evans, the aged burglar,
smiling furtively at me from the line.   Far in the distance seems the day when I read his marginal note upon
a magazine article I sent him, concerning the stupendous
cost of crime.   I had felt quite piqued at the flippancy of
his comment, "We come high, but they must have us."
With the severe intellectuality of revolutionary tradition, I thought of him and his kind as inevitable fungus
growths, the rotten fruit of a decaying society.   Unfortunate derelicts, indeed, yet parasites, almost devoid
of humanity.   But the threads of comradeship have
slowly been woven by common misery.   The touch of
sympathy has discovered the man beneath the criminal;
the crust of sullen suspicion has melted at the breath of
kindness, warming into view the palpitating human heart.
Old Evans and Sammy and Bob,—what suffering and
pain must have chilled their fiery souls with the winter
of savage bitterness!   And the resurrection trembles
within!   How terrible man's ignorance, that forever condemns itself to be scourged by its own blind fury!   And
these my friends, Davis and Russell, these innocently
guilty,—what worse punishment could society inflict upon
itself, than the loss of their latent nobility which it had
killed? . . . Not entirely in vain are the years of suffering that have wakened my kinship with the humanity
of *les misérables,* whom social stupidity has cast into the
valley of death.

CHAPTER XXXIX

A NEW PLAN OF ESCAPE

I

My new neighbor turns my thoughts into a different channel. It is "Fighting" Tom, returned after several years of absence. By means of a string attached to a wire we "swing" notes to each other at night, and Tom startles me by the confession that he was the author of the mysterious note I had received soon after my arrival in the penitentiary. An escape was being planned, he informs me, and I was to be "let in," by his recommendation. But one of the conspirators getting "cold feet," the plot was betrayed to the Warden, whereupon Tom "sent the snitch to the hospital." As a result, however, he was kept in solitary till his release. In the prison he had become proficient as a broom-maker, and it was his intention to follow the trade. There was nothing in the crooked line, he thought; and he resolved to be honest. But on the day of his discharge he was arrested at the gate by officers from Illinois on an old charge. He swore vengeance against Assistant Deputy Hopkins, before whom he had once accidentally let drop the remark that he would never return to Illinois, because he was "wanted" there. He lived the five years in the Joliet prison in the sole hope of "getting square" with the man who had so meanly betrayed him. Upon his release, he returned to Pittsburgh, determined to

kill Hopkins.   On the night of his arrival he broke into
the latter's residence, prepared to avenge his wrongs.
But the Assistant Deputy had left the previous day on
his vacation.   Furious at being baffled, Tom was about
to set fire to the house, when the light of his match fell
upon a silver trinket on the bureau of the bedroom.   It
fascinated him.   He could not take his eyes off it.   Suddenly he was seized with the desire to examine the contents of the house.   The old passion was upon him.   He
could not resist.   Hardly conscious of his actions, he
gathered the silverware into a tablecloth, and quietly
stole out of the house.   He was arrested the next day,
as he was trying to pawn his booty.   An old offender,
he received a sentence of ten years.   Since his arrival,
eight months ago, he has been kept in solitary.   His
health is broken; he has no hope of surviving his sentence.   But if he is to die—he swears—he is going to
take "his man" along.

Aware of the determination of "Fighting" Tom, I
realize that the safety of the hated officer is conditioned
by Tom's lack of opportunity to carry out his revenge.   I
feel little sympathy for Hopkins, whose craftiness in
worming out the secrets of prisoners has placed him on
the pay-roll of the Pinkerton agency; but I exert myself
to persuade Tom that it would be sheer insanity thus
deliberately to put his head in the noose.   He is still a
young man; barely thirty.   It is not worth while sacrificing his life for a sneak of a guard.

However, Tom remains stubborn.   My arguments
seem merely to rouse his resistance, and strengthen his
resolution.   But closer acquaintance reveals to me his
exceeding conceit over his art and technic, as a second-
story expert.   I play upon his vanity, scoffing at the
crudity of his plans of revenge.   Would it not be more
in conformity with his reputation as a skilled "gun," I

argue, to "do the job" in a "smoother" manner? Tom assumes a skeptical attitude, but by degrees grows more interested. Presently, with unexpected enthusiasm, he warms to the suggestion of "a break." Once outside, well—"I'll get 'im all right," he chuckles.

II

The plan of escape completely absorbs us. On alternate nights we take turns in timing the rounds of the guards, the appearance of the Night Captain, the opening of the rotunda door. Numerous details, seemingly insignificant, yet potentially fatal, are to be mastered. Many obstacles bar the way of success, but time and perseverance will surmount them. Tom is thoroughly engrossed with the project. I realize the desperation of the undertaking, but the sole alternative is slow death in the solitary. It is the last resort.

With utmost care we make our preparations. The summer is long past; the dense fogs of the season will aid our escape. We hasten to complete all details, in great nervous tension with the excitement of the work. The time is drawing near for deciding upon a definite date. But Tom's state of mind fills me with apprehension. He has become taciturn of late. Yesterday he seemed peculiarly glum, sullenly refusing to answer my signal. Again and again I knock on the wall, calling for a reply to my last note. Tom remains silent. Occasionally a heavy groan issues from his cell, but my repeated signals remain unanswered. In alarm I stay awake all night, in the hope of inducing a guard to investigate the cause of the groaning. But my attempts to speak to the officers are ignored. The next morning I behold Tom carried on a stretcher from his cell, and learn with horror that he had bled to death during the night.

III

The peculiar death of my friend preys on my mind. Was it suicide or accident? Tom had been weakened by long confinement; in some manner he may have ruptured a blood vessel, dying for lack of medical aid. It is hardly probable that he would commit suicide on the eve of our attempt. Yet certain references in his notes of late, ignored at the time, assume new significance. He was apparently under the delusion that Hopkins was "after him." Once or twice my friend had expressed fear for his safety. He might be poisoned, he hinted. I had laughed the matter away, familiar with the sporadic delusions of men in solitary. Close confinement exerts a similar effect upon the majority of prisoners. Some are especially predisposed to auto-suggestion; Young Sid used to manifest every symptom of the diseases he read about. Perhaps poor Tom's delusion was responsible for his death. Spencer, too, had committed suicide a month before his release, in the firm conviction that the Warden would not permit his discharge. It may be that in a sudden fit of despondency, Tom had ended his life. Perhaps I could have saved my friend: I did not realize how constantly he brooded over the danger he believed himself threatened with. How little I knew of the terrible struggle that must have been going on in his tortured heart! Yet we were so intimate; I believed I understood his every feeling and emotion.

The thought of Tom possesses my mind. The news from the Girl about Bresci's execution of the King of Italy rouses little interest in me. Bresci avenged the

peasants and the women and children shot before the
palace for humbly begging bread. He did well, and the
agitation resulting from his act may advance the Cause.
But it will have no bearing on my fate. The last hope
of escape has departed with my poor friend. I am
doomed to perish here. And Bresci will perish in
prison, but the comrades will eulogize him and his act,
and continue their efforts to regenerate the world. Yet
I feel that the individual, in certain cases, is of more
direct and immediate consequence than humanity. What
is the latter but the aggregate of individual existences—
and shall these, the best of them, forever be sacrificed
for the metaphysical collectivity? Here, all around me,
a thousand unfortunates daily suffer the torture of Calvary, forsaken by God and man. They bleed and
struggle and suicide, with the desperate cry for a little
sunshine and life. How shall they be helped? How
helped amid the injustice and brutality of a society whose
chief monuments are prisons? And so we must suffer
and suicide, and countless others after us, till the play of
social forces shall transform human history into the
history of true humanity,—and meanwhile our bones
will bleach on the long, dreary road.

Bereft of the last hope of freedom, I grow indifferent to life. The monotony of the narrow cell daily becomes more loathsome. My whole being longs for rest.
Rest, no more to awaken. The world will not miss me.
An atom of matter, I shall return to endless space.
Everything will pursue its wonted course, but I shall
know no more of the bitter struggle and strife. My
friends will sorrow, and yet be glad my pain is over,
and continue on their way. And new Brescis will arise,
and more kings will fall, and then all, friend and enemy,
will go my way, and new generations will be born and

400 PRISON MEMOIRS OF AN ANARCHIST

die, and humanity and the world be whirled into space
and disappear, and again the little stage will be set, and
the same history and the same facts will come and go,
the playthings of cosmic forces renewing and transforming forever.

How insignificant it all is in the eye of reason, how
small and puny life and all its pain and travail! . . .
With eyes closed, I behold myself suspended by the
neck from the upper bars of the cell. My body swings
gently against the door, striking it softly, once, twice,
—just like Pasquale, when he hanged himself in the
cell next to mine, some months ago. A few twitches,
and the last breath is gone. My face grows livid, my
body rigid; slowly it cools. The night guard passes.
"What's this, eh?" He rings the rotunda bell. Keys
clang; the lever is drawn, and my door unlocked. An
officer draws a knife sharply across the rope at the
bars: my body sinks to the floor, my head striking against
the iron bedstead. The doctor kneels at my side; I feel
his hand over my heart. Now he rises.

"Good job, Doc?" I recognize the Deputy's voice.

The physician nods.

"Damn glad of it," Hopkins sneers.

The Warden enters, a grin on his parchment face.
With an oath I spring to my feet. In terror the officers
rush from the cell. "Ah, I fooled you, didn't I, you
murderers!"

.   .   .   .

The thought of the enemy's triumph fans the embers
of life. It engenders defiance, and strengthens stubborn
resistance.

CHAPTER XL

DONE TO DEATH

I

In my utter isolation, the world outside appears like a faint memory, unreal and dim. The deprivation of newspapers has entirely severed me from the living. Letters from my comrades have become rare and irregular; they sound strangely cold and impersonal. The life of the prison is also receding; no communication reaches me from my friends. "Pious" John, the rangeman, is unsympathetic; he still bears me ill will from the days of the jail. Only young Russell still remembers me. I tremble for the reckless boy as I hear his low cough, apprising me of the "stiff" he unerringly shoots between the bars, while the double file of prisoners marches past my door. He looks pale and haggard, the old buoyant step now languid and heavy. A tone of apprehension pervades his notes. He is constantly harassed by the officers, he writes; his task has been increased; he is nervous and weak, and his health is declining. In the broken sentences, I sense some vague misgiving, as of impending calamity.

With intense thankfulness I think of Russell. Again I live through the hopes and fears that drew us into closer friendship, the days of terrible anxiety incident to the tunnel project. My heart goes out to the faithful boy, whose loyalty and discretion have so much aided the

safety of my comrades. A strange longing for his companionship possesses me. In the gnawing loneliness, his
face floats before me, casting the spell of a friendly
presence, his strong features softened by sorrow, his
eyes grown large with the same sweet sadness of "Little
Felipe." A peculiar tenderness steals into my thoughts
of the boy; I look forward eagerly to his notes. Impatiently I scan the faces in the passing line, wistful for
the sight of the youth, and my heart beats faster at
his fleeting smile.

How sorrowful he looks! Now he is gone. The
hours are weary with silence and solitude. Listlessly I
turn the pages of my library book. If only I had the
birds! I should find solace in their thoughtful eyes:
Dick and Sis would understand and feel with me. But
my poor little friends have disappeared; only Russell remains. My only friend! I shall not see him when he
returns to the cell at noon: the line passes on the opposite
side of the hall. But in the afternoon, when the men
are again unlocked for work, I shall look into his eyes
for a happy moment, and perhaps the dear boy will
have a message for me. He is so tender-hearted: his
correspondence is full of sympathy and encouragement,
and he strives to cheer me with the good news: another
day is gone, his sentence is nearing its end; he will at
once secure a position, and save every penny to aid in
my release. Tacitly I concur in his ardent hope,—it
would break his heart to be disillusioned.

II

The passing weeks and months bring no break in the
dreary monotony. The call of the robin on the river
bank rouses no echo in my heart. No sign of awakening spring brightens the constant semi-darkness of the

solitary. The dampness of the cell is piercing my bones;
every movement racks my body with pain. My eyes
are tortured with the eternal white of the walls. Sombre
shadows brood around me.

I long for a bit of sunshine. I wait patiently at the
door: perhaps it is clear to-day. My cell faces west; may
be the setting sun will steal a glance upon me. For
hours I stand with naked breast close to the bars: I must
not miss a friendly ray; it may suddenly peep into the
cell, and turn away from me, unseen in the gloom. Now
a bright beam plays on my neck and shoulders, and I
press closer to the door to welcome the dear stranger.
He caresses me with soft touch,—perhaps it is the soul
of little Dick pouring out his tender greeting in this song
of light,—or may be the astral aura of my beloved Uncle
Maxim, bringing warmth and hope. Sweet conceit of
Oriental thought, barren of joy in life. . . . The sun
is fading. It feels chilly in the twilight,—and now the
solitary is once more bleak and cold.

As his release approaches, the tone of native confidence becomes more assertive in Russell's letter. The
boy is jubilant and full of vitality: within three months
he will breathe the air of freedom. A note of sadness at
leaving me behind permeates his communications, but
he is enthusiastic over his project of aiding me to liberty.

Eagerly every day I anticipate his mute greeting, as
he passes in the line. This morning I saw him hold up
two fingers, the third crooked, in sign of the remaining
"two and a stump." A joyous light is in his eyes, his
step firmer, more elastic.

But in the afternoon he is missing from the line.
With sudden apprehension I wonder at his absence.
Could I have overlooked him in the closely walking

ranks? It is barely possible. Perhaps he has remained in the cell, not feeling well. It may be nothing serious; he will surely be in line to-morrow.

For three days, every morning and afternoon, I anxiously scrutinize the faces of the passing men; but Russell is not among them. His absence torments me with a thousand fears. May be the Warden has renewed his inquisition of the boy—perhaps he got into a fight in the shop—in the dungeon now—he'll lose his commutation time. . . . Unable to bear the suspense, I am about to appeal to the Chaplain, when a friendly runner surreptitiously hands me a note.

With difficulty I recognize my friend's bold handwriting in the uneven, nervous scrawl. Russell is in the hospital! At work in the shop, he writes, he had suffered a chill. The doctor committed him to the ward for observation, but the officers and the convict nurses accuse him of shamming to evade work. They threaten to have him returned to the shop, and he implores me to have the Chaplain intercede for him. He feels weak and feverish, and the thought of being left alone in the cell in his present condition fills him with horror.

I send an urgent request to see the Chaplain. But the guard informs me that Mr. Milligan is absent; he is not expected at the office till the following week. I prevail upon the kindly Mitchell, recently transferred to the South Block, to deliver a note to the Warden, in which I appeal on behalf of Russell. But several days pass, and still no reply from Captain Wright. Finally I pretend severe pains in the bowels, to afford Frank, the doctor's assistant, an opportunity to pause at my cell. As the "medicine boy" pours the prescribed pint of "horse salts" through the funnel inserted between the bars, I hastily inquire:

"Is Russell still in the ward, Frank? How is he?"

"What Russell?" he asks indifferently.

"Russell Schroyer, put four days ago under observation."

"Oh, that poor kid! Why, he is paralyzed."

For an instant I am speechless with terror. No, it cannot be. Some mistake.

"Frank, I mean young Schroyer, from the construction shop. He's Number 2608."

"Your friend Russell; I know who you mean. I'm sorry for the boy. He is paralyzed, all right."

"But . . . No, it can't be! Why, Frank, it was just a chill and a little weakness."

"Look here, Aleck. I know you're square, and you can keep a secret all right. I'll tell you something if you won't give me away."

"Yes, yes, Frank. What is it?"

"Sh-sh. You know Flem, the night nurse? Doing a five spot for murder. His father and the Warden are old cronies. That's how he got to be nurse; don't know a damn thing about it, an' careless as hell. Always makes mistakes. Well, Doc ordered an injection for Russell. Now don't ever say I told you. Flem got the wrong bottle; gave the poor boy some acid in the injection. Paralyzed the kid; he did, the damn murderer."

I pass the night in anguish, clutching desperately at the faint hope that it cannot be—some mistake—perhaps Frank has exaggerated. But in the morning the "medicine boy" confirms my worst fears: the doctor has said the boy will die. Russell does not realize the situation: there is something wrong with his legs, the poor boy writes; he is unable to move them, and suffers great pain. It can't be fever, he thinks; but the physician will not tell him what is the matter. . . .

The kindly Frank is sympathetic; every day he passes notes between us, and I try to encourage Russell. He will improve, I assure him; his time is short, and fresh air and liberty will soon restore him. My words seem to soothe my friend, and he grows more cheerful, when unexpectedly he learns the truth from the wrangling nurses. His notes grow piteous with misery. Tears fill my eyes as I read his despairing cry, "Oh, Aleck, I am so young. I don't want to die." He implores me to visit him; if I could only come to nurse him, he is sure he would improve. He distrusts the convict attendants who harry and banter the country lad; their heartless abuse is irritating the sick boy beyond patience. Exasperated by the taunts of the night nurse, Russell yesterday threw a saucer at him. He was reported to the doctor, who threatened to send the paralyzed youth to the dungeon. Plagued and tormented, in great suffering, Russell grows bitter and complaining. The nurses and officers are persecuting him, he writes; they will soon do him to death, if I will not come to his rescue. If he could go to an outside hospital, he is sure to recover.

Every evening Frank brings sadder news: Russell is feeling worse; he is so nervous, the doctor has ordered the nurses to wear slippers; the doors in the ward have been lined with cotton, to deaden the noise of slamming; but even the sight of a moving figure throws Russell into convulsions. There is no hope, Frank reports; decomposition has already set in. The boy is in terrible agony; he is constantly crying with pain, and calling for me.

Distraught with anxiety and yearning to see my sick friend, I resolve upon a way to visit the hospital. In the morning, as the guard hands me the bread ration and shuts my cell, I slip my hand between the sill and door. With an involuntary cry I withdraw my maimed and bleeding fingers. The overseer conducts me to the dispensary. By tacit permission of the friendly "medicine boy" I pass to the second floor, where the wards are located, and quickly steal to Russell's bedside. The look of mute joy on the agonized face subdues the excruciating pain in my hand. "Oh, dear Aleck," he whispers, "I'm so glad they let you come. I'll get well if you'll nurse me." The shadow of death is in his eyes; the body exudes decomposition. Bereft of speech, I gently press his white, emaciated hand. The weary eyes close, and the boy falls into slumber. Silently I touch his dry lips, and steal away.

In the afternoon I appeal to the Warden to permit me to nurse my friend. It is the boy's dying wish; it will ease his last hours. The Captain refers me to the Inspectors, but Mr. Reed informs me that it would be subversive of discipline to grant my request. Thereupon I ask permission to arrange a collection among the prisoners: Russell firmly believes that he would improve in an outside hospital, and the Pardon Board might grant the petition. Friendless prisoners are often allowed to circulate subscription lists among the inmates, and two years previously I had collected a hundred and twenty-three dollars for the pardon of a lifetimer. But the Warden curtly refuses my plea, remarking that it is dangerous to permit me to associate with the men. I suggest the Chaplain for the mission, or some prisoner selected by the authorities. But this offer is also vetoed, the Warden berating me for having taken advantage of my presence in the dispensary to see Russell clandestinely, and threatening to punish me with the dungeon. I plead with him for permission to visit the sick boy who is hungry for a friendly presence, and constantly calling for me. Apparently touched by my emotion, the Captain yields. He will permit me to visit Russell, he informs me, on condition that a guard be present at the meeting. For a moment I hesitate. The desire to see my friend struggles against the fear of irritating him by the sight of the hated uniform; but I cannot expose the dying youth to this indignity and pain. Angered by my refusal, perhaps disappointed in the hope of learning the secret of the tunnel from the visit, the Warden forbids me hereafter to enter the hospital.

Late at night Frank appears at my cell. He looks very grave, as he whispers:

"Aleck, you must bear up."

"Russell—?"

"Yes, Aleck."

"Worse? Tell me, Frank."

"He is dead. Bear up, Aleck. His last thought was of you. He was unconscious all afternoon, but just before the end—it was 9.33—he sat up in bed so suddenly, he frightened me. His arm shot out, and he cried, 'Good bye, Aleck.'"

CHAPTER XLI

THE SHOCK AT BUFFALO

I

July 10, 1901.

DEAR GIRL:

This is from the hospital, *sub rosa*. Just out of the strait-jacket, after eight days.

For over a year I was in the strictest solitary; for a long time mail and reading matter were denied me. I have no words to describe the horror of the last months. . . . I have passed through a great crisis. Two of my best friends died in a frightful manner. The death of Russell, especially, affected me. He was very young, and my dearest and most devoted friend, and he died a terrible death. The doctor charged the boy with shamming, but now he says it was spinal meningitis. I cannot tell you the awful truth,—it was nothing short of murder, and my poor friend rotted away by inches. When he died they found his back one mass of bedsores. If you could read the pitiful letters he wrote, begging to see me, and to be nursed by me! But the Warden wouldn't permit it. In some manner his agony seemed to affect me, and I began to experience the pains and symptoms that Russell described in his notes. I knew it was my sick fancy; I strove against it, but presently my legs showed signs of paralysis, and I suffered excruciating pain in the spinal column, just like Russell. I was afraid that I would be done to death like my poor friend. I grew suspicious of every guard, and would barely touch the food, for fear of its being poisoned. My "head was workin'," they said. And all the time I knew it was my diseased imagination, and I was in terror of going mad. . . . I tried so hard to fight it, but it would always creep up, and get hold of me stronger and stronger. Another week of solitary would have killed me.

I was on the verge of suicide. I demanded to be relieved

from the cell, and the Warden ordered me punished. I was put
in the strait-jacket. They bound my body in canvas, strapped
my arms to the bed, and chained my feet to the posts. I was
kept that way eight days, unable to move, rotting in my own
excrement. Released prisoners called the attention of our new
Inspector to my case. He refused to believe that such things
were being done in the penitentiary. Reports spread that I was
going blind and insane. Then the Inspector visited the hospital
and had me released from the jacket.

I am in pretty bad shape, but they put me in the general
ward now, and I am glad of the chance to send you this note.

Sasha.

II

Direct to Box A 7,
Allegheny City, Pa.
July 25th, 1901.

DEAR SONYA:

I cannot tell you how happy I am to be allowed to write
to you again. My privileges have been restored by our new
Inspector, a very kindly man. He has relieved me from the
cell, and now I am again on the range. The Inspector requested
me to deny to my friends the reports which have recently
appeared in the papers concerning my condition. I have not
been well of late, but now I hope to improve. My eyes are very
poor. The Inspector has given me permission to have a specialist examine them. Please arrange for it through our local comrades.

There is another piece of very good news, dear friend. A
new commutation law has been passed, which reduces my
sentence by 2½ years. It still leaves me a long time, of course;
almost 4 years here, and another year to the workhouse. However, it is a considerable gain, and if I should not get into solitary again, I may—I am almost afraid to utter the thought—
I may live to come out. I feel as if I am being resurrected.

The new law benefits the short-timers proportionately much
more than the men with longer sentences. Only the poor lifers
do not share in it. We were very anxious for a while, as there
were many rumors that the law would be declared unconstitutional. Fortunately, the attempt to nullify its benefits proved

ineffectual. Think of men who will see something unconstitutional in allowing the prisoners a little more good time than the commutation statute of 40 years ago. As if a little kindness to the unfortunates—really justice—is incompatible with the spirit of Jefferson! We were greatly worried over the fate of this statute, but at last the first batch has been released, and there is much rejoicing over it.

There is a peculiar history about this new law, which may interest you; it sheds a significant side light. It was especially designed for the benefit of a high Federal officer who was recently convicted of aiding two wealthy Philadelphia tobacco manufacturers to defraud the government of a few millions, by using counterfeit tax stamps. Their influence secured the introduction of the commutation bill and its hasty passage. The law would have cut their sentences almost in two, but certain newspapers seem to have taken offence at having been kept in ignorance of the "deal," and protests began to be voiced. The matter finally came up before the Attorney General of the United States, who decided that the men in whose special interest the law was engineered, could not benefit by it, because a State law does not affect U. S. prisoners, the latter being subject to the Federal commutation act. Imagine the discomfiture of the politicians! An attempt was even made to suspend the operation of the statute. Fortunately it failed, and now the "common" State prisoners, who were not at all meant to profit, are being released. The legislature has unwittingly given some unfortunates here much happiness.

I was interrupted in this writing by being called out for a visit. I could hardly credit it: the first comrade I have been allowed to see in nine years! It was Harry Gordon, and I was so overcome by the sight of the dear friend, I could barely speak. He must have prevailed upon the new Inspector to issue a permit. The latter is now Acting Warden, owing to the serious illness of Captain Wright. Perhaps he will allow me to see my sister. Will you kindly communicate with her at once? Meantime I shall try to secure a pass. With renewed hope, and always with green memory of you,

Alex.

III

Sub Rosa,
Dec. 20, 1901.

DEAREST GIRL:

I know how your visit and my strange behavior have affected you. . . . The sight of your face after all these years completely unnerved me. I could not think, I could not speak. It was as if all my dreams of freedom, the whole world of the living, were concentrated in the shiny little trinket that was dangling from your watch chain. . . . I couldn't take my eyes off it, I couldn't keep my hand from playing with it. It absorbed my whole being. . . . And all the time I felt how nervous you were at my silence, and I couldn't utter a word.

Perhaps it would have been better for us not to have seen each other under the present conditions. It was lucky they did not recognize you: they took you for my "sister," though I believe your identity was suspected after you had left. You would surely not have been permitted the visit, had the old Warden been here. He was ill at the time. He never got over the shock of the tunnel, and finally he has been persuaded by the prison physician (who has secret aspirations to the Wardenship) that the anxieties of his position are a menace to his advanced age. Considerable dissatisfaction has also developed of late against the Warden among the Inspectors. Well, he has resigned at last, thank goodness! The prisoners have been praying for it for years, and some of the boys on the range celebrated the event by getting drunk on wood alcohol. The new Warden has just assumed charge, and we hope for improvement. He is a physician by profession, with the title of Major in the Pennsylvania militia.

It was entirely uncalled for on the part of the officious friend, whoever he may have been, to cause you unnecessary worry over my health, and my renewed persecution. You remember that in July the new Inspector released me from the strait-jacket and assigned me to work on the range. But I was locked up again in October, after the McKinley incident. The President of the Board of Inspectors was at the time in New York. He inquired by wire what I was doing. Upon being informed that I was working on the range, he ordered me into solitary. The new Warden, on assuming office, sent for me. "They give you a bad reputation," he said; "but I

will let you out of the cell if you'll promise to do what is right
by me." He spoke brusquely, in the manner of a man closing
a business deal, with the power of dictating terms. He reminded
me of Bismarck at Versailles. Yet he did not seem unkind;
the thought of escape was probably in his mind. But the new
law has germinated the hope of survival; my weakened condition and the unexpected shortening of my sentence have at last
decided me to abandon the idea of escape. I therefore replied
to the Warden: "I will do what is right by you, if you treat
me right." Thereupon he assigned me to work on the range.
It is almost like liberty to have the freedom of the cell-house
after the close solitary.

And you, dear friend? In your letters I feel how terribly
torn you are by the events of the recent months. I lived in
great fear for your safety, and I can barely credit the good
news that you are at liberty. It seems almost a miracle.

I followed the newspapers with great anxiety. The whole
country seemed to be swept with the fury of revenge. To a
considerable extent the press fanned the fires of persecution.
Here in the prison very little sincere grief was manifested. Out
of hearing of the guards, the men passed very uncomplimentary
remarks about the dead president. The average prisoner cor-
responds to the average citizen—their patriotism is very passive,
except when stimulated by personal interest, or artificially
excited. But if the press mirrored the sentiment of the people,
the Nation must have suddenly relapsed into cannibalism. There
were moments when I was in mortal dread for your very life,
and for the safety of the other arrested comrades. In previous
letters you hinted that it was official rivalry and jealousy, and
your absence from New York, to which you owe your release.
You may be right; yet I believe that your attitude of proud self-
respect and your admirable self-control contributed much to the
result. You were splendid, dear; and I was especially moved by
your remark that you would faithfully nurse the wounded man,
if he required your services, but that the poor boy, condemned
and deserted by all, needed and deserved your sympathy and aid
more than the president. More strikingly than your letters, that
remark discovered to me the great change wrought in us by the
ripening years. Yes, in us, in both, for my heart echoed your
beautiful sentiment. How impossible such a thought would
have been to us in the days of a decade ago! We should have

considered it treason to the spirit of revolution; it would have outraged all our traditions even to admit the humanity of an official representative of capitalism. Is it not very significant that we two—you living in the very heart of Anarchist thought and activity, and I in the atmosphere of absolute suppression and solitude—should have arrived at the same evolutionary point after a decade of divergent paths?

You have alluded in a recent letter to the ennobling and broadening influence of sorrow. Yet not upon every one does it exert a similar effect. Some natures grow embittered, and shrink with the poison of misery. I often wonder at my lack of bitterness and enmity, even against the old Warden—and surely I have good cause to hate him. Is it because of greater maturity? I rather think it is temperamentally conditioned. The love of the people, the hatred of oppression of our younger days, vital as these sentiments were with us, were mental rather than emotional. Fortunately so, I think. For those like Fedya and Lewis and Pauline, and numerous others, soon have their emotionally inflated idealism punctured on the thorny path of the social protestant. Only aspirations that spontaneously leap from the depths of our soul persist in the face of antagonistic forces. The revolutionist is born. Beneath our love and hatred of former days lay inherent rebellion, and the passionate desire for liberty and life.

In the long years of isolation I have looked deeply into my heart. With open mind and sincere purpose, I have revised every emotion and every thought. Away from my former atmosphere and the disturbing influence of the world's turmoil, I have divested myself of all traditions and accepted beliefs. I have studied the sciences and the humanities, contemplated life, and pondered over human destiny. For weeks and months I would be absorbed in the domain of "pure reason," or discuss with Leibnitz the question of free will, and seek to penetrate, beyond Spencer, into the Unknowable. Political science and economics, law and criminology—I studied them with unprejudiced mind, and sought to slacken my soul's thirst by delving deeply into religion and theology, seeking the "Key to Life" at the feet of Mrs. Eddy, expectantly listening for the voice of the disembodied, studying Koreshanity and Theosophy, absorbing the *prana* of knowledge and power, and concentrating upon the wisdom of the Yogi. And after years of contemplation and study, chastened by much sorrow and suffering, I arise from the broken fetters of the world's folly and delusions, to behold the threshold of a new life of liberty and equality. My youth's ideal of a free humanity in the vague future has become clarified and crystallized into the living truth of Anarchy, as the sustaining elemental force of my every-day existence.

Often I have wondered in the years gone by, was not wisdom dear at the price of enthusiasm? At 30 one is not so reckless, not so fanatical and one-sided as at 20. With maturity we become more universal; but life is a Shylock that cannot be cheated of his due. For every lesson it teaches us, we have a wound or a scar to show. We grow broader; but too often the heart contracts as the mind expands, and the fires are burning down while we are learning. At such moments my mind would revert to the days when the momentarily expected approach of the Social Revolution absorbed our exclusive interest. The raging present and its conflicting currents passed us by, while our eyes were riveted upon the Dawn, in thrilling expectancy of the sunrise. Life and its manifold expressions were vexatious to the spirit of revolt; and poetry, literature, and art were scorned as hindrances to progress, unless they sounded the tocsin of immediate revolution. Humanity was sharply divided in two warring camps,—the noble People, the producers, who yearned for the light of the new gospel, and the hated oppressors, the exploiters, who craftily strove to obscure the rising day that was to give back to man his heritage. If only "the good People" were given an opportunity to hear the great truth, how joyfully they would embrace Anarchy and walk in triumph into the promised land!

The splendid naivety of the days that resented as a personal reflection the least misgiving of the future; the enthusiasm that discounted the power of inherent prejudice and predilection! Magnificent was the day of hearts on fire with the hatred of oppression and the love of liberty! Woe indeed to the man or the people whose soul never warmed with the spark of Prometheus,—for it is youth that has climbed the heights. . . . But maturity has clarified the way, and the stupendous task of human regeneration will be accomplished only by the purified vision of hearts that grow not cold.

And you, my dear friend, with the deeper insight of time, you have yet happily kept your heart young. I have rejoiced

at it in your letters of recent years, and it is especially evident
from the sentiments you have expressed regarding the happening at Buffalo. I share your view entirely; for that very
reason, it is the more distressing to disagree with you in one
very important particular: the value of Leon's act. I know
the terrible ordeal you have passed through, the fiendish persecution to which you have been subjected. Worse than all must
have been to you the general lack of understanding for such
phenomena; and, sadder yet, the despicable attitude of some
would-be radicals in denouncing the man and his act. But
I am confident you will not mistake my expressed disagreement for condemnation.

We need not discuss the phase of the *Attentat* which manifested the rebellion of a tortured soul, the individual protest
against social wrong. Such phenomena are the natural result
of evil conditions, as inevitable as the flooding of the river
banks by the swelling mountain torrents. But I cannot agree
with you regarding the social value of Leon's act.

I have read of the beautiful personality of the youth, of
his inability to adapt himself to brutal conditions, and the rebellion of his soul. It throws a significant light upon the causes
of the *Attentat*. Indeed, it is at once the greatest tragedy of
martyrdom, and the most terrible indictment of society, that
it forces the noblest men and women to shed human blood,
though their souls shrink from it. But the more imperative
it is that drastic methods of this character be resorted to only
as a last extremity. To prove of value, they must be motived
by social rather than individual necessity, and be directed against
a real and immediate enemy of the people. The significance
of such a deed is understood by the popular mind—and in that
alone is the propagandistic, educational importance of an *Attentat,* except if it is exclusively an act of terrorism.

Now, I do not believe that this deed was terroristic; and
I doubt whether it was educational, because the social necessity
for its performance was not manifest. That you may not
misunderstand, I repeat: as an expression of personal revolt
it was inevitable, and in itself an indictment of existing conditions. But the background of social necessity was lacking,
and therefore the value of the act was to a great extent
nullified.

In Russia, where political oppression is popularly felt,

such a deed would be of great value. But the scheme of political subjection is more subtle in America. And though McKinley was the chief representative of our modern slavery, he could not be considered in the light of a direct and immediate enemy of the people; while in an absolutism, the autocrat is visible and tangible. The real despotism of republican institutions is far deeper, more insidious, because it rests on the popular delusion of self-government and independence. That is the subtle source of democratic tyranny, and, as such, it cannot be reached with a bullet.

In modern capitalism, exploitation rather than oppression is the real enemy of the people. Oppression is but its handmaid. Hence the battle is to be waged in the economic rather than the political field. It is therefore that I regard my own act as far more significant and educational than Leon's. It was directed against a tangible, real oppressor, visualized as such by the people.

As long as misery and tyranny fill the world, social contrasts and consequent hatreds will persist, and the noblest of the race—our Czolgoszes—burst forth in "rockets of iron." But does this lightning really illumine the social horizon, or merely confuse minds with the succeeding darkness? The struggle of labor against capital is a class war, essentially and chiefly economic. In that arena the battles must be fought.

It was not these considerations, of course, that inspired the nation-wide man-hunt, or the attitude even of alleged radicals. Their cowardice has filled me with loathing and sadness. The brutal farce of the trial, the hypocrisy of the whole proceeding, the thirst for the blood of the martyr,—these make one almost despair of humanity.

I must close. The friend to smuggle out this letter will be uneasy about its bulk. Send me sign of receipt, and I hope that you may be permitted a little rest and peace, to recover from the nightmare of the last months.

SASHA.

CHAPTER XLII

MARRED LIVES

I

THE discussion with the Girl is a source of much mortification. Harassed on every side, persecuted by the authorities, and hounded even into the street, my friend, in her hour of bitterness, confounds my appreciative disagreement with the denunciation of stupidity and inertia. I realize the inadequacy of the written word, and despair at the hopelessness of human understanding, as I vainly seek to elucidate the meaning of the Buffalo tragedy to friendly guards and prisoners. Continued correspondence with the Girl accentuates the divergence of our views, painfully discovering the fundamental difference of attitude underlying even common conclusions.

By degrees the stress of activities reacts upon my friend's correspondence. Our discussion lags, and soon ceases entirely. The world of the outside, temporarily brought closer, again recedes, and the urgency of the immediate absorbs me in the life of the prison.

II

A spirit of hopefulness breathes in the cell-house. The new commutation law is bringing liberty appreciably nearer. In the shops and yard the men excitedly discuss

the increased "good time," and prisoners flit about with
paper and pencil, seeking a tutored friend to "figure out"
their time of release. Even the solitaries, on the verge of
despair, and the long-timers facing a vista of cheerless
years, are instilled with new courage and hope.

The tenor of conversation is altered. With the ap-
pointment of the new Warden the constant grumbling
over the food has ceased. Pleasant surprise is manifest
at the welcome change in "the grub." I wonder at the
tolerant silence regarding the disappointing Christmas
dinner. The men impatiently frown down the occasional "kicker." The Warden is "green," they argue; he
did not know that we are supposed to get currant bread
for the holidays; he will do better, "jest give 'im a
chanc't." The improvement in the daily meals is enlarged upon, and the men thrill with amazed expectancy
at the incredible report, "Oysters for New Year's dinner!" With gratification we hear the Major's expression of disgust at the filthy condition of the prison, his
condemnation of the basket cell and dungeon as barbarous, and the promise of radical reforms. As an
earnest of his régime he has released from solitary the
men whom Warden Wright had punished for having
served as witnesses in the defence of Murphy and Mong.
Greedy for the large reward, Hopkins and his stools had
accused the two men of a mysterious murder committed
in Elk City several years previously. The criminal trial,
involving the suicide of an officer* whom the Warden
had forced to testify against the defendants, resulted in
the acquittal of the prisoners, whereupon Captain Wright

* Officer Robert G. Hunter, who committed suicide August
30, 1901, in Clarion, Pa. (where the trial took place). He left
a written confession, in which he accused Warden E. S. Wright
of forcing him to testify against men whom he knew to be
innocent.

ordered the convict-witnesses for the defence to be punished.

The new Warden, himself a physician, introduces hygienic rules, abolishes the "holy-stoning"* of the cell-house floor because of the detrimental effect of the dust, and decides to separate the consumptive and syphilitic prisoners from the comparatively healthy ones. Upon examination, 40 per cent. of the population are discovered in various stages of tuberculosis, and 20 per cent. insane. The death rate from consumption is found to range between 25 and 60 per cent. At light tasks in the block and the yard the Major finds employment for the sickly inmates; special gangs are assigned to keeping the prison clean, the rest of the men at work in the shop. With the exception of a number of dangerously insane, who are to be committed to an asylum, every prisoner in the institution is at work, and the vexed problem of idleness resulting from the anti-convict labor law is thus solved.

The change of diet, better hygiene, and the abolition of the dungeon, produce a noticeable improvement in the life of the prison. The gloom of the cell-house perceptibly lifts, and presently the men are surprised at music hour, between six and seven in the evening, with the strains of merry ragtime by the newly organized penitentiary band.

III

New faces greet me on the range. But many old friends are missing. Billy Ryan is dead of consumption; "Frenchy" and Ben have become insane; Little Mat, the

---

* The process of whitening stone floors by pulverizing sand into their surfaces.

Duquesne striker, committed suicide. In sad remembrance I think of them, grown close and dear in the years of mutual suffering. Some of the old-timers have survived, but broken in spirit and health. "Praying" Andy is still in the block, his mind clouded, his lips constantly moving in prayer. "Me innocent," the old man reiterates, "God him know." Last month the Board has again refused to pardon the lifetimer, and now he is bereft of hope. "Me have no more money. My children they save and save, and bring me for pardon, and now no more money." Aleck Killain has also been refused by the Board at the same session. He is the oldest man in the prison, in point of service, and the most popular lifer. His innocence of murder is one of the traditions of Riverside. In the boat he had rented to a party of picnickers, a woman was found dead. No clew could be discovered, and Aleck was sentenced to life, because he could not be forced to divulge the names of the men who had hired his boat. He pauses to tell me the sad news: the authorities have opposed his pardon, demanding that he furnish the information desired by them. He looks sere with confinement, his eyes full of a mute sadness that can find no words. His face is deeply seamed, his features grave, almost immobile. In the long years of our friendship I have never seen Aleck laugh. Once or twice he smiled, and his whole being seemed radiant with rare sweetness. He speaks abruptly, with a perceptible effort.

"Yes, Aleck," he is saying, "it's true. They refused me."

"But they pardoned Mac," I retort hotly. "He confessed to a cold-blooded murder, and he's only been in four years."

"Good luck," he remarks.

"How, good luck?"

"Mac's father accidentally struck oil on his farm."

"Well, what of it?"

"Three hundred barrels a day. Rich. Got his son a pardon."

"But on what ground did they dismiss your application? They know you are innocent."

"District Attorney came to me. 'You're innocent, we know. Tell us who did the murder.' I had nothing to tell. Pardon refused."

"Is there any hope later on, Aleck?"

"When the present administration are all dead, perhaps."

Slowly he passes on, at the approach of a guard. He walks weakly, with halting step.

"Old Sammy" is back again, his limp heavier, shoulders bent lower. "I'm here again, friend Aleck," he smiles apologetically. "What could I do? The old woman died, an' my boys went off somewhere. Th' farm was sold that I was borned in," his voice trembles with emotion. "I couldn't find th' boys, an' no one wanted me, an' wouldn't give me any work. 'Go to th' pogy',* they told me. I couldn't, Aleck. I've worked all me life; I don't want no charity. I made a bluff," he smiles between tears,—"Broke into a store, and here I am."

With surprise I recognize "Tough" Monk among the first-grade men. For years he had been kept in stripes, and constantly punished for bad work in the hosiery department. He was called the laziest man in the prison: not once in five years had he accomplished his task. But the new Warden transferred him to the construction shop, where Monk was employed at his trade

---

* Poorhouse.

of blacksmith. "I hated that damn sock makin'," he tells me. "I've struck it right now, an' the Major says I'm the best worker in th' shop. Wouldn't believe it, eh, would you? Major promised me a ten-spot for the fancy iron work I did for them 'lectric posts in th' yard. Says it's artistic, see? That's me all right; it's work I like. I won't lose any time, either. Warden says Old Sandy was a fool for makin' me knit socks with them big paws of mine. Th' Major is aw' right, aw' right."

With a glow of pleasure I meet "Smiling" Al, my colored friend from the jail. The good-natured boy looks old and infirm. His kindness has involved him in much trouble; he has been repeatedly punished for shouldering the faults of others, and now the Inspectors have informed him that he is to lose the greater part of his commutation time. He has grown wan with worry over the uncertainty of release. Every morning is tense with expectation. "Might be Ah goes to-day, Aleck," he hopefully smiles as I pause at his cell. But the weeks pass. The suspense is torturing the young negro, and he is visibly failing day by day.

A familiar voice greets me. "Hello, Berk, ain't you glad t' see an old pal?" Big Dave beams on me with his cheerful smile.

"No, Davy. I hoped you wouldn't come back."

He becomes very grave. "Yes, I swore I'd swing sooner than come back. Didn't get a chanc't. You see," he explains, his tone full of bitterness, "I goes t' work and gets a job, good job, too; an' I keeps 'way from th' booze an' me pals. But th' damn bulls was after me. Got me sacked from me job three times, an' den I knocked one of 'em on th' head. Damn his soul to hell, wish I'd killed 'im. 'Old offender,' they says to the jedge, and he soaks me for a seven spot. I was a sucker all right for tryin' t' be straight."

IV

In the large cage at the centre of the block, the men employed about the cell-house congregate in their idle moments. The shadows steal silently in and out of the inclosure, watchful of the approach of a guard. Within sounds the hum of subdued conversation, the men lounging about the sawdust barrel, absorbed in "Snakes" Wilson's recital of his protracted struggle with "Old Sandy." He relates vividly his persistent waking at night, violent stamping on the floor, cries of "Murder! I see snakes!" With admiring glances the young prisoners hang upon the lips of the old criminal, whose perseverance in shamming finally forced the former Warden to assign "Snakes" a special room in the hospital, where his snake-seeing propensities would become dormant, to suffer again violent awakening the moment he would be transferred to a cell. For ten years the struggle continued, involving numerous clubbings, the dungeon, and the strait-jacket, till the Warden yielded, and "Snakes" was permanently established in the comparative freedom of the special room.

Little groups stand about the cage, boisterous with the wit of the "Four-eyed Yegg," who styles himself "Bill Nye," or excitedly discussing the intricacies of the commutation law, the chances of Pittsburgh winning the baseball pennant the following season, and next Sunday's dinner. With much animation, the rumored resignation of the Deputy Warden is discussed. The Major is gradually weeding out the "old gang," it is gossiped. A colonel of the militia is to secure the position of assistant to the Warden. This source of conversation is inex-

haustible, every detail of local life serving for endless
discussion and heated debate. But at the 'lookout's'
whispered warning of an approaching guard, the circle
breaks up, each man pretending to be busy dusting
and cleaning. Officer Mitchell passes by; with short legs
wide apart, he stands surveying the assembled idlers
from beneath his fierce-looking eyebrows.

"Quiet as me grandmother at church, ain't ye? All
of a sudden, too. And mighty busy, every damn one of
you. You 'Snakes' there, what business you got here,
eh?"

"I've jest come in fer a broom."

"You old reprobate, you, I saw you sneak in there
an hour ago, and you've been chawin' the rag to beat
the band. Think this a barroom, do you? Get to your
cells, all of you."

He trudges slowly away, mumbling: "You loafers,
when I catch you here again, don't you dare talk so
loud."

One by one the men steal back into the cage, jokingly
teasing each other upon their happy escape. Presently
several rangemen join the group. Conversation becomes
animated; voices are raised in dispute. But anger subsides, and a hush falls upon the men, as Blind Charley
gropes his way along the wall. Bill Nye reaches for
his hand, and leads him to a seat on the barrel. "Feelin'
better to-day, Charley?" he asks gently.

"Ye-es, I—think a little—better," the blind man says
in an uncertain, hesitating manner. His face wears a
bewildered expression, as if he has not yet become resigned to his great misfortune. It happened only a few
months ago. In company with two friends, considerably
the worse for liquor, he was passing a house on the out-
skirts of Allegheny. It was growing dark, and they
wanted a drink. Charley knocked at the door. A head

appeared at an upper window. "Robbers!" some one suddenly cried. There was a flash. With a cry of pain, Charley caught at his eyes. He staggered, then turned round and round, helpless, in a daze. He couldn't see his companions, the house and the street disappeared, and all was utter darkness. The ground seemed to give beneath his feet, and Charley fell down upon his face, moaning and calling to his friends. But they had fled in terror, and he was alone in the darkness,—alone and blind.

"I'm glad you feel better, Charley," Bill Nye says kindly. "How are your eyes?"

"I think—a bit—better."

The gunshot had severed the optic nerves in both eyes. His sight is destroyed forever; but with the incomplete realization of sudden calamity, Charley believes his eyesight only temporarily injured.

"Billy," he says presently, "when I woke this morning, it—didn't seem so—dark. It was like—a film over my eyes. Perhaps—it may—get better yet," his voice quivers with the expectancy of having his hope confirmed.

"Ah, whatcher kiddin' yourself for," "Snakes" interposes.

"Shut up, you big stiff," Bill flares up, grabbing "Snakes" by the throat. "Charley," he adds, "I once got paralyzed in my left eye. It looked just like yours now, and I felt as if there was a film on it. Do you see things like in a fog, Charley?"

"Yes, yes, just like that."

"Well, that's the way it was with me. But little by little things got to be lighter, and now the eye is as good as ever."

"Is that right, Billy?" Charley inquires anxiously. "What did you do?"

"Well, the doc put things in my eye. The croaker here is giving you some applications, ain't he?"

"Yes; but he says it's for the inflammation."

"That's right. That's what the doctors told me. You just take it easy, Charley; don't worry. You'll come out all right, see if you don't."

Bill reddens guiltily at the unintended expression, but quickly holds up a warning finger to silence the giggling "Snowball Kid." Then, with sudden vehemence, he exclaims: "By God, Charley, if I ever meet that Judge of yours on a dark night, I'll choke him with these here hands, so help me! It's a damn shame to send you here in this condition. You should have gone to a hospital, that's what I say. But cheer up, old boy, you won't have to serve your three years; you can bet on that. We'll all club together to get your case up for a pardon, won't we, boys?"

With unwonted energy the old yegg makes the rounds of the cage, taking pledges of contributions. "Doctor George" appears around the corner, industriously polishing the brasswork, and Bill appeals to him to corroborate his diagnosis of the blind man's condition. A smile of timid joy suffuses the sightless face, as Bill Nye slaps him on the shoulder, crying jovially, "What did I tell you, eh? You'll be O. K. soon, and meantime keep your mind busy how to avenge the injustice done you," and with a violent wink in the direction of "Snakes," the yegg launches upon a reminiscence of his youth. As far as he can remember, he relates, the spirit of vengeance was strong within him. He has always religiously revenged any wrong he was made to suffer, but the incident that afforded him the greatest joy was an experience of his boyhood. He was fifteen then, and living with his widowed mother and three elder sisters in a small country place. One evening, as the family gathered in the large sitting-room, his sister Mary said something which deeply offended him. In great rage he left the house. Just as he was crossing the street, he was met by a tall, well-dressed gentleman, evidently a stranger in the town. The man guardedly inquired whether the boy could direct him to some address where one might pass the evening pleasantly. "Quick as a flash a brilliant idea struck me," Bill narrates, warming to his story. "Never short of them, anyhow," he remarks parenthetically, "but here was my revenge! 'You mean a whore-house, don't you?' I ask the fellow. Yes, that's what was wanted, my man says. 'Why,' says I to him, kind of suddenly, 'see the house there right across the street? That's the place you want,' and I point out to him the house where the old lady and my three sisters are all sitting around the table, expectant-like—waiting for me, you know. Well, the man gives me a quarter, and up he goes, knocks on the door, and steps right in. I hide in a dark corner to see what's coming, you know, and sure enough, presently the door opens with a bang and something comes out with a rush, and falls on the veranda, and mother she's got a broom in her hand, and the girls, every blessed one of them, out with flatiron and dustpan, and biff, baff, they rain it upon that thing on the steps. I thought I'd split my sides laughing. By an' by I return to the house, and mother and sisters are kind of excited, and I says, innocent-like, 'What's up, girls?' Well, you ought to hear 'em! Talk, did they? 'That beast of a man, the dirty thing that came to the house and insulted us with—' they couldn't even mention the awful things he said; and Mary—that's the sis I got mad at—she cries, 'Oh, Billie, you're so big and strong, I wish you was here when that nasty old thing came up.'"

The boys are hilarious over the story, and "Doctor George" motions me aside to talk over "old times." With a hearty pressure I greet my friend, whom I had not seen since the days of the first investigation. Suspected of complicity, he had been removed to the shops, and only recently returned to his former position in the block. His beautiful thick hair has grown thin and gray; he looks aged and worn. With sadness I notice his tone of bitterness. "They almost killed me, Aleck!" he says; "if it wasn't for my wife, I'd murder that old Warden." Throughout his long confinement, his wife had faithfully stood by him, her unfailing courage and devotion sustaining him in the hours of darkness and despair. "The dear girl," he muses, "I'd be dead if it wasn't for her." But his release is approaching. He has almost served the sentence of sixteen years for alleged complicity in the bank robbery at Leechburg, during which the cashier was killed. The other two men convicted of the crime have both died in prison. The Doctor alone has survived, "thanks to the dear girl," he repeats. But the six months at the workhouse fill him with apprehension. He has been informed that the place is a veritable inferno, even worse than the penitentiary. However, his wife is faithfully at work, trying to have the workhouse sentence suspended, and full liberty may be at hand.

CHAPTER XLIII

"PASSING THE LOVE OF WOMAN"

THE presence of my old friend is a source of much pleasure. George is an intelligent man; the long years of incarceration have not circumscribed his intellectual horizon. The approach of release is intensifying his interest in the life beyond the gates, and we pass the idle hours conversing over subjects of mutual interest, discussing social theories and problems of the day. He has a broad grasp of affairs, but his temperament and Catholic traditions are antagonistic to the ideas dear to me. Yet his attitude is free from personalities and narrow prejudice, and our talks are conducted along scientific and philosophical lines. The recent death of Liebknecht and the American lecture tour of Peter Kropotkin afford opportunity for the discussion of modern social questions. There are many subjects of mutual interest, and my friend, whose great-grandfather was among the signers of the Declaration, waxes eloquent in denunciation of his country's policy of extermination in the Philippines and the growing imperialistic tendencies of the Republic. A Democrat of the Jeffersonian type, he is virulent against the old Warden on account of his favoritism and discrimination. His prison experience, he informs me, has considerably altered the views of democracy he once entertained.

"Why, Aleck, there *is* no justice," he says vehemently; "no, not even in the best democracy. Ten years ago

I would have staked my life on the courts. To-day I know they are a failure; our whole jurisprudence is wrong. You see, I have been here nine years. I have met and made friends with hundreds of criminals. Some were pretty desperate, and many of them scoundrels. But I have to meet one yet in whom I couldn't discover some good quality, if he's scratched right. Look at that fellow there," he points to a young prisoner scrubbing an upper range, "that's 'Johnny the Hunk.' He's in for murder. Now what did the judge and jury know about him? Just this: he was a hard-working boy in the mills. One Saturday he attended a wedding, with a chum of his. They were both drunk when they went out into the street. They were boisterous, and a policeman tried to arrest them. Johnny's chum resisted. The cop must have lost his head—he shot the fellow dead. It was right near Johnny's home, and he ran in and got a pistol, and killed the policeman. Must have been crazy with drink. Well, they were going to hang him, but he was only a kid, hardly sixteen. They gave him fifteen years. Now he's all in—they've just ruined the boy's life. And what kind of a boy is he, do you know? Guess what he did. It was only a few months ago. Some screw told him that the widow of the cop he shot is hard up; she has three children, and takes in washing. Do you know what Johnny did? He went around among the cons, and got together fifty dollars on the fancy paper-work he is making; he's an artist at it. He sent the woman the money, and begged her to forgive him."

"Is that true, Doctor?"

"Every word. I went to Milligan's office on some business, and the boy had just sent the money to the woman. The Chaplain was so much moved by it, he told me the whole story. But wait, that isn't all. You know what that woman did?"

"What?"

"She wrote to Johnny that he was a dirty murderer, and that if he ever goes up for a pardon, she will oppose it. She didn't want anything to do with him, she wrote. But she kept the money."

"How did Johnny take it?"

"It's really wonderful about human nature. The boy cried over the letter, and told the Chaplain that he wouldn't write to her again. But every minute he can spare he works on that fancy work, and every month he sends her money. That's the *criminal* the judge sentenced to fifteen years in this hell!"

My friend is firmly convinced that the law is entirely impotent to deal with our social ills. "Why, look at the courts!" he exclaims, "they don't concern themselves with crime. They merely punish the criminal, absolutely indifferent to his antecedents and environment, and the predisposing causes."

"But, George," I rejoin, "it is the economic system of exploitation, the dependence upon a master for your livelihood, want and the fear of want, which are responsible for most crimes."

"Only partly so, Aleck. If it wasn't for the corruption in our public life, and the commercial scourge that holds everything for sale, and the spirit of materialism which has cheapened human life, there would not be so much violence and crime, even under what you call the capitalist system. At any rate, there is no doubt the law is an absolute failure in dealing with crime. The criminal belongs to the sphere of therapeutics. Give him to the doctor instead of the jailer."

"You mean, George, that the criminal is to be considered a product of anthropological and physical factors. But don't you see that you must also examine society, to determine to what extent social conditions are responsible for criminal actions? And if that were done, I believe most crimes would be found to be misdirected energy—misdirected because of false standards, wrong environment, and unenlightened self-interest."

"Well, I haven't given much thought to that phase of the question. But aside of social conditions, see what a botch the penal institutions are making of it. For one thing, the promiscuous mingling of young and old, without regard to relative depravity and criminality, is converting prisons into veritable schools of crime and vice. The blackjack and the dungeon are surely not the proper means of reclamation, no matter what the social causes of crime. Restraint and penal methods can't reform. The very idea of punishment precludes betterment. True reformation can emanate only from voluntary impulse, inspired and cultivated by intelligent advice and kind treatment. But reformation which is the result of fear, lacks the very essentials of its object, and will vanish like smoke the moment fear abates. And you know, Aleck, the reformatories are even worse than the prisons. Look at the fellows here from the various reform schools. Why, it's a disgrace! The boys who come from the outside are decent fellows. But those kids from the reformatories—one-third of the cons here have graduated there—they are terrible. You can spot them by looking at them. They are worse than street prostitutes."

My friend is very bitter against the prison element variously known as "the girls," "Sallies," and "punks," who for gain traffic in sexual gratification. But he takes a broad view of the moral aspect of homosexuality; his denunciation is against the commerce in carnal desires. As a medical man, and a student, he is deeply interested in the manifestations of suppressed sex. He speaks with profound sympathy of the brilliant English

man-of-letters, whom the world of cant and stupidity
has driven to prison and to death because his sex life
did not conform to the accepted standards. In detail, my
friend traces the various phases of his psychic development since his imprisonment, and I warm toward him
with a sense of intense humanity, as he reveals the intimate emotions of his being. A general medical practi-
tioner, he had not come in personal contact with cases
of homosexuality. He had heard of pederasty; but
like the majority of his colleagues, he had neither understanding for nor sympathy with the sex practices he
considered abnormal and vicious. In prison he was
horrified at the perversion that frequently came under
his observation. For two years the very thought of
such matters filled him with disgust; he even refused
to speak to the men and boys known to be homosexual,
unconditionally condemning them—"with my prejudices
rather than my reason," he remarks. But the forces of
suppression were at work. "Now, this is in confidence,
Aleck," he cautions me. "I know you will understand.
Probably you yourself have experienced the same thing.
I'm glad I can talk to some one about it; the other fellows here wouldn't understand it. It makes me sick to
see how they all grow indignant over a fellow who is
caught. And the officers, too, though you know as well
as I that quite a number of them are addicted to these
practices. Well, I'll tell you. I suppose it's the same
story with every one here, especially the long-timers.
I was terribly dejected and hopeless when I came. Sixteen years—I didn't believe for a moment I could live
through it. I was abusing myself pretty badly. Still,
after a while, when I got work and began to take an interest in this life, I got over it. But as time went, the sex
instinct awakened. I was young: about twenty-five,
strong and healthy. Sometimes I thought I'd get crazy

with passion. You remember when we were celling together on that upper range, on R; you were in the stocking shop then, weren't you? Don't you remember?"

"Of course I remember, George. You were in the cell next mine. We could see out on the river. It was in the summer: we could hear the excursion boats, and the girls singing and dancing."

"That, too, helped to turn me back to onanism. I really believe the whole blessed range used to 'indulge' then. Think of the precious material fed to the fishes," he smiles; "the privies, you know, empty into the river."

"Some geniuses may have been lost to the world in those orgies."

"Yes, orgies; that's just what they were. As a matter of fact, I don't believe there is a single man in the prison who doesn't abuse himself, at one time or another."

"If there is, he's a mighty exception. I have known some men to masturbate four and five times a day. Kept it up for months, too."

"Yes, and they either get the con, or go bugs. As a medical man I think that self-abuse, if practised no more frequently than ordinary coition, would be no more injurious than the latter. But it can't be done. It grows on you terribly. And the second stage is more dangerous than the first."

"What do you call the second?"

"Well, the first is the dejection stage. Hopeless and despondent, you seek forgetfulness in onanism. You don't care what happens. It's what I might call mechanical self-abuse, not induced by actual sex desire. This stage passes with your dejection, as soon as you begin to take an interest in the new life, as all of us are forced to do, before long. The second stage is the psychic and mental. It is not the result of dejection. With the gradual adaptation to the new conditions, a comparatively normal life begins, manifesting sexual desires. At this stage your self-abuse is induced by actual need. It is the more dangerous phase, because the frequency of the practice grows with the recurring thought of home, your wife or sweetheart. While the first was mechanical, giving no special pleasure, and resulting only in increasing lassitude, the second stage revolves about the charms of some loved woman, or one desired, and affords intense joy. Therein is its allurement and danger; and that's why the habit gains in strength. The more miserable the life, the more frequently you will fall back upon your sole source of pleasure. Many become helpless victims. I have noticed that prisoners of lower intelligence are the worst in this respect."

"I have had the same experience. The narrower your mental horizon, the more you dwell upon your personal troubles and wrongs. That is probably the reason why the more illiterate go insane with confinement."

"No doubt of it. You have had exceptional opportunities for observation of the solitaries and the new men. What did you notice, Aleck?"

"Well, in some respects the existence of a prisoner is like the life of a factory worker. As a rule, men used to outdoor life suffer most from solitary. They are less able to adapt themselves to the close quarters, and the foul air quickly attacks their lungs. Besides, those who have no interests beyond their personal life, soon become victims of insanity. I've always advised new men to interest themselves in some study or fancy work,—it's their only salvation."

"If you yourself have survived, it's because you lived in your theories and ideals; I'm sure of it. And I continued my medical studies, and sought to absorb myself in scientific subjects."

For a moment George pauses. The veins of his forehead protrude, as if he is undergoing a severe mental struggle. Presently he says: "Aleck, I'm going to speak very frankly to you. I'm much interested in the subject. I'll give you my intimate experiences, and I want you to be just as frank with me. I think it's one of the most important things, and I want to learn all I can about it. Very little is known about it, and much less understood."

"About what, George?"

"About homosexuality. I have spoken of the second phase of onanism. With a strong effort I overcame it. Not entirely, of course. But I have succeeded in regulating the practice, indulging in it at certain intervals. But as the months and years passed, my emotions manifested themselves. It was like a psychic awakening. The desire to love something was strong upon me. Once I caught a little mouse in my cell, and tamed it a bit. It would eat out of my hand, and come around at meal times, and by and by it would stay all evening to play with me. I learned to love it. Honestly, Aleck, I cried when it died. And then, for a long time, I felt as if there was a void in my heart. I wanted something to love. It just swept me with a wild craving for affection. Somehow the thought of woman gradually faded from my mind. When I saw my wife, it was just like a dear friend. But I didn't feel toward her sexually. One day, as I was passing in the hall, I noticed a young boy. He had been in only a short time, and he was rosy-cheeked, with a smooth little face and sweet lips—he reminded me of a girl I used to court before I married. After that I frequently surprised myself thinking of the lad. I felt no desire toward

him, except just to know him and get friendly. I became
acquainted with him, and when he heard I was a medical man, he would often call to consult me about the
stomach trouble he suffered. The doctor here persisted
in giving the poor kid salts and physics all the time.
Well, Aleck, I could hardly believe it myself, but I grew
so fond of the boy, I was miserable when a day passed
without my seeing him. I would take big chances to
get near him. I was rangeman then, and he was
assistant on a top tier. We often had opportunities to
talk. I got him interested in literature, and advised
him what to read, for he didn't know what to do with
his time. He had a fine character, that boy, and he was
bright and intelligent. At first it was only a liking
for him, but it increased all the time, till I couldn't
think of any woman. But don't misunderstand me,
Aleck; it wasn't that I wanted a 'kid.' I swear to you,
the other youths had no attraction for me whatever;
but this boy—his name was Floyd—he became so dear
to me, why, I used to give him everything I could get.
I had a friendly guard, and he'd bring me fruit and
things. Sometimes I'd just die to eat it, but I always
gave it to Floyd. And, Aleck—you remember when I
was down in the dungeon six days? Well, it was for
the sake of that boy. He did something, and I took
the blame on myself. And the last time—they kept
me nine days chained up—I hit a fellow for abusing
Floyd: he was small and couldn't defend himself. I
did not realize it at the time, Aleck, but I know now
that I was simply in love with the boy; wildly, madly
in love. It came very gradually. For two years I loved
him without the least taint of sex desire. It was the
purest affection I ever felt in my life. It was all-
absorbing, and I would have sacrificed my life for him
if he had asked it. But by degrees the psychic stage

began to manifest all the expressions of love between the opposite sexes. I remember the first time he kissed me. It was early in the morning; only the range-men were out, and I stole up to his cell to give him a delicacy. He put both hands between the bars, and pressed his lips to mine. Aleck, I tell you, never in my life had I experienced such bliss as at that moment. It's five years ago, but it thrills me every time I think of it. It came suddenly; I didn't expect it. It was entirely spontaneous: our eyes met, and it seemed as if something drew us together. He told me he was very fond of me. From then on we became lovers. I used to neglect my work, and risk great danger to get a chance to kiss and embrace him. I grew terribly jealous, too, though I had no cause. I passed through every phase of a passionate love. With this difference, though —I felt a touch of the old disgust at the thought of actual sex contact. That I didn't do. It seemed to me a desecration of the boy, and of my love for him. But after a while that feeling also wore off, and I desired sexual relation with him. He said he loved me enough to do even that for me, though he had never done it before. He hadn't been in any reformatory, you know. And yet, somehow I couldn't bring myself to do it; I loved the lad too much for it. Perhaps you will smile, Aleck, but it was real, true love. When Floyd was unexpectedly transferred to the other block, I felt that I would be the happiest man if I could only touch his hand again, or get one more kiss. You—you're laughing?" he asks abruptly, a touch of anxiety in his voice.

"No, George. I am grateful for your confidence. I think it is a wonderful thing; and, George—I had felt the same horror and disgust at these things, as you did. But now I think quite differently about them."

"Really, Aleck? I'm glad you say so. Often I was

troubled—is it viciousness or what, I wondered; but I could never talk to any one about it. They take everything here in such a filthy sense. Yet I knew in my heart that it was a true, honest emotion."

"George, I think it a very beautiful emotion. Just as beautiful as love for a woman. I had a friend here; his name was Russell; perhaps you remember him. I felt no physical passion toward him, but I think I loved him with all my heart. His death was a most terrible shock to me. It almost drove me insane."

Silently George holds out his hand.

CHAPTER XLIV

LOVE'S DARING

Castle on the Ohio,
Aug. 18, 1902.

MY DEAR CAROLUS:

You know the saying, "Der eine hat den Beutel, der andere das Geld." I find it a difficult problem to keep in touch with my correspondents. I have the leisure, but theirs is the advantage of the paper supply. Thus runs the world. But you, a most faithful correspondent, have been neglected a long while. Therefore this unexpected *sub rosa* chance is for you.

My dear boy, whatever your experiences since you left me, don't fashion your philosophy in the image of disappointment. All life is a multiplied pain; its highest expressions, love and friendship, are sources of the most heart-breaking sorrow. That has been my experience; no doubt, yours also. And you are aware that here, under prison conditions, the disappointments, the grief and anguish, are so much more acute, more bitter and lasting. What then? Shall one seal his emotions, or barricade his heart? Ah, if it were possible, it would be wiser, some claim. But remember, dear Carl, mere wisdom is a barren life.

I think it a natural reaction against your prison existence that you feel the need of self-indulgence. But it is a temporary phase, I hope. You want to live and enjoy, you say. But surely you are mistaken to believe that the time is past when we cheerfully sacrificed all to the needs of the cause. The first flush of emotional enthusiasm may have paled, but in its place there is the deeper and more lasting conviction that permeates one's whole being. There come moments when one asks himself the justification of his existence, the meaning of his life. No torment is more excruciating and overwhelming than the failure to find an answer. You will discover it neither in physical indulgence nor in coldly intellectual pleasure. Something more substantial is needed. In this regard, life outside does not differ so very much from prison existence. The narrower

your horizon—the more absorbed you are in your immediate
environment, and dependent upon it—the sooner you decay,
morally and mentally.   You can, in a measure, escape the
sordidness of life only by living for something higher.

Perhaps that is the secret of my survival. .Wider interests
have given me strength. And other phases there are. From
your own experience you know what sustaining satisfaction is
found in prison in the constant fight for the feeling of human
dignity, because of the constant attempt to strangle your sense
of self-respect. I have seen prisoners offer most desperate resistance in defence of their manhood. On my part it has been
a continuous struggle. Do you remember the last time I was
in the dungeon? It was on the occasion of Comrade Kropotkin's presence in this country, during his last lecture tour. The
old Warden was here then; he informed me that I would not
be permitted to see our Grand Old Man. I had a tilt with him,
but I did not succeed in procuring a visiting card. A few days
later I received·a letter from Peter. On the envelope, under my
name, was marked, "Political prisoner." The Warden was
furious. "We have no political prisoners in a free country,"
he thundered, tearing up the envelope. "But you have political
grafters," I retorted. We argued the matter heatedly, and I
demanded the envelope. The Warden insisted that I apologize.
Of course I refused, and I had to spend three days in the
dungeon.

There have been many changes since then. Your coming
to Pittsburgh last year, and the threat to expose this place
(they knew you had the facts) helped to bring matters to a
point. They assigned me to a range, and I am still holding the
position. The new Warden is treating me more decently. He
"wants no trouble with me," he told me. But he has proved
a great disappointment. He started in with promising reforms,
but gradually he has fallen into the old ways. In some respects
his régime is even worse than the previous one. He has introduced a system of "economy" which barely affords us sufficient
food. The dungeon and basket, which he had at first abolished,
are in operation again, and the discipline is daily becoming
more drastic. The result is more brutality and clubbings, more
fights and cutting affairs, and general discontent. The new
management cannot plead ignorance, for the last 4th of July
the men gave a demonstration of the effects of humane treat-

ment. The Warden had assembled the inmates in the chapel, promising to let them pass the day in the yard, on condition of good behavior. The Inspectors and the old guards advised against it, arguing the "great risk" of such a proceeding. But the Major decided to try the experiment. He put the men on their honor, and turned them loose in the yard. He was not disappointed; the day passed beautifully, without the least mishap; there was not even a single report. We began to breathe easier, when presently the whole system was reversed. It was partly due to the influence of the old officers upon the Warden; and the latter completely lost his head when a trusty made his escape from the hospital. It seems to have terrorized the Warden into abandoning all reforms. He has also been censured by the Inspectors because of the reduced profits from the industries. Now the tasks have been increased, and even the sick and consumptives are forced to work. The labor bodies of the State have been protesting in vain. How miserably weak is the Giant of Toil, because unconscious of his strength!

The men are groaning, and wishing Old Sandy back. In short, things are just as they were during your time. Men and Wardens may come and go, but the system prevails. More and more I am persuaded of the great truth: given authority and the opportunity for exploitation, the results will be essentially the same, no matter what particular set of men, or of "principles," happens to be in the saddle.

Fortunately I am on the "home run." I'm glad you felt that the failure of my application to the Superior Court would not depress me. I built no castles upon it. Yet I am glad it has been tried. It was well to demonstrate once more that neither lower courts, pardon boards, nor higher tribunals, are interested in doing justice. My lawyers had such a strong case, from the legal standpoint, that the State Pardon Board resorted to every possible trick to avoid the presentation of it. And now the Superior Court thought it the better part of wisdom to ignore the argument that I am being illegally detained. They simply refused the application, with a few meaningless phrases that entirely evade the question at issue.

Well, to hell with them. I have "2 an' a stump" (stump, 11 months) and I feel the courage of perseverance. But I hope that the next legislature will not repeal the new commutation law. There is considerable talk of it, for the politicians are angry that their efforts in behalf of the wealthy U. S. grafters in the Eastern Penitentiary failed. They begrudge the "common" prisoner the increased allowance of good time. However, I shall "make" it. Of course, you understand that both French leave and Dutch act are out of the question now. I have decided to stay—till I can *walk* through the gates.

In reference to French leave, have you read about the Biddle affair? I think it was the most remarkable attempt in the history of the country. Think of the wife of the Jail Warden helping prisoners to escape! The boys here were simply wild with joy. Every one hoped they would make good their escape, and old Sammy told me he prayed they shouldn't be caught. But all the bloodhounds of the law were unchained; the Biddle boys got no chance at all.

The story is this. The brothers Biddle, Jack and Ed, and Walter Dorman, while in the act of robbing a store, killed a man. It was Dorman who fired the shot, but he turned State's evidence. The State rewards treachery. Dorman escaped the noose, but the two brothers were sentenced to die. As is customary, they were visited in the jail by the "gospel ladies," among them the wife of the Warden. You probably remember him—Soffel; he was Deputy Warden when we were in the jail, and a rat he was, too. Well, Ed was a good-looking man, with soft manners, and so forth. Mrs. Soffel fell in love with him. It was mutual, I believe. Now witness the heroism a woman is capable of, when she loves. Mrs. Soffel determined to save the two brothers; I understand they promised her to quit their criminal life. Every day she would visit the condemned men, to console them. Pretending to read the gospel, she would stand close to the doors, to give them an opportunity to saw through the bars. She supplied them with revolvers, and they agreed to escape together. Of course, she could not go back to her husband, for she loved Ed, loved him well enough never even to see her children again. The night for the escape was set. The brothers intended to separate immediately after the break, subsequently to meet together with Mrs. Soffel. But the latter insisted on going with them. Ed begged her not to. He knew that it was sheer suicide for all of them. But she persisted, and Ed acquiesced, fully realizing that it would prove fatal. Don't you think it showed a noble trait in the boy? He did not want her to think that he was deserting her. The escape from the jail was made successfully; they even had several hours' start. But snow had fallen, and it was easy to trace two men and a woman in a sleigh. The brutality of the man-hunters is past belief. When the detectives came upon the boys, they fired their Winchesters into the two brothers. Even when the wounded were stretched on the ground, bleeding and helpless, a detective emptied his revolver into Ed, killing him. Jack died later, and Mrs. Soffel was placed in jail. You can imagine the savage fury of the respectable mob. Mrs. Soffel was denounced by her husband, and all the good Christian women cried "Unclean!" and clamored for the punishment of their unfortunate sister. She is now here, serving two years for aiding in the escape. I caught a glimpse of her when she came in. She has a sympathetic face, that bears signs of deep suffering; she must have gone through a terrible ordeal. Think of the struggle before she decided upon the desperate step; then the days and weeks of anxiety, as the boys were sawing the bars and preparing for the last chance! I should appreciate the love of a woman whose affection is stronger than the iron fetters of convention. In some ways this woman reminds me of the Girl—the type that possesses the courage and strength to rise above all considerations for the sake of the man or the cause held dear. How little the world understands the vital forces of life!

                                                    A.

CHAPTER XLV

THE BLOOM OF "THE BARREN STAFF"

I

It is September the nineteenth. The cell-house is silent and gray in the afternoon dusk. In the yard the rain walks with long strides, hastening in the dim twilight, hastening whither the shadows have gone. I stand at the door, in reverie. In the sombre light, I see myself led through the gate yonder,—it was ten years ago this day. The walls towered menacingly in the dark, the iron gripped my heart, and I was lost in despair. I should not have believed then that I could survive the long years of misery and pain. But the nimble feet of the rain patter hopefully; its tears dissipate the clouds, and bring light; and soon I shall step into the sunshine, and come forth grown and matured, as the world must have grown in the struggle of suffering—

"Fresh fish!" a rangeman announces, pointing to the long line of striped men, trudging dejectedly across the yard, and stumbling against each other in the unaccustomed lockstep. The door opens, and Aleck Killain, the lifetimer, motions to me. He walks with measured, even step along the hall. Rangeman "Coz" and Harry, my young assistant, stealthily crowd with him into my cell. The air of mystery about them arouses my apprehension.

446

"What's the matter, boys?" I ask.

They hesitate and glance at each other, smiling diffidently.

"*You* speak, Killain," Harry whispers.

The lifetimer carefully unwraps a little package, and I become aware of the sweet scent of flowers perfuming the cell. The old prisoner stammers in confusion, as he presents me with a rose, big and red. "We swiped it in the greenhouse," he says.

"Fer you, Aleck," Harry adds.

"For your tenth anniversary," corrects "Coz." "Good luck to you, Aleck."

Mutely they grip my hand, and steal out of the cell.

In solitude I muse over the touching remembrance. These men—they are the shame Society hides within the gray walls. These, and others like them. Daily they come to be buried alive in this grave; all through the long years they have been coming, and the end is not yet. Robbed of joy and life, their being is discounted in the economy of existence. And all the while the world has been advancing, it is said; science and philosophy, art and letters, have made great strides. But wherein is the improvement that augments misery and crowds the prisons? The discovery of the X-ray will further scientific research, I am told. But where is the X-ray of social insight that will discover in human understanding and mutual aid the elements of true progress? Deceptive is the advance that involves the ruthless sacrifice of peace and health and life; superficial and unstable the civilization that rests upon the treacherous sands of strife and warfare. The progress of science and industry, far from promoting man's happiness and social harmony, merely accentuates discontent and sharpens the contrasts. The knowledge gained at so much cost of suffering and sacrifice bears bitter fruit, for lack of wisdom to apply the lessons learned. There are no limits to the achievements of man, were not humanity divided against itself, exhausting its best energies in sanguinary conflict, suicidal and unnecessary. And these, the thousands stepmothered by cruel stupidity, are the victims castigated by Society for her own folly and sins. There is Young Harry. A child of the slums, he has never known the touch of a loving hand. Motherless, his father a drunkard, the heavy arm of the law was laid upon him at the age of ten. From reform school to reformatory the social orphan has been driven about.—"You know, Aleck," he says, "I nev'r had no real square meal, to feel full, you know; 'cept once, on Christmas, in de ref." At the age of nineteen, he has not seen a day of liberty since early childhood.

Three years ago he was transferred to the penitentiary, under a sentence of sixteen years for an attempted escape from the Morganza reform school, which resulted in the death of a keeper. The latter was foreman in the tailor shop, in which Harry was employed together with a number of other youths. The officer had induced Harry to do overwork, above the regular task, for which he rewarded the boy with an occasional dainty of buttered bread or a piece of corn-cake. By degrees Harry's voluntary effort became part of his routine work, and the reward in delicacies came more rarely. But when they entirely ceased the boy rebelled, refusing to exert himself above the required task. He was reported, but the Superintendent censured the keeper for the unauthorized increase of work. Harry was elated; but presently began systematic persecution that made the boy's life daily more unbearable. In innumerable ways the hostile guard sought to revenge his defeat upon the lad, till at last, driven to desperation, Harry resolved upon escape. With several other inmates the fourteen-year-old boy planned to flee to the Rocky Mountains, there to hunt the "wild" Indians, and live the independent and care-free life of Jesse James. "You know, Aleck," Harry confides to me, reminiscently, "we could have made it easy; dere was eleven of us. But de kids was all sore on de foreman. He 'bused and beat us, an' some of de boys wouldn' go 'cept we knock de screw out first. It was me pal Nacky that hit 'im foist, good an' hard, an' den I hit 'im, lightly. But dey all said in court that I hit 'im both times. Nacky's people had money, an' he beat de case, but I got soaked sixteen years." His eyes fill with tears and he says plaintively: "I haven't been outside since I was a little kid, an' now I'm sick, an' will die here mebbe."

II

Conversing in low tones, we sweep the range. I shorten my strokes to enable Harry to keep pace. Weakly he drags the broom across the floor. His appearance is pitifully grotesque. The sickly features, pale with the color of the prison whitewash, resemble a little child's. But the eyes look oldish in their wrinkled sockets, the head painfully out of proportion with the puny, stunted body. Now and again he turns his gaze on me, and in his face there is melancholy wonder, as if he is seeking something that has passed him by. Often I ponder, Is there a crime more appalling and heinous than the one Society has committed upon him, who is neither man nor youth and never was child? Crushed by the heel of brutality, this plant had never budded. Yet there is the making of a true man in him. His mentality is pathetically primitive, but he possesses character and courage, and latent virgin forces. His emotional frankness borders on the incredible; he is unmoral and unsocial, as a field daisy might be, surrounded by giant trees, yet timidly tenacious of its own being. It distresses me to witness the yearning that comes into his eyes at the mention of the "outside." Often he asks: "Tell me, Aleck, how does it feel to walk on de street, to know that you're free t' go where you damn please, wid no screw to foller you?" Ah, if he'd only have a chance, he reiterates, he'd be so careful not to get into trouble! He would like to keep company with a nice girl, he confides, blushingly; he had never had one. But he fears his days are numbered. His lungs are getting very bad, and now that his father has died, he has no one to help him get a pardon. Perhaps father wouldn't have helped him, either; he was always drunk, and never cared for his children. "He had no business t' have any children," Harry comments passionately. And he can't expect any assistance from his sister; the poor girl barely makes a living in the factory. "She's been workin' ev'r so long in the pickle works," Harry explains. "That feller, the boss there, must be rich; it's a big factory," he adds, naïvely, "he oughter give 'er enough to marry on." But he fears he will die in the prison. There is no one to aid him, and he has no friends. "I never had no friend," he says, wistfully; "there ain't no real friends. De older boys in de ref always used me, an' dey use all de kids. But dey was no friends, an' every one was against me in de court, an' dey put all de blame on me. Everybody was always against me," he repeats bitterly.

Alone in the cell, I ponder over his words. "Everybody was always against me," I hear the boy say. I wake at night, with the quivering cry in the darkness, "Everybody against me!" Motherless in childhood, reared in the fumes of brutal inebriation, cast into the slums to be crushed under the wheels of the law's Juggernaut, was the fate of this social orphan. Is this the fruit of progress? this the spirit of our Christian civilization? In the hours of solitude, the scheme of existence unfolds in kaleidoscope before me. In variegated design and divergent angle it presents an endless panorama of stunted minds and tortured bodies, of universal misery and wretchedness, in the elemental aspect of the boy's desolate life. And I behold all the suffering and agony resolve themselves in the dominance of the established, in tradition and custom that heavily encrust humanity, weighing down the already fettered soul till its wings break and it beats helplessly against the artificial barriers. . . . The blanched face of Misery is silhouetted against the night. The silence sobs with the piteous cry of the crushed boy. And I hear the cry, and it fills my whole being with the sense of terrible wrong and injustice, with the shame of my kind, that sheds crocodile tears while it swallows its helpless prey. The submerged moan in the dark. I will echo their agony to the ears of the world. I have suffered with them, I have looked into the heart of Pain, and with its voice and anguish I will speak to humanity, to wake it from sloth and apathy, and lend hope to despair.

The months speed in preparation for the great work. I must equip myself for the mission, for the combat with the world that struggles so desperately to defend its chains. The day of my resurrection is approaching, and I will devote my new life to the service of my fellow-sufferers. The world shall hear the tortured; it shall behold the shame it has buried within these walls, yet not eliminated. The ghost of its crimes shall rise and harrow its ears, till the social conscience is roused to the cry of its victims. And perhaps with eyes once opened, it will behold the misery and suffering in the world beyond, and Man will pause in his strife and mad race to ask himself, wherefore? whither?

CHAPTER XLVI

A CHILD'S HEART-HUNGER

I

WITH deep gratification I observe the unfoldment of Harry's mind. My friendship has wakened in him hope and interest in life. Merely to please me, he smilingly reiterated, he would apply himself to reading the mapped-out course. But as time passed he became absorbed in the studies, developing a thirst for knowledge that is transforming his primitive intelligence into a mentality of great power and character. Often I marvel at the peculiar strength and aspiration springing from the depths of a prison friendship. "I did not believe in friendship, Aleck," Harry says, as we ply our brooms in the day's work, "but now I feel that I wouldn't be here, if I had had then a real friend. It isn't only that we suffer together, but you have made me feel that our minds can rise above these rules and bars. You know, the screws have warned me against you, and I was afraid of you. I don't know how to put it, Aleck, but the first time we had that long talk last year, I felt as if something walked right over from you to me. And since then I have had something to live for. You know, I have seen so much of the priests, I have no use for the church, and I don't believe in immortality. But the idea I got from you clung to me, and it was so persistent, I really think there is such a thing as immortality of an idea."

For an instant the old look of helpless wonder is in his face, as if he is at a loss to master the thought. He pauses in his work, his eyes fastened on mine. "I got it, Aleck," he says, an eager smile lighting up his pallid features. "You remember the story you told me about them fellers—Oh,"—he quickly corrects himself—"when I get excited, I drop into my former bad English. Well, you know the story you told me of the prisoners in Siberia; how they escape sometimes, and the peasants, though forbidden to house them, put food outside of their huts, so that an escaped man may not starve to death. You remember, Aleck?"

"Yes, Harry. I'm glad you haven't forgotten it."

"Forgotten? Why, Aleck, a few weeks ago, sitting at my door, I saw a sparrow hopping about in the hall. It looked cold and hungry. I threw a piece of bread to it, but the Warden came by and made me pick it up, and drive the bird away. Somehow I thought of the peasants in Siberia, and how they share their food with escaped men. Why should the bird starve as long as I have bread? Now every night I place a few pieces near the door, and in the morning, just when it begins to dawn, and every one is asleep, the bird steals up and gets her breakfast. It's the immortality of an idea, Aleck."

II

The inclement winter has laid a heavy hand upon Harry. The foul hot air of the cell-house is aggravating his complaint, and now the physician has pronounced him in an advanced stage of consumption. The disease is ravaging the population. Hygienic rules

are ignored, and no precautions are taken against contagion. Harry's health is fast failing. He walks with
an evident effort, but bravely straightens as he meets my
gaze. "I feel quite strong, Aleck," he says, "I don't believe it's the con. It's just a bad cold."

He clings tenaciously to the slender hope; but now
and then the cunning of suspicion tests my faith. Pretending to wash his hands, he asks: "Can I use your
towel, Aleck? Sure you're not afraid?" My apparent
confidence seems to allay his fears, and he visibly rallies
with renewed hope. I strive to lighten his work on the
range, and his friend "Coz," who attends the officers'
table, shares with the sick boy the scraps of fruit and
cake left after their meals. The kind-hearted Italian,
serving a sentence of twenty years, spends his leisure
weaving hair chains in the dim light of the cell, and in-
vests the proceeds in warm underwear for his consumptive friend. "I don't need it myself, I'm too hot-blooded,
anyhow," he lightly waves aside Harry's objections. He
shudders as the hollow cough shakes the feeble frame,
and anxiously hovers over the boy, mothering him with
unobtrusive tenderness.

At the first sign of spring, "Coz" conspires with me
to procure for Harry the privilege of the yard. The
consumptives are deprived of air, immured in the shop
or block, and in the evening locked in the cells. In
view of my long service and the shortness of my remaining time, the Inspectors have promised me fifteen minutes' exercise in the yard. I have not touched the soil
since the discovery of the tunnel, in July 1900, almost
four years ago. But Harry is in greater need of fresh
air, and perhaps we shall be able to procure the privilege
for him, instead. His health would improve, and in the
meantime we will bring his case before the Pardon

Board. It was an outrage to send him to the penitentiary, "Coz" asserts vehemently. "Harry was barely fourteen then, a mere child. Think of a judge who will give such a kid sixteen years! Why, it means death. But what can you expect! Remember the little boy who was sent here—it was somewhere around '97—he was just twelve years old, and he didn't look more than ten. They brought him here in knickerbockers, and the fellows had to bend over double to keep in lockstep with him. He looked just like a baby in the line. The first pair of long pants he ever put on was stripes, and he was so frightened, he'd stand at the door and cry all the time. Well, they got ashamed of themselves after a while, and sent him away to some reformatory, but he spent about six months here then. Oh, what's the use talking," "Coz" concludes hopelessly; "it's a rotten world all right. But may be we can get Harry a pardon. Honest, Aleck, I feel as if he's my own child. We've been friends since the day he came in, and he's a good boy, only he never had a chance. Make a list, Aleck. I'll ask the Chaplain how much I've got in the office. I think it's twenty-two or may be twenty-three dollars. It's all for Harry."

The spring warms into summer before the dime and quarter donations total the amount required by the attorney to carry Harry's case to the Pardon Board. But the sick boy is missing from the range. For weeks his dry, hacking cough resounded in the night, keeping the men awake, till at last the doctor ordered him transferred to the hospital. His place on the range has been taken by "Big Swede," a tall, sallow-faced man who shuffles along the hall, moaning in pain. The passing guards mimic him, and poke him jocularly in the ribs. "Hey, you! Get a move on, and quit your shammin'." He starts in affright; pressing both hands against his side, he shrinks at the officer's touch. "You fakir, we're next to *you*, all right." An uncomprehending, sickly smile spreads over the sere face, as he murmurs plaintively, "Yis, sir, me seek, very seek."

CHAPTER XLVII

CHUM

I

THE able-bodied men have been withdrawn to the shops, and only the old and decrepit remain in the cell-house. But even the light duties of assistant prove too difficult for the Swede. The guards insist that he is shamming. Every night he is placed in a strait-jacket, and gagged to stifle his groans. I protest against the mistreatment, and am cited to the office. The Deputy's desk is occupied by "Bighead," the officer of the hosiery department, now promoted to the position of Second Assistant Deputy. He greets me with a malicious grin. "I knew you wouldn't behave," he chuckles; "know you too damn well from the stockin' shop."

The gigantic Colonel, the new Deputy, loose-jointed and broad, strolls in with long, swinging step. He glances over the report against me. "Is that all?" he inquires of the guard, in cold, impassive voice.

"Yes, sir."

"Go back to your work, Berkman."

But in the afternoon, Officer "Bighead" struts into the cell-house, in charge of the barber gang. As I take my turn in the first chair, the guard hastens toward me. "Get out of that chair," he commands. "It ain't your turn. You take *that* chair," pointing toward the second barber, a former boilermaker, dreaded by the men as a "butcher."

458

"It *is* my turn in this chair," I reply, keeping my seat.

"Dat so, Mr. Officer," the negro barber chimes in.

"Shut up!" the officer bellows. "Will you get out of that chair?" He advances toward me threateningly.

"I won't," I retort, looking him squarely in the eye.

Suppressed giggling passes along the waiting line. The keeper turns purple, and strides toward the office to report me.

II

"This is awful, Aleck. I'm so sorry you're locked up. You were in the right, too," "Coz" whispers at my cell. "But never min', old boy," he smiles reassuringly, "you can count on me, all right. And you've got other friends. Here's a stiff some one sends you. He wants an answer right away. I'll call for it."

The note mystifies me. The large, bold writing is unfamiliar; I cannot identify the signature, "Jim M." The contents are puzzling. His sympathies are with me, the writer says. He has learned all the details of the trouble, and feels that I acted in the defence of my rights. It is an outrage to lock me up for resenting undeserved humiliation at the hands of an unfriendly guard; and he cannot bear to see me thus persecuted. My time is short, and the present trouble, if not corrected, may cause the loss of my commutation. He will immediately appeal to the Warden to do me justice; but he should like to hear from me before taking action.

I wonder at the identity of the writer. Evidently not a prisoner; intercession with the Warden would be out of the question. Yet I cannot account for any officer who would take this attitude, or employ such means of communicating with me.

Presently "Coz" saunters past the cell. "Got your answer ready?" he whispers.

"Who gave you the note, Coz?"

"I don't know if I should tell you."

"Of course you must tell me. I won't answer this note unless I know to whom I am writing."

"Well, Aleck," he hesitates, "he didn't say if I may tell you."

"Then better go and ask him first."

Considerable time elapses before "Coz" returns. From the delay I judge that the man is in a distant part of the institution, or not easily accessible. At last the kindly face of the Italian appears at the cell.

"It's all right, Aleck," he says.

"Who is he?" I ask impatiently.

"I'll bet you'll never guess."

"Tell me, then."

"Well, I'll tell you. He is not a screw."

"Can't be a prisoner?"

"No."

"Who, then?"

"He is a fine fellow, Aleck."

"Come now, tell me."

"He is a citizen. The foreman of the new shop."

"The weaving department?"

"That's the man. Here's another stiff from him. Answer at once."

III

DEAR MR. J. M.:

I hardly know how to write to you. It is the most remarkable thing that has happened to me in all the years of my confinement. To think that you, a perfect stranger —and not a prisoner, at that—should offer to intercede in

my behalf because you feel that an injustice has been done!
It is almost incredible, but "Coz" has informed me that
you are determined to see the Warden in this matter. I
assure you I appreciate your sense of justice more than I
can express it. But I most urgently request you not to
carry out your plan. With the best of intentions, your
intercession will prove disastrous, to yourself as well as
to me. A shop foreman, you are not supposed to know
what is happening in the block. The Warden is a martinet,
and extremely vain of his authority. He will resent your
interference. I don't know who you are, but your indignation at what you believe an injustice characterizes you
as a man of principle, and you are evidently inclined to be
friendly toward me. I should be very unhappy to be the
cause of your discharge. You need your job, or you would
not be here. I am very, very thankful to you, but I urge
you most earnestly to drop the matter. I must fight my
own battles. Moreover, the situation is not very serious,
and I shall come out all right.

                         With much appreciation,
                                              A. B.

Dear Mr. M.:
      I feel much relieved by your promise to accede to my
request. It is best so. You need not worry about me. I
expect to receive a hearing before the Deputy, and he
seems a decent chap. You will pardon me when I confess
that I smiled at your question whether your correspondence
is welcome. Your notes are a ray of sunshine in the darkness, and I am intensely interested in the personality of a
man whose sense of justice transcends considerations of
personal interest. You know, no great heroism is required
to demand justice for oneself, in the furtherance of our
own advantage. But where the other fellow is concerned,
especially a stranger, it becomes a question of "abstract"
justice—and but few people possess the manhood to jeopardize their reputation or comfort for that.
      Since our correspondence began, I have had occasion to
speak to some of the men in your charge. I want to thank

you in their name for your considerate and humane treatment of them.

"Coz" is at the door, and I must hurry. Trust no one with notes, except him. We have been friends for years, and he can tell you all you wish to know about my life here.

Cordially,

B.

My Dear M.:

There is no need whatever for your anxiety regarding the effects of the solitary upon me. I do not think they will keep me in long; at any rate, remember that I do not wish you to intercede.

You will be pleased to know that my friend Harry shows signs of improvement, thanks to your generosity. "Coz" has managed to deliver to him the tid-bits and wine you sent. You know the story of the boy. He has never known the love of a mother, nor the care of a father. A typical child of the disinherited, he was thrown, almost in infancy, upon the tender mercies of the world. At the age of ten the law declared him a criminal. He has never since seen a day of liberty. At twenty he is dying of prison consumption. Was the Spanish Inquisition ever guilty of such organized child murder? With desperate will-power he clutches at life, in the hope of a pardon. He is firmly convinced that fresh air would cure him, but the new rules confine him to the hospital. His friends here have collected a fund to bring his case before the Pardon Board; it is to be heard next month. That devoted soul, "Coz," has induced the doctor to issue a certificate of Harry's critical condition, and he may be released soon. I have grown very fond of the boy so much sinned against. I have watched his heart and mind blossom in the sunshine of a little kindness, and now—I hope that at least his last wish will be gratified: just once to walk on the street, and not hear the harsh command of the guard. He begs me to express to his unknown friend his deepest gratitude.

B.

DEAR M.:

The Deputy has just released me. I am happy with a double happiness, for I know how pleased you will be at the good turn of affairs. It is probably due to the fact that my neighbor, the Big Swede—you've heard about him—was found dead in the strait-jacket this morning. The doctor and officers all along pretended that he was shamming. It was a most cruel murder; by the Warden's order the sick Swede was kept gagged and bound every night. I understand that the Deputy opposed such brutal methods, and now it is rumored that he intends to resign. But I hope he will remain. There is something big and broad-minded about the gigantic Colonel. He tries to be fair, and he has saved many a prisoner from the cruelty of the Major. The latter is continually inventing new modes of punishment; it is characteristic that his methods involve curtailment of rations, and consequent saving, which is not accounted for on the books. He has recently cut the milk allowance of the hospital patients, notwithstanding the protests of the doctor. He has also introduced severe punishment for talking. You know, when you have not uttered a word for days and weeks, you are often seized with an uncontrollable desire to give vent to your feelings. These infractions of the rules are now punished by depriving you of tobacco and of your Sunday dinner. Every Sunday from 30 to 50 men are locked up on the top range, to remain without food all day. The system is called "Killicure" (kill or cure) and it involves considerable graft, for I know numbers of men who have not received tobacco or a Sunday dinner for months.

Warden Wm. Johnston seems innately cruel. Recently he introduced the "blind" cell,—door covered with solid sheet iron. It is much worse than the basket cell, for it virtually admits no air, and men are kept in it from 30 to 60 days. Prisoner Varnell was locked up in such a cell 79 days, becoming paralyzed. But even worse than these punishments is the more refined brutality of torturing the boys with the uncertainty of release and the increasing deprivation of good time. This system is developing insanity to an alarming extent.

Amid all this heartlessness and cruelty, the Chaplain is a refreshing oasis of humanity. I noticed in one of your

letters the expression, "because of economic necessity," and
—I wondered. To be sure, the effects of economic causes
are not to be underestimated. But the extremists of the
materialistic conception discount character, and thus help to
vitiate it. The factor of personality is too often ignored
by them. Take the Chaplain, for instance. In spite of the
surrounding swamp of cupidity and brutality, notwithstanding all disappointment and ingratitude, he is to-day, after
30 years of incumbency, as full of faith in human nature
and as sympathetic and helpful, as years ago. He has had to
contend against the various administrations, and he is a
poor man; necessity has not stifled his innate kindness.

And this is why I wondered. "Economic necessity"—
has Socialism pierced the prison walls?

B.

DEAR, DEAR COMRADE:

Can you realize how your words, "I am socialistically
inclined," warmed my heart? I wish I could express to you
all the intensity of what I feel, my dear *friend* and *comrade*.
To have so unexpectedly found both in you, unutterably
lightens this miserable existence. What matter that you
do not entirely share my views,—we are comrades in the
common cause of human emancipation. It was indeed well
worth while getting in trouble to have found you, dear
friend. Surely I have good cause to be content, even happy.
Your friendship is a source of great strength, and I feel
equal to struggling through the ten months, encouraged and
inspired by your comradeship and devotion. Every evening
I cross the date off my calendar, joyous with the thought
that I am a day nearer to the precious moment when I shall
turn my back upon these walls, to join my friends in the
great work, and to meet you, dear Chum, face to face, to
grip your hand and salute you, my friend and comrade!

Most fraternally,

Alex.

CHAPTER XLVIII

LAST DAYS

On the Homestretch,
Sub Rosa, April 15, 1905.

MY DEAR GIRL:

The last spring is here, and a song is in my heart. Only three more months, and I shall have settled accounts with Father Penn. There is the year in the workhouse, of course, and that prison, I am told, is even a worse hell than this one. But I feel strong with the suffering that is past, and perhaps even more so with the wonderful jewel I have found. The man I mentioned in former letters has proved a most beautiful soul and sincere friend. In every possible way he has been trying to make my existence more endurable. With what little he may, he says, he wants to make amends for the injustice and brutality of society. He is a Socialist, with a broad outlook upon life. Our lengthy discussions (per notes) afford me many moments of pleasure and joy.

It is chiefly to his exertions that I shall owe my commutation time. The sentiment of the Inspectors was not favorable. I believe it was intended to deprive me of two years' good time. Think what it would mean to us! But my friend—my dear Chum, as I affectionately call him—has quietly but persistently been at work, with the result that the Inspectors have "seen the light." It is now definite that I shall be released in July. The date is still uncertain. I can barely realize that I am soon to leave this place. The anxiety and restlessness of the last month would be almost unbearable, but for the soothing presence of my devoted friend. I hope some day you will meet him,—perhaps even soon, for he is not of the quality that can long remain a helpless witness of the torture of men. He wants to work in the broader field, where he may join hands with those who strive to reconstruct the conditions that are bulwarked with prison bars.

But while necessity forces him to remain here, his character is in evidence. He devotes his time and means to lightening the burden of the prisoners. His generous interest kept my sick friend Harry alive, in the hope of a pardon. You will be saddened to hear that the Board refused to release him, on the ground that he was not "sufficiently ill." The poor boy, who had never been out of sight of a guard since he was a child of ten, died a week after the pardon was refused.

But though my Chum could not give freedom to Harry, he was instrumental in saving another young life from the hands of the hangman. It was the case of young Paul, typical of prison as the nursery of crime. The youth was forced to work alongside of a man who persecuted and abused him because he resented improper advances. Repeatedly Paul begged the Warden to transfer him to another department; but his appeals were ignored. The two prisoners worked in the bakery. Early one morning, left alone, the man attempted to violate the boy. In the struggle that followed the former was killed. The prison management was determined to hang the lad, "in the interests of discipline." The officers openly avowed they would "fix his clock." Permission for a collection, to engage an attorney for Paul, was refused. Prisoners who spoke in his behalf were severely punished; the boy was completely isolated preparatory to his trial. He stood absolutely helpless, alone. But the dear Chum came to the rescue of Paul. The work had to be done secretly, and it was a most difficult task to secure witnesses for the defence among the prisoners terrorized by the guards. But Chum threw himself into the work with heart and soul. Day and night he labored to give the boy a chance for his life. He almost broke down before the ordeal was over. But the boy was saved; the jury acquitted him on the ground of self-defence.

The proximity of release, if only to change cells, is nerve-racking in the extreme. But even the mere change will be a relief. Meanwhile my faithful friend does everything in his power to help me bear the strain. Besides ministering to my physical comforts, he generously supplies me with books and publications. It helps to while away the leaden-heeled days, and keeps me abreast of the world's work. The Chum is enthusiastic over the growing strength of Socialism, and we often discuss the subject with much vigor. It appears to me, however, that the Socialist anxiety for success is by degrees perverting essential principles. It is with much sorrow I have learned that political activity, formerly viewed merely as a means of spreading Socialist ideas, has gradually become an end in itself. Straining for political power weakens the fibres of character and ideals. Daily contact with authority has strengthened my conviction that control of the governmental power is an illusory remedy for social evils. Inevitable consequences of false conceptions are not to be legislated out of existence. It is not merely the conditions, but the fundamental ideas of present civilization, that are to be transvalued, to give place to new social and individual relations. The emancipation of labor is the necessary first step along the road of a regenerated humanity; but even that can be accomplished only through the awakened consciousness of the toilers, acting on their own initiative and strength.

On these and other points Chum differs with me, but his intense friendship knows no intellectual distinctions. He is to visit you during his August vacation. I know you will make him feel my gratitude, for I can never repay his boundless devotion.

Sasha.

DEAREST CHUM:

It seemed as if all aspiration and hope suddenly went out of my life when you disappeared so mysteriously. I was tormented by the fear of some disaster. Your return has filled me with joy, and I am happy to know that you heard and responded unhestitatingly to the call of a sacred cause.

I greatly envy your activity in the P. circle. The revolution in Russia has stirred me to the very depths. The giant is awakening, the mute giant that has suffered so patiently, voicing his misery and agony only in the anguish-laden song and on the pages of his Gorkys.

Dear friend, you remember our discussion regarding Plehve. I may have been in error when I expressed the view that the execution of the monster, encouraging sign of individual revolu-

tionary activity as it was, could not be regarded as a manifestation of social awakening. But the present uprising undoubtedly
points to widespread rebellion permeating Russian life. Yet
it would probably be too optimistic to hope for a very radical
change. I have been absent from my native land for many
years; but in my youth I was close to the life and thought of
the peasant. Large, heavy bodies move slowly. The proletariat
of the cities has surely become impregnated with revolutionary
ideas, but the vital element of Russia is the agrarian population.
I fear, moreover, that the dominant reaction is still very strong,
though it has no doubt been somewhat weakened by the discontent manifesting in the army and, especially, in the navy.
With all my heart I hope that the revolution will be successful.
Perhaps a constitution is the most we can expect. But whatever the result, the bare fact of a revolution in long-suffering
Russia is a tremendous inspiration. I should be the happiest
of men to join in the glorious struggle.

Long live the Revolution!

A.

Dear Chum:

Thanks for your kind offer. But I am absolutely opposed
to having any steps taken to eliminate the workhouse sentence.
I have served these many years and I shall survive one more.
I will ask no favors of the enemy. They will even twist their
own law to deprive me of the five months' good time, to which
I am entitled on the last year. I understand that I shall be
allowed only two months off, on the preposterous ground that
the workhouse term constitutes the first year of a *new* sentence!
But I do not wish you to trouble about the matter. You have
more important work to do. Give all your energies to the good
cause. Prepare the field for the mission of Tchaikovsky and
Babushka, and I shall be with you in spirit when you embrace
our brave comrades of the Russian Revolution, whose dear names
were a hallowed treasure of my youth.

May success reward the efforts of our brothers in Russia.

A.

CHUM:

Just got word from the Deputy that my papers are signed. I didn't wish to cause you anxiety, but I was apprehensive of some hitch. But it's positive and settled now,—I go out on the 19th. Just one more week! This is the happiest day in thirteen years. Shake, Comrade.

A.

DEAREST CHUM:

My hand trembles as I write this last good-bye. I'll be gone in an hour. My heart is too full for words. Please send enclosed notes to my friends, and embrace them all as I embrace you now. I shall live in the hope of meeting you all next year. Good-bye, dear, devoted friend.

With my whole heart,

Your Comrade and Chum.

July 19, 1905.

DEAREST GIRL:

It's Wednesday morning, the 19th, at last!

> Geh stiller meines Herzens Schlag
> > Und schliesst euch alle meine alten Wunden,
> Denn dieses ist mein letzter Tag
> > Und dies sind seine letzten Stunden.

My last thoughts within these walls are of you, my dear, dear Sonya, the Immutable!

Sasha.

PART III

THE WORKHOUSE

THE WORKHOUSE

I

THE gates of the penitentiary open to leave me out, and I pause involuntarily at the fascinating sight. It is a street: a line of houses stretches before me; a woman, young and wonderfully sweet-faced, is passing on the opposite side. My eyes follow her graceful lines, as she turns the corner. Men stand about. They wear citizen clothes, and scan me with curious, insistent gaze. . . . The handcuff grows taut on my wrist, and I follow the sheriff into the waiting carriage. A little child runs by. I lean out of the window to look at the rosy-cheeked, strangely youthful face. But the guard impatiently lowers the blind, and we sit in gloomy silence.

The spell of the civilian garb is upon me. It gives an exhilarating sense of manhood. Again and again I glance at my clothes, and verify the numerous pockets to reassure myself of the reality of the situation. I am free, past the dismal gray walls! Free? Yet even now captive of the law. The law! . . .

The engine puffs and shrieks, and my mind speeds back to another journey. It was thirteen years and one week ago this day. On the wings of an all-absorbing love I hastened to join the struggle of the oppressed people. I left home and friends, sacrificed liberty, and risked life. But human justice is blind: it will not see the soul on fire. Only the shot was heard, by the Law

473

that is deaf to the agony of Toil. "Vengeance is mine," it saith. To the uttermost drop it will shed the blood to exact its full pound of flesh. Twelve years and ten months! And still another year. What horrors await me at the new prison? Poor, faithful "Horsethief" will nevermore smile his greeting: he did not survive six months in the terrible workhouse. But my spirit is strong; I shall not be daunted. This garb is the visible, tangible token of resurrection. The devotion of staunch friends will solace and cheer me. The call of the great Cause will give strength to live, to struggle, to conquer.

II

Humiliation overwhelms me as I don the loathed suit of striped black and gray. The insolent look of the guard rouses my bitter resentment, as he closely scrutinizes my naked body. But presently, the examination over, a sense of gratification steals over me at the assertiveness of my self-respect.

The ordeal of the day's routine is full of inexpressible anguish. Accustomed to prison conditions, I yet find existence in the workhouse a nightmare of cruelty, infinitely worse than the most inhuman aspects of the penitentiary. The guards are surly and brutal; the food foul and inadequate; punishment for the slightest offence instantaneous and ruthless. The cells are even smaller than in the penitentiary, and contain neither chair nor table. They are unspeakably ill-smelling with the privy buckets, for the purposes of which no scrap of waste paper is allowed. The sole ablutions of the day are performed in the morning, when the men form in the hall and march past the spigot of running water, snatching a handful in the constantly moving line. Absolute silence prevails in cell-house and shop. The slightest motion of the lips is punished with the blackjack or the dungeon, referred to with caustic satire as the "White House."

The perverse logic of the law that visits the utmost limit of barbarity upon men admittedly guilty of minor transgressions! Throughout the breadth of the land the workhouses are notoriously more atrocious in every respect than the penitentiaries and State prisons, in which are confined men convicted of felonies. The Allegheny County Workhouse of the great Commonwealth of Pennsylvania enjoys infamous distinction as the blackest of hells where men expiate the sins of society.

At work in the broom shop, I find myself in peculiarly familiar surroundings. The cupidity of the management has evolved methods even more inhuman than those obtaining in the State prison. The tasks imposed upon the men necessitate feverish exertion. Insufficient product or deficient work is not palliated by physical inability or illness. In the conduct of the various industries, every artifice prevalent in the penitentiary is practised to evade the law limiting convict competition. The number of men employed in productive work by far exceeds the legally permitted percentage; the provisions for the protection of free labor are skilfully circumvented; the tags attached to the shop products are designed to be obliterated as soon as the wares have left the prison; the words "convict-made" stamped on the broom-handles are pasted over with labels giving no indication of the place of manufacture. The anti-convict-labor law, symbolic of the political achievements of labor, is frustrated at every point, its element of protection a "lame and impotent conclusion."

How significant the travesty of the law in its holy of holies! Here legal justice immures its victims; here are buried the disinherited, whose rags and tatters annoy respectability; here offenders are punished for breaking the law. And here the Law is daily and hourly violated by its pious high priests.

III

The immediate is straining at the leash that holds memory in the environment of the penitentiary, yet the veins of the terminated existence still palpitate with the recollection of friends and common suffering. The messages from Riverside are wet with tears of misery, but Johnny, the young Magyar, strikes a note of cheer: his sentence is about to expire; he will devote himself to the support of the little children he had so unwittingly robbed of a father. Meanwhile he bids me courage and hope, enclosing two dollars from the proceeds of his fancy work, "to help along." He was much grieved, he writes, at his inability to bid me a last farewell, because the Warden refused the request, signed by two hundred prisoners, that I be allowed to pass along the tiers to say good-bye. But soon, soon we shall see each other in freedom.

Words of friendship glow brightly in the darkness of the present, and charm my visions of the near future. Coming liberty casts warming rays, and I dwell in the atmosphere of my comrades. The Girl and the Chum are aglow with the fires of Young Russia. Busily my mind shapes pictures of the great struggle that transplant me to the days of my youth. In the little tenement flat in New York we had sketched with bold stroke the fortunes of the world—the Girl, the Twin, and I. In the dark, cage-like kitchen, amid the smoke of the asthmatic stove, we had planned our conspirative work in Russia. But the need of the hour had willed it otherwise. Homestead had sounded the prelude of awakening, and my heart had echoed the inspiring strains.

The banked fires of aspiration burst into life. What matter the immediate outcome of the revolution in Russia? The yearning of my youth wells up with spontaneous power. To live is to struggle! To struggle against Caesar, side by side with the people: to suffer with them, and to die, if need be. That is life. It will sadden me to part with Chum even before I had looked deeply into the devoted face. But the Girl is aflame with the spirit of Russia: it will be joyous work in common. The soil of Monongahela, laden with years of anguish, has grown dear to me. Like the moan of a broken chord wails the thought of departure. But no ties of affection will strain at my heartstrings. Yet— the sweet face of a little girl breaks in on my reverie, a look of reproaching sadness in the large, wistful eyes. It is little Stella. The last years of my penitentiary life have snatched many a grace from her charming correspondence. Often I have sought consolation in the beautiful likeness of her soulful face. With mute tenderness she had shared my grief at the loss of Harry, her lips breathing sweet balm. Gray days had warmed at her smile, and I lavished upon her all the affection with which I was surcharged. It will be a violent stifling of her voice in my heart, but the call of the *muzhik* rings clear, compelling. Yet who knows? The revolution may be over before my resurrection. In republican Russia, with her enlightened social protestantism, life would be fuller, richer than in this pitifully *bourgeois* democracy. Freedom will present the unaccustomed problem of self-support, but it is premature to form

definite plans. Long imprisonment has probably incapacitated me for hard work, but I shall find means to
earn my simple needs when I have cast off the fetters
of my involuntary parasitism.

The thought of affection, the love of woman, thrills
me with ecstasy, and colors my existence with emotions
of strange bliss. But the solitary hours are filled with
recurring dread lest my life forever remain bare of
woman's love. Often the fear possesses me with the
intensity of despair, as my mind increasingly dwells on
the opposite sex. Thoughts of woman eclipse the
memory of the prison affections, and the darkness of
the present is threaded with the silver needle of love-
hopes.

IV

The monotony of the routine, the degradation and
humiliation weigh heavier in the shadow of liberty. My
strength is failing with the hard task in the shop, but
the hope of receiving my full commutation sustains me.
The law allows five months' "good time" on every year
beginning with the ninth year of a sentence. But the
Superintendent has intimated to me that I may be
granted the benefit of only two months, as a "new"
prisoner, serving the first year of a workhouse sentence.
The Board of Directors will undoubtedly take that view,
he often taunts me. Exasperation at his treatment,
coupled with my protest against the abuse of a fellow
prisoner, have caused me to be ordered into the solitary.
Dear Chum is insistent on legal steps to secure my full
commutation; notwithstanding my unconditional refusal
to resort to the courts, he has initiated a *sub rosa* campaign to achieve his object. The time drags in torturing
uncertainty. With each day the solitary grows more

stifling, maddening, till my brain reels with terror of the graveyard silence. Like glad music sounds the stern command, "Exercise!"

In step we circle the yard, the clanking of Charley's chain mournfully beating time. He had made an unsuccessful attempt to escape, for which he is punished with the ball and chain. The iron cuts into his ankle, and he trudges painfully under the heavy weight. Near me staggers Billy, his left side completely paralyzed since he was released from the "White House." All about me are cripples. I am in the midst of the social refuse: the lame and the halt, the broken in body and spirit, past work, past even crime. These were the blessed of the Nazarene; these a Christian world breaks on the wheel. They, too, are within the scope of my mission, they above all others—these the living indictments of a leprous system, the excommunicated of God and man.

The threshold of liberty is thickly sown with misery and torment. The days are unbearable with nervous restlessness, the nights hideous with the hours of agonizing stillness,—the endless, endless hours. Feverishly I pace the cell. The day will pass, it *must* pass. With reverent emotion I bless the shamed sun as he dips beyond the western sky. One day nearer to the liberty that awaits me, with unrestricted sunshine and air and life beyond the hated walls of gray, out in the daylight, in the open. The open world! . . . The scent of fresh-mown hay is in my nostrils; green fields and forests stretch before me; sweetly ripples the mountain spring. Up to the mountain crest, to the breezes and the sunshine, where the storm breaks in its wild fury upon my uncovered head. Welcome the rain and the wind that sweep the foul prison dust off my heart, and blow life and strength into my being! Tremblingly rapturous is the thought of freedom. Out in the woods, away from the stench of the cannibal world I shall wander, nor lift my foot from soil or sod. Close to the breath of Nature I will press my parched lips, on her bosom I will pass my days, drinking sustenance and strength from the universal mother. And there, in liberty and independence, in the vision of the mountain peaks, I shall voice the cry of the social orphans, of the buried and the disinherited, and visualize to the living the yearning, menacing Face of Pain.

PART IV

THE RESURRECTION

THE RESURRECTION

I

ALL night I toss sleeplessly on the cot, and pace the cell in nervous agitation, waiting for the dawn. With restless joy I watch the darkness melt, as the first rays herald the coming of the day. It is the 18th of May—my last day, my very last! A few more hours, and I shall walk through the gates, and drink in the warm sunshine and the balmy air, and be free to go and come as I please, after the nightmare of thirteen years and ten months in jail, penitentiary, and workhouse.

My step quickens with the excitement of the outside, and I try to while away the heavy hours thinking of freedom and of friends. But my brain is in a turmoil; I cannot concentrate my thoughts. Visions of the near future, images of the past, flash before me, and crowd each other in bewildering confusion.

Again and again my mind reverts to the unnecessary cruelty that has kept me in prison three months over and above my time. It was sheer sophistry to consider me a "new" prisoner, entitled only to two months' commutation. As a matter of fact, I was serving the last year of a twenty-two-year sentence, and therefore I should have received five months time off. The Superintendent had repeatedly promised to inform me of the decision of the Board of Directors, and every day, for weeks and months, I anxiously waited for word from

483

them.   None ever came, and I had to serve the full ten months.

Ah, well, it is almost over now!   I have passed my last night in the cell, and the morning is here, the precious, blessed morning!

How slowly the minutes creep!   I listen intently, and catch the sound of bars being unlocked on the bottom range: it is the Night Captain turning the kitchen men out to prepare breakfast—5 A. M! Two and a half hours yet before I shall be called; two endless hours, and then another thirty long minutes.   Will they ever pass? . . . And again I pace the cell.

II

The gong rings the rising hour.   In great agitation I gather up my blankets, tincup and spoon, which must be delivered at the office before I am discharged.   My heart beats turbulently, as I stand at the door, waiting to be called.   But the guard unlocks the range and orders me to "fall in for breakfast."

The striped line winds down the stairs, past the lynx-eyed Deputy standing in the middle of the hallway, and slowly circles through the centre, where each man receives his portion of bread for the day and returns to his tier.   The turnkey, on his rounds of the range, casts a glance into my cell.   "Not workin'," he says mechanically, shutting the door in my face.

"I'm going out," I protest.

"Not till you're called," he retorts, locking me in.

I stand at the door, tense with suspense.   I strain my ear for the approach of a guard to call me to the office, but all remains quiet.   A vague fear steals over me: perhaps they will not release me to-day; I may be losing time. . . . A feeling of nausea overcomes me, but by a strong effort I throw off the dreadful fancy, and quicken my step. I must not think—not think. . . .

At last! The lever is pulled, my cell unlocked, and with a dozen other men I am marched to the clothes-room, in single file and lockstep. I await my turn impatiently, as several men are undressed and their naked bodies scrutinized for contraband or hidden messages. The overseer flings a small bag at each man, containing the prisoner's civilian garb, shouting boisterously: "Hey, you! Take off them clothes, and put your rags on."

I dress hurriedly. A guard accompanies me to the office, where my belongings are returned to me: some money friends had sent, my watch, and the piece of ivory the penitentiary turnkey had stolen from me, and which I had insisted on getting back before I left Riverside. The officer in charge hands me a railroad ticket to Pittsburgh (the fare costing about thirty cents), and I am conducted to the prison gate.

III

The sun shines brightly in the yard, the sky is clear, the air fresh and bracing. Now the last gate will be thrown open, and I shall be out of sight of the guard, beyond the bars,—alone! How I have hungered for this hour, how often in the past years have I dreamed of this rapturous moment—to be alone, out in the open, away from the insolent eyes of my keepers! I'll rush away from these walls and kneel on the warm sod, and kiss the soil and embrace the trees, and with a song of joy give thanks to Nature for the blessings of sunshine and air.

The outer door opens before me, and I am confronted by reporters with cameras. Several tall men approach me. One of them touches me on the shoulder, turns back the lapel of his coat, revealing a police officer's star, and says:

"Berkman, you are to leave the city before night, by order of the Chief."

The detectives and reporters trailing me to the nearby railway station attract a curious crowd. I hasten into a car to escape their insistent gaze, feeling glad that I have prevailed upon my friends not to meet me at the prison.

My mind is busy with plans to outwit the detectives, who have entered the same compartment. I have arranged to join the Girl in Detroit. I have no particular reason to mask my movements, but I resent the surveillance. I must get rid of the spies, somehow; I don't want their hateful eyes to desecrate my meeting with the Girl.

I feel dazed. The short ride to Pittsburgh is over before I can collect my thoughts. The din and noise rend my ears; the rushing cars, the clanging bells, bewilder me. I am afraid to cross the street; the flying monsters pursue me on every side. The crowds jostle me on the sidewalk, and I am constantly running into the passers-by. The turmoil, the ceaseless movement, disconcerts me. A horseless carriage whizzes close by me; I turn to look at the first automobile I have ever seen, but the living current sweeps me helplessly along. A woman passes me, with a child in her arms. The baby looks strangely diminutive, a rosy dimple in the laughing face. I smile back at the little cherub, and my eyes meet the gaze of the detectives. A wild thought to escape, to get away from them, possesses me, and I turn quickly into a side street, and walk blindly, faster and faster. A sudden impulse seizes me at the sight of a passing car, and I dash after it.

"Fare, please!" the conductor sings out, and I almost laugh out aloud at the fleeting sense of the material reality of freedom. Conscious of the strangeness of my action, I produce a dollar bill, and a sense of exhilarating independence comes over me, as the man counts out the silver coins. I watch him closely for a sign of recognition. Does he realize that I am just out of prison? He turns away, and I feel thankful to the dear Chum for having so thoughtfully provided me with a new suit of clothes. It is peculiar, however, that the conductor has failed to notice my closely cropped hair. But the man in the seat opposite seems to be watching me. Perhaps he has recognized me by my picture in the newspapers; or may be it is my straw hat that has attracted his attention. I glance about me. No one wears summer headgear yet; it must be too early in the season. I ought to change it: the detectives could not follow me so easily then. Why, there they are on the back platform!

At the next stop I jump off the car. A hat sign arrests my eye, and I walk into the store, and then slip quietly through a side entrance, a dark derby on my head. I walk quickly, for a long, long time, board several cars, and then walk again, till I find myself on a deserted street. No one is following me now; the detectives must have lost track of me. I feel worn and tired. Where could I rest up, I wonder, when I suddenly recollect that I was to go directly from the prison to the drugstore of Comrade M——. My friends must be worried, and M—— is waiting to wire to the Girl about my release.

It is long past noon when I enter the drugstore.

M—— seems highly wrought up over something; he
shakes my hand violently, and plies me with questions, as
he leads me into his apartments in the rear of the store.
It seems strange to be in a regular room: there is paper
on the walls, and it feels so peculiar to the touch, so
different from the whitewashed cell. I pass my hand
over it caressingly, with a keen sense of pleasure. The
chairs, too, look strange, and those quaint things on the
table. The bric-a-brac absorbs my attention—the people
in the room look hazy, their voices sound distant and
confused.

"Why don't you sit down, Aleck?" the tones are
musical and tender; a woman's, no doubt.

"Yes," I reply, walking around the table, and picking
up a bright toy. It represents Undine, rising from the
water, the spray glistening in the sun. . . .

"Are you tired, Aleck?"

"N—no."

"You have just come out?"

"Yes."

It requires an effort to talk. The last year, in the
workhouse, I have barely spoken a dozen words; there
was always absolute silence. The voices disturb me. The
presence of so many people—there are three or four
about me—is oppressive. The room reminds me of the
cell, and the desire seizes me to rush out into the open,
to breathe the air and see the sky.

"I'm going," I say, snatching up my hat.

IV

The train speeds me to Detroit, and I wonder
vaguely how I reached the station. My brain is numb;
I cannot think. Field and forest flit by in the gathering
dusk, but the surroundings wake no interest in me. "I

am rid of the detectives"—the thought persists in my mind, and I feel something relax within me, and leave me cold, without emotion or desire.

With an effort I descend to the platform, and sway from side to side, as I cross the station at Detroit. A man and a girl hasten toward me, and grasp me by the hand. I recognize Carl. The dear boy, he was a most faithful and cheering correspondent all these years since he left the penitentiary. But who is the girl with him, I wonder, when my gaze falls on a woman leaning against a pillar. She looks intently at me. The wave of her hair, the familiar eyes—why, it's the Girl! How little she has changed! I take a few steps forward, somewhat surprised that she did not rush up to me like the others. I feel pleased at her self-possession: the excited voices, the quick motions, disturb me. I walk slowly toward her, but she does not move. She seems rooted to the spot, her hand grasping the pillar, a look of awe and terror in her face. Suddenly she throws her arms around me. Her lips move, but no sound reaches my ear.

We walk in silence. The Girl presses a bouquet into my hand. My heart is full, but I cannot talk. I hold the flowers to my face, and mechanically bite the petals.

V

Detroit, Chicago, and Milwaukee pass before me like a troubled dream. I have a faint recollection of a sea of faces, restless and turbulent, and I in its midst. Confused voices beat like hammers on my head, and then all is very still. I stand in full view of the audience. Eyes are turned on me from every side, and I grow embarrassed. The crowd looks dim and hazy; I feel hot and cold, and a great longing to flee. The perspiration is running down my back; my knees tremble violently, the floor is slipping from under my feet—there is a tumult of hand clapping, loud cheers and bravos.

We return to Carl's house, and men and women grasp my hand and look at me with eyes of curious awe. I fancy a touch of pity in their tones, and am impatient of their sympathy. A sense of suffocation possesses me within doors, and I dread the presence of people. It is torture to talk; the sound of voices agonizes me. I watch for an opportunity to steal out of the house. It soothes me to lose myself among the crowds, and a sense of quiet pervades me at the thought that I am a stranger to every one about me. I roam the city at night, and seek the outlying country, conscious only of a desire to be alone.

VI

I am in the Waldheim, the Girl at my side. All is quiet in the cemetery, and I feel a great peace. No emotion stirs me at the sight of the monument, save a feeling of quiet sadness. It represents a woman, with one hand placing a wreath on the fallen, with the other grasping a sword. The marble features mirror unutterable grief and proud defiance.

I glance at the Girl. Her face is averted, but the droop of her head speaks of suffering. I hold out my hand to her, and we stand in mute sorrow at the graves of our martyred comrades. . . . I have a vision of Stenka Razin, as I had seen him pictured in my youth, and at his side hang the bodies of the men buried beneath my feet. Why are they dead? I wonder. Why should I live? And a great desire to lie down with them is upon me. I clutch the iron post, to keep from falling.

Steps sound behind me, and I turn to see a girl hastening toward us. She is radiant with young womanhood; her presence breathes life and the joy of it. Her bosom heaves with panting; her face struggles with a solemn look.

"I ran all the way," her voice is soft and low; "I was afraid I might miss you."

The Girl smiles. "Let us go in somewhere to rest up, Alice." Turning to me, she adds, "She ran to see— you."

How peculiar the Girl should conceive such an idea! It is absurd. Why should Alice be anxious to see me? I look old and worn; my step is languid, unsteady. . . . Bitter thoughts fill my mind, as we ride back on the train to Chicago.

"You are sad," the Girl remarks. "Alice is very much taken with you. Aren't you glad?"

"You are mistaken," I reply.

"I'm sure of it," the Girl persists. "Shall I ask her?" She turns to Alice.

"Oh, I like you so much, Sasha," Alice whispers. I look up timidly at her. She is leaning toward me in the abandon of artless tenderness, and a great joy steals over me, as I read in her eyes frank affection.

VII

New York looks unexpectedly familiar, though I miss many old landmarks. It is torture to be indoors, and I roam the streets, experiencing a thrill of kinship when I locate one of my old haunts.

I feel little interest in the large meeting arranged to greet me back into the world. Yet I am conscious of some curiosity about the comrades I may meet there. Few of the old guard have remained. Some dropped from the ranks; others died. John Most will not be there. I cherished the hope of meeting him again, but he died a few months before my release. He had been unjust to me; but who is free from moments of weakness? The passage of time has mellowed the bitterness of my resentment, and I think of him, my first teacher of Anarchy, with old-time admiration. His unique personality stands out in strong relief upon the flat background of his time. His life was the tragedy of the ever unpopular pioneer. A social Lear, his whitening years brought only increasing isolation and greater lack of understanding, even within his own circle. He had struggled and suffered much; he gave his whole life to advance the Cause, only to find at the last that he who crosses the threshold must leave all behind, even friendship, even comradeship.

My old friend, Justus Schwab, is also gone, and Brady, the big Austrian. Few of the comrades of my day have survived. The younger generation seems different, unsatisfactory. The Ghetto I had known has also disappeared. Primitive Orchard Street, the scene of our pioneer meetings, has conformed to business respectability; the historic lecture hall, that rang with the breaking chains of the awakening people, has been turned into a dancing-school; the little café "around the corner," the intellectual arena of former years, is now a counting-house. The fervid enthusiasm of the past, the spontaneous comradeship in the common cause, the intoxication of world-liberating zeal—all are gone with the days of my youth. I sense the spirit of cold deliberation in the new set, and a tone of disillusioned wisdom that chills and estranges me.

The Girl has also changed. The little Sailor, my companion of the days that thrilled with the approach of the Social Revolution, has become a woman of the world. Her mind has matured, but her wider interests antagonize my old revolutionary traditions that inspired every day and colored our every act with the direct perception of the momentarily expected great upheaval. I feel an instinctive disapproval of many things, though particular instances are intangible and elude my analysis. I sense a foreign element in the circle she has gathered about her, and feel myself a stranger among them. Her friends and admirers crowd her home, and turn it into a sort of salon. They talk art and literature; discuss science and philosophize over the disharmony of life. But the groans of the dungeon find no gripping echo there. The Girl is the most revolutionary of them all; but even she has been infected by the air of intellectual aloofness, false tolerance and everlasting pessimism. I resent the situation, the more I become conscious of the chasm between the Girl and myself. It seems unbridgeable; we cannot recover the intimate note of our former comradeship. With pain I witness her evident misery. She is untiring in her care and affection; the whole circle lavishes on me sympathy and tenderness. But through it all I feel the commiserating tolerance toward a sick child. I shun the atmosphere of the house, and flee to seek the solitude of the crowded streets and the companionship of the plain, untutored underworld.

In a Bowery resort I come across Dan, my assistant on the range during my last year in the penitentiary.

"Hello, Aleck," he says, taking me aside, "awful glad to see you out of hell. Doing all right?"

"So, so, Dan. And you?"

"Rotten, Aleck, rotten. You know it was my first bit, and I swore I'd never do a crooked job again. Well, they turned me out with a five-spot, after four years' steady work, mind you, and three of them working my head off on a loom. Then they handed me a pair of Kentucky jeans, that any fly-cop could spot a mile off. My friends went back on me—that five-spot was all I had in the world, and it didn't go a long way. Liberty ain't what it looks to a fellow through the bars, Aleck, but it's hell to go back. I don't know what to do."

"How do you happen here, Dan? Could you get no work at home, in Oil City?"

"Home, hell! I wish I had a home and friends, like you, Aleck. Christ, d'you think I'd ever turn another trick? But I got no home and no friends. Mother died before I came out, and I found no home. I got a job in Oil City, but the bulls tipped me off for an ex-con, and I beat my way here. I tried to do the square thing, Aleck, but where's a fellow to turn? I haven't a cent and not a friend in the world."

Poor Dan! I feel powerless to help him, even with advice. Without friends or money, his "liberty" is a hollow mockery, even worse than mine. Five years ago he was a strong, healthy young man. He committed a burglary, and was sent to prison. Now he is out, his body weakened, his spirit broken; he is less capable than ever to survive in the struggle. What is he to do but commit another crime and be returned to prison? Even I, with so many advantages that Dan is lacking, with kind comrades and helpful friends, I can find no place in this world of the outside. I have been torn out, and I seem unable to take root again. Everything looks so different, changed. And yet I feel a great hunger for life. I could enjoy the sunshine, the open, and freedom of action.

I could make my life and my prison experience useful to the world. But I am incapacitated for the struggle. I do not fit in any more, not even in the circle of my comrades. And this seething life, the turmoil and the noises of the city, agonize me. Perhaps it would be best for me to retire to the country, and there lead a simple life, close to nature.

VIII

The summer is fragrant with a thousand perfumes, and a great peace is in the woods. The Hudson River shimmers in the distance, a solitary sail on its broad bosom. The Palisades on the opposite side look immutable, eternal, their undulating tops melting in the grayish-blue horizon.

Puffs of smoke rise from the valley. Here, too, has penetrated the restless spirit. The muffled thunder of blasting breaks in upon the silence. The greedy hand of man is desecrating the Palisades, as it has desecrated the race. But the big river flows quietly, and the sailboat glides serenely on the waters. It skips over the foaming waves, near the spot I stand on, toward the great, busy city. Now it is floating past the high towers, with their forbidding aspect. It is Sing Sing prison. Men groan and suffer there, and are tortured in the dungeon. And I—I am a useless cog, an idler, while others toil; and I keep mute, while others suffer.

My mind dwells in the prison. The silence rings with the cry of pain; the woods echo the agony of the dungeon. I start at the murmur of the leaves; the trees with their outstretched arms bar my way, menacing me like the guards on the prison walls. Their monster shapes follow me in the valley.

At night I wake in cold terror. The agonized cry of
Crazy Smithy is in my ears, and again I hear the sickening thud of the riot clubs on the prisoner's head. The
solitude is harrowing with the memory of the prison; it
haunts me with the horrors of the basket cell. Away, I
must away, to seek relief amidst the people!

Back in the city, I face the problem of support. The
sense of dependence gnaws me. The hospitality of my
friends is boundless, but I cannot continue as the beneficiary of their generosity. I had declined the money
gift presented to me on my release by the comrades: I
felt I could not accept even their well-meant offering.
The question of earning my living is growing acute.
I cannot remain idle. But what shall I turn to? I am
too weak for factory work. I had hoped to secure employment as a compositor, but the linotype has made me
superfluous. I might be engaged as a proof-reader.
My former membership in the Typographical Union will
enable me to join the ranks of labor.

My physical condition, however, precludes the immediate realization of my plans. Meanwhile some comrades suggest the advisability of a short lecture tour: it
will bring me in closer contact with the world, and serve
to awaken new interest in life. The idea appeals to me.
I shall be doing work, useful work. I shall voice the cry
of the depths, and perhaps the people will listen, and
some may understand!

IX

With a great effort I persevere on the tour. The
strain is exhausting my strength, and I feel weary and
discontented. My innate dread of public speaking is

aggravated by the necessity of constant association with people. The comrades are sympathetic and attentive, but their very care is a source of annoyance. I long for solitude and quiet. In the midst of people, the old prison instinct of escape possesses me. Once or twice the wild idea of terminating the tour has crossed my mind. The thought is preposterous, impossible. Meetings have already been arranged in various cities, and my appearance widely announced. It would disgrace me, and injure the movement, were I to prove myself so irresponsible. I owe it to the Cause, and to my comrades, to keep my appointments. I must fight off this morbid notion.

My engagement in Pittsburgh aids my determination. Little did I dream in the penitentiary that I should live to see that city again, even to appear in public there! Looking back over the long years of imprisonment, of persecution and torture, I marvel that I have survived. Surely it was not alone physical capacity to suffer—how often had I touched the threshold of death, and trembled on the brink of insanity and self-destruction! Whatever strength and perseverance I possessed, they alone could not have saved my reason in the night of the dungeon, or preserved me in the despair of the solitary. Poor Wingie, Ed Sloane, and "Fighting" Tom; Harry, Russell, Crazy Smithy—how many of my friends have perished there! It was the vision of an ideal, the consciousness that I suffered for a great Cause, that sustained me. The very exaggeration of my self-estimate was a source of strength: I looked upon myself as a representative of a world movement; it was my duty to exemplify the spirit and dignity of the ideas it embodied. I was not a prisoner, merely; I was an Anarchist in the hands of the enemy; as such, it devolved upon me to

maintain the manhood and self-respect my ideals signified. The example of the political prisoners in Russia
inspired me, and my stay in the penitentiary was a continuous struggle that was the breath of life.

Was it the extreme self-consciousness of the idealist,
the power of revolutionary traditions, or simply the persistent will to be? Most likely, it was the fusing of all
three, that shaped my attitude in prison and kept me
alive. And now, on my way to Pittsburgh, I feel the
same spirit within me, at the threat of the local authorities to prevent my appearance in the city. Some
friends seek to persuade me to cancel my lecture there,
alarmed at the police preparations to arrest me. Something might happen, they warn me: legally I am still a
prisoner out on parole. I am liable to be returned to the
penitentiary, without trial, for the period of my commutation time—eight years and two months—if convicted of
a felony before the expiration of my full sentence of
twenty-two years.

But the menace of the enemy stirs me from apathy,
and all my old revolutionary defiance is roused within
me. For the first time during the tour, I feel a vital interest in life, and am eager to ascend the platform.

An unfortunate delay on the road brings me into
Pittsburgh two hours late for the lecture. Comrade
M—— is impatiently waiting for me, and we hasten to
the meeting. On the way he informs me that the hall
is filled with police and prison guards; the audience is in
a state of great suspense; the rumor has gone about that
the authorities are determined to prevent my appearance.

I sense an air of suppressed excitement, as I enter
the hall, and elbow my way through the crowded aisle.
Some one grips my arm, and I recognize "Southside"
Johnny, the friendly prison runner. "Aleck, take care,"
he warns me, "the bulls are layin' for you."

X

The meeting is over, the danger past. I feel worn and tired with the effort of the evening.

My next lecture is to take place in Cleveland, Ohio. The all-night ride in the stuffy smoker aggravates my fatigue, and sets my nerves on edge. I arrive in the city feeling feverish and sick. To engage a room in a hotel would require an extra expense from the proceeds of the tour, which are intended for the movement; moreover, it would be sybaritism, contrary to the traditional practice of Anarchist lecturers. I decide to accept the hospitality of some friend during my stay in the city.

For hours I try to locate the comrade who has charge of arranging the meetings. At his home I am told that he is absent. His parents, pious Jews, look at me askance, and refuse to inform me of their son's whereabouts. The unfriendly attitude of the old folks drives me into the street again, and I seek out another comrade. His family gathers about me. Their curious gaze is embarrassing; their questions idle. My pulse is feverish, my head heavy. I should like to rest up before the lecture, but a constant stream of comrades flows in on me, and the house rings with their joy of meeting me. The talking wearies me; their ardent interest searches my soul with rude hands. These men and women— they, too, are different from the comrades of my day; their very language echoes the spirit that has so depressed me in the new Ghetto. The abyss in our feeling and thought appals me.

With failing heart I ascend the platform in the evening. It is chilly outdoors, and the large hall, sparsely filled and badly lit, breathes the cold of the grave upon me. The audience is unresponsive. The lecture on

Crime and Prisons that so thrilled my Pittsburgh meeting, wakes no vital chord. I feel dispirited. My voice is weak and expressionless; at times it drops to a hoarse whisper. I seem to stand at the mouth of a deep cavern, and everything is dark within. I speak into the blackness; my words strike metallically against the walls, and are thrown back at me with mocking emphasis. A sense of weariness and hopelessness possesses me, and I conclude the lecture abruptly.

The comrades surround me, grasp my hand, and ply me with questions about my prison life, the joy of liberty and of work. They are undisguisedly disappointed at my anxiety to retire, but presently it is decided that I should accept the proffered hospitality of a comrade who owns a large house in the suburbs.

The ride is interminable, the comrade apparently living several miles out in the country. On the way he talks incessantly, assuring me repeatedly that he considers it a great privilege to entertain me. I nod sleepily.

Finally we arrive. The place is large, but squalid. The low ceilings press down on my head; the rooms look cheerless and uninhabited. Exhausted by the day's exertion, I fall into heavy sleep.

Awakening in the morning, I am startled to find a stranger in my bed. His coat and hat are on the floor, and he lies snoring at my side, with overshirt and trousers on. He must have fallen into bed very tired, without even detaching the large cuffs, torn and soiled, that rattle on his hands.

The sight fills me with inexpressible disgust. All through the years of my prison life, my nights had been passed in absolute solitude. The presence of another in my bed is unutterably horrifying. I dress hurriedly, and rush out of the house.

A heavy drizzle is falling; the air is close and damp. The country looks cheerless and dreary. But one thought possesses me: to get away from the stranger snoring in my bed, away from the suffocating atmosphere of the house with its low ceilings, out into the open, away from the presence of man. The sight of a human being repels me, the sound of a voice is torture to me. I want to be alone, always alone, to have peace and quiet, to lead a simple life in close communion with nature. Ah, nature! That, too, I have tried, and found more impossible even than the turmoil of the city. The silence of the woods threatened to drive me mad, as did the solitude of the dungeon. A curse upon the thing that has incapacitated me for life, made solitude as hateful as the face of man, made life itself impossible to me! And is it for this I have yearned and suffered, for this spectre that haunts my steps, and turns day into a nightmare—this distortion, Life? Oh, where is the joy of expectation, the tremulous rapture, as I stood at the door of my cell, hailing the blush of the dawn, the day of resurrection! Where the happy moments that lit up the night of misery with the ecstasy of freedom, which was to give me back to work and joy! Where, where is it all? Is liberty sweet only in the anticipation, and life a bitter awakening?

The rain has ceased. The sun peeps through the clouds, and glints its rays upon a shop window. My eye falls on the gleaming barrel of a revolver. I enter the place, and purchase the weapon.

I walk aimlessly, in a daze. It is beginning to rain again; my body is chilled to the bone, and I seek the shelter of a saloon on an obscure street.

In the corner of the dingy back room I notice a girl. She is very young, with an air of gentility about her, that is somewhat marred by her quick, restless look.

502 PRISON MEMOIRS OF AN ANARCHIST

We sit in silence, watching the heavy downpour out-doors. The girl is toying with a glass of whiskey.

Angry voices reach us from the street. There is a heavy shuffling of feet, and a suppressed cry. A woman lurches through the swinging door, and falls against a table.

The girl rushes to the side of the woman, and assists her into a chair. "Are you hurt, Madge?" she asks sym-pathetically.

The woman looks up at her with bleary eyes. She raises her hand, passes it slowly across her mouth, and spits violently.

"He hit me, the dirty brute," she whimpers, "he hit me. But I sha'n't give him no money; I just won't, Frenchy."

The girl is tenderly wiping her friend's bleeding face. "Sh-sh, Madge, sh—sh!" she warns her, with a glance at the approaching waiter.

"Drunk again, you old bitch," the man growls. "You'd better vamoose now."

"Oh, let her be, Charley, won't you?" the girl coaxes. "And, say, bring me a bitters."

"The dirty loafer! It's money, always gimme money," the woman mumbles; "and I've had such bad luck, Frenchy. You know it's true. Don't you, Frenchy?"

"Yes, yes, dear," the girl soothes her. "Don't talk now. Lean your head on my shoulder, so! You'll be all right in a minute."

The girl sways to and fro, gently patting the woman on the head, and all is still in the room. The woman's breathing grows regular and louder. She snores, and the young girl slowly unwinds her arms and resumes her seat.

I motion to her. "Will you have a drink with me?"

"With pleasure," she smiles. "Poor thing," she nods toward the sleeper, "her fellow beats her and takes all she makes."

"You have a kind heart, Frenchy."

"We girls must be good to each other; no one else will. Some men are so mean, just too mean to live or let others live. But some are nice. Of course, some girls are bad, but we ain't all like that and—" she hesitates.

"And what?"

"Well, some have seen better days. I wasn't always like this," she adds, gulping down her drink.

Her face is pensive; her large black eyes look dreamy. She asks abruptly:

"You like poetry?"

"Ye—es. Why?"

"I write. Oh, you don't believe me, do you? Here's something of mine," and with a preliminary cough, she begins to recite with exaggerated feeling:

> Mother dear, the days were young
> When posies in our garden hung.
> Upon your lap my golden head I laid,
> With pure and happy heart I prayed.

"I remember those days," she adds wistfully.

We sit in the dusk, without speaking. The lights are turned on, and my eye falls on a paper lying on the table. The large black print announces an excursion to Buffalo:

"Will you come with me?" I ask the girl, pointing to the advertisement.

"To Buffalo?"

"Yes."

"You're kidding."

"No. Will you come?"

"Sure."

Alone with me in the stateroom, "Frenchy" grows tender and playful. She notices my sadness, and tries to amuse me. But I am thinking of the lecture that is to take place in Cleveland this very hour: the anxiety of my comrades, the disappointment of the audience, my absence, all prey on my mind. But who am I, to presume to teach? I have lost my bearings; there is no place for me in life. My bridges are burned.

The girl is in high spirits, but her jollity angers me. I crave to speak to her, to share my misery and my grief. I hint at the impossibility of life, and my superfluity in the world, but she looks bored, not grasping the significance of my words.

"Don't talk so foolish, boy," she scoffs. "What do you care about work or a place? You've got money; what more do you want? You better go down now and fetch something to drink."

Returning to the stateroom, I find "Frenchy" missing. In a sheltered nook on the deck I recognize her in the lap of a stranger. Heart-sore and utterly disgusted, I retire to my berth. In the morning I slip quietly off the boat.

The streets are deserted; the city is asleep. In the fog and rain, the gray buildings resemble the prison walls, the tall factory chimneys standing guard like monster sentinels. I hasten away from the hated sight, and wander along the docks. The mist weaves phantom shapes, and I see a multitude of people and in their midst a boy, pale, with large, lustrous eyes. The crowd curses and yells in frenzied passion, and arms are raised, and blows rain down on the lad's head. The rain beats heavier, and every drop is a blow. The boy totters and falls to the ground. The wistful face, the dreamy eyes —why, it is Czolgosz!

Accursed spot! I cannot die here. I must to New York, to be near my friends in death!

XI

Loud knocking wakes me.

"Say, Mister," a voice calls behind the door, "are you all right?"

"Yes."

"Will you have a bite, or something?"

"No."

"Well, as you please. But you haven't left your room going on two days now."

Two days, and still alive? The road to death is so short, why suffer? An instant, and I shall be no more, and only the memory of me will abide for a little while in this world. *This* world? Is there another? If there is anything in Spiritualism, Carl will learn of it. In the prison we had been interested in the subject, and we had made a compact that he who is the first to die, should appear in spirit to the other. Pretty fancy of foolish man, born of immortal vanity! Hereafter, life after death—children of earth's misery. The disharmony of life bears dreams of peace and bliss, but there is no harmony save in death. Who knows but that even then the atoms of my lifeless clay will find no rest, tossed about in space to form new shapes and new thoughts for aeons of human anguish.

And so Carl will not see me after death. Our compact will not be kept, for nothing will remain of my "soul" when I am dead, as nothing remains of the sum when its units are gone. Dear Carl, he will be dis-

506 PRISON MEMOIRS OF AN ANARCHIST

traught at my failure to come to Detroit. He had arranged a lecture there, following Cleveland. It is peculiar that I should not have thought of wiring him that I was unable to attend. He might have suspended preparations. But it did not occur to me, and now it is too late.

The Girl, too, will be in despair over my disappearance. I cannot notify her now—I am virtually dead. Yet I crave to see her once more before I depart, even at a distance. But that also is too late. I am almost dead.

I dress mechanically, and step into the street. The brilliant sunshine, the people passing me by, the children playing about, strike on my consciousness with pleasing familiarity. The desire grips me to be one of them, to participate in their life. And yet it seems strange to think of myself as part of this moving, breathing humanity. Am I not dead?

I roam about all day. At dusk I am surprised to find myself near the Girl's home. The fear seizes me that I might be seen and recognized. A sense of guilt steals over me, and I shrink away, only to return again and again to the familiar spot.

I pass the night in the park. An old man, a sailor out of work, huddles close to me, seeking the warmth of my body. But I am cold and cheerless, and all next day I haunt again the neighborhood of the Girl. An irresistible force attracts me to the house. Repeatedly I return to my room and snatch up the weapon, and then rush out again. I am fearful of being seen near the "Den," and I make long detours to the Battery and the Bronx, but again and again I find myself watching the entrance and speculating on the people passing in and out of the house. My mind pictures the Girl, with her friends about her. What are they discussing, I wonder.

"Why, myself!" it flits through my mind. The thought appalls me. They must be distraught with anxiety over my disappearance. Perhaps they think me dead!

I hasten to a telegraph office, and quickly pen a message to the Girl: "Come. I am waiting here."

In a flurry of suspense I wait for the return of the messenger. A little girl steps in, and I recognize Tess, and inwardly resent that the Girl did not come herself.

"Aleck," she falters, "Sonya wasn't home when your message came. I'll run to find her."

The old dread of people is upon me, and I rush out of the place, hoping to avoid meeting the Girl. I stumble through the streets, retrace my steps to the telegraph office, and suddenly come face to face with her.

Her appearance startles me. The fear of death is in her face, mute horror in her eyes.

"Sasha!" Her hand grips my arm, and she steadies my faltering step.

XII

I open my eyes. The room is light and airy; a soothing quiet pervades the place. The portières part noiselessly, and the Girl looks in.

"Awake, Sasha?" She brightens with a happy smile.

"Yes. When did I come here?"

"Several days ago. You've been very sick, but you feel better now, don't you, dear?"

Several days? I try to recollect my trip to Buffalo, the room on the Bowery. Was it all a dream?

"Where was I before I came here?" I ask.

"You—you were—absent," she stammers, and in her face is visioned the experience of my disappearance.

With tender care the Girl ministers to me. I feel like

one recovering from a long illness: very weak, but with a touch of joy in life. No one is permitted to see me, save one or two of the Girl's nearest friends, who slip in quietly, pat my hand in mute sympathy, and discreetly retire. I sense their understanding, and am grateful that they make no allusion to the events of the past days.

The care of the Girl is unwavering. By degrees I gain strength. The room is bright and cheerful; the silence of the house soothes me. The warm sunshine is streaming through the open window; I can see the blue sky, and the silvery cloudlets. A little bird hops upon the sill, looks steadily at me, and chirps a greeting. It brings back the memory of Dick, my feathered pet, and of my friends in prison. I have done nothing for the agonized men in the dungeon darkness—have I forgotten them? I have the opportunity; why am I idle?

The Girl calls cheerfully: "Sasha, our friend Philo is here. Would you like to see him?"

I welcome the comrade whose gentle manner and deep sympathy have endeared him to me in the days since my return. There is something unutterably tender about him. The circle had christened him "the philosopher," and his breadth of understanding and non-invasive personality have been a great comfort to me.

His voice is low and caressing, like the soft crooning of a mother rocking her child to sleep. "Life is a problem," he is saying, "a problem whose solution consists in trying to solve it. Schopenhauer may have been right," he smiles, with a humorous twinkle in his eyes, "but his love of life was so strong, his need for expression so compelling, he had to write a big book to prove how useless is all effort. But his very sincerity disproves him. Life is its own justification. The disharmony of life is more seeming than real; and what is real of it, is the folly and blindness of man. To struggle against that folly, is to create greater harmony, wider possibilities. Artificial barriers circumscribe and dwarf life, and stifle its manifestations. To break those barriers down, is to find a vent, to expand, to express oneself. And that is life, Aleck: a continuous struggle for expression. It mirrors itself in nature, as in all the phases of man's existence. Look at the little vine struggling against the fury of the storm, and clinging with all its might to preserve its hold. Then see it stretch toward the sunshine, to absorb the light and the warmth, and then freely give back of itself in multiple form and wealth of color. We call it beautiful then, for it has found expression. That is life, Aleck, and thus it manifests itself through all the gradations we call evolution. The higher the scale, the more varied and complex the manifestations, and, in turn, the greater the need for expression. To suppress or thwart it, means decay, death. And in this, Aleck, is to be found the main source of suffering and misery. The hunger of life storms at the gates that exclude it from the joy of being, and the individual soul multiplies its expressions by being mirrored in the collective, as the little vine mirrors itself in its many flowers, or as the acorn individualizes itself a thousandfold in the many-leafed oak. But I am tiring you, Aleck."

"No, no, Philo. Continue; I want to hear more."

"Well, Aleck, as with nature, so with man. Life is never at a standstill; everywhere and ever it seeks new manifestations, more expansion. In art, in literature, as in the affairs of men, the struggle is continual for higher and more intimate expression. That is progress—the vine reaching for more sunshine and light. Translated into the language of social life, it means the individualization of the mass, the finding of a higher level, the climbing over the fences that shut out life. Everywhere

you see this reaching out. The process is individual and
social at the same time, for the species lives in the individual as much as the individual persists in the species.
The individual comes first; his clarified vision is multiplied in his immediate environment, and gradually permeates through his generation and time, deepening the
social consciousness and widening the scope of existence.
But perhaps you have not found it so, Aleck, after your
many years of absence?"

"No, dear Philo. What you have said appeals to
me very deeply. But I have found things so different
from what I had pictured them. Our comrades, the
movement—it is not what I thought it would be."

"It is quite natural, Aleck. A change has taken place,
but its meaning is apt to be distorted through the dim
vision of your long absence. I know well what you miss,
dear friend: the old mode of existence, the living on the
very threshold of the revolution, so to speak. And
everything looks strange to you, and out of joint.
But as you stay a little longer with us, you will see that
it is merely a change of form; the essence is the same.
We are the same as before, Aleck, only made deeper and
broader by years and experience. Anarchism has cast
off the swaddling bands of the small, intimate circles of
former days; it has grown to greater maturity, and become a factor in the larger life of Society. You remember it only as a little mountain spring, around which
clustered a few thirsty travelers in the dreariness of the
capitalist desert. It has since broadened and spread as a
strong current that covers a wide area and forces its
way even into the very ocean of life. You see, dear
Aleck, the philosophy of Anarchism is beginning to
pervade every phase of human endeavor. In science, in
art, in literature, everywhere the influence of Anarchist
thought is creating new values; its spirit is vitalizing

social movements, and finding interpretation in life.
Indeed, Aleck, we have not worked in vain. Throughout the world there is a great awakening. Even in this
socially most backward country, the seeds sown are beginning to bear fruit. Times have changed, indeed; but
encouragingly so, Aleck. The leaven of discontent, ever
more conscious and intelligent, is moulding new social
thought and new action. To-day our industrial conditions, for instance, present a different aspect from those
of twenty years ago. It was then possible for the mas--
ters of life to sacrifice to their interests the best friends
of the people. But to-day the spontaneous solidarity
and awakened consciousness of large strata of labor is a
guarantee against the repetition of such judicial murders.
It is a most significant sign, Aleck, and a great inspiration to renewed effort."

The Girl enters. "Are you crooning Sasha to sleep,
Philo?" she laughs.

"Oh, no!" I protest, "I'm wide awake and much interested in Philo's conversation."

"It is getting late," he rejoins. "I must be off to the
meeting."

"What meeting?" I inquire.

"The Czolgosz anniversary commemoration."

"I think—I'd like to come along."

"Better not, Sasha," my friend advises. "You need
some light distraction."

"Perhaps you would like to go to the theatre," the
Girl suggests. "Stella has tickets. She'd be happy to
have you come, Sasha."

.   .   .   .

Returning home in the evening, I find the "Den" in
great excitement. The assembled comrades look wor-

ried, talk in whispers, and seem to avoid my glance. I miss several familiar faces.

"Where are the others?" I ask.

The comrades exchange troubled looks, and are silent.

"Has anything happened? Where are they?" I insist.

"I may as well tell you," Philo replies, "but be calm, Sasha. The police have broken up our meeting. They have clubbed the audience, and arrested a dozen comrades."

"Is it serious, Philo?"

"I am afraid it is. They are going to make a test case. Under the new 'Criminal Anarchy Law' our comrades may get long terms in prison. They have taken our most active friends."

The news electrifies me. I feel myself transported into the past, the days of struggle and persecution. Philo was right! The enemy is challenging, the struggle is going on! . . . I see the graves of Waldheim open, and hear the voices from the tomb.

A deep peace pervades me, and I feel a great joy in my heart.

"Sasha, what is it?" Philo cries in alarm.

"My resurrection, dear friend. I have found work to do."